Ancient Egyptian Imperialism

Ancient Egyptian Imperialism

Ellen Morris

WILEY Blackwell

Registered Office(s)
John Wiley & Sons, Inc., 111 River Street, Hoboken, NJ 07030, USA
John Wiley & Sons Ltd, The Atrium, Southern Gate, Chichester, West Sussex, PO19 8SQ, UK

Editorial Office
101 Station Landing, Medford, MA 02155, USA

For details of our global editorial offices, customer services, and more information about Wiley products visit us at www.wiley.com.

Wiley also publishes its books in a variety of electronic formats and by print-on-demand. Some content that appears in standard print versions of this book may not be available in other formats.

Library of Congress Cataloging-in-Publication Data

Name: Morris, Ellen, author.
Title: Ancient Egyptian Imperialism / by Ellen Morris.
Description: Hoboken, NJ : Wiley, 2018. | Includes index. |
Identifiers: LCCN 2018001068 (print) | LCCN 2018004511 (ebook) | ISBN 9781119467670 (pdf)
    | ISBN 9781119467663 (epub) | ISBN 9781405136778 (cloth) | ISBN 9781405136785 (pbk.)
Subjects: LCSH: Egypt–History–To 332 B.C. | Egypt–Politics and government–To 332 B.C. |
    Egypt–Foreign relations. | Imperialism.
Classification: LCC DT83 (ebook) | LCC DT83 .M67 2018 (print) | DDC 932/.01–dc23
LC record available at https://lccn.loc.gov/2018001068

Cover Design: Wiley
Cover Images: (front cover) Facsimile of a wall painting in the Tomb of Anen by Nina de Garis Davies, Metropolitan Museum 33.8.8, Rogers Fund 1933; (back cover) © OnstOn/iStockphoto

Set in 10/12pt Warnock by SPi Global, Pondicherry, India
Printed in Singapore by C.O.S. Printers Pte Ltd

10   9   8   7   6   5   4   3   2   1

This book is dedicated to Sev and Jules with love and gratitude.

Contents

Acknowledgments

Chapters of this book have been written in many different places. I would like to express my gratitude to the curators at the Metropolitan Museum of Art, where I held a Jane and Morgan Whitney Art History Fellowship in 2008–2009. Special thanks are due to Dorothea Arnold, Diana Craig Patch, and Janice Kamrin. Chapters for the book were also written while I was employed at the Institute for the Study of the Ancient World, and I am particularly grateful to Roger Bagnall and Chuck Jones for their support. I would also like to thank Michael Brown and Laura Holt—the latter of whom worked many miracles obtaining particularly tricky interlibrary loans during the time I spent resident at the School for Advanced Research in Santa Fe. My former student and research assistant, Rachel Kronberg, was also a great help to me that year on this and other projects. Finally, I am deeply appreciative of the support of my colleagues in the Department of Classics at Barnard College and at Columbia University, especially Helene Foley, Kristina Milnor, Nancy Worman, and John Ma. Meredith Wisner, Barnard's resident expert on permissions, also provided valuable assistance in the final stages of preparing the images.

In terms of individual scholars and friends, Josef and Jennifer Wegner have been very generous in sharing information on their research and also in granting me rights to utilize their detailed illustration of the scene from Meryre II's tomb that is discussed in the Epilogue. I am also extremely grateful to Georges Soukiassian, Clara Jeuthe, Julia Budka, Amihai Mazar, and Tony Mills for permission to utilize up-to-date plans of their excavations as well as to Franck Monnier for allowing me to publish his illustration of Aniba. My thanks are also due to Stuart Tyson Smith, Jeff Blakely, Amihai Mazar, Julia Budka, Vincent Francigny, Nadine Moeller, Jana Mynářová, Aaron Burke, James Hoffmeier, Lindsey Weglarz, Jacob Damm, Tony Mills, Colin Hope, Olaf Kaper, Laurent Bavay, and to numerous other scholars who have shared their insights and the results of their investigations into Egypt's imperial endeavors with me. The main challenge in writing this book has been keeping up with all of the recent excavations and re-examinations of Egypt's imperial past. The amount of new work published within the past few years alone is both daunting and exciting, and I hope that I have done at least some of it justice.

Finally, I appreciate the thoughtful commentary of three anonymous reviewers and also the graduate student participants in Egypt and the Outside World, a seminar at UCLA taught by Kara Cooney, who all read and commented on an earlier draft of this manuscript. Participants in the seminar were Danielle Candelora, Nadia Ben-Marzouk, Carolyn Arbuckle MacLeod, Jordan Galczynski, Jeffrey Newman, Marissa Stevens, Luke Brenig, Vera Rondano, Rose Campbell, and Michael Moore. I look forward to enjoying the work of these scholars in the years to come.

Most directly responsible for the success of this project are Haze Humbert and Janani Govindankutty, my editor and project editor at John Wiley & Sons, to whom I owe a great deal of thanks for their skill and patience. Finally, I am deeply grateful to Severin Fowles, whose love, support, artistic ability, and various areas of expertise I have drawn upon throughout this project, as well as to Andrew Miller and my parents (Dee Morris, Wendy Deutelbaum, and David Morris), who read over the page proofs and helped me see the text with new eyes. The encouragement of a great many more family, friends, and colleagues, was crucial and, moreover, much appreciated!

Chronology of Ancient Egypt

Late Predynastic (Nagada II) Period		**3500–3200**
Protodynastic (Nagada III) Period		**3200–3000**
Early Dynastic Period (Dynasties 1–2)		**3000–2686**
First Dynasty	3000–2890	
Second Dynasty	2890–2686	
Old Kingdom (Dynasties 3–6)		**2686–2160**
Third Dynasty	2686–2613	
Fourth Dynasty	2613–2494	
Fifth Dynasty	2494–2345	
Sixth Dynasty	2345–2181	
First Intermediate Period		**2181–2055**
Seventh and Eighth Dynasties	2180–2160	
Ninth and Tenth Dynasties	2160–2025	
Early Eleventh Dynasty	2125–2055	
Middle Kingdom		**2055–1650**
Late Eleventh Dynasty	2055–1985	
Twelfth Dynasty	1985–1773	
Thirteenth Dynasty	1773–after 1650	
Fourteenth Dynasty	1773–1650	
Second Intermediate Period		**1650–1550**
Fifteenth Dynasty	1650–1550	
Sixteenth Dynasty	1650–1580	
Seventeenth Dynasty	1580–1550	
New Kingdom		**1550–1069**
Eighteenth Dynasty	1550–1295	
Nineteenth Dynasty	1295–1186	
Twentieth Dynasty	1186–1069	

Introduction

Every book has its germ of inspiration, which, mostly, long precedes its publication date. In the case of this book, I trace the idea back to the winter semester of 2003, when I taught a class titled State and Empire in the Ancient Near East at the University of Michigan. Between the first meeting and the final exam, the American government had rattled its saber at Saddam Hussein, scrambled for allies, declared war, arguably shocked and awed its opposing army, declared "mission accomplished," and installed its second American governor.

Although I appreciate the numerous ways in which global media coverage, smart bombs, corporate interests, and other facets of modernity have transformed the practices of war in the past 3500 years, what struck me repeatedly as I covered the empires of the Hittites, the Assyrians, and the Persians, was how much remained fundamentally recognizable. As I lectured on the elaborate lengths to which the Hittites and the Assyrians would typically go to assemble allied forces[1] and to justify their *casus belli* before their enemies and their gods,[2] the American government spent January, February, and much of March mounting a case for war before the United Nations and assembling a Coalition of the Willing. The Hittites and Assyrians both likewise anticipated the American PSYOP (psychological operations) campaigns of aerial leaflet distribution over Iraq by yelling up exhortations directly to the people who peered down from besieged city walls, urging them to abandon loyalty to their ruler.[3]

As the specter of war loomed closer, the Americans bargained long and hard, though eventually to no avail, to be allowed to invade northern Iraq from Turkish soil. This proposed point of entry was the same as Mursili I of Hatti had employed to demolish Babylon in 1595 BCE, a pyrrhic victory that the king did not long survive. Indeed, in the centuries that followed, this ancient road would be the main highway traveled—now in the opposite direction—by countless Assyrian, Babylonian, and Persian armies looking to extend their influence into lands formerly under Hittite sovereignty.

Ancient Egyptian Imperialism, First Edition. Ellen Morris.
© 2018 Ellen Morris. Published 2018 by John Wiley & Sons Ltd.

In mid-March, after a final ultimatum of the type typically offered by the Hittites and Assyrians to rival rulers,[4] the Americans declared war and attempted—via a spectacular display of power—to cow Saddam Hussein's forces into submission. While the United States deployed 1,700 air sorties in order to induce feelings of hopelessness among Iraqi soldiers, the ancient imperialists mustered massive armies against city-states, obliterated as much as possible of their enemy's agricultural and industrial wealth, and liberally applied the most gruesome of terror tactics. Of his attack on the fortified city of Tela, for example, Ashurnasirpal II records:

> In strife and conflict I besieged (and) conquered the city. I felled 3,000 of their fighting men with the sword. I carried off prisoners, possessions, oxen, (and) cattle from them. I burnt many captives from them. I captured many troops alive: from some I cut off their arms (and) hands; from others I cut off their noses, ears, (and) *extremities*. I gouged out the eyes of many troops. I made one pile of the living (and) one of heads. I hung their heads on trees around the city. I burnt their adolescent boys (and) girls. I razed, destroyed, burnt, (and) consumed the city.[5]

Such displays were far in excess of the effort necessary to achieve a military victory and clearly were designed to communicate the message that resistance was, and always would be, futile.

Assyrian campaigns, at least those recorded in the official annals, by and large achieved the same quick blush of (often ephemeral) success as met the Americans. In the immediate aftermath of the fall of Saddam Hussein's regime, the country was to be governed by an American, just as the rulers of the Hittites, Assyrians, and Persians had once sent members of their own inner courts to administer areas deemed too politically unstable to rule themselves in a manner acceptable to imperial interests. By term's end, then, our class had witnessed a drama that in many essential facets had been playing out in the same geographical region for millennia. But such dynamics are not tied to place.

Imperialism in Ancient Egypt

While I am fascinated by the structure and trajectory of empires generally, my area of expertise and special interest is pharaonic Egypt. Many of the same issues I explored with my class in 2003, therefore, brought Egypt to mind as well. At various points in its expansive history, Egypt exercised dominion over a heterogeneous assortment of polities and people (from Nilotic villages, to "kingdoms" based in mountain strongholds, to cosmopolitan port cities, to the arid haunts and oases frequented by Bedouin). The many examples of Egypt's experimentation with empire remain largely unknown to scholars interested in the comparative studies of imperial systems, although the work of individuals such as Barry Kemp, Stuart Tyson Smith, Robert Morkot, Bruce Trigger, W. Paul van Pelt, and a handful of others who have published in cross-disciplinary venues has done much to remedy this situation. In general, however, it may be safely stated that Egyptologists tend to write for other Egyptologists and for specialists in the ancient Near East when undertaking the crucial work of analyzing particular campaigns, archives, or excavations.

My own contribution to the study of Egyptian imperialism can easily be enfolded into this last critique. The question I pose in my book *The Architecture of Imperialism: Military Bases and the Evolution of Foreign Policy in Egypt's New Kingdom* is big: namely, how do Egypt's military bases, as they evolved over the course of the New Kingdom, enlighten shifts in its imperial priorities? Yet the great mass of data brought to bear on this question limits its readership to scholars already invested in regional specifics. It is a pleasure, then, to step back and to craft a book with a much wider focus for a more diverse audience. As its title implies, *Ancient Egyptian Imperialism* is intended to interest equally readers for whom Egypt is the main attraction and also those whose curiosity is piqued primarily by investigations into grand strategy, low-level insurgencies, back-room deals, and all the internal complexities of empire. It seeks therefore to explore not only the actions of empires but also—just as importantly—the reactions to them, divergent as these often are.

This book is organized around central imperial themes, each of which is explored in depth at a particular place and time in Egypt's history. Chapter 1, "Trade Before Empire; Empire Before the State," takes as its premise that strong parallels can be drawn between the formation of Egypt's first unified government and the country's later imperial interventions. Escalating tensions between regional centers in Upper Egypt in late prehistory (c. 3500–3200),[6] for example, led to an elite preoccupation with obtaining exotic goods in order to express power and to augment it. Just as trade proceeded, prompted, and facilitated empire in the colonial scramble for Africa, so expeditions to the north and south assumed a much more martial character just prior to the advent of the First Dynasty, when the political unification of the state was unambiguously accomplished. Within the Nile Valley and in southern Canaan, Protodynastic and Early Dynastic (c. 3200–2686) efforts were made to eliminate middlemen, to regularize extraction, and to co-opt resources, just as would be accomplished later when Egypt's frontiers were farther flung. This early internal colonization, then, which sought to harness the resources of a newly defined nation-state for the benefit of its ruling elite, not only provided a backbone for the pharaonic state; it also created a foundational template for the expansion and consolidation of political power.

Chapter 2, "Settler Colonialism," traces another imperial project, this time undertaken at the end of the Old Kingdom in the late Fifth and Sixth Dynasties

(c. 2400–2181). At this time Egyptian settlers were drawn in large numbers to a remote oasis in Egypt's Western Desert. Motivations for this venture are difficult to decipher. Large-scale settlement certainly followed initial explorations for minerals and other resources. Dakhla's special allure at this juncture, however, may have been due to the combined effect of a string of perilously low floods in the Nile Valley (likely decreasing agricultural profits and putting pressure on individual farmers) and the rise of increasingly ambitious rulers in Lower Nubia (whose internal conflicts and ambivalent relations with Egypt threatened the profitability of state-sponsored trading ventures). These dual factors provided strong economic incentives for potential settlers to farm oasis land and for the central government to exploit desert routes to Nubia. This chapter discusses what is presently known about the evolution and nature of this state-sanctioned settlement as well as the relations between the Egyptian colonists and the indigenous inhabitants of Dakhla Oasis.

Egypt's Middle Kingdom (c. 1985–1650) occupation of Lower Nubia and the legacy thereof is the subject of Chapters 3 and 4. "Military Occupation" explores how Twelfth-Dynasty pharaohs attempted to assure themselves unfettered access to highly valued Nubian resources (such as gold, valuable stones and minerals, as well as sub-Saharan trade goods) by erecting a series of massive mud-brick fortresses in Lower Nubia, each of which was at first staffed primarily by rotating garrisons. Throughout the Twelfth Dynasty, archaeological and textual evidence suggests that the Egyptian and the riparian Nubian population kept their interactions to a minimum, perhaps due to mutual enmity. As has been noted by various scholars, conquered populations for whom armed resistance is not an option often practice aggressive boundary maintenance. Evidence from this period in Nubia's history is thus brought into dialogue with Britain's ultimately unsuccessful efforts in the early portion of the twentieth century CE to lure the largely pastoralist population of occupied Sudan into abetting their own subjugation.

In the early Thirteenth Dynasty (c. 1773–1650), due to worsening economic conditions in Egypt's core, imperial soldiers began to settle permanently in the Nubian fortresses and to engage in a much more collaborative manner with the surrounding communities. When the state finally collapsed during the Second Intermediate period (c. 1650–1550), Egyptian and Nubian interactions intensified further, and the former occupiers even unabashedly switched loyalties to the Nubian kingdom of Kush! Chapter 4, "Transculturation, Collaboration, Colonization," follows this initial cultural détente between Egyptian and Nubian communities to a point in the mid-Eighteenth Dynasty (c. 1450), at which time pharaonic armies had reconquered and secured their hold on the region. The inhabitants of Lower Nubia had of their own accord selectively adopted aspects of Egypt's material culture, and this process intensified markedly post-conquest, such that in the absence of strong contextual clues it is extremely difficult to distinguish "Egyptians" from "Nubians" north of the Third Cataract.

Chapter 4, thus, considers two important factors in the turn toward the expression of an apparent Egyptian identity in New Kingdom Nubia. The first is the well-attested practice on frontiers and in colonial settings of men from the imperial culture and local women raising families together that are culturally neither "his" nor "hers." As generations progress, bicultural families often curate socially significant aspects of their paternal heritage, while continuing to embrace aspects of a more deeply rooted local culture, such as foodways, that tend to be passed down through the maternal line—a dynamic that highlights the vital importance of gender in any nuanced discussion of empire. By virtue of sustained interaction and transculturation, ethnically mixed communities not only forge a hybrid that is all their own but also retain the ability to deploy aspects of their dual heritage strategically. Thus, in the Second Intermediate period, Nubio-Egyptians might highlight their indigenous identity when seeking to interact with Nubian neighbors and with the Kerman forces that controlled their land. Descendants of the same community, however, seem to have played up their status as Egyptians-by-descent when pharaonic armies once again reasserted their dominance.

The second factor in such a seeming switch of cultural allegiance in the New Kingdom is the effect of imperial policies for promotion—policies dictating that individuals could only rise in the new regime if they shed outward signs of their indigeneity and, presumably, encouraged their family to do likewise. This process, well attested in Ptolemaic Egypt among other colonial situations, results in the rather ironic situation that the more indigenous a local leadership becomes under colonial rule, the *less* indigenous it looks. Neither abandoned nor forgotten, traditional material signatures typically become for a time far less visible.

Chapter 5 shifts northward in space and back slightly in time to the very beginnings of Egypt's New Kingdom empire in Syria-Palestine (c. 1550). "Motivation, Intimidation, Enticement" argues that Egypt's empire wasn't envisioned at its origins. After Theban rulers succeeded in defeating and expelling the Syro-Palestinians who had dominated the Delta during the Second Intermediate period, they launched a series of pre-emptive strikes to protect their realm. The lucrative nature of the booty, the relative ease with which Egypt could extend its area of influence, and the seduction of international power, it is argued, were unexpected and exciting. Once the Egyptians decided not to retreat back behind their borders but rather to keep control, however, they needed to rely on methods other than brute force. Increasingly included in their imperial arsenal, then, were veiled threats, deft diplomacy, and even outright bribery. Despite these efforts at incentivizing collaboration, Egypt's empire in the early Eighteenth Dynasty remained essentially informal and, as such, inherently unstable.

Rulers like Pachacuti, Gengis Khan, Shaka Zulu, and Qin Shi Huang are primarily famous for their radical reorganizations of army, infrastructure, and empire. The keystone of any successful empire, of course, is the creation of an efficient infrastructure that allows people, goods, and information to travel from the peripheries to the core (and vice versa) with maximum speed and safety. The reforms of these rulers and those of Thutmose III (c. 1479–1425)—their Egyptian counterpart—helped extend and stabilize their conquests. Under Thutmose III's watch, the Egyptian empire was transformed from an intermittent smash-and-grab operation to an efficient and predictable machine. Thutmose's reforms—the subject of the sixth chapter, "Organization and Infrastructure"—aimed to naturalize Egypt's control, facilitate resource extraction, reliably provision armies and imperial functionaries, and ensure that local rulers internalized early on a healthy dose of Egyptian ideology, such that they would accept their new status as mayors (rather than kings). With the aid of imperial tutelage and infrastructure, the pharaoh intended that locals, with limited oversight, would administer their country for the twin benefits of Egypt's revenue and reputation.

Chapter 7, "Outwitting the State," argues the perhaps unsurprising point that Egypt's vassals had no desire to run their realms for Egypt's benefit. Nor did the population of Syria-Palestine necessarily appreciate the extra overlay of extraction. An archive of diplomatic correspondence, unearthed at the city of Amarna in Egypt and covering roughly three decades (c. 1362–1332), offers an invaluable glimpse into the ways that the region's inhabitants and vassals managed to subvert Egypt's authority. From the reports of vassals, we learn that disaffected subjects did not hesitate to stage coups against rulers they felt were too tightly intertwined with imperial interests. Others simply voted with their feet, heading for mountainous zones where everyone knew Egypt's armies were loath to tread. If situated in the contested border zone between rival powers, vassals had the unique opportunity—and one that they routinely took advantage of—to play one great power against another. Even for those closer to the core, however, it was still possible to "safeguard" Egyptian stores in the absence of an Egyptian official, to employ dissimulation to mask seditious acts, and to impugn one's rivals such that imperial armies might be manipulated into acting against them.

Perhaps because the many loopholes that locals could utilize to exploit the system had become increasingly apparent over time, the Egyptians again restructured their system of governance at the very end of the Eighteenth Dynasty or the beginning of the Nineteenth (c. 1300). Chapter 8, "Conversions and Contractions in Egypt's Northern Empire," focuses on the manner in which Egypt intensified its presence in the heart of its territory, thereby rendering it much more visible to Canaanites and archaeologists alike. As part of this strategic conversion, the pharaonic state created purpose-built bases stocked with many of the comforts of home. Egyptians stationed abroad could live in an Egyptian-style dwelling, eat Nilotic fish, savor the taste of geese, and drink "Egyptian" beer from Egyptian-style jars. The more pious and patriotic among them could also, increasingly, worship Amun and his close associate, the divine king, in an Egyptian-affiliated temple. At such temples, too, Canaanites were evidently encouraged to deliver taxes to Amun, although locals may have greeted this particular reform in religio-economic practice with muted enthusiasm. Indeed, the notion of discrepant experiences of empire, especially with regard to the co-existing highs and lows in prosperity observed in the most securely held areas of Egypt's northern empire at this time, is crucial to the chapter's project. Considerations of contractions—both of foreign mercenaries to staff Egyptian bases and, in another sense, of the sphere of Egypt's effective control in the decades following the death of Ramesses III—round out these meditations on the country's northern empire.

The final chapter, "Conversions and Contractions in Egypt's Southern Empire," redirects focus southward again to Egyptian-held Nubia. While Chapter 4 already considered numerous conversions—of soldiers to settlers, troop commanders to mayors, and Nubian rulers to Egyptian-style nobles— this chapter considers two further fundamental changes wrought by Egyptian imperialism. First, when Egypt extended its authority into Upper Nubia at the beginning of the New Kingdom, it chose not to emulate the fortress system by which its Middle Kingdom predecessors had governed Lower Nubia. Rather, it sponsored the building of a number of lightly fortified Egyptian-style towns, each of which possessed a temple at its heart. Such administrative temple-towns, it must have been believed, would not only attract Egyptian settlers but would also encourage Nubians from this previously unconquered region to move into them and thereby to settle into an Egyptian pattern of life.

Not surprisingly, given the nature of the towns, the New Kingdom imperial government also oversaw a number of conversions in the sphere of religion. For instance, in the south especially they strategically altered the visage of the god Amun into a ram-headed manifestation, likely intended to attract the devotion of Nubians. With similar intent, the Egyptian government re-envisioned a prominent—and no doubt spiritually significant—mountain as the heart of a complex dedicated to Amun's worship. Finally, in the Eighteenth and Nineteenth Dynasties especially, they constructed massive stone-built temples throughout Nubia in an effort to convert the southernmost portion of the empire into a temple-based economy capable of subsidizing a variety of extractive enterprises. Scattered evidence suggests, however, that many of these temples may have been administered by Nubians, both in order to secure the loyalty of prominent families and also in acknowledgment of the fact that the "Egyptian" administration in Nubia was increasingly Nubian. Such incorporation of influential Nubians into Amun's cult no doubt accounts for the fact that the god's reign in Nubia far outlasted that of Egypt's New Kingdom pharaohs.

The contractions noted in the chapter's title refer not only to the progressive diminishments of the territory over which Egypt claimed dominance, but also metaphorically to the contractions that herald a birth. As Egypt's control in the region became ever more precarious at the very end of the Twentieth Dynasty, Nubians seemed to become increasingly invested in resuscitating elements of their traditional material culture. This trend intensified after Egypt ceded control completely, and it resulted finally in the birth of a powerful Nubian kingdom based at Napata, the site of the aforementioned holy mountain. In legitimizing their own expanding empire, these new indigenous rulers drew quite deliberately upon both Nubian and Egyptian models. Indeed, fittingly enough, it was none other than the divine, ram-headed Amun who would give his blessing to Nubia's invasion and annexation of Egypt (c. 730). An investigation of imperial conquests both *by* Egypt and *of* Egypt could, of course, go on well into modern times. The end of this book is not the end of the story. It is but a preface.

Ancient Egyptian Imperialism and its Project

Political scientists, anthropologists, and comparative historians have added immeasurably to our understandings of empire, crafting models and charts that claim (with varying degrees of success) to fashion order out of chaos and find method in madness. This book is indebted to the insights of these theorists and draws upon their work throughout. The creation and/or reification of classificatory schemes, however, is not an end goal of this work. Empires, like sharks, must swim or die, and as such, I would argue, constitute moving targets. These predatory beasts are difficult to classify, not only because they adjust their tactics rapidly in response to challenges to their authority, but also because even the very same empire at the very same period may look quite different in its various nooks and crannies. As Sue Alcock has cogently observed:

> ...to manufacture a rigid typology into which any individual empire slots neatly is neither feasible nor desirable, for more often than not *all* of the above strategies are to be seen at work in one and the same empire, operating in different locations.... There is the additional complication that these different strategies could be implemented at different stages in the rise or decline of an empire.... Imperial systems are nothing if not *dynamic* in nature.[7]

Neither uniformly "direct" nor "indirect" in their rule, Egypt's empires most often combined aspects of multiple—often seemingly contradictory—organizational models, because what worked well in some contexts failed abysmally in others.

Empires are complex entities, and I am interested in the experimental nature of imperialism—how a whole host of variables affected decisions regarding the structure of government. A jostling crowd of related questions thus vies for attention. How, for instance, did the goals at the outset of empire change over time in dialogue with the responses of individual peoples and with unforeseen logistical challenges? What pre-existing political structures (and infrastructures) were to be found in a given region, and how did their presence influence choices made and policies implemented? What pushback or support did imperial administrators receive in various regions? Did factional schisms in dominated peripheries or in central administrations influence imperial decisions and trajectories? What experiments failed (from the perspective of either the ruler or the ruled), and how did these failures influence subsequent decisions? How often and to what degree did imperial blueprints undergo revisions, and when did it happen that they were scrapped entirely? What factors, it is crucial to ask, accounted most fundamentally for the discrepant experiences of empire?

Throughout this work analogies are drawn to tactics employed by imperial governments and by dominated peoples in a wide variety of historically documented empires, both old world and new. These comparative examples are not intended to obscure vital differences that distinguish one society and situation from another. Rather, I draw upon these comparisons especially when the rationale behind a given choice is more clearly explicated than it is in Egypt's own empire and when it adds extra nuance or perspective to the discussion. These comparative examples are good to think with. They likewise help combat any notions either of Egyptian exceptionalism or that the somewhat small scale of Egypt's expansionary efforts (by comparison perhaps to those of Assyria, Persia, or Rome) would disqualify it from the status of empire. Critiqued often for its insularity, Egyptology stands to benefit from attending to contemporary dialogues. As should be evident, however, it also has a vast amount to contribute to such conversations. It is in the spirit of abetting such disciplinary cross-fertilization, then, that *Ancient Egyptian Imperialism* is offered.

Notes

1 For example: "[The Hittite king] had left no silver in his land. He had stripped it of all its possessions and had given them to all the foreign countries in order to bring them with him to fight" (Kadesh "Poem," trans. Lichtheim 1976, 64).
2 Oded 1992, 177–81 et passim; Elgavish 2008.
3 See Beal 1995, 552; Grayson 1995, 961.
4 See Gurney 1990, 94–5; Kuhrt 1995, 509–10.
5 Grayson 1991, 201.
6 The chronology presented in *The Oxford History of Ancient Egypt* is utilized throughout this book.
7 Alcock 1989, 92. For a very similar assessment, see Sowell 1998, 15.

1

Trade Before Empire; Empire Before the State (c. 3500–2686)

Trade is said to follow the flag. More often than not, however—at least at first—the reverse is true.[1] This is one of two main arguments this chapter pursues with regard to Protodynastic and Early Dynastic Egypt. The other is that nations are often a product of empires, rather than simply a producer of them. As history and archaeology demonstrate, many of the world's greatest pre-modern states arose—by virtue of sudden, successful military action—out of a constellation of relatively comparable polities to unite vast swaths of territory under their rule. In some cases, these polities were already recognizably urban (such as Teotihuacan, Uruk, and Rome), while in others thriving metropolitan centers followed on the heels of empire (as with the Inka empire and Achaemenid Persia). Regardless, the salient point is that just prior to expansion, the polity that was to become an empire may have closely resembled its peers and even have been dominated by one or another among them for a period of time. Such seems to have been the trajectory of Abydos, whose political fortune lagged behind those of Hierakonpolis and Nagada—its more precocious southern neighbors—for much of early and mid-prehistory, at least so far as it is possible to ascertain archaeologically (see Figure 1.1).

Colin Renfrew and John Cherry have termed the type of competitive milieu in which similarly sized political units tend to operate "peer polity interaction."[2] The city-states of the Mayan heartland and Early Dynastic Mesopotamia are classic exemplars of this potentially generative dynamic. Two cities in such a system might ally themselves against a mutual foe one century, might attack one another's territory the next, and might exist for a time in the relationship of vassal and overlord. Typically, however, any suzerainty enjoyed by one city remained on a relatively small scale and was balanced by similar relationships negotiated among its peers. As Renfrew and Cherry note, over the course of such intense and ever-shifting interaction, the material culture of such cities tended to become ever more homogenized, heightening the impression that one differed little from the others.

The point at which a polity switches from exercising political paramountcy to wielding imperial power is related primarily to the unprecedented size of the

Ancient Egyptian Imperialism, First Edition. Ellen Morris.
© 2018 Ellen Morris. Published 2018 by John Wiley & Sons Ltd.

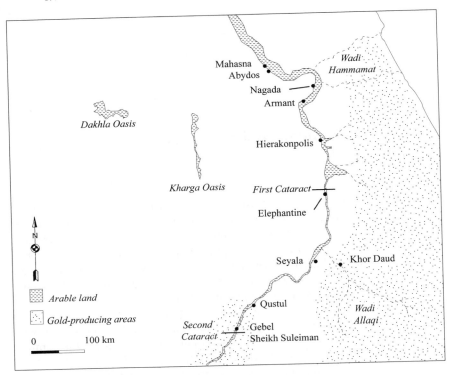

Figure 1.1 Sites from southern Egypt and Nubia mentioned in the chapter.

new dominion and to the complexity of the mechanisms necessary to govern it effectively. Definitions of empire differ widely, but one tenet that most scholars agree upon is that in order to qualify, a polity must lay claim to a vast expanse of land and great numbers of people. Further, these new subjects should lie outside the constellation of peers traditionally feuded with and include a heterogeneous assortment of cultures. Carla Sinopoli offers a pithy, yet broadly representative, definition of empires as "geographically and politically expansive polities, composed of a diversity of localized communities and ethnic groups."[3]

It is interesting, therefore, to compare this definition of an empire with Robert Carneiro's definition of a state as "an autonomous political unit, encompassing many communities within its territory and having a centralized government with the power to collect taxes, draft men for work or war, and decree and enforce laws."[4] A close look shows the two to be inextricable to some degree, for without the initial conquests typical of an empire, the consolidation of many hundreds of communities into a state is difficult to envision. By the same token, an imperial project—whether launched by a local leader, a city, or a state—is only distinguished from a series of predatory razzias by the erection of an administration capable of doing what states do: regularly gathering resources, mustering manpower, and imposing political will.

The initial scalar leap necessary for the transformation of a relatively small polity into what was first an empire and then a consolidated (and more or less expansive) territorial state often occurred with remarkable speed.[5] While groundwork may have been laid in peaceful as well as martial interactions that occurred many years prior, the leap into unknown territory and scale often came within the reign of one highly organized and ambitious ruler, such as Sargon or Shaka. The genius of such forgers of states and empires, however, was their ability to figure out not just how to conquer but also how to consolidate and keep—how to reorganize their own political structure to cope with a massive increase in the number of communities ruled and resources requisitioned.

In the Nagada II period (c. 3500–3200),[6] Upper Egypt had been a land divided among a number of competing polities, each of which developed local industry, engaged in trade, constructed monuments, and buried its leaders in sumptuous style. The large-scale diversion of power from the courts of individual regional leaders to that of a single ruler of Upper Egypt seems to have first taken place in the Nagada IIIA period (c. 3200). This conclusion stems from the massive, symbolically potent, and extravagantly wealthy tomb U-j at Abydos; from the lack of other comparable "royal" tombs north of the First Cataract; and from the fact that the majority of known Nagada III kings (Iry-Hor, Ka, Narmer) and all of the First Dynasty kings (c. 3000–2890) were subsequently buried at Abydos. It would be foolhardy to assume, however, that the process of establishing Abydene political supremacy was easy or linear. Indeed, the fact that U-j was larger than any of the other Protodynastic tombs at Abydos—including Narmer's tomb—points to the complexity of this process.

It was Narmer, after all, whose economic and political influence is most notably attested from Upper Egypt all the way to the southern coastal plain of Canaan. While this king undoubtedly stood firmly on the shoulders of the rulers who came before him, it is Narmer whose serekhs litter the Nile Valley, the eastern Delta, and Canaan; Narmer whose victories over enemies are most coherently broadcast and whose royal iconography is most elaborately expressed; and Narmer whose achievements allowed Hor-Aha (c. 3000) to ascend to the throne of a united Upper and Lower Egypt as the first god-king of the First Dynasty. While much of our evidence concerning this Protodynastic king's purported accomplishments is gleaned from the iconography on votive gifts—sources that should not be accepted uncritically—the very fact that this king sponsored such ideologically laden pictorial statements speaks volumes about the political sophistication of his rule.

This chapter does not attempt to construct a chronological narrative of how the unification of Upper—and then Upper and Lower—Egypt progressed; such would be unabashed guesswork and would require far more space than is available here. Rather, its aim is to bring to the fore a sampling of the many strategies employed by the Abydene kings of Nagada III and the First Dynasty to co-opt economic, political, and spiritual sources of power from the peoples they conquered and to consolidate their political grip. Many of the techniques utilized in this initial project and discussed below bear strong similarities to those that pharaohs, millennia later, were to deploy with good effect in Syria-Palestine and Nubia. The bulk of these state-forging strategies should likewise strike notes resonant to those whose investments reside in other empires.

Establish Unmitigated Access to Highly Valued Resources

Agriculture, livestock, and labor formed the basis of Egypt's economy and the building blocks of power—a power that first began to be co-opted by local rulers in the late Nagada I period at Hierakonpolis (c. 3600) and throughout Upper Egypt in Nagada II. Social prestige might be gained from gathering resources and from using these staple goods to fete others or to fund projects. The industrial breweries discovered at Hierakonpolis, capable of producing beer for hundreds of individuals at a time, represent early efforts to this end, and by the Nagada IIA period similar industrial establishments could be found at Abydos and the nearby site of Mahasna.[7]

An essential second step for rulers seeking to build and articulate power in Upper Egypt for themselves and for their earthly and divine supporters, however, seems to have been to co-opt all that inspired awe. In anthropological terms, in the Nagada II period there can be no doubt that Egypt entered into a prestige-goods economy in which items accessible only through external exchange and which lacked any practical function with regard to the physical welfare of their users became a fetishistic source of power. As Randall McGuire puts it,

> The artefacts derive their power from ideology, and their exchange and distribution maintains the ideology. Goods that are rare, that require unusual skill to produce, or that are associated with more powerful social systems provide the best candidates for valuables.[8]

Some of these marvels would be disbursed as gifts and rewards, while others (it was surely hoped) would endow the ruler, if kept by him alone, with a similar capacity to excite wonder. Such extraordinary entities, of course, did not need to be fetched from afar. At Hierakonpolis, for example, archaeologists exhumed the bones of monstrously large perch from a ceremonial precinct and the bones of a dwarf from a grave sunk into the funerary chapel of a royal tomb.[9] Admittedly, however, by far the most effective way to obtain items the likes of which had never yet been seen was to seek them out from foreign lands.

As early as the Nagada IIC period, an influx of items, images, and ideas from the greater Mesopotamian world arrived in Egypt. Their effect on the elite of Upper Egypt—a stratum of society eager to adopt new vocabularies of power into its semiotic system—was to inspire immense creativity. Although the duration of this interchange was short, ideas introduced at this time (especially regarding the technology of sealing in order to mark ownership, the utility of writing, the communicative power of heraldic imagery, and the design of niched buildings of monumental proportions) helped forge the visual insignias of high social status in the late Predynastic and Protodynastic period as well as pharaonic iconography throughout the Early Dynastic period and beyond.[10]

When this contact ceased, Upper Egyptian rulers did not have the resources to sponsor their own expeditions to Syria, but they do appear to have emulated their Mesopotamian counterparts in sending out traders in order to facilitate the importation of yet more wonders. Thus, already in the late Nagada II period caches of hundreds of Egyptian storage jars at Khor Daud (located at the mouth of the resource-rich Wadi Allaqi) betray a thriving trade between Upper Egyptian polities and contemporary peoples in northern Nubia. In such exchanges, exotica funneled up from sub-Saharan Africa and perhaps also minerals exhumed from the Wadi Allaqi were exchanged for Egyptian foodstuffs (such as jars of beer, oil, honey, cheese, and grain) and manufactured items (such as linen, metal tools, and sundry items typical of court culture).[11]

Similar ventures took place also in the foreign territories of Lower Egypt and Canaan (see Figure 1.2). Upper Egyptian material was found in greater quantities at the settlement of Maadi than at any other excavated site in Lower Egypt in the Nagada I and early Nagada II periods, suggesting a robust trade relationship. Moreover, local and imported pottery from Maadi, or settlements very much like it, was recovered from the contemporary cultic precinct at Hierakonpolis as well as from elite burials at the same site—including one belonging to a ruler's elephant![12]

Upper Egyptian traders may have been particularly attracted to Maadi due to the site's close relationships with settlements located across the Sinai in the southern coastal plains of Canaan. Archaeologists discovered that the inhabitants of the town had stockpiled goods such as shells and catfish barbs for export. Such trade commodities would likely have been supplemented with ivory and a variety of other raw and manufactured items as well as the foodstuffs originally contained in the Black Ware drop-pots commonly attested at Maadi and in the assemblages of Early Bronze IA sites such as Taur Ikhbeineh, Tel Halif Terrace, and Fara H. Egyptian-style pottery, presumably manufactured in Canaan for the use of resident traders, was also discovered in limited quantities at these sites.[13] From such enclaves, the merchants evidently loaded copper, bitumen, resins, tabular flints, and vessels (most likely originally containing wine and oil) onto donkeys for transport to Maadi. Drawing on Colin Renfrew's

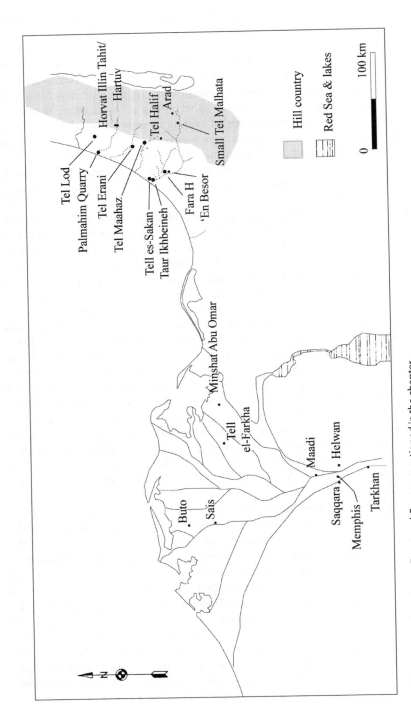

Figure 1.2 Sites from Lower Egypt and Canaan mentioned in the chapter.

typology of exchange, Tim Harrison has characterized Maadi as an entrepôt and its relations with its Canaanite partners as "freelance middleman trading."[14]

Just who initiated the early trade ventures that linked the commercial hub of Maadi with polities in Upper Egypt is unclear. One might speculate that elites from Abydos focused on fostering trade with the north, elites from Hierakonpolis on trade with the south, and elites from Nagada (ancient Nubt, meaning "gold town") on extracting gold from veins in the Wadi Hammamat. As Stephen Savage has demonstrated, however, there were more political players than only these three in the latter half of the Nagada II period, and even within specific settlements certain lineages may have specialized in obtaining access to a variety of trade goods.[15]

The manner in which the rulers of Abydos came to assert their sovereignty over their rivals in other polities is not clear. Superiority in military matters may well have played an important role. Signs of large-scale violence and militarization are difficult to discern in the archaeological record, but the numerous scenes of combat and of prisoners that ornamented the walls of the Painted Tomb at Hierakonpolis, the ivory hilts of knives, and the most elaborate of cosmetic palettes provide evidence that elite identity and martial prowess were already closely entwined in the transition between the late Nagada II and the early Nagada III periods.[16] Regardless of any practical reasons for engaging in internecine warfare (such as settling disagreements over rights to land, mineral resources, or trade routes), the ideology that victory in war brought personal glory and the reality that it also provided an occasion for plunder undoubtedly fueled the violence and encouraged the participation of all levels of society in it.

What is certain—and of paramount importance for the argument that trade often excites imperial ambition—is that after the political unification of Upper Egypt, the Abydene kings moved quickly to establish unmitigated access to the high-value resources the court desired most fervently in both Nubia and Canaan. This too is typical of early complex societies. As McGuire explains,

> Lineage heads gain power relative to their subordinates when they come to control the production or source of the valuables used in the system. The greater this control the less dependent the lineage heads are on foreign lineage heads, and the more they are able to monopolize access to valuables. This means less redistribution to dependents and an increasingly restricted circulation of valuables only to those in the elite group.[17]

Although McGuire wrote in order to elucidate the process by which the elites at Chaco Canyon assumed power, his description fits what we know of Egypt during this period as well. In Protodynastic Egypt, however, as in European colonialism, the elites mustered martial force to retain access to what had become for them crucial resources. As in European colonialism, in Egypt the flag followed quickly on the heels of trade. The guiding policy of the new Protodynastic and early First-Dynasty rulers seems to have been to eliminate middlemen and to seize direct control of both resources and trade contacts.

Lower Nubia and the Early State

As early as the Nagada IIIA period—the time when the ruler buried in U-j and his close contemporaries flourished—the elites of Sayala in Lower Nubia may well have augmented their own power by exploiting the Wadi Allaqi, a region rich in both copper and gold. Two maces found in one exceptionally rich grave in Sayala's cemetery 137 each had handles sheathed in gold, and one was decorated with lines of animals, a motif imported to the Nile Valley from Mesopotamia. Whether these maces were diplomatic gifts from rulers at Abydos or early examples of an "international style" of luxury good is unclear. What *is* clear, however, is that local power brokers in Lower Nubia must have interacted with their northern counterparts on an equal footing.

The growing power of elites at Sayala may well have excited the envy of their counterparts at Qustul, a rival polity situated just upstream of the nearly 20-km-long outcropping of granite that disrupted the Nile and constituted its Second Cataract. Certainly, in the course of the Nagada IIIA–IIIC period, the rulers of Qustul appear to have taken the bulk of Egypto-Nubian material exchange under their stewardship and to have dictated the terms of trade. The site's most select cemetery, rich in imports from Egypt, contained several tombs that virtually all assessors deem royal. Of contemporary tombs in Egypt or Nubia, only U-j at Abydos exceeded them in size.[18]

In addition to quintessentially Nubian luxury goods and a few imports from Canaan, many of the tombs at Qustul included among their associated artifacts either Egyptian imports or objects exhibiting a similar iconographic vocabulary. The famous Qustul incense burner, discovered in the very largest of the Qustul graves (L24), provides the most interesting example of the latter category. This quintessentially Nubian object bore a carved representation of a king wearing the "white crown," which would later characterize Upper Egypt, traveling toward a niched palace façade in a high-prowed boat. The king appears in the company of the Horus falcon, a bound prisoner, and a rosette, reminiscent of the rosettes witnessed on the Narmer Palette and Macehead (see Figure 1.3a and c). The style in which this southern ruler was portrayed would not have been out of place in Upper Egypt and suggests that prior to Qustul's destruction, it and Abydos constituted each other's most prestigious peers.[19]

The amount of Egyptian pottery recovered at Qustul (at a minimum some 271 vessels) and at Khor Daud is indicative presumably of only a portion of the vast amount of Egyptian wealth expended in obtaining exotic goods from Nubia. The option to cut costs, then, by eliminating middlemen—middlemen

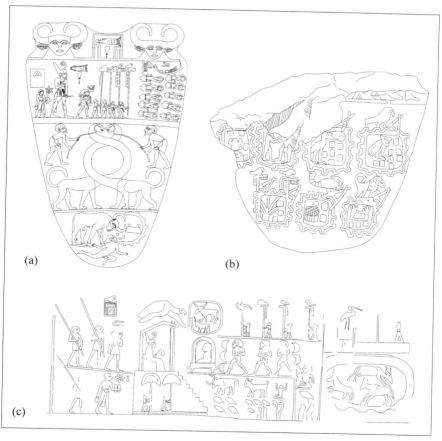

Figure 1.3 Three representations of conquest and its aftermath from the Protodynastic period. (a) The Narmer Palette (redrawn from Quibell 1898, pl. 12); (b) the Cities Palette (redrawn from Quibell 1905, 233, no. 14238); (c) the Narmer Macehead (redrawn from Millet 1990, 54, figure 1).

who held the power potentially to deny Egypt the rare and precious items its prestige-goods economy increasingly demanded, to threaten its southern borders, and ideologically to challenge the uniqueness of the role of the divine sovereign—may have been seen as increasingly attractive. Just how this program of elimination proceeded, however, is unclear and can only be surmised through clues such as the badly burned and plundered tombs at Qustul, the martial graffito just north of the Second Cataract at Gebel Sheikh Suleiman, and, most profoundly, the eerie and abrupt disappearance of robust evidence for indigenous settlement in Lower Nubia. All three of these occurrences seem to have taken place relatively early in the First Dynasty.[20]

Stuart Tyson Smith has suggested that the Egyptians practiced what Ronald Horvath has classified as Eradication Imperialism, meaning that the Egyptians preferred to rid the area of occupants rather than to attempt to politically dominate a subject people.[21] Certainly the archaeological record betrays virtually no signs of any indigenous settlements or cemeteries until some time in the late Old Kingdom. Eradication Imperialism may well be an apt characterization given the iconographic and archaeological evidence for violence. It is also important, however, to stress that the Nubians possessed agency in the matter and likely preferred, like many aggressed peoples, to withdraw beyond the imperialist reach rather than to live in subjugation.[22] Interestingly, with the exception of relatively limited mining and quarrying activity, there is little evidence that the Egyptians chose to exploit this now eminently exploitable region. Instead, the Early Dynastic and Early Old Kingdom rulers (c. 3000–2400) seem content to have left Lower Nubia as a buffer zone. Akin to the supposed tactics of the Romans in Britain, the Egyptians may well have created a wasteland and called it peace.[23]

Southern Canaan and the Early State

If Upper Egyptian elites had been obtaining Canaanite goods via freelance traders who operated out of sites like Maadi in Lower Egypt, this arrangement seems at some point to have been deemed unsatisfactory. As is well known, beginning in the Nagada IIC period, the material culture of Lower Egypt transitioned to more closely resemble that of Upper Egypt, implying that levels of interaction between the north and the south had ratcheted up significantly. Minshat Abu Omar, a site newly established in the eastern Delta in the Nagada IIC period, was built according to southern norms, and its inhabitants appear initially to have traded with the same sites as Maadi. They may, however, have acted relatively early on to establish a monopoly on this lucrative trade. Certainly it is notable that Maadi would be abruptly abandoned prior to the end of Nagada IIC, while the fortunes of Minshat Abu Omar rose such that eventually only the elites of Abydos interred more Canaanite pottery within their graves.[24]

Trade between Egypt and Canaan intensified in the Nagada IIC–D period, and imports of pottery and raw materials appeared in unprecedented quantities in the graves of Upper Egypt's wealthiest citizens.[25] Following the unification of Upper Egypt in Nagada IIIA, however, markedly elite graves and also graves containing Canaanite imports narrowed to only two sites: Abydos and (to a far lesser degree) Hierakonpolis. At this point trade emissaries were stationed at sites like Tel Erani (level C) and Hartuv, in order to contract with local vintners, who now produced, at least in part, with Egypt's market in mind.[26] The several hundred wine jars originally interred in tomb U-j—amounting to an estimated 4,500 liters—are well known, but lesser quantities of similar storage jars were discovered in other Nagada IIIA tombs at Abydos.[27] Clearly, the power of wine to intoxicate and to impress was a factor the new court was eager to use to its advantage.

Demand for such imports evidently expanded along with the size of the state, for slightly before the reign of the Protodynastic King Ka the organization of trade shifted again, with the government moving to enhance production and profitability.[28] Along the Sinai land bridge, the number of significant scatters of Egyptian storage vessels and bread molds escalated abruptly in the Nagada IIIA or Early Bronze IB period.[29] Roughly 80% of the ceramics along the route were now Egyptian in style, and the finds of paired-falcon royal serekhs strongly suggest that the state had assumed direct responsibility for facilitating cross-Sinai trade. If so, as Eliezer Oren has pointed out, they would have anticipated by a millennium and a half or so the system of way stations that New Kingdom rulers erected when safe and efficient passage along the northern Sinai was a state priority (see Chapter 8).[30]

In Canaan as well, the change in policy had a dramatic effect on the archaeological record, leading to the establishment not only of Egyptian enclaves within Canaanite settlements (e.g. Tel Erani B, Tel Halif II, Tel Lod IV) but also to new settlements that exhibited a primarily Egyptian-style material culture (at 'En Besor III, Tel Ma'ahaz I, and Tell es-Sakan).[31] The pottery at both types of sites typically included significant quantities of imported Egyptian wavy-handled transport vessels as well as numerous Egyptian-style bowls and breadmolds fashioned in local clays. The assemblage strongly suggests a resident Egyptian population that oversaw a thriving Egypto-Canaanite commercial enterprise.[32] The percentages of Egyptian-style pottery at these sites varies between roughly 10 and 35% for the enclaves and up to 80–90% for the Egyptian-dominated settlements, yet even the more modest numbers are significant. Indeed, the Syro-Palestinian style pottery seen at Tell el-Dab'a during the Fifteenth Dynasty—when this site served as the capital of the Levantine Hyksos kingdom based in the Eastern Delta of Egypt—only hovered between 30 and 40%! Interestingly, such quantities of utilitarian Egyptian-style pottery would not again be discovered in southern Canaan until the Nineteenth Dynasty, when the area was under military occupation, as is discussed in Chapter 8.

In addition to the style and manufacturing techniques of much of the pottery, Egyptian influence on these settlements is evident in lithic technologies ('En Besor, Tel Erani, and Tel Lod), Egyptian-style architecture and masonry ('En Besor and Tel Erani), and sealing technology ('En Besor, Tel Erani, Tel Halif, and Tel Lod). Uniformly fashioned out of Canaanite clays, the mud used for sealing was either unimpressed or was impressed with designs or hieroglyphic signs typical of cylinder seals in Egypt. At the site of 'En Besor, for example, 90 such sealings were discovered—a huge amount for a site that consisted of a single building and only a dozen or so estimated inhabitants.[33]

Significantly, at all of the Egyptian sites and enclaves so far discussed, except the as yet poorly sampled Tell es-Sakan, serekhs of late Nagada III rulers were discovered etched onto Egyptian storage jars as well as their locally manufactured equivalents.

Egyptian activity in Early Bronze IB Canaan seems to have focused primarily upon two relatively large, fortified sites located along the southern coast: the "mother colony" of Tell es-Sakan, which was Egyptian-dominated and roughly 20–30 acres in size, and an enclave at the 62-acre site of Tel Erani. Tell es-Sakan, interestingly enough, was located at the juncture of Canaan's main north–south trunk route and an east–west route much favored by Bedouin that led toward mining districts to the east. These same factors accounted for the region's vital strategic importance in later times as well. Tell es-Sakan and Tel Erani were then in very close communication with a series of much smaller (1–10-acre) unfortified settlements, some of which may have served as trading posts, checkpoints, or provisioning stations. Other sites and enclaves, more functionally varied in scope, included among their populations Egyptian officials, potters, and even perhaps agriculturalists, based on the lithic evidence for Egyptian-style sickle blades.[34]

This phase of Egyptian-dominated trade is estimated to have lasted roughly a century, to have involved perhaps as many as several hundred Egyptians, and to have reached a peak of intensity in the reign of Narmer, whose serekhs have been identified on locally made and/or imported storage vessels at Tel Ma'ahaz, Tel Erani, Tel Arad, 'En Besor, Halif Terrace, as well as Small Tel Malhata, Palmahim Quarry, and Horvat Illin Tahtit.[35] Egyptian occupation of southern Canaan at this time is intensive enough that some scholars have suggested that the government actively colonized the region between the Besor Brook and the Yarkon River in the late Nagada III period.[36] Relying on martial imagery on the Narmer Palette as well as on somewhat ambiguous archaeological evidence, these scholars view Egypt's presence as established by force and maintained by military control—a textbook instance of informal imperialism.[37]

Other scholars, proponents of the "commercialization model," however, envision the relationship as having been peaceful and collaborative. Certainly the evidence seems to fit the model of a trade diaspora that Abner Cohen developed with respect to Hausa enclaves in Yoruba communities. He defined these settlements as

> interregional exchange networks composed of spatially dispersed specialized merchant groups which are culturally distinct, organizationally cohesive, and socially independent from their host communities while maintaining a high level of economic and social ties with related communities who define themselves in terms of the same general cultural identity.[38]

The arrival of foreigners with lucrative trade ties may thus have been welcomed, if profits from newly stimulated production and trade reached an unprecedented proportion of the local population. The intermingling of Egyptian-style and Canaanite ceramics likewise suggests a relationship of mutual benefit. Indeed on the basis of the distribution of Egyptian cylindrical jars and palettes in contemporary Canaanite settlements, Stan Hendrickx and Laurent Bavay have suggested that Egyptians imported oil for use in cosmetics and returned to Canaan a portion of the finished product. If so, this exchange of raw materials for manufactured goods would be paralleled in countless historical world systems.[39] In support of a model of cooperative co-existence, it has also been noted that the Egyptian-style lithic remains in southern Canaan consist largely of sickle blades, while arrowheads and other weapons are almost entirely absent.[40]

Oddly enough, within a few generations following Narmer's reign, Egyptian investment in these settlements seems mostly to have ceased. With the notable exception of 'En Besor, royal names postdating that of Hor-Aha are scarcely attested on sealings or as serekhs.[41] The rationale behind this large-scale economic withdrawal from Canaan is not understood. Like many governments that have established permanent outposts devoted to the procural (and sometimes production) of desired resources, the First Dynasty court may simply have come to the conclusion that maintaining such settlements represented an unnecessarily complicated and costly method of achieving their aims.[42] Grapes for wine, as it turned out, could be cultivated on the fringes of the Nile Delta, and rulers were quick to usurp such lands for royal domains. Likewise, even the most expensive Canaanite wine purchased for special occasions would represent a financial bargain if the cost of its production did not need to be underwritten!

From the mid-First through the Fourth Dynasties (c. 2950–2494), then, the Egyptians evidently preferred intensive contacts with far-off trading centers like Byblos and perhaps also Yam to relations with their nearest neighbors. In addition, as discussed in the following chapter, the court sponsored exploratory expeditions aimed at identifying mines, quarries, and other means of accessing wealth. By and large, however, the government's focus had shifted to a more direct harnessing of the human, animal, and agricultural resources of the Nile Valley.

Considering the near-simultaneous expulsion of the indigenous A-Group from Lower Nubia, however, it is important to note that the early First-Dynasty rulers may also have been invested in creating and maintaining depopulated buffer zones at their outer edges. Certainly it is notable that Egypt's abandonment of sites in southern Canaan coincided with what Eliezer Oren described as a "total abandonment" of Early Bronze Age sites along the Sinai land bridge.[43] While the steep drop in visibility for indigenous material culture is no doubt tied to the shift in trade patterns, documented campaigns against

Canaanite and nomadic populations in the First Dynasty may also have prompted local out-migration to regions beyond state control. Certainly, it is important to note that—as in Lower Nubia—a robust indigenous presence in the archaeological record of the North Sinai would not reappear until the Egyptian state showed signs of weakening in the late Old Kingdom (Early Bronze IV).[44]

Disrupt the Traditional Power Structures of Enemies

For the kings of Abydos, the first and most pressing task internally was to unify Upper Egypt under their rule. If we lack the scorched earth or mass graves that would unambiguously signal the political defeat of Nagada and Hierakonpolis sometime around the transition to the Nagada III period, other subtler signs betray the newly subordinate status of these polities. At Nagada, an economic downturn is evident throughout the mortuary record, and most dramatically in Cemetery T, which previously had been the burial ground of the town's rulers and their circle of intimates.[45] Although the cemetery continued in use, it no longer contained the type of opulent tombs that suggest an unmitigated access to power. The substantive shift from the South Town toward what would become the Dynastic town of Nubt may also have taken place at this period.[46] Analogously, the Painted Tomb cemetery at Hierakonpolis hosted no more painted tombs, and the center of gravity for the town as a whole shifted toward the floodplain. Although it has been suggested that the latter settlement shift was prompted by a series of low floods, it is worthwhile to note that, following the conquest of the powerful Nubian capital of Kerma in the early Eighteenth Dynasty, the older town was largely abandoned—its population having been transferred closer to the river.[47] Such mandatory evictions, as the Inca knew, acted to unsettle a vanquished population and to render it vulnerable.[48]

The loss of political autonomy at Nagada and Hierakonpolis, as well as at other sites in Upper Egypt, seems to have stripped much of the power from the traditional elites and much of the ambition from those who occupied the social strata just below. Certainly, at numerous sites in Upper Egypt the social competition that surrounded the fashioning and provisioning of tombs seems to have become much more muted, as if rank and status were no longer a matter to be decided locally.[49] What is notable in the late Nagada III and early First Dynasty, in fact, is the establishment of entirely new cemeteries or portions of cemeteries in which sizable mastaba tombs are for the first time found. The intrusive and extravagant mastaba tombs at Nagada, Armant, and Tarkhan, for instance, are representative of a burial style closely associated with the royal court, and their appearance seems to indicate that the occupants of these tombs gained their status by virtue of having been hand-picked by the Abydene kings. Whether or not these individuals bore any ties to the previous elites, the shift in cemetery location, tomb type, and manner of provisioning abruptly and clearly signified that their closest connections were now with the court.[50]

Create Allies where Enemies had Existed Before

Defeating military rivals may have been the shortest of the many steps on the path to political unification. If the Abydene conquerors were to rule a stable realm, however, they required followers outside their own immediate circle—willing participants who were personally invested in the success of the venture. To convert enemies into allies is a delicate business and better accomplished with incentives than with threats. One of the classic strategies for new rulers eager to expand their authority, therefore, is to make at least a pretense of power-sharing. Courting the old elite and restoring back to them a portion of the power they had thought lost forever is one method for doing so. Another is elevating the fortunes of a new lineage or faction, perhaps one that had considered itself slighted under the former regime. Such freshly empowered collaborators are particularly valuable to a new government for their authority depends entirely on their patrons' success.

Something akin to this latter scenario may perhaps have taken place at Hierakonpolis. In the late Nagada II period, when Hierakonpolis was a major power in the region, its ruler was interred in a painted tomb close to the settlement. Following the site's demotion in the Nagada III period, however, burials of elites did not cease. Sumptuous sepulchres did, however, retreat 2.5 km back inside the adjacent wadi to the hallowed ground where the first rulers of Hierakonpolis had been buried in the late Nagada I and early Nagada II period. The new tombs not only consciously emulated the old but were indeed occasionally placed above or even inside these structures! Whether the new elite claimed a relationship of blood or only of ideological outlook with these earlier rulers is not known, but judging from the shift in cemeteries and perhaps also from a smashed life-size statue, this earlier line may well have been actively suppressed or neglected during much of the period that Hierakonpolis vied for paramountcy with its neighbors.[51] If a political alliance with Abydos allowed a rival faction to rise ascendant and (re)claim roots with the past, the new partnership may not have been unpalatable to at least some residents of the city.

Indeed, it appears likely that in the Nagada III period the Abydene rulers and the newly empowered elites of Hierakonpolis moved the religious center of gravity from the precinct at HK29A (which continued to function, albeit in a much more muted fashion)[52] to a newly built temple mount. Nothing remains of the structure erected there except the votive offerings that were later cached when the temple was rebuilt in the early Old Kingdom. What is fascinating, however, is that this temple—intended to serve as the new spiritual focus of the city—was dedicated to the falcon god Horus. During the Nagada III period, while the rulers of Abydos were incorporating the falcon into their own names or titles, rival polities also drew upon falcon imagery to legitimize their own leaders. Thus, in entrusting to Hierakonpolis stewardship of the divine avatar of the rightful ruling king, the Abydene monarchs placed the city at the sacred core of the newly expanded kingdom, inextricably enfolding it into the royal project as a whole.

Indeed, the importance of Hierakonpolis's allegiance to the rulers of Abydos is showcased on the gigantic palette and macehead that Narmer dedicated to Horus of Hierakonpolis and deposited in his temple (see Figure 1.3a and c). On the macehead, Narmer sits enthroned under the protective wings of the goddess Nekhbet—another local deity of greater Hierakonpolis awarded elevated status as a divine protector of the king. Meanwhile, on the obverse of the palette, the king and Horus are depicted working together to subdue their enemies. On other Protodynastic votive objects and luxury goods, the gods of various regions—often depicted as anthropomorphized standards—fight beside the king, likely in visual acknowledgment of the crucial aid their followers had offered in battle.

Among the most tangible expressions of the king's gratitude to his celestial and terrestrial allies may have been the expensive gifts he donated to the temples of gods and to the tombs of men. At Hierakonpolis, the temple of Horus received a lion's share of prestigious royal gifts. Moreover, the precious materials deposited in the tombs of the town's leading citizens—such as the lapis lazuli, silver, gold, turquoise, obsidian, crystal, garnet, cornelian, and ivory objects discovered in tomb 11—suggest the largess of the apparently contemporary king of Abydos, owner of the far grander and more opulent tomb U-j. It is of more than passing interest, then, that "small sandstone carvings of birds, animal-shaped blanks, some with base sockets suitable for carrying on poles"[53] were also discovered within Hierakonpolis tomb 11. So here, with the remnants of this lord and his fetishes, we find the potent fusion of local religious and political authority marshaled in service to the state.

While the archaeological remains of the vast majority of early cult centers are long lost and parallels are thus difficult to come by for polities other than Hierakonpolis and Abydos, excavations in the environs of the Ptolemaic temple of Min at Coptos yielded three colossal statues of the city's patron deity that have been dated to the transition between late Nagada III and the early First Dynasty. If Bruce Williams is correct in reading Narmer's name etched into one,[54] it may be that the reward for the loyalty of Coptos to the new regime was an awe-inspiring set of cultic statues, each originally towering some 4 m tall and weighing in at roughly 2 tons. The fashioning of cult statues in Dynastic Egypt was a closely guarded royal prerogative and so important an endeavor that entire years could be named after the "birth" of a statue-god. The co-option of such vital religious power and creativity by the Abydene kings was, of course, yet another important strategy to portray the institution of kingship as ideologically indispensable.

Before leaving the topic of how the early kings of Upper (and then Upper and Lower) Egypt gained the long-term support of local elites in conquered polities, it is worthwhile returning briefly to Nagada. This locale, which in Dynastic times was sacred to the god Seth, may well be represented by one of the two Seth animal fetishes on the Scorpion Macehead. Seth was rewarded as early as the First Dynasty in Egypt with a privileged position beside Horus as one of the "Two Lords" embodied on earth by the king. A former rival of Horus of Hierakonpolis, Seth of Nagada was transformed into his partner—his other half. Interestingly, the unease of this arranged détente is clearly revealed by the negotiations that took place in Egypt's Second Dynasty, when Seth briefly displaced Horus in the throne name of King Peribsen and then was placed alongside Horus in the name of his successor, King Khasekhemwy (lit. "The Two Powers Have Risen"). Given that Khasekhemwy claimed victory over numerous rebels, it is difficult to imagine that this struggle was not as political as it was religious.

In addition to the elevation of Seth as a patron of kingship, the town of Nagada may well have bestowed its Red Crown upon the Abydene king of Upper and Lower Egypt. The earliest-known depiction of a Red Crown, after all, ornamented a jar interred in a grave at Nagada from a period that long predated the ascendancy of Abydos.[55] Further, the town may also have provided this king with his first queen. Certainly, the palace-façade mastaba tombs of Queen Neithhotep (c. 3000) and her unknown near-contemporary discovered at Nagada suggest that the Abydene kings at the dawn of the First Dynasty saw fit to broker a diplomatic marriage with Nagada's post-conquest elite, thereby strengthening the ties of this group to the king. Significantly, this new elite apparently did not claim descent from the old guard elite whose burial ground had been Cemetery T. The close identification of both the Red Crown and the goddess Neith—who often wore it in religious iconography—with Lower Egypt and the Deltaic town of Sais, may have been a result of the Egyptian predilection for "symbolic geography"[56] whereby a dualism perhaps formerly relevant only to Upper Egypt (i.e. the "Lower" Kingdom of Nagada vs. the "Upper" Kingdom of Hierakonpolis) was transposed onto an entirely new political reality once Upper Egypt had united and imposed its rule on the Delta.

It is unknown whether the remaining First-Dynasty queens bearing theophoric names incorporating the goddess (Merneith and Herneith, for example) came from Nagada or from Lower Egypt (perhaps even from the lineage of the ruler Ny-Neith, who is as yet attested solely on a wine jar from Helwan[57]). A Lower Egyptian origin is not improbable, however, as the first kings of the First Dynasty cultivated the loyalty of former Lower Egyptian power centers in much the same way that their predecessors had courted the elites of Hierakonpolis and Nagada. Thus, at the start of the First Dynasty, the cobra goddess of Buto gained a seat beside the vulture goddess of greater Hierakonpolis to become the second of the divine "Two Ladies" that protected and aided the king. Likewise, the Narmer Macehead seems to suggest that earlier—perhaps as a reward for its alliance with the Abydene kings—triumphal ceremonies took place at Buto, and that its shrine quite likely reaped a percentage of the booty Narmer accrued in his battles for control over the entirety of the Nile Valley (see Figure 1.3c).

Just what the relationship between Buto and the Upper Egyptian powers had been prior to this point would be fascinating to ascertain. Recent excavations have revealed the town's precocious engagements with Syrian traders, and archaeological evidence suggests that lucrative maritime connections may have prompted southern elites as early as the mid-Nagada II period to establish a commercial enclave at Buto.[58] Certainly by the time that the ruler of Upper Egypt was laid to rest in tomb U-j, the southern court and the same heron-topped shrine of Buto that Narmer would later honor for its collaboration were in close contact. Ivory tags from the tomb imply that the heron-shrine (or the polity it represented[59]) sent the deceased ruler parting gifts to take into the afterlife—though it is unclear whether these gifts imply a relationship of dominance and submission, of an enclave to its sponsor, or of diplomatic courtesy.

By the reign of Narmer, Buto had clearly become a key member of the Abydene alliance and found itself well remunerated. While the site's traditional heron-shrine seems to have received booty from Narmer, Thomas von der Way suggests that Narmer or Hor-Aha sponsored the construction at the site of an additional place of worship. Based on images of bulls found within, it may have been that this second cultic locus was dedicated to the king-as-bull, just as the Horus temple at Hierakonpolis honored the king-as-falcon.[60] Regardless, recorded visits of early First-Dynasty rulers to pay their respects to the gods of Buto and to Neith of Sais demonstrate that even in the aftermath of conquest Egypt's earliest kings viewed cultic alliances with vital political players as a keystone of their internal policy.[61]

Crush Resistance

Narmer's votive macehead, which touts his apparent largess toward his divine (and accordingly also earthly) collaborators in Buto, carries an attendant understanding: those who do not *receive* booty are in danger of becoming booty (see Figure 1.3c). At the bottom of the scene, next to the livestock being donated to the temple, is a depiction of a pinioned individual with the numeric notation 120,000 written out below. This number, like the even more exuberant totals for the cows and smaller livestock, must be viewed as an exaggeration or perhaps as an assertion that all his erstwhile enemies now constituted chattel. Whether these conquered foes were Libyans, Lower Egyptians, Eastern Bedouin, or denizens of Canaan's southern coastal plain is uncertain and perhaps immaterial. By the reign of Narmer's successor, Hor-Aha, the Abydene kingdom had likely imposed its authority as far north as modern Tel Aviv and as far south as the Second Cataract in Nubia.

Polities do not typically cede their sovereignty lightly, even if they share a superficially similar material culture with their would-be overlords. As discussed above, the rulers of Abydos no doubt offered potential allies (and subjects) enticements or signing bonuses in order to economize on violence. Willing partners in the imperial venture would be acknowledged in official iconography and ideology as well as by gifts of booty and awe-inspiring divine images and accoutrements. Likewise by virtue of diplomatic marriages, elites from the most powerful polities might mingle their bloodline with that of the royal house. In other cases, however, when such carrots were refused (or withheld), submission could only be accomplished through violent means. Indeed, when opponents possessed walls to retreat behind or enjoyed the mobility to escape to regions beyond the control of the invaders, violence was almost inevitable. Certainly this seems to be the story told by much of the early imagery.[62]

It is an imperial truism that the more trouble a polity has caused a conqueror, the harsher the retribution afterwards. The wholesale elimination of particularly determined foes is in many ways a wise (if not a merciful) move, for it accomplishes many goals at once. Sieges, if difficult, are potentially demoralizing and debilitating for an army. The eminent Chinese strategist who penned *The Art of War* in the fifth century BCE advises,

> When you engage in actual fighting, if victory is long in coming, then men's weapons will grow dull and their ardor will be damped. If you lay siege to a town, you will exhaust your strength. Again, if the campaign is protracted, the resources of the State will not be equal to the strain.[63]

Machiavelli warned likewise: "worldly things are so variable that it is next to impossible for one to stand with his armies idle in a siege for a year."[64] At various points in Egypt's history, its armies did lay siege to cities, but this was generally undertaken only when deemed absolutely necessary, such as at the end of the Second Intermediate period (when the enemies were Hyksos) or else when the allied city-states of Canaan held out at Megiddo under the encouragement of the King of Kadesh, as will be discussed in Chapter 5. The walled city depicted on Narmer's Palette was no doubt also worth the expenditure of extraordinary effort, given that its defeat graced a gift fit for a god (see Figure 1.3a).

Following the successful conquest of a walled town, there are a number of particularly effective methods of dramatically reducing the chances of backsliding and future sedition. The first is razing the city or fortress walls, a tactic Machiavelli and Philippe Maigret both found had much to recommend it.[65] The concerted destruction of city walls by the king's animal avatars is depicted in the Cities Palette (see Figure 1.3b). Although the images could simply depict the moment of breaching walls as the necessary prelude to victory, the notable lack of city walls in Dynastic Egypt suggests that—with the exception of state bastions of security (such as the newly erected southern border fortress of Elephantine and the "White Walls" of Memphis)—the new administration forbade their (re)construction. Analogously, when Egypt was to assume control of Canaan in the Late Bronze Age, the formidable defenses of most Middle Bronze Age polities were destroyed and the vast majority of cities remained unwalled until Egypt ceded control of the region in the early Iron Age.[66]

Because of the frustration that sieges entail, their aftermaths are famously bloody. In innumerable historical accounts, once an army gained entrance to a particularly recalcitrant city, wholesale slaughter ensued. After the victory depicted on the Narmer Palette, executions of prisoners may well have served psychologically to sate the army's frustration, yet the killing itself appears to have been methodical and controlled. Prior to their deaths, males had been tied up, with their arms pinioned behind their backs, and lined in a row. Following the quick stroke of decapitation, each man's head had been tucked between his legs. Surmounting one horror with another, the prisoners were apparently also castrated, and, in all but one case, each man's genitals were placed above his decapitated head—firmly denying the dead any chance of resurrection or regeneration.[67] Once so arranged, the palette implies that the corpses were viewed by the king, his court, and no doubt also by the army, the city's survivors, and numerous individuals from the surrounding countryside. News of the new regime's brutal treatment of enemies no doubt circulated widely and served its purpose as a cautionary tale, all the more memorable for its horror.

Assume Direct and Indirect Control over Large Quantities of Land and Labor

The fate of the women, children, and any remaining men of the defeated city is not publicized on Narmer's Palette, but given the scene depicted on his macehead (see Figure 1.3c), many prisoners may have been donated to regime-friendly temples, as they were to be in later times, to serve as a dependent workforce. Others, it is quite likely, were resettled in domains and royal estates of the type that were set up throughout the country—but particularly in the Delta—in Early Dynastic times. Such settlements, established by and for the state, moved people into areas where their labor could be harnessed for productive purposes, such as farming uncultivated land, tending the many animals accrued by the state, engaging in massive building or agricultural reclamation works, or even simply (re)populating vulnerable frontier zones. Such efforts at internal colonization, undertaken at the dawn of the pharaonic state, molded it for millennia to come.[68]

Massive resettlement programs are typical of many imperial regimes, particularly in the aftermath of military activity. The Assyrian king Assur-dan boasted that he

> ...brought back the exhausted [people] of Assyria [who] had abandoned [their cities (and) houses in the face of] want, hunger, (and) famine (and) [had gone up] to other lands. [I settled] them in cities (and) houses [which were suitable] (and) they dwelt in peace. I constructed [palaces in] the (various) districts of my land ... (and thereby) [piled up] more grain than ever before.[69]

Resettlement programs have the virtue of accomplishing a variety of goals simultaneously. Resistant populations may be rendered dependent on the state if they are relocated far from their extended families and provided with previously uncultivated land that would take a few years to become profitable. During this time the population would be entirely dependent on the state for sustenance and supplies. The Inca recognized the benefits of this tactic and used it to great effect, relocating several million people in less than a century. The case of the Inca is remarkable only for its scale, however, for forcible relocation is a staple strategy of states and empires worldwide.[70]

So far as can be ascertained, Early Dynastic *ḥwt*-estates were large state-owned tracts of land that had been provided with a dependent population and livestock in order to provide revenue for the pharaoh and his administration. While some of the profits may well have been funneled back to the court in the newly founded capital at Memphis, much of the produce appears to have been stored locally and to have funded the travel expenses of court functionaries as well as numerous government initiatives such as alabaster quarrying.[71] The survival of this system throughout the entire Old Kingdom and the fact that Thutmose III emulated important aspects of it when he reorganized the administration of his northern empire—as will be discussed in Chapter 6—is evidence of its success.

Another category of state-owned land was the royal "domain," which was devoted to supplying the funerary equipment and perpetual cult needs of a particular pharaoh. Perhaps already evidenced in the provisioning of tomb U-j, royal domains survived throughout the Old Kingdom, though their functions seem increasingly to have been co-opted by those of "new towns" and "pyramid towns" as the era wore on.[72] Like *ḥwt*-estates, these purpose-built settlements ensured that potential laborers for state projects were centralized, that land was brought into cultivation, and that a great quantity of produce was funneled from the peripheries into the coffers of the court. These eternal domains of the dead may also have been partially intended to provide collateral relatives of deceased pharaohs with a perpetual source of income so that their upkeep did not become a burden to the current ruler. Certainly, many of the officials that supervised such settlements were indeed descendants of the royal founder.[73] Situated on a different continent, thousands of years later, the Inca would also apportion royal mortuary estates to relatives of deceased rulers so as to provision and placate a noble class that swelled with each successive reign.

The Gebelein archive of papyri, which pertain to two related Upper Egyptian funerary settlements established in the Fourth Dynasty, is of particular importance for understanding this type of funerary domain. It contains corvée labor lists for the construction of a temple of King Snefru (c. 2613–2589), ration lists for grain and cloth, and a census which demonstrates that, while there were some officials and craft specialists resident within the settlement, the bulk of the population was made up of agricultural laborers, many of whom were classified as "servants" or "slaves" of the king (*ḥm-nswt*).[74] Significantly, the hieroglyphs designating both estates and domains depicted walled and occasionally fortified structures, while their administration—as well as that of "royal colonists"—was occasionally paired with the administration of watchtowers.[75] Flight from forced agricultural labor occurred throughout pharaonic history, as records from the Middle Kingdom and the Roman period attest.[76] Such evasion was no doubt especially acute, however, at a time when forced labor had not yet been naturalized by innumerable centuries of state imposition.

Erect an Infrastructure so that Resources may be Cultivated and Collected in an Orderly and Efficient Manner

Establishing direct ownership over land and labor in a conquered region is an effective strategy for securing a stable, steady stream of income to the imperial government. Regardless of how lucrative this method of resource extraction might be, however, empires and states typically aim also to impose taxes on the greater population as a whole. Broad-based taxation in goods and labor obviously vastly increases crown revenue, but it also serves the more insidious purpose of social engineering, such that conquered people become subjects of the state and excess income, which might have fueled personal ambitions, is siphoned off into the royal treasury.[77]

In order to requisition its share of surplus, a state relies upon intelligence, intimidation, and ideology. Conquering governments must quickly understand just who and what in their new realms can and/or should be taxed.

Likewise, unless they are comfortable encountering near-constant resistance, they must develop an ideology that legitimizes their extraction. One of the first moves typical of imperial governments is establishing a census to survey and document human and material resources in their realm.[78] Intimidation and ideology are, in effect, the stick and the carrot of resource extraction. Subjects must be made aware of the consequences of tax evasion, but they should ideally be convinced that in surrendering the profits of their labors, they derive benefit.

Although the evidence is frustratingly sparse, it seems that already in the Nagada III period, the Abydene kings had instituted a regular "royal progress" to address all three concerns, which is a tactic common to old and new world empires alike.[79] Royal annals and early year names demonstrate that every other year an event called the "Following of Horus" took place. Judging from its determinative, the travel occurred by boat, and the reference to Horus as well as the prominence of this event in the records strongly suggest the personal participation of the king. When attested in the Second Dynasty (c. 2890–2686) this progress could take place in conjunction with a "count"—sometimes specified as assessing fields or gold. The combination of these two events has convinced many scholars that the progress had always served in part as a census and/or resource assessment. As the government became naturalized, however, more of a state than an empire, the personal participation of the pharaoh appears no longer to have been deemed necessary, and the system was replaced at least in part by a biennial cattle count.[80] From that time on, highly ritualized royal journeys throughout the length of the country seem to have been undertaken primarily upon a ruler's accession to the throne.

Archaeological and textual information combine to form the impression that Egypt was highly centralized in its first four dynasties, such that power, high-density population, wealth, and awe-inspiring monumentality were all tightly localized at the new capital at Memphis, despite the southern origin of the kings. As in later times, certain court ceremonies periodically drew all the nation's elites (the most important of men and gods alike) to the center. Such ceremonies, which generally involved the reciprocal giving of gifts, enfolded local elites in a personal relationship with the king and situated their tribute within an ideologically charged ritual setting. The bulk of the nation's population, however, would never make this journey or form such bonds. Thus, in a time before the mass distribution of imperial propaganda, the best way to create an investment in the power of the ruler among the widely dispersed population of the countryside was to bring him to them in what may have been, perhaps, an ancient version of shock and awe.

One feature of territorial empires, such as those forged by the Inca and the Egyptians, was that, by and large, artistic and technological production was highly localized in the imperial center and its most vital outposts. The rest of the country existed in much the same state as it always had.[81] To introduce the ornate, exotic, and richly dazzling pomp of the court into the provinces, then, was to create a study in contrasts. In First-Dynasty Egypt, where the government was especially invested in promoting the bold fiction that the pharaoh was a god on earth, the smoke and mirrors intended to create the atmosphere of otherworldly power must have been particularly intense.[82]

So the progress was a chance to exhibit the divine personage of the ruler before his people, and it was also a chance for the king and court to assess for themselves the wealth and loyalty of the provinces. Typically, on such journeys the king received gifts and thus augmented his treasury with whatever prestige goods could be mustered locally, but the progress also occasionally served an ulterior motive of simultaneously assessing and consuming local surplus. Receiving the king was a great honor, but it typically incurred fantastic expense for the host, as feasts fit for a king (and his elaborate retinue) needed to be assembled and prepared and ceremonial architecture fit to receive a king constructed. Thus, such visits were best spaced at least a couple of years apart, as was the Following of Horus, to give the provinces time to recover from the expenditure of the last royal visit and to accumulate adequate supplies for the next.[83]

The exploitative nature of such visits was recognized by European colonial officials in Africa, who—perhaps jealous of the profits being consumed by the indigenous kings—frowned on such royal progresses. British authorities in Uganda, for example, held suspicions

> ...that the Mukama used them as a means of economizing on his palace expenses. They were also growing increasingly unpopular with the people, who were required to contribute labor and foodstuffs to support them, and saw little or no return for their efforts. But they were important traditionally, both in enabling the Mukama to keep an eye on the activities of his chiefs of all ranks in their areas, and also in keeping him in touch with trends in public opinion throughout the country.[84]

If the full-blown ceremonial that accompanied the Following of Horus eventually came to be seen by Egypt's population more as a burden than an honor, this may account for the fact that the custom is poorly attested following the First Dynasty. Indeed it is possible that the rulers of the Second Dynasty largely abandoned the custom of participating in the biennial progress—along with the even more egregious custom of retainer sacrifice—as part of a set of reforms intended to distinguish this dynasty from its predecessor. As will be discussed in Chapter 6, Thutmose III's annual armed visitation to Syria-Palestine in the New Kingdom bore many similarities to a royal progress, but it too would be abandoned in a relatively short time, presumably due to being deemed unnecessary, exploitative, and/or ineffective.

Conclusion

The two arguments presented here find cross-cultural parallels elsewhere. The notion that the flag follows trade is not at odds with the more famous reverse statement that trade follows the flag. It simply places emphasis not on the role of the colonies in trade but on the role of trade in inciting an acquisitive desire on the part of one polity to control the resources of another directly. Thus, the very prosperity that the Nubian rulers enjoyed as a result of trade with Upper Egyptian aggrandizers is what eventually brought Egypt's armies upon them. Likewise, trade between Upper and Lower Egypt resulted in an increasing drive on the part of the former to control not only Lower Egypt, but also, eventually, that region's trading partners in southern Canaan. Those polities that traded with Europe in the nineteenth and early twentieth centuries found similarly that military men followed quickly upon the heels of merchants. Indeed, innumerable examples of much the same phenomenon could be culled from ancient times up until the present day.

Regarding the second key argument of this chapter—that states often *follow* empire rather than precede it—Thomas Barfield has written,

> It could be argued that these definitions could be equally applied to large states, not just empires. This should not be surprising because from an archaeological perspective it appears that empires were the templates for large states, and not the reverse. Historically, empires were the crucibles in which the possibility of large states was realized. Indeed, it is difficult to find examples of large states in areas that were not first united by an empire.[85]

For most of its history, pharaonic Egypt stretched—at bare minimum—all along the Nile's floodplain from the First Cataract to the Mediterranean Sea. Yet at the dawn of the state there was nothing traditional about these borders, and neither was there any precedent for the rule of a single god-king over a nation. Local peoples and polities, it seemed, required persuasion before this particular ideological "truth" would be accepted as self-evident. As William J. Adams rather cynically summed up their project, Egypt's pharaohs, for the first several centuries they held power, "were chiefly engaged in consolidating the realm and subjugating their own people."[86]

The late Nagada III and Early Dynastic rulers employed many strategies besides those so far discussed to augment their power and incorporate their newly conquered territory into a functioning state. The Abydene kings, for example, moved into the newly conquered region—perhaps as early as the reign of Narmer's predecessor Ka—established a lavish and sacred capital, and administered their new country from its most strategic point.[87] Located at the juncture between Upper and Lower Egypt, Memphis remains even today at the political heart of the country, absorbed into the sprawling megalopolis of Cairo. Moreover, as the thousands of tombs at Helwan attest, the Abydene court created and cultivated an efficient team of bureaucrats and nobles to share in their power and to aid in resource extraction. Whether the government as yet acted to ensure the allegiance of its most important officials by raising their children at court is uncertain, but this practice would be in place by the Fourth Dynasty.[88] Such youths—whose futures would either be glorious or cut quite short, depending on the behavior of their fathers—would be joined in the New Kingdom by the sons of Nubian and Syro-Palestinian vassals. This topic, however, is one that must await Chapter 7.

Thus, in addition to ensuring that the threat of force was always implicit and to moving their court so as to occupy the geographic lynchpin of their new realm, the first rulers proceeded to force their entry into pre-existing natural and cosmological systems by performing agricultural rites, founding and visiting temples, creating statues of gods, marshaling the most important gods in their retinue (on standards), and even by promoting themselves to the ranks of the divine. The fact that this ideology endured for well over three millennia testifies to the success of these early efforts in forging a nation. As the generations cycled and new governments attempted to extend their authority on various frontiers, some of these early strategies would be resuscitated and others amended. Still others were to be invented as circumstance demanded. Exploring these heavily creased imperial blueprints—rubbed raw with revisions and smudged by annotations—is, of course, the central project of the chapters that follow.

Notes

1 Fullerton 1913, 206.
2 Renfrew and Cherry 1986.
3 Sinopoli 1994, 159.
4 Carneiro 1970, 733.
5 Flannery 1999, 5–18.
6 For consistency's sake, all dates given are those provided in Shaw 2003. For a revised dating, see Stevenson 2016.
7 Mączyńska 2014, 199. In this technology, Lower Egypt was not far behind, as evidenced by a brewery dating to Nagada IIB at Tell el-Farkha (Adamski and Rosińska-Balik 2014, 23).
8 McGuire 1989, 50.
9 Linseele and Van Neer 2003, 7; Pieri 2011, 7–8.
10 Stevenson 2013.
11 Török 2009, 36–8; Roy 2014.
12 Adams and Friedman 1992, 321; Adams 1996, 5; Friedman 2003, 10; Mączyńska 2014, 194.

13 The nature of Egypto-Canaanite trade at Buto and Maadi in the Chalcolithic period is poorly understood (Mączyńska 2014, 184–8). For an overview of Early Bronze IA trade, see Harrison 1993.

14 Harrison 1993, 89.

15 Savage 1997.

16 Bestock 2017, 24–77.

17 McGuire 1989, 50.

18 O'Connor 1993, 21.

19 Williams 1986, 138–45.

20 Török 2009, 49–51.

21 Horvath 1972, 47; Smith 1991, 83.

22 For examples of societies that chose to withdraw from their homeland rather than to suffer oppression, see Sowell 1998, 44, 271, 299.

23 Tacitus, *Agricola*, chapter 30.

24 Anđelković 1995, 63; Hartung 2002, 446; Mączyńska 2014, 188–90.

25 Hendrickx and Bavay 2002, 72.

26 Braun and van den Brink 1998; Hendrickx and Bavay 2002, 66–7, 73–4.

27 Anđelković 1995, 57, 60; Hendrickx and Bavay 2002, 67.

28 Hartung 2002, 447–8; Braun 2014, 37.

29 Oren 1989, 393, 400–1; Miroschedji 2002, 43.

30 Oren 1989, 393, 402–4.

31 Braun 2014.

32 Porat 1992, 433–5.

33 Brandl 1992; Braun 2003.

34 Gophna 1987, 16–18; Schulman 1992, 410–11; Beit-Arieh and Gophna 1999, 197–8, 206.

35 Ben-Tor 1991, 8; Amiran and van den Brink 2001, 47; Miroschedji 2002, 44.

36 Braun 2014.

37 Doyle 1986, 143; Schulman 1992, 409.

38 Abner Cohen quoted in Stein 2002, 30.

39 Levy et al. 1997, 6; Hendrickx and Bavay 2002, 74.

40 Ben-Tor 1991, 5–6.

41 Schulman 1992, 410.

42 Stein 2005b, 152.

43 Oren 1989, 400, 403–4.

44 Yekutieli 2002.

45 Bard 1989, 240–2, 245.

46 Wilkinson 1999, 336–7.

47 Bonnet 1991, 114; Wilkinson 1996, 87–8.

48 D'Altroy 2003, 248–9.

49 For a discussion of this dynamic in Egypt and cross-culturally, see Morris 2006a.

50 Wilkinson 1996, 73, 86.

51 Adams 1996; Friedman 2005, 11–12.

52 Friedman 2009, 98.
53 Adams 1996, 13.
54 Williams 1988, 36–7.
55 Wainwright 1923.
56 Kemp 1989, 41.
57 Köhler 2004, 310.
58 von der Way 1992, 3–4, 9.
59 Wilkinson 1999, 317–19.
60 von der Way 1992, 7.
61 Wilkinson 1996, 8.
62 For a comprehensive survey of violent imagery from the period of state formation, see Bestock 2017, 40–77.
63 Sun Tzu, *Art of War*, chapter II, 2–3.
64 Machiavelli *Prince*, ch. X, 44.
65 Machiavelli *Prince*, ch. XX, 83, 86–7; Maigret 1747, 231–2.
66 Gonen 1992a, 218.
67 Davies and Friedman 2002, 244–6.
68 Wengrow 2006, 142–6; Scott 2017, 150–82.
69 Kuhrt 1995, 48.
70 D'Altroy 2003, 20; Scott 2017, 150–5.
71 Wilkinson 1999, 118, 123–4; Moreno García 1999, 233–8; Moreno García 2007, 317–18, 325.
72 Dreyer 1992, 296–7; Gillam 1995, 226; Wilkinson 1999, 118–22.
73 Breasted 1906a, 88–90; Troy 2003, 13–14; Muhs 2016, 16–17.
74 Troy 2003, 11; Posener-Kriéger 2004; Moreno García 2007, 320.
75 Strudwick 2005, 423; Moreno García 2007, 320.
76 Wilkinson 1999, 119–20; Williams 1999, 444–5, n. 35; Given 2004, 103–4; Moreno García 2007, 317.
77 See the discussion in Cromer 1910, 57.
78 Given 2004, 30, 37–40.
79 Hendrickx et al. 2012.
80 Wilkinson 1999, 113–14, 220–1; Muhs 2016, 15–16.
81 Trigger 1993, 10–11.
82 See Morris 2013.
83 For descriptions of such elaborate royal progresses, see Beattie 1971, 138–9; Wiesehöfer 2001, 40–1; Given 2004, 94.
84 Beattie 1971, 139.
85 Barfield 2001, 33. See Diamond 1974, 1, who asserted that the rise of state-based societies began with "conquest abroad and repression at home."
86 Adams 1984, 37.
87 Wilkinson 1996, 8.
88 Breasted 1906a, 117.

2

Settler Colonialism (c. 2400–2181)

In the late Old Kingdom, the Egyptian state sanctioned the settlement of Dakhla Oasis, a large but relatively resource-poor patch of green located some 275 km deep into the Sahara Desert. Prior to this time, Fourth Dynasty (c. 2589–2566) prospectors had visited it in passing, but evidence for Nilotic peoples is otherwise difficult to identify. Of interest in this chapter are the motivations of the state, the progressive demilitarization of the colonial settlements, the relations between the Egyptians and the semi-pastoral peoples they settled amidst, the unusual power exercised by the oasis's quasi-independent governors in the late Sixth Dynasty (c. 2278–2184), and the ultimate reaction against these rulers.

Given that Egypt's last large-scale experiment with settling regions beyond its borders was abandoned by the mid-First Dynasty (c. 2900), it is useful to begin by stating that rulers of Egypt from that time all the way through the Fourth Dynasty were isolationist in outlook. Raiding, trading, mining, and prospecting took place prior to the late Old Kingdom, but the state made virtually no effort to colonize or methodically control land that lay outside the Nile floodplain north of the First Cataract or much beyond the narrow routes leading to quarries, mines, or Red Sea harbors. Moreover, it is difficult to give much credence to the scant surviving records of purported military ventures in Nubia.[1]

With the late Fifth and Sixth Dynasty, however, the textual record for Egyptian engagements with surrounding lands increases, perhaps because a general waning of Egyptian power was conversely balanced by a resurgence in the indigenous populations of both Canaan and Lower Nubia. Thus, the royal agent Weni in the Sixth Dynasty (c. 2330–2278) was ordered to lead an army of Egyptian and allied troops into Canaan to punish the "Sand-dwellers" six times! Likewise, two Sixth-Dynasty Egyptian tomb biographies show the great lengths that Egyptian troops and traders had to go through just to reclaim the bodies of their fallen compatriots. In the case of a sole companion and ritual priest who had died in Nubia, the delivery of 100 donkeys loaded with produce was required to ransom the body, while the corpse of a sole companion and ship's

Ancient Egyptian Imperialism, First Edition. Ellen Morris.
© 2018 Ellen Morris. Published 2018 by John Wiley & Sons Ltd.

captain, who had been ambushed on the shores of the Red Sea by Bedouin, had to be seized by force.[2]

When one takes into account both the internal focus of the Old Kingdom and its increasingly beleaguered border zones in the Sixth Dynasty (c. 2345–2181), it is especially surprising to find Egypt's first large-scale experiment in settler colonialism occurring in Dakhla, an oasis so remote that even today—in an age of paved highways and fast cars—the vast majority of Nile Valley Egyptians have never visited it. Roughly a full week of arduous trekking through waterless terrain would have been necessary to reach Dakhla in the Old Kingdom. Moreover, as will be discussed shortly, the donkey caravans that most travelers employed in order to make the journey feasible would have been expensive and logistically challenging to arrange.

Even with the aid of camels, which were employed by later travelers, the journey was not for the faint of heart. As narratives of desert travel attest, water stored in goatskin bags became ever more rancid as the journey progressed, and the threat of accident or ambush was ever present. Indeed, common wisdom held that the easiest way to identify a desert route was by the numerous camel bones that littered it. Such bleak remnants served as a constant reminder that the end of the road for some would come in a slow death by dehydration.[3] Given the arduous task of simply reaching the oasis and the comparative dearth of natural resources to be found there in comparison to the Nile Valley, Ahmed Fakhry's discovery in 1947 of the ruins of a once-thriving late Old Kingdom colony was entirely unforeseen.

Settler Colonialism and an Encounter Between Others

Europe's colonial ventures in the past few centuries have shaped the modern world such that a great many nations can be aptly described as "post-colonial," having been governed by an outside power in the relatively recent past. Perhaps ironically, the same colonial powers that so influenced the trajectory of the peoples over whom they exerted authority were in many cases themselves indelibly imprinted with the experience of their *own* colonization under the Roman empire. Although this earlier colonial experience took place roughly two millennia ago, it left its mark on the Romance languages still spoken in many European countries as well as on religious, social, and political spheres that were in turn fundamental to the culture of the colonizer in modern times.

Perhaps not surprisingly, then, when Europeans looked for models and precedents for their own imperial governments and colonies, they often looked back to the Roman empire and to the methods by which their own ancestors and countless others in the ancient Mediterranean world had been dominated.[4] Settler colonialism—both ancient and modern—is thus an especially vibrant area of study, as it occurred in virtually all areas of the world at different historical junctures. According to Gil Stein, a colony can be understood as

> an implanted settlement established by one society in the territory of another society. The implanted settlement is established for long-term residence by all or part of the population and is both spatially and socially distinguishable from the communities of the host society. The settlement at least begins with a distinct formal or informal corporate identity as a community with some level of cultural, economic, military, or political ties to its homeland....[5]

Colonial experiences differ according to the purpose for which the colony was established, the backgrounds and motivations of the colonists, and, most especially, the nature of the relationship between the colonists and the indigenous population. Given that archaeological research at Dakhla is relatively recently established and that, consequently, opinions are ever in flux as to the meaning of various categories of material culture, much remains to be understood about the nature of the colonial experience during the late Old Kingdom. This chapter aims to present an overview of the dynamics involved in this early experiment, while acknowledging that ongoing excavations by members of the Dakhleh Oasis Project, the Institut français d'archéologie orientale, the ACACIA project, and other expeditions have the potential to radically change our perceptions of this process.

For an encounter to be classified as "colonial" in its common understanding, scholars generally stipulate that there should be stark societal differences between the newcomers and the indigenous occupants of the land. Moreover, these differences should have resulted in an imbalance in power that worked in favor, initially at least, of the settlers. Colonists were often distinguished by their possession of highly effective tools and weapons unavailable to the local inhabitants, by the fact that they included many more full-time specialists among their ranks, and by a radically incongruous understanding of property and set of socio-economic priorities. According to this understanding of colonialism, it has been stated that those colonized were typically "technically backward, small scale in their political organization, incapable of concerted action, as compared with their ... conquerors. Above all, they were ... hopelessly outclassed in their ability to apply force."[6] While many scholars have rightly contested the notion that such technological and organizational differences need be inherent to the colonial dynamic, in the case of Dakhla such caveats are beside the point. It would be difficult to find two more dissimilarly structured societies than those of the Old Kingdom colonists and the oasis population they settled amidst.

Archaeologists refer to Dakhla's indigenous inhabitants from the late Predynastic period through the First Intermediate period as "Sheikh Muftah," after a village located in the vicinity of an early activity zone. The name (or names) that these people would have used to describe themselves is unknown, though the Egyptians may have designated them rather generically as Tjemehu or Tjehenu—two poorly understood terms that referenced inhabitants of the Western Desert during this time period.[7] Akin perhaps to the modern use of "Bedouin," such terms may have lumped together those who followed similar lifeways, yet who almost certainly viewed themselves as internally heterogeneous and often, perhaps, at odds. Without linguistic or archaeological evidence to suggest alliances or rivalries between various subsets of Dakhla's indigenous inhabitants, our understanding of colonial relations remains as yet unnuanced.

In the sixth and fifth millennia, when increasing aridity encouraged migration toward the Nile Valley, the cultures that flourished in Dakhla may have been more complex socially, technologically, and economically than their riparian counterparts. Many cultural traits typical of early Predynastic Egypt are, after all, first witnessed in the Western Desert, such as the adoption of cattle herding, circular architecture, and various lithic technologies.[8] By the time the Sheikh Muftah culture is first recognized, however, the situation had reversed. Isolated finds of artifacts typical of the Nile Valley at Dakhla as well as oasis-ware ceramics in the Valley indicate that there were indeed sporadic communications between the two regions, yet long before the advent of the First Dynasty their cultural trajectories had diverged markedly. In the Nile Valley, agriculture quickly took root as the basis of the economy, encouraging long-term sedentism and allowing surplus to be accumulated that would increasingly support craft specialists as well as, eventually, nobles and bureaucrats. Metallurgy, the arts, the technology of writing, and monumental architecture flourished under the patronage of the court.

Given that oasis dwellers who traveled to the Nile Valley over the course of nearly a millennium would have been capable of seeing first-hand the potential of agriculture to transform society and of then communicating this potential to other oasis dwellers, it is significant that this way of life was *not* adopted. Perhaps the initial investment of time and energy was deemed daunting and the resources of the oasis were regarded as better suited to the herding and gathering economy of the semi-nomadic pastoralist. While it could have been that the Sheikh Muftah subsisted quite comfortably without agriculture, the archaeological remains tell a story of relative hardship. The few skeletons discovered so far exhibit signs of nutritional stress and/or disease—symptoms of life in an unforgiving environment. Likewise, the remains of campsites demonstrate that protein was scarce enough that the bones of animals were routinely reduced to smithereens in the attempt to extract even the marrow within them.[9]

The Sheikh Muftah do not appear to have belonged to the original affluent society, as Marshall Sahlins has characterized those who did not choose to practice agriculture because their nutritional needs could be met much more simply by living off the land.[10] Thus, it is tempting to suggest that the basis of the Sheikh Muftah's aversion to agriculture was ideological rather than practical. Perhaps the oasis inhabitants who had visited the Nile Valley did not like what they saw and specifically chose to engage in a very different life. The antipathy traditionally felt for fellahin by Bedouin is well known, and it may have been that the oasis pastoralists likewise to some extent defined themselves in opposition to Nilotic farmers, whom they viewed as tethered to their lands and mercilessly taxed. In view of the burdens piled upon the peasants by an exploitative elite, the Sheikh Muftah may have emphatically privileged the relatively free and egalitarian existence of the semi-nomadic pastoralist. Dakhla remained an oasis free from state control, where homes and material possessions did not tie an individual down and neither did there exist a rigid class hierarchy that set one man far below his fellow. Certainly the scarcity of remains for the Sheikh Muftah and the complete absence of any archaeologically recognizable architecture whatsoever over the course of nearly a millennia and a half argues persuasively that, prior to the immigration of Old Kingdom settlers to Dakhla, a relatively modest oasis population lived lightly on the land.[11]

Close Encounters Prior to Intensive Colonialism

Prior to the Fourth Dynasty, evidence within Dakhla for Nile Valley pots and people is extremely limited. A few graves with imported material that may possibly have belonged to Nile Valley individuals have been dated to the Early Dynastic period.[12] Likewise, imported Early Dynastic ceramics were found together in a deep sounding with Sheikh Muftah pottery at the site of Mut. While the greater context of this mixed assemblage is not known, Colin Hope has suggested that by the early Old Kingdom both Egyptian and Sheikh Muftah potters worked at Mut and that the latter experimented on occasion with incorporating Nilotic influences into the design of their vessels.[13] Whether this experimentation is indicative of a general openness toward Nilotic culture is impossible to ascertain, but similarly hybrid Sheikh Muftah ceramics do not otherwise appear at this early date.

In the Fourth Dynasty, pharaonic interest in Dakhla seems to have coincided with a renewed royal focus on prospecting, as is amply evident in the Sinai and Nubia. A recently discovered hillock, located roughly 100 km into the desert southwest of Dakhla, bears evidence of two expeditions launched by the court (see Figure 2.1). The first took place in Khufu's 25th year (c. 2584) and consisted of 200 men, while another, twice that size, took place two years later. The stated purpose of the latter expedition was to "...produce *mfȝt*-powder from the *sš*-pigment of the desert district. They (both) took the *minw*-sacks/semi-precious

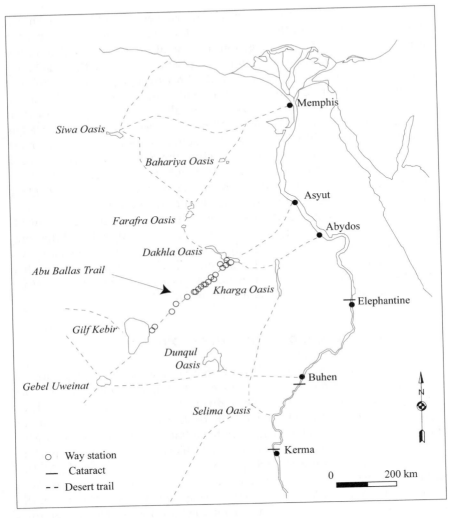

Figure 2.1 Desert routes and way stations.

minerals."[14] The powder referred to is most commonly presumed to have been red ochre, though the value of ochre would seem unequal to the resources expended in obtaining it. Just how far the men and beasts journeyed past "Khufu Hill" is unclear, as is the question of whether the prospectors might have doubled as long-distance traders.

The many tethering stones discovered along routes extending to the southwest of Dakhla demonstrate that expeditions undertaken in the third millennium relied heavily upon donkey transport—hardly surprising given that it is extremely difficult for an individual to transport more than three days' worth of provisions unaided. These expeditions, led by Egyptian overseers of recruits, involved hundreds of men and their equipment, foodstuffs, water, and mineral products. If they were to succeed, then, donkey trains consisting of an estimated 50–100 beasts would necessarily be involved in the provisioning, adding their own water and fodder to the collective burden. Such a system was certainly operative in the late Old Kingdom, when the nearby route that extended hundreds of kilometers southwest to the oases of Gilf Kebir and Gebel Uweinat became well established.[15] Thus, taking into account the scale of the expeditions, the appearance of the names of Khufu and Djedefre (c. 2566–2558) at Khufu Hill, the accompanying royal smiting scene, and the upwards of 60 or so inscribed clay seals found at the site, there is little doubt that the expeditions based out of Dakhla in the Fourth Dynasty were court financed.[16]

Even the most carefully provisioned expedition would be destined to failure, however, if the state neglected to equip itself with local knowledge and allies. Thus, the finds at Khufu Hill of shale-tempered sherds characteristic of Dakhla's indigenous population were perhaps to be expected. Certainly, expeditions deep into the desert undertaken by Europeans and Egyptians alike in the nineteenth and early twentieth centuries invariably employed Bedouin guides and relied upon them to safely navigate the shifting sands, to steer by the stars, and to advise correctly on vital logistical matters. Segments of the Sheikh Muftah population appear to have been seasoned desert travelers, judging from the distribution of their pottery on the trails radiating from Dakhla and the uniquely dense clustering of enigmatic artifacts called "Clayton rings" in the environs of the oasis. These distinctive sets of rings and lids have been discovered in lesser numbers at desert sites from Farafra to Kerma throughout the Predynastic period and the Old Kingdom, though their purpose remains unclear.[17] The presence of shale-tempered Clayton rings at Khufu Hill, then, strongly suggests that Sheikh Muftah guides had agreed—for whatever reason and remuneration—to collaborate with Egyptian expedition leaders as early as the Fourth Dynasty.[18]

The narratives of desert travel referenced above agree on two things: first, that Bedouin allies and guides were absolutely crucial to a successful journey, and second, that predatory attacks by unaffiliated Bedouin constituted an ever-present danger.[19] Similar concerns evidently led Fourth-Dynasty expedition leaders to establish a series of watch-posts on high hillocks located around the southern and eastern flanks of Dakhla Oasis (see Figure 2.2). Significantly, the fact that these watch-posts were associated with pottery imported from the Nile Valley suggests that in matters of security the government felt safest with their own men on watch. Given that permanent civilian settlements of Egyptians—with the possible exception of Mut—do not appear to have been established in the oasis at that time, these posts surely delineate the route the prospectors followed.[20] There would, it seems, have been little else to surveil.

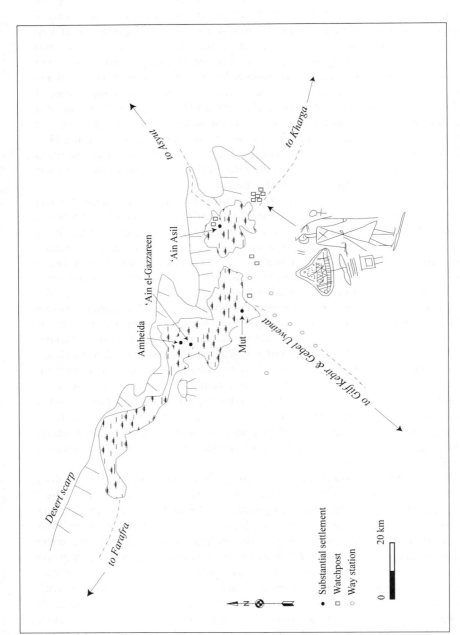

Figure 2.2 Dakhla Oasis in the Old Kingdom and a graffito of a soldier found at a desert watch post (redrawn from Kaper and Willems 2002, 85, figure 4).

Motivations for Colonization

Given that expeditions into the desert southwest of Dakhla continued to be mounted and that soldiers sat sentinel at many of the same watch-towers during the high point of Egypt's colonial experiment in the oasis, it may be that these expeditions represent the primary rationale for the establishment of the colony. If so, however, the scope of such ventures radically expanded. By the Sixth Dynasty large-scale expeditions were routinely setting off some 400 km southwest of Dakhla to the region of Gilf Kebir, Gebel Uweinat, and possibly beyond. The route they took is defined by refueling stations that punctuated the most direct path at roughly 80-km intervals—the distance a donkey can travel before needing to drink deeply—as well as by minor campsites situated a day's travel or so apart.[21] Cairns, donkey bones and droppings, and cleared pathways point to the passage of numerous men and beasts along this route in the late Old Kingdom and First Intermediate period. Maintaining this infrastructure would have been extremely expensive, however, as it was crucial that these stations be continually provisioned—an increasingly difficult task the more distant the destination.[22]

Significantly, parallels to the pottery commonly found at staging posts—vats used for mixing industrial quantities of dough, storage jars, Clayton rings, and smaller versions of the characteristic large water jars—have all been identified at the Sixth-Dynasty site of 'Ain Asil, the undisputed capital of the colony established at Dakhla (see Figure 2.3). Along the trail and at 'Ain Asil, this pottery was invariably Egyptian in style but fashioned out of local fabric. Many of the potmarks found on vessels along the trail are likewise attested at 'Ain Asil. Clearly, then, part of the function of the oasis capital, and perhaps the colony as a whole, was to provision and facilitate long-distance desert trading expeditions.[23]

In the Fourth Dynasty, official activity appears to have centered on Mut, where imported Fourth to Fifth-Dynasty Meidum bowls and Sheikh Muftah sherds have been found together in some numbers along with what looks to have been substantial Egyptian-style architecture of both domestic and seemingly more official character. Whether this architecture belonged to a modest settlement or to a seasonally occupied outpost remains unknown. Egyptian and Egyptian-style ceramic at Mut was always discovered in conjunction with Sheikh Muftah pottery—though, significantly, the percentage of the latter dwindled over time. If the mixing is not due to later disturbance, then it would appear that the earliest Old Kingdom agents had formed an enclave in or adjacent to a Sheikh Muftah settlement, strongly suggesting a collaborative relationship. The location of Mut, nestled to the southwest of the oasis, is eminently logical for staging desert expeditions to the region of Gebel Uweinat and Gilf Kebir, and it is notable that modern expeditions to this region still

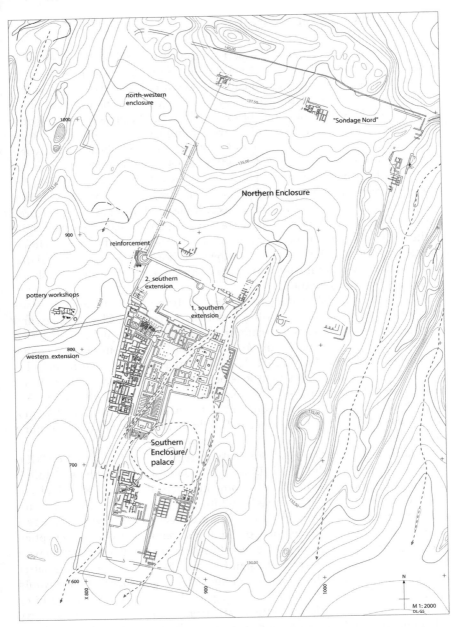

Figure 2.3 Map of the Sixth Dynasty and First Intermediate period levels at 'Ain Asil from Jeuthe 2012, figure 1 © IFAO. Republished with the generous permission of Clara Jeuthe and Georges Soukiassian.

leave from Mut. It is therefore puzzling that with the establishment of 'Ain Asil, the settlement at Mut seems to have been largely abandoned.[24]

The logic behind 'Ain Asil's placement was not its proximity to trailheads south but rather to those that facilitated contact with the Nile Valley. The settlement lay in the shadow of the Darb el-Tawil, the most sensible path for donkey caravans from Egypt to descend the 300-m scarp into the oasis. 'Ain Asil was likewise convenient to the Darb el-Ghubbari trail that led to Kharga and thence to the Nile Valley. Proximity to Egypt's core was presumably of foremost concern to the new colony, given that all metals and numerous other staples of "civilized" life would have had to have come from this direction, as would reinforcements in times of trouble. This refocus to the east of the oasis need not imply a diminishment in the importance of mining or trading ventures, however. 'Ain Asil's governors, after all, typically held a title that indicated their authority over state-sanctioned expeditions, and correspondence discovered in the administrative complex indicates their involvement in facilitating the arrival ("prepar[ing] the road") of a visiting ruler (the *ḥḳз* of *dmi-iw*).[25]

The governors of Dakhla Oasis in the Old Kingdom, then, were apparently charged with engaging in diplomatic or trade relations with desert chiefs and also with provisioning desert transit routes with food and water. This seems, however, like a tremendous investment for the Sixth-Dynasty court, when increasing aridity and decreasing Nile floods were beginning to significantly erode the country's economic health. Why, then, did the government of Egypt pick that particular time to invest in a full-fledged colony?

A Safer Trade Route

One answer may perhaps be divined from the inscriptions of Harkhuf, an official normally based out of Elephantine, who undertook a series of journeys to the polity of Yam, located somewhere south of Egypt's Second Cataract. Harkhuf journeyed on behalf of the crown in order to trade and thereby obtain the sorts of southern exotica craved by the court: primarily, ebony, ivory, incense, and animal skins. For his first two journeys, Harkhuf went south along a route leading from Elephantine to Yam likely by way of Selima and Kurkur Oases.[26] In passing through Lower Nubia on his return, however, he found that the region—far from being the depopulated zone that it had been for the majority of the Old Kingdom—was now split into three different chiefdoms or polities. Over the course of Harkhuf's journeys, one ruler managed to exert his control over all three of these political entities. Based on analogies with the unification of Egypt during the late Predynastic and subsequent Intermediate periods, the process was likely to have been bloody, rendering the region and its adjacent oases far too unsafe for unescorted traders to traverse with goods in tow.

Whether because of a desire to avoid a politically unstable region or because he wished to safeguard his own trade goods from taxes that might be levied en route, Harkhuf decided on his third journey to Yam that he would take the "oasis road" and return via Lower Nubia only with the relative safety of an armed escort from Yam. Because he left from Abydos to start his journey, it has traditionally been assumed that he went to Kharga and from there traveled south along the Darb el-Arba'in route. Given the contrast between the paucity of Old Kingdom remains in Kharga and the intensive colonization of Dakhla, however, many scholars now believe that Harkhuf passed through Kharga but continued on to Dakhla, where he perhaps refreshed his provisions and donkeys. Harkhuf would have then swung southward, either back to the Darb el-Arba'in or along the trail to Gebel Uweinat where he could perhaps gain information as to the whereabouts of the ruler of Yam.[27] The latter possibility has recently been rendered much more plausible given the discovery of an inscription at Gebel Uweinat that depicts Mentuhotep II (c. 2055–2004) receiving gifts from an emissary of Yam. While it is unlikely that the king would indeed have undertaken such a time-consuming and hazardous journey, the inscription certainly implies that Gebel Uweinat served as a meeting point for traders from Egypt and Yam at the end of the First Intermediate period. Similar connections may well have been made in the Old Kingdom, thanks to the faithful provisioning of the transit route.[28] Given that Yam was one of Egypt's most highly valued trading partners, the much-beleaguered late Old Kingdom government may have found it worthwhile, even at great cost, to maintain the feasibility of this overland trade route.

The reason that Harkhuf, fellow caravan leaders, and Old Kingdom colonists may have preferred Dakhla to Kharga, despite the fact that reaching the former entailed three extra days of trekking through the desert, must be due to the oasis's comparative abundance of springs. With minimal redirecting, the water around spring mounds irrigated surrounding lands, providing an abundance of fertile fields. Thus, the oasis provided plenty of grazing land for donkeys as well as a healthy agricultural surplus capable of supporting both traveling caravans and the many resident personnel whose job it was to attend to the provisioning of the trail.

Food Security

If political turmoil in Nubia in the Sixth Dynasty was one incentive to invest in the permanent maintenance of a viable secondary route to Yam, Dakhla's notable fertility may have provided a second incentive for investment in an Egyptian colony at that particular moment in time. Environmental research has demonstrated that toward the end of the third millennium widespread aridification placed increasing stress upon the agricultural economy of the Nile Valley. At the source of the Nile, rains were radically reduced, having profound effects on the levels of the river in Egypt. Coring suggests that Lake Qarun, a massive 65-m deep lake fed by a channel in the Nile, shrunk substantially at this time. To exacerbate the situation, sandstorms and traveling dunes were prevalent, blanketing arable fields and settlements alike. Coring at Memphis has revealed a large-scale settlement shift at the end of the Old Kingdom due to the vast quantities of sand that swamped the city, and strata indicating extremely dry conditions have been found even at the heart of the Delta.[29] The stress on available food supplies caused by a dramatic reduction in viable farmland seems to have contributed to a countrywide famine that is evoked not only in the so-called lamentation literature (which sought to frame the political chaos of the First Intermediate period in the worst possible light) but also in contemporary autobiographies of provincial leaders (which sought to showcase the ingenuity and generosity of their subjects in the *best* possible light).[30]

While some critiques have judged as histrionic both the scientists and the historians who set too much stock in ecological evidence for the fall of the state, horrifying famines have beset Egypt in the much more recent past—and the narratives contemporary with them include many of the same tropes evoked by the authors of the lamentation literature, including societal recourse to infanticide and cannibalism.[31] Thus, it may have been that if large amounts of land were no longer available to farmers, those that lived on this land may have been amenable to resettling in Dakhla, a region where the water supply did not depend on the Nile and where, moreover, crops could be grown year-round due to the absence of the inundation. 'Ain Asil was located in close proximity to a profusion of spring mounds and so would have been particularly lush. Likewise, most other major Old Kingdom settlements were established in the western portion of the oasis, an area in which spring mounds were particularly dense.[32] Further, if the social unrest described as accompanying the descent into anarchy in the First Intermediate period was preceded by unrest in the cities of Egypt during the late Old Kingdom, then the Egyptian government may have anticipated Pericles' motivation for implanting Athenian colonists abroad, believing that, as Plutarch expressed it, such colonies

> ...relieved the city of a large number of idlers and agitators, raised the standards of the poorest classes, and, by installing garrisons among the allies, implemented at the same time a fear of rebellion.[33]

The word "colony" originally came from the Latin *colere* (to cultivate, till, or inhabit), which referred to the agricultural settlements in conquered territories that were allotted to veterans. This was done in part to reward military service but more practically to provide Rome with strong, permanent footholds in potentially problematic regions.[34] While the situation is not exactly analogous, the oasis may have struck the crown as particularly attractive, being an agriculturally rich area in a strategic location. If the widespread aridification was dusting semi-nomadic Libyans out of their already marginal grazing lands, Dakhla may have been at risk of becoming populated by groups that could endanger Egyptian trading missions or even utilize the oasis as a base from whence to launch predatory raids to the Nile Valley. Certainly it seems that both Harkhuf and the ruler of Yam had been united in their interest in smiting the Tjemehu-Libyans, for this task had to be accomplished prior to the initiation of trade negotiations. Settling Dakhla may thus have accomplished simultaneously three important tasks: securing the oasis from potentially hostile others, protecting and facilitating trade, and providing agricultural security to a vulnerable population. Significantly, security, trade, and sustenance have been cited as three of the most important driving forces in settler colonialism worldwide.[35]

The Beginning of the Colony

The formidable walls that surrounded the settlement at 'Ain Asil and the elaborate system of watch-posts that continued to be established and manned are two indications that the settlers who came to Dakhla in or slightly before the early Sixth Dynasty felt insecure about their own safety. The site of 'Ain Asil in its early incarnation had the character of a military fortress, and it is quite possible that the very first occupants were soldiers, who served short stints on a rotating basis, as is presumed to have been the case at the Twelfth-Dynasty fortress of Buhen (see Chapter 3).[36] Settlements of non-permanent military men, of course, tend to operate very differently (at least at first) from settlements founded by families of farmers; thus, a better understanding of the site's earliest demographics would undoubtedly shed much light on its intended function.

Regardless of their ratio at the beginning, however, soldiers certainly made up a significant portion of the population as late as the reign of Pepi II (c. 2278–2184), as is indicated by a cache of administrative triangular pendants that were found in the governor's mansion. The heading inscribed on some of these read "soldier," while the reverse bore a single name. On others, perhaps designating a civilian population, the sign for "house" marked one side, while two names appeared on the other. Many more tablets bore nothing but lists of men called up presumably for corvée labor or else for military service.[37]

The architecture of the fortress and earliest settlement is not yet known in detail, and certain aspects continue to be debated. At its core, the square fortress extended 171 m to a side. Engineered to withstand sieges, substantial towers protected its entrance, and its bastioned and battered enclosure walls stood 4 m thick and upwards of 4.5 m high.[38] Roughly similar in size to Buhen and to the enclosure walls that surrounded major state temples like Medinet Habu in the New Kingdom, the fortress at 'Ain Asil could presumably have accommodated a few hundred people without undue discomfort.

The soldiers stationed at 'Ain Asil were placed under the control of a Commander of the Oasis (ꜣṯw wḥꜣt),[39] and two of their duties may have been to accompany expeditions and to man hilltop watch-posts. In contrast to their earlier counterparts, the soldiers stationed in Sixth-Dynasty surveillance out-posts used pottery that had been manufactured locally, presumably in the ceramic workshop that constituted the only substantial extramural settle-ment in the early days of the fortress.[40] The logic of these watch-posts stayed consistent, however, as they still monitored trailheads leading to the Nile Valley and to Yam, as well as the southeastern regions of the oasis, which played host to an especially dense Sheikh Muftah population.

Sentry duty at such lonely outposts must have been dreaded. Most guard stations consisted of two or three semicircular windbreaks perched atop a hill with another at its base. A raised northern wall and ephemeral roofing offered some protection against sandstorms and extreme heat, but cooked food did not number among the amenities. Hearths lacked the charred remains of edible substances, suggesting that fires were generally reserved for signaling purposes. Sequences of ticks, like the mute accounts found also at 'Ain Asil, aided soldiers invested in counting off the days spent on their 20-day shifts, while the numer-ous etched pubic triangles perhaps afforded distraction. Significantly, one of these pubic triangles had been annotated with the word "love" (*mr*).

The simple hieroglyphic captions that accompanied the pubic triangle and a few other petroglyphs found at these watch-posts suggest that at least some of the men stationed at the site were literate Egyptians. Most fascinating of all is a petroglyph labeled "soldier" (*ʿnḫ*), which depicted a military man with all his gear: kilt, crossed leather chest straps, bow, arrows, wrist guard, and even the feather worn in his hair (see Figure 2.2). The verisimilitude of this sketch is suggested by the fact that a wrist guard, similar to the one depicted, has indeed been discovered in such a context.[41] Although the label for the petroglyph was written in good Egyptian, it is notable that the man's garb is characteristic of the Medjay—the Nubian desert tribesmen that by the late Old Kingdom were routinely contracted into Egyptian service. Heavily shale-tempered pottery, characteristic of the Sheikh Muftah and found at a few hilltop sites, further complicates efforts to assign a singular ethnic identity to the personnel that manned these posts.[42]

It is not unlikely that the Egyptians enlisted locals, not only to serve as guides for caravans but also as desert scouts, in much the same way as the semi-nomadic Medjay tribesmen worked in conjunction with Egyptian soldiers in safeguarding Middle Kingdom Nubian fortresses, as will be discussed in the following chapter. A similar alliance seems to have been made in the New Kingdom, if the model letter P. Anastasi IV 10,8–11,8 was indeed, as is likely, fashioned after an original document. This note of reprimand was addressed to an overseer of the treasury who had sent a scribe to requisition from "the oasis" certain members of the Tjukten tribe, who hunted and scouted on the govern-ment's behalf, presumably for some sort of state labor. Given the overseer's reaction, this act must have violated existing agreements with the tribe.

The writer thus sternly warned the offending overseer that should he attempt to remove any more of these scouts,

> You will be taken away and put there [i.e. in the oasis] to be a Tjukten-convict.... Beware of meddling with the Tjukten [even] to remove just only one of them, or else it will be reckoned against you as a capital offense.[43]

Quite clearly, Egypt's government preferred to court rather than to coerce the cooperation of a tribe that could, if angered, cause them a tremendous amount of trouble.

The Colony at its Zenith

It has been stated that relations between colonists and local populations typically fall under the rubrics of alliance, domination, long-term competition, or some variegated combination of the three.[44] Examples of "middle ground colonialism"—in which both sides maintain an impression that they are more or less in control of their own destinies and that the association between them is mutually beneficial—is found in many instances of colonial interaction, especially in its early stages. The economic links forged between the Algonkian Native Americans and Europeans in the fur trade is a classic example, and Rufus Churcher suggests that the Old Kingdom immigrants and the Sheikh Muftah enjoyed a similar relationship.[45]

The idea that the Sheikh Muftah might act as guides and scouts takes little imagination, but it is less clear how to interpret the small amounts of shale-tempered ware in Old Kingdom domestic contexts, which consisted mostly of storage jars and cooking pots.[46] Were the storage vessels a result of trade? Did Old Kingdom potters adopt shale-tempered ware for its properties? Or did at least some of the Sheikh Muftah abandon their semi-nomadic ways and come to live in Old Kingdom settlements? If so, how were they integrated into the community? Did the Sheikh Muftah cement peaceful relations through the formation of familial ties? Such has happened on a great many frontiers, and intermarriages are a famously powerful tool for integrating otherwise separate communities. In such cases, female presence is often signaled in the material record by the juxtaposition of indigenous cookpots and other domestic ware with colonial serving ware, as will be discussed in more depth in Chapter 4. Barring an adaptation based solely upon thermal properties, the shale-tempered cookpots found in Old Kingdom settlements might suggest this scenario. Due to gender and power relations in the ancient world, however, the hiring of indigenous domestic servants might well result in a similar archaeological footprint.

The discussion is ongoing and the ramifications of various conclusions are important. The dates of "Terminal Sheikh Muftah" ware remain the subject of much debate. Ashten Warfe has argued that the Sixth-Dynasty shale-tempered pottery is different enough from its earlier equivalents that it should not be taken as a cultural signifier. Thus, according to this view, the end of the Sheikh Muftah would have coincided with the beginning of intensive Egyptian presence at Mut.[47] If this dating were correct, then, the Old Kingdom occupation of Dakhla would presumably constitute an instance of "eradication colonialism" in which the local population was driven out or else elected to evacuate rather than to face life under a radically changed power dynamic. Anthony Mills suggests that perhaps, as in the American West, pastoralists and farmers had found it difficult to share space and the former finally left to seek less crowded, if not greener, pastures elsewhere.[48] Other archaeologists working at Dakhla, however, see a clear overlap between Terminal Sheikh Muftah and Sixth-Dynasty material.[49] The only aspect of the Terminal Sheikh Muftah that is clear, then, is that much remains to be clarified.

Whether the situation was one of cooperation and cohabitation, of domination, or else of the indigenous population abandoning the oasis in the wake of Egypt's invasive settlement, one ramification seems to have been the same. Within a relatively short time the wariness that the Egyptians felt when establishing their initial settlement dissipated. At 'Ain Asil, this is witnessed by the presence of an apparently contemporary Sheikh Muftah base camp only 90 m from the fortress walls, by the apparent domestication of the fortress, and by the erection of an unfortified administrative quarters located just south of the fortress, where it would presumably have been extremely vulnerable had real threats been expected. Another site, 'Ain el-Gazzareen, which was located in the western portion of the oasis and will be discussed below, exhibited a similar trajectory whereby maintaining the integrity of the settlement's substantial walls was at some point deprioritized.

Although very little of the fortress at 'Ain Asil has been excavated, it would appear that the structure's cramped, specialized rooms became redundant over the course of the Sixth Dynasty. There is evidence that certain areas were largely abandoned and were later altered and used for purposes other than those for which they were originally intended.[50] The transformation of the pillared fore-court into an apparent animal pen is reminiscent of the formation of "sacred slums" inside many Fourth and Fifth-Dynasty mortuary temples as the descendants of the priests originally charged with looking after these temples set up residence inside them.[51] Lisa Giddy, who participated in the excavation of the fortress, compared the archaeological situation of the structure to that of the Middle Kingdom fortress of Buhen, when the garrisons ceased to rotate and soldiers settled down as citizens (see Chapter 4).[52] Sealings found in some of these fortress rooms, however, indicate that a certain amount of official activity did persist.

Sometime during the reign of Pepi II, however, the fortress outlived its original purpose. The rooms were infilled with rubble, and a carefully-built mudbrick platform was prepared, perhaps as a podium for a monumental construction, such as a temple.[53] Certainly, a resident cult of the god Igai is attested in inscriptional evidence at 'Ain Asil, as were *mrt*-temples devoted to the royal cults of Pepi I (c. 2321–2287) and Pepi II.[54] Whatever the podium's purpose, it was evidently *not* intended to provide the foundation for the governor's mansion and the divine chapels to the governors' ka-souls, for these were found directly south of it and bear eloquent testimony to the vast power of these governors during the reign of Pepi II.

Textual evidence indicates that the governors possessed the power to requisition labor and goods from polities outside Dakhla, even including Bahariya Oasis, located many hundreds of kilometers to the north.[55] That the governor's abode was sumptuous, then, is hardly surprising. At its core, a 10-pillared hall fronted a suite with two spacious bed- or reception rooms, complete with large hearths, small side chambers, and stone footings for baldachins or bed legs. Surrounding this central core and extending to the west were numerous smaller rooms likely intended for officials, servants, and storage, as well as another grand pillared hall that also seemed to front more intimate reception or sleeping rooms. The thickness of the walls, the width of the rooms, and the purposeful preparation of floors and walls in the main areas of the building clearly broadcasted the importance of these rulers, despite (or, perhaps, precisely *because* of) their position at the geographic margins of the state.[56]

Yet another vivid attestation of the comparative wealth of the provincial rulers in Dakhla vis-à-vis their Nile Valley counterparts is the line of massive mastaba tombs erected a kilometer or so outside 'Ain Asil, all of which would have been easily visible to the citizens of the town. The mastabas had been erected over the reigns of Pepi I, Merenre (2287–2278), and Pepi II, a period of time that saw Egypt's economy progressively plummet. While a number of sizable mastabas and rock-cut tombs had been erected in the Nile Valley at the start of Pepi II's reign, by its midpoint even the highest elites do not appear to have possessed funds enough to commission impressive monuments.[57] At Dakhla, however, the trajectory was different. Six governors held power sequentially during Pepi II's reign, and the mastabas belonging to Ima-Pepi II, Khentika, Khentikau-Pepi, and Medunefer outshone the monuments of virtually all of their more centrally located contemporaries. The unexcavated mastaba of Khentikau-Pepi, for example, although much denuded, still stands over 10 m high. Likewise, the goods stored in the subterranean chambers of Medunefer's tomb, preserved due to a ceiling collapse, included vast quantities of wealth, much of it imported.[58]

Ka-chapels, erected within the town for the perpetual benefit of the souls of four of Dakhla's last and most powerful governors, provide further testimony to the unusual honor bestowed upon these men. A stone stele found at the site read:

> A royal decree to the boat commander, the ruler of the oasis, the overseer of priests.... My majesty has commanded [both] the building for you of

a soul chapel in the oasis, and the establishment for you of soul priests dedicated to provisioning you. This has been previously done for your father, the ruler of the oasis Khentyka, [son of] Desheru, [son of] Iduwy.... Sealed in the presence of the king himself.[59]

As Sixth-Dynasty pharaohs strove to make themselves more relevant to their subjects, chapels dedicated to the ka-soul of the pharaoh began to appear in regional temples, so that the king might be worshiped alongside local divinities. Very quickly, however, pharaohs were convinced of the utility of extending this privilege to family members and to certain key elites. The private citizens permitted by the king to possess ka-chapels were few and far between and generally excluded officials below the rank of vizier.[60] Thus, the fact that no fewer than four governors of Dakhla received the right to have their souls propitiated by court-appointed priests demonstrates that Pepi II must have been especially eager to cement ties with the individuals who ruled their far-off oasis in his name.

It is no doubt significant that these governors were semantically distinguished from their peers in being designated "rulers" (*ḥḳꜣ*), rather than "mayors" (*ḥꜣty-ꜥ*) or "regional governors" (*ḥry-tp ꜥꜣ*). The use of the term *ḥḳꜣ* suggests official acknowledgment that the Egyptian colony by this point enjoyed a relatively high degree of political autonomy. As Dakhla was still peripheral to Egypt's core, the pharaohs attempted to keep ties strong by allowing sons to ascend to their fathers' positions, provided these heirs apparent completed a stay at court.[61] Such was common practice both for high officials in the Old Kingdom and for the sons of vassals in the New Kingdom. Its benefits, discussed in Chapters 1 and 6, need not be restated.

Likewise, judging from numerous alabaster vessels and items bearing cartouches of Pepi II, Medunefer appears to have been invited to at least one of this king's Sed-festivals. Pharaohs sent such gifts to grandees in far-flung kingdoms like Ebla, Byblos, and Kerma, whose leaders if they attended such jubilees did so only by proxy. Provincial leaders would, however, have been expected to attend royal festivals. Such occasions were intended in part to cement relationships between the king and regional rulers but also to demonstrate to the latter the true nature of the power dynamic between them (for a New Kingdom parallel, see the Epilogue). One suspects, however, that Dakhla's rulers—whose spirits were worshiped at ka-chapels and whose dependents crowded around their graves at death—may have preferred to remain in the oasis, as the centers of their *own* world, rather than to travel to the Nile Valley for the purpose of being positioned at the periphery of another.

Over the time that 'Ain Asil flourished, its wealth stemmed in part, it seems, from purpose-built settlements established in the even more fertile areas of the western oasis. The Dakhleh Oasis Survey discovered over 50 sites dating to the Old Kingdom, more than existed at any point prior to the Roman period. Two of the most important, 'Ain el-Gazzareen and Amheida, were located a short walk from one another and were extremely similar in purpose and design (see Figure 2.4).[62] Oriented northwest–southeast, both walled sites were built to almost identical dimensions (54×112 m at 'Ain el-Gazzareen and 56×108 m at Amheida) and seem to have been divided internally by a wall that delineated a specific zone, downwind, to the southeast.[63] At 'Ain el-Gazzareen this area was

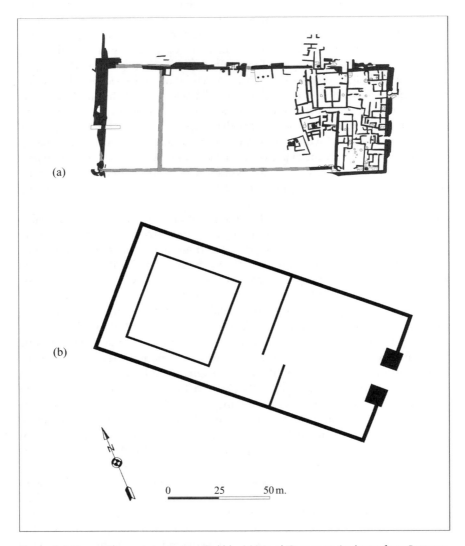

Figure 2.4 Two settlements in western Dakhla. (a) 'Ain el-Gazzareen (redrawn from Pettman 2012, 182, figure 2); (b) Amheida, magnetometry plan (redrawn from Smekalova and Smekalov, n.d., figure 8b).

devoted to industrial baking, as is signaled by the tremendous quantities of ash, grinding stones, grain storage facilities, and bread molds found there.[64] Although its equivalent at Amheida is known only through magnetometry and conductivity surveys, similar disturbed debris has been recovered from its environs. Whether the bread baked at these centers primarily served to provision passing caravans or to supply residents dependent on rations is not clear.

Like 'Ain Asil, with which it was largely contemporary, 'Ain el-Gazzareen seems to have been established at a time when thick, buttressed walls and watch-towers were deemed prudent.[65] In at least one area, these walls were associated with a significant quantity of Sheikh Muftah pottery, which, in turn, lay over earlier Old Kingdom material. Whether this indicated contemporaneous habitation or a short-lived Sheikh Muftah reclaiming of the site is unclear. 'Ain el-Gazzareen's location in close proximity to a spring would have made it especially amenable to settlement, and the Sheikh Muftah pottery, in conjunction with the quite substantial material evidence for butchering, might indicate that the indigenous residents of the oasis had found a market for their animals among the Egyptian immigrants.[66] Certainly, the fact that the settlement's thick walls were quickly deemed inessential speaks volumes.

Excavation at 'Ain el-Gazzareen has demonstrated that habitation extended outside these walls, and indeed the most impressive building yet excavated at the site was constructed directly atop them! This structure, dubbed Building C, resembled the interior of the palace at 'Ain Asil in its symmetrical alignment and in the prominence of two large and formal hearths. Painted and plastered, the rooms were kept unusually pristine and boasted a far finer pottery assemblage than was typical. The fact that both hearths were filled with clean white ash has led some to suggest that the building may have served a cultic function.[67] If so, perhaps the bakeries helped to solidify connections between settlers and Sheikh Muftah, as the two groups broke bread together at festivals or exchanged bread and meat between them. The fact that seals discovered on bread molds and other containers at 'Ain el-Gazzareen bore striking similarities to those found at 'Ain Asil suggests that whatever purpose the bread was put to, it bore the stamp of authority.[68]

The End of the Colony

While a deep economic depression may have settled upon the Nile Valley, Dakhla Oasis apparently thrived. The men who ruled Dakhla were able to command tremendous resources and appear for all intents and purposes to have acted independently. What is not known is the way in which this great wealth was viewed by the indigenous and settler populations who shared the oasis. While the bulk of their subjects may have been supportive and have viewed the prosperity of Dakhla's rulers with civic pride, this need not necessarily have been the case. The inhabitants of circumscribed areas are among the most notoriously vulnerable to exploitation, for the prospect of "voting with one's feet" is less appealing if the journey elsewhere is extremely hazardous.[69] Certainly, a tale set in the late Twentieth Dynasty, a comparably tumultuous time in Egypt's history, paints a vivid picture of a landowner based in one of Egypt's southern oases who cheated, oppressed, and abused his tenants to the breaking point.[70] Whether such a scenario was anomalous or typical is not known.

It is, however, perhaps telling that right at the juncture between the late Old Kingdom and the First Intermediate period, the gubernatorial mansion went up in flames. This fire raged so hot that the massive wooden doors seared indelible impressions onto the floor. The large sunken braziers in the main rooms indicate that incendiary materials would have been common within the palace itself, and so the fire could have been accidental. There are several clues, however, that it was deliberately set. Most significantly, the sumptuous residential suites of the palace were never rebuilt or refurbished, unlike adjacent areas that were either rebuilt or remained unscathed.[71] Whether the burning and plundering witnessed in mastaba II, which belonged to the recent governor Ima-Pepi II, dated to the destruction of the palace is unclear. If so, it perhaps indicates that deceased rulers were not exempt from acts of rage, retribution, or income redistribution.[72]

An exception may perhaps prove the rule. Alone among the burial chambers excavated, that of Medunefer remained unmolested, and, while this may have been due to the fact that an internal collapse had rendered the chamber difficult to access, there are other indications that this governor may have been remembered with more fondness than many of the others. Certainly it is notable that Medunefer's mastaba was comparatively modest, and his ka-chapel was restored after the fire, with a statue of the governor returned to its place of honor.[73] Significantly, his ka-chapel stood separately from those of his fellow governors. If this was not a purely practical decision, it might suggest that Medunefer came from a separate lineage than the rest of the rulers or that he wished to consciously differentiate himself from them.

There are, of course, numerous possible suspects for the burning of the palace. Pepi II could have sent soldiers to prevent the polity of Dakhla from seceding from his realm or to punish a perceived slight. Admittedly, however, the general impression is that Pepi II did not have the resources to mount such a campaign in the latter portion of his reign, even if he still had the will to do so. Alternatively, the attack might have come from desert raiders, such as those who periodically plagued the oasis for much of the next four millennia. Such men would no doubt focus on the palace and tombs of the rulers as these targets would yield the greatest amount of plunder. Arguing against both of these scenarios, however, is the fact that those who rebuilt the town did not feel it necessary to construct a formidable enclosure wall or to otherwise bolster the settlement's defenses.[74]

The notion that the violence to 'Ain Asil had come from within the community is interesting to consider given several intriguing references to internal revolts in the later lamentation literature. This genre—however tendentious its intent—conveyed much in its description of governmental collapse that is reminiscent of first-hand reports of upheaval and anarchy even today. Certainly, it seems as if the movement to depose Pepi II (or perhaps one of his ephemeral successors) was either orchestrated by the people or, at the very least, enjoyed popular support. Ipuwer, a purported eyewitness to such events, states,

> ...the king has been overthrown by the rabble.... Behold now, the land begins to lose the kingship at the hands of a few men who ignore tradition. Behold now, there arises rebellion against the mighty Uraeus of Re who contents the Two Lands. Behold, the secret of the land, whose limits are unknown, is laid bare, and the Residence could fall at any moment.... Behold, the Residence is fearful because of want, and everyone will arouse strife with no opposition. Behold, the land is fettered by mobs....[75]

Such treatment was apparently not reserved for the king but extended to regional leaders as well. Ipuwer also reports, "Behold, the judges of the land are driven away throughout the land." And again, "...every city says, 'Let us drive out the mighty from our midst.'"[76] Certainly, weakness at the core seems to have inspired provincial peoples throughout Egypt to throw off the yokes that had bound them since rulers of the First Dynasty had assumed control nearly a millennium previously. Such social movements are often contagious—as is amply illustrated by the American and French revolutions in the late eighteenth century, the numerous revolutions of 1968 and 1989 in Europe, and also those of 2011 in the Arab world. It would be remarkable, but not at all implausible, for the spread of such revolutionary ideas at the end of the Sixth Dynasty to have extended even to a desert oasis located many hundreds of kilometers from Memphis.

Postscript

The Old Kingdom settlers of Dakhla would have relied upon the Nile Valley for all of their metal and also for any prestige goods that would have provided long-distance traders with precious items to barter. Thus, one might have assumed that a cessation of relations with Egypt would have damaged the colony's economy. What is fascinating and counterintuitive, however, is that the settlements at 'Ain Asil, at Amheida, and elsewhere continued for some time into the First Intermediate period and that the most intensive utilization of the Abu Ballas trail that stretched southward to Gilf Kebir seems to have occurred after the destruction of the palace.⁷⁷ Where the funds to launch such expeditions came from is unclear. While there is reference in Ipuwer to continued low-level trading between the oases and the Nile Valley, this appears to have been so low-level as to have been either laughable or lamentable.⁷⁸ Directly after conquering the oasis and annexing it to his expanding kingdom, Mentuhotep II sent his own representatives to meet with counterparts from Yam, as an inscription at Gebel Uweinat implies. Thus, lines of communication between the two regions may well have remained open during the interim.⁷⁹

How did Dakhla's inhabitants view the royal reconquest of their oasis? An incised design on one intriguing vessel is perhaps suggestive. At one of the desert way stations along the Abu Ballas trail, archaeologists discovered the remains of an industrial vat for making dough, which bore on its base a depiction of a king of Upper and Lower Egypt.⁸⁰ While there is nothing in the schematic drawing itself that would necessarily relegate it to the realm of social commentary, the positioning of the depiction on the underside of a vat speaks volumes. In ancient Egypt, as in modern Egypt, the idea of being placed beneath the sole of another individual's foot was particularly insulting. Throughout Egyptian history depictions of foreigners were placed on sandals, on footstools, and along palace walkways, while in the most obsequious greeting formulae, a vassal would claim to be the footstool of the pharaoh. The pharaoh's image, on the other hand, was so sacred that until the end of the Middle Kingdom it was not permissible for a depiction of the king to be included in the tomb or on a stele of a private person. The idea that a depiction of the god-king might be placed face down beneath so humble a vessel would have been bad enough on its own. Judging from tomb scenes and models, however, a low-status individual would likely have stood barefoot inside such a vat and repeatedly stamped his feet to mix the dough! A stronger subversive statement of anti-royalist sentiments would be difficult to envision.

After its reconquest by Mentuhotep II, Dakhla was utilized by the state for many purposes—such as banishment and viticulture—but it is notable that comparable archaeological evidence for intensive settlement does not appear for well over a millennium. Evidently, the special social, economic, and ecological circumstances that made the settlement of Dakhla particularly attractive in the Sixth Dynasty—namely, low Nile floods and a strife-ridden Lower Nubia—no longer applied. What is fascinating, however, is that the large-scale withdrawal of settlers was not balanced by an influx of archaeologically visible desert pastoralists. Unless such peoples lived very, very lightly upon the land, they either chose to avoid Dakhla or were actively warded off by military personnel that may yet have patrolled the region. Likewise, regardless of whether the Sheikh Muftah had departed long before or had masked their culture behind the material signatures of the immigrants they had lived amidst, by the end of the First Intermediate period, their trail had grown irrevocably cold.

Notes

1 The Palermo Stone records a Nubian campaign in which Snefru netted 7,000 captives and 200,000 livestock. Considering the lack of contemporary evidence for habitation in Lower Nubia, the numbers seem high. While the campaign could have been mounted against Kerma (Török 2009, 55–6), such a far-flung military venture is uncharacteristic for the time, and one would have expected luxury items to have been listed among the booty. The high numbers of Egyptian soldiers (20,000) and Nubian prisoners (17,000) attested on poorly dated Old Kingdom rock inscriptions from Khor el-Aquiba are similarly perplexing (Strudwick 2005, 149–50).

2 Strudwick 2005, 335–6, 354–5.

3 Cf. the discussion and references cited in Morris *forthcoming*.

4 Cf. Cromer 1910; Haverfield et al. 1910; Dietler 2005, 42–6.

5 Stein 1999, 70.

6 Finley 1976, 184, but see the critiques in Gosden 2004, 3; Stein 2005a, 10.

7 Hope 2007.

8 McDonald 1996; Warfe 2003.

9 McDonald 2001, 9; Thompson 2002, 43–5.

10 Sahlins 1972, 1–39.

11 McDonald 2001, 8–9.

12 Mills 1999, 174, 258; Hope and Pettman 2012, 161.

13 Hope 2007, 405.

14 Kuhlmann 2002, 136; Kuhlmann 2005, 245–51, figures 1–8.

15 Förster 2007, 5.

16 Förster 2008, 18–21.

17 Ethnobotanical experiments undertaken by Carlo Bergmann (2016) suggest the Clayton rings may have been utilized to roast the bitter seeds of the colocynthis fruit to produce a palatable form of protein.

18 Hope and Pettman 2012, 160.

19 For relevant discussions of desert travel to the oases, see Morris 2010a, 130–2 and *forthcoming*.

20 It is puzzling that the early watch-tower pottery was generally imported given that Egyptian potters were fashioning pottery out of local clays in the Fourth Dynasty (Kaper and Willems 2002, 90; Hope and Pettman 2012, 158–9). Further excavation should clarify the nature of the earliest levels at Mut.

21 Förster 2007, 1, 5.

22 Förster 2007, 3–5.

23 Riemer 2004, 975, 979; Förster 2007, 3.

24 Hope and Pettman 2012, 158–9.

25 Förster 2007, 7–8; Cooper 2012, 11; Pantalacci 2013, 199.

26 See Simpson 2003, 407–12 for Harkhuf's inscription and Cooper 2012 for a recent discussion of the location of Yam and the logistics of Harkhuf's travels.

27 Giddy 1987, 52; Förster 2007, 8–9.
28 Clayton et al. 2008.
29 Hassan et al. 2006, 40; Hassan 2007, 360; but see Moeller 2005, who argues that climate change is unlikely to have been dramatic enough to lead to the demise of the Old Kingdom government.
30 See Bell 1971, 8–21; Moreno García 1997, 1–87.
31 See Al-Baghdādī 1231/1964, 223–43.
32 Mills 1999, 175.
33 Plutarch, *Pericles*, chapter 11.
34 Gosden 2004, 1.
35 Gosden 2004, 2.
36 Giddy 1987, 186, 197, 207.
37 Giddy 1987, 201.
38 Giddy 1987, 185–6; Kaper and Willems 2002, 79–80; Moeller 2016, 175.
39 Kaper and Willems 2002, 90.
40 This information and the rest concerning the watch-towers comes from Kaper and Willems 2002.
41 Kaper and Willems 2002, 85, 88, figure 4.
42 Hope 2007, 404.
43 Caminos 1954, 176–7.
44 Stein 2005a, 14.
45 Churcher quoted in Thurston 2004, 136; Gosden 2004, 26, 30–2.
46 Giddy 1987, 199.
47 Hope and Pettman 2012, 156.
48 Mills 1999, 177–8.
49 McDonald 2002, 113; Hope 2007, 405; Jeuthe 2014.
50 Giddy 1987, 191.
51 Giddy 1987, 186–8; Kemp 1989, 146–8.
52 Giddy 1987, 207.
53 Giddy 1987, 195.
54 Hubschmann 2010, 46–7; Pantalacci 2013, 201.
55 Pantalacci 2013, 199, 204.
56 Soukiassian et al. 2002.
57 Snape 2011, 86–104; Barta 2013, 269.
58 For summary overviews, see Giddy 1987, 174–84; Valloggia 1999. The mastaba tombs are individually published by the Institut français d'archéologie orientale.
59 Strudwick 2005, 115.
60 Valbelle 2002, 109.
61 Pantalacci 2013, 199.
62 Mills 1999, 174–6, 258–9.
63 Smekalova and Smekalov n.d., 6–8.
64 Mills 2002, 76–7.

65 Mills 2002, 76–7; Mills 2012; Pettman 2012, 198.
66 Mills 2002, 75–6; Mills 2012, 180.
67 Mills and Kaper 2003, 127–8; Pettman 2012, 184, 196–8; compare with the plan in Soukiassian 1997, 16.
68 Mills 2002, 77.
69 Carneiro 1970, 735.
70 Caminos 1977, 44–5.
71 Soukiassian 1997, 17; Kaper and Willems 2002, 79–80; Moeller 2016, 242.
72 Giddy 1987, 179.
73 Soukiassian et al. 2002, 57–76.
74 Kaper and Willems 2002, 79–80.
75 Simpson 2003, 198.
76 Simpson 2003, 191, 199.
77 Giddy 1987, 168; Kaper and Willems 2002, 79–80; Soukiassian et al. 2002, 10–12, 521–3, figures 1, 5; Förster 2007, 6.
78 Giddy 1987, 64–5; Simpson 2003, 193.
79 Giddy 1987, 53; Clayton et al. 2008.
80 Förster 2007, 4–5, figures 27–28.

3

Military Occupation (c. 2055–1773)

This chapter begins where the last ended, with the ascension to power of Mentuhotep II (c. 2055–2004) in the mid-Eleventh Dynasty and with an examination of Egypt's motivations for sending its army southward. After a brief discussion of this king's institution of indirect rule in Lower Nubia, the chapter focuses upon the Twelfth-Dynasty government's rejection of this policy in favor of a strategy of military occupation. Elaborate fortresses were constructed between the First and Second Cataracts by Amenemhet I (c. 1985–1956) and his successors in order to guard agricultural and mineral resources, to monitor local populations, and to protect against incursions from the increasingly powerful polity based at Kerma (see Figure 3.1). The nature of the relations between the occupiers and the occupied at this time is of particular interest, due to the contrast between the physical proximity of the two populations and the near mutual exclusivity of their material assemblages.

When considering Egypt's motivations for extending control over Lower Nubia in the mid-Eleventh Dynasty, it is useful to return quickly to the late Old Kingdom. At this time the active resettlement of Lower Nubia by a predominantly pastoral population, known to scholars as the C-Group, complicated matters for Egyptian traders, who had previously enjoyed right of way through this territory on their journeys southward to meet their trading partners in the polities of Yam and Punt—located somewhere south of the Second Cataract and near the Horn of Africa, respectively. In the reigns of the last two kings of the Sixth Dynasty (c. 2287–2184), the trader Harkhuf was forced to cope with complex shifts in the socio-political terrain of Lower Nubia.

Between Harkhuf's first trip to Yam and his third, he saw the discrete polities of Wawat, Irtjet, and Setjau fall under the control of a single ruler. Well-argued opinions differ as to whether these toponyms should be equated with the three fertile zones of Lower Nubia, centered in the vicinity of Kubban, Aniba, and Faras, or whether the latter two extended significantly upstream of the Second Cataract.[1] Whatever the case, the upheaval that attended this unification seems to have prompted Harkhuf to switch his route from the "Elephantine road" to

Ancient Egyptian Imperialism, First Edition. Ellen Morris.
© 2018 Ellen Morris. Published 2018 by John Wiley & Sons Ltd.

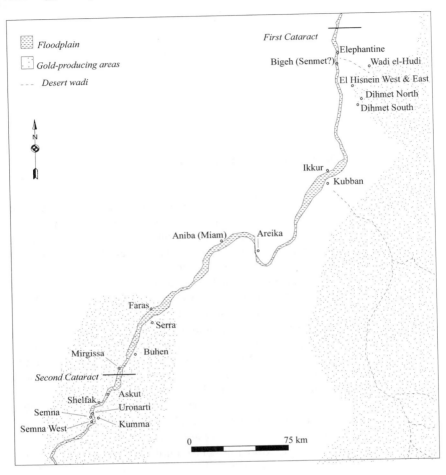

Figure 3.1 Egyptian installations in Middle Kingdom Nubia.

the much more arduous "oasis road," which almost certainly utilized 'Ain Asil as a key staging post.

As discussed in the previous chapter, the roughly 600 km journey from Dakhla to Gebel Uweinat—the next site that offered a permanent water supply—would have been unpleasant, unsafe, and a logistical nightmare (see Figure 2.1). For Harkhuf, then, this detour must have been born of necessity. Moreover, on the return leg of this third trip both he and the ruler of Yam seem to have felt it prudent that his caravan be escorted by a "strong and numerous" contingent of warriors. A donkey train full of southern luxury goods—including ebony, ivory, panther skins, incense, and more—would certainly have made a tempting target for an ambitious ruler, who might have coveted such cargo or at least demanded a handsome share of the profits for allowing the caravan to pass through his land unmolested.

Harkhuf's third mission, then, likely bore the costs of his additional escort of soldiers from Yam, of his use of the oasis route (with its elaborate series of water depots stretching hundreds of kilometers into the desert), and also likely of at least a token customs fee to the ruler of Irtjet, Setjau, and Wawat. On balance, these costs must have threatened to render the venture ultimately unprofitable. The situation had evidently not improved by the beginning of Mentuhotep II's reign, however, judging from an inscription at Gebel Uweinat that commemorated a meeting between traders working for the king and representatives from Yam.[2]

In terms of imperial motivations for intervention in Lower Nubia, then, one important factor may have been the same as that which ultimately spelled ruin for the A-Group at the dawn of the Egyptian state. The pharaoh and his court evidently desired to eliminate interference in their importation of the types of southern prestige goods that adorned them in life and death and decorated (or suffused) their temples, palaces, and mortuary chapels. Indeed, whether the kingdom was Old, Middle, or New, the steady and reliable acquisition of these goods constituted a strong state interest.

The territory of Yam likely incorporated—or else enjoyed close contact with—an extremely powerful polity based at the site of Kerma, located just upstream of the Third Cataract. By the Sixth Dynasty, Kerma possessed all the hallmarks of a political powerhouse: markedly elite graves, temples, workshops, and what look to have been large audience halls and administrative buildings. Moreover, numerous alabaster vessels engraved with cartouches and a stele bearing the names of two Egyptian captains demonstrate that Kerma's government was in reasonably close communication with Egypt's court in the late Old Kingdom.[3] From Egypt's point of view, then, the trade missions that passed through Lower Nubia to Kerma—or even to lands beyond—required safe passage, and it was thus imperative that the population of Lower Nubia refrain from raiding Egyptian caravans or from extorting exorbitant customs fees.

Egypt's court evidently also desired to regain the unhindered access to Lower Nubian mineral resources that it had enjoyed in the absence of a robust Nubian population from the middle of the First Dynasty until the late Fifth Dynasty. Of paramount importance were the veins of copper and gold to be found in Wadi Allaqi, Wadi Gabgaba, Wadi Hagar Shams, and in the Batn el-Hagar (the "Belly of the Rock") at the Second Cataract (see Figure 3.1). The diorite mines accessible from the region of Aniba and the amethyst mines and granite quarries of the First Cataract region, however, also attracted the interest of these new rulers, who were eager both to showcase their power and to set it in stone. While there is very little evidence that the

C-Group actively exploited any of these resources prior to the Egyptian occupation, they certainly possessed the means to thwart Egypt's operations, judging from the fact that copper smelting at Buhen ceased at roughly the same point that these peoples first appear in the archaeological record (c. 2445–2421).[4]

If the Egyptians were interested in subduing the population of Lower Nubia so as to obtain control over their resources, they may also have been concerned that the elites of Kerma not turn a covetous eye toward the north. Pastoral groups have the advantage of mobility and can be fierce and formidable raiders, but the Egyptians may have been far more apprehensive of the potential challenge to their authority that armed soldiers called up by a rich and powerful political center like Kerma would constitute. This apprehension is observable in the pre-emptive nature of many Middle Kingdom military campaigns, in the rhetoric of royal inscriptions, and in the defensive architecture that the Egyptian government was to erect at the Second Cataract.

Such fears may not have been unfounded. Archaeologically, all evidence from the Middle Kerman settlement and cemetery zones, contemporary with the Twelfth and Thirteenth Dynasties, suggests not only that Kerma was prosperous but also that its elites were deeply enmeshed in the project of advertising and augmenting their power. For example, the 4,351 bucrania arrayed to the south of one of the more elite Kerman tumuli serve as a clear indication that the deceased had stood at the nexus of a vast socioeconomic network.[5]

Twelfth-Dynasty execration texts, intended to harm enemies of the state through sympathetic magic, designate at least two Kerman rulers by name— Awa'a and Utatrerses—as constituting threats to Egypt's national security. Given the expansive power of this kingdom, the pharaonic government no doubt felt that Kerman kings would not hesitate to extend their reach northward to gain control over Lower Nubian gold mines and quarries if the Egyptians were to show the least sign of weakness. Judging from the elaborate bastioned enclosure walls, defensive ditches, and palisades excavated at contemporary Kerma, however, the inhabitants of this city evidently viewed Egypt with a similar suspicion.[6] Sun Tzu, the famous Chinese strategist of the sixth century BCE, is credited with the following observation:

> The art of war teaches us to rely not on the likelihood of the enemy's not coming, but on our own readiness to receive him; not on the chance of his not attacking, but rather on the fact that we have made our position unassailable.[7]

Both the Egyptians and the Kermans, it seems, had anticipated his advice.

Fortification

Egyptian forces could not realistically contemplate a conquest of Lower Nubia until their own country was reunited in the 39th regnal year of Mentuhotep II (c. 2016). Following this unification, however, assumption of control over Lower Nubia was evidently among the top priorities. In the same year that Mentuhotep II effected his reunification, he sent a campaign south of the First Cataract. This campaign or subsequent ones resulted in the annexation of Lower Nubia down to the former Old Kingdom industrial outpost at Buhen, a move made perhaps following on the heels of Mentuhotep's conquest of the western oases and his resumption of relations with Yam.[8]

The recent discovery at Abydos of a 2-m-high stele of Idudju-iker, who seems to have participated in the annual procession of Osiris at that site and who bore the title "Foremost One of the Rulers of Lower Nubia" (*ḥ3t ḥk3w nw w3tw3t*), is intriguing. Josef Wegner states that the iconography and the palaeography of the stele fit within the reigns of Intef II or Mentuhotep II, though he suggests that the conquest of Abydos in the reign of the former renders this king stronger candidate.[9] It would seem equally plausible, however, that instead of being an ally of Intef II, Idudju-iker served Mentuhotep II as an honored vassal. If so, he may well have spent time as a youth at the Theban court and thereby have developed the strong affinity for Egyptian culture and religious rites that his act of commissioning the monument implies.

There are other reasons to think that Mentuhotep II preferred to employ diplomacy in his relations with Nubian rulers. Scholars have long noted that in certain funerary monuments, the black skin of Mentuhotep's subsidiary wives is deliberately contrasted with the pale pigmentation of their maidservants as well as with the ruddy brown skin of male attendants (see Figure 3.2). Given

Figure 3.2 Facsimile of a painting on the sarcophagus of Mentuhotep II's wife Aashyt by Charles K. Wilkinson. Metropolitan Museum of Art 48.105.31. Rogers Fund, 1948. *Source:* http://www.metmuseum.org/art/collection/search/544536

that diplomatic marriage is an age-old strategy to neutralize hostile relationships and to transform them, it is likely that these women had been wed to the king in order to seal vassal agreements with C-Group leaders as well as perhaps a parity agreement with the ruler of Kerma.[10]

Certainly, Mentuhotep II is known to have actively recruited Nubian soldiers, and so keeping relations positive would presumably have been a priority. Likewise, it is notable that, although the king appears to have quartered troops in the fortress at Elephantine, there are no signs of Egyptian domination in his reign further south. Thus, control of Nubia at this point was almost assuredly indirect or hegemonic, that is, administered through relationships with subordinate local rulers. Such relationships, however, are inherently unstable, and it is thus interesting that this tactic, if indeed adopted, was abandoned in the reign of the first Twelfth-Dynasty ruler, Amenemhet I, despite the fact that Amenemhet's own mother was apparently of Nubian origin.[11]

Like Mentuhotep II, Amenemhet I had to wage an extended campaign to unify Egypt under his rule, and, in the course of doing so, he must have gained an appreciation both for the fragility of vassal relationships and for the utility of strong fortifications. Machiavelli once wrote,

> It has been the custom of princes, so as to be able to hold their states more securely, to build fortresses that would be a bridle and a bit for those who might plan to act against them, and to have a secure refuge from sudden attack. I praise this mode because it has been used since antiquity.[12]

Machiavelli's advice was anticipated in recommendations purportedly dispensed by at least one First Intermediate period ruler to his heir: "Fortify your borders and your buffer zones, for it is expedient to work for the future.... Keep guard over your border, and strengthen your forts."[13] Multiple lines of evidence, however, suggest that such advice may well have been widely dispensed in the politically volatile First Intermediate period.

A roughly contemporary regional ruler in the south of Egypt named Ankhtify, for instance, reported that his attempts to expand his realm northward were thwarted, given that his would-be foes repeatedly chose to retreat behind strong walls rather than to fight.[14] Likewise, Amenemhet I was himself forced to lay siege to heavily fortified citadels, such as were prominently depicted on the walls of his allies at the Middle Egyptian site of Beni Hassan. These tomb paintings are remarkable for their depiction of Egyptians battling Egyptians, a motif that is understandably rare in pharaonic art. The battered bodies of 60 soldiers, who—as tell-tale wounds attest—evidently died while besieging a fortress and were buried together in the environs of Amenemhet I's aborted mortuary temple at Deir el-Bahari, provide visceral testament to the dangers inherent in siege warfare.[15]

Archaeological remains of First Intermediate period fortifications are generally inaccessible due to changes in the course of the Nile, to intensive overbuilding, or to the damage caused by farmers harvesting ruins for fertilizer. The military innovations developed under fire during this turbulent period, however, are evident in the architecture of the archaeologically accessible fortresses that Amenemhet I and his successors erected and maintained along the banks of the Nile between the First and Second Cataracts in Lower Nubia. These Twelfth-Dynasty military installations were certainly capable of withstanding siege engines, sappers, and virtually all other offensive techniques of warfare known at the beginning of the second millennium BCE (see Figure 3.3).[16]

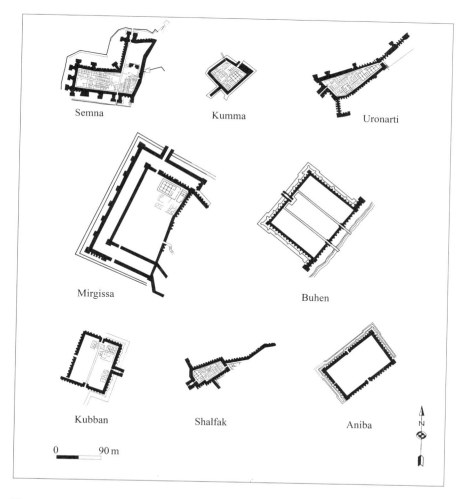

Figure 3.3 Middle Kingdom Nubian fortresses (redrawn from Emery 1965, 144–51).

Relatively early in his reign, Amenemhet I established control of Lower Nubia and began construction of a pair of gateway fortresses at Kubban and Ikkur. Together these fortresses served to guard the entrance to the Wadi Allaqi and Wadi Gabgaba mines (Kubban) and to monitor the C-Group settlements in the fertile plain on the western side of the river (Ikkur). This twinning of fortresses, with one situated opposite the other on the Nile's two banks, is observed also at Faras and Serra as well as at Semna and Kumma.[17] In other cases, the Egyptians chose to cluster their Nubian fortresses at cataracts, such as Elephantine and Senmet in the First Cataract; Buhen and Mirgissa toward the northern end of the Second Cataract; and finally Askut, Shelfak, Uronarti, and Semna South—all marshaled together with Semna and Kumma to render the southern end of the Second Cataract inviolable.

The military rationale for twinning or clustering fortresses, as was favored by military architects from the reigns of Amenemhet I until Senusret III (1870–1831), is not difficult to discern. In Philippe Maigret's treatise on the usefulness of fortresses, written in 1747 CE, he stresses that fortresses are dangerous to an invading army whether they are placed under siege or bypassed. In the first case, the resources of the attacker are put under strain; the army is delayed and weakened before reaching its ultimate goal; and the siege buys the aggressed government time to muster a suitable defensive army. On the other hand, if an attacker chooses to bypass a fortress, with soldiers inside, the invading army risks being attacked from the rear or else realizing that its passage out of enemy territory is blocked by the inhabitants of the bypassed fortress.[18] Such dangers, he asserts, are multiplied when fortresses are located in relatively close proximity and have the ability to communicate with and reinforce one another.

Maigret goes on to state that fortresses situated on rivers are often optimal as, generally speaking, rivers serve as the fastest means to move messengers, troops, and supplies into a region. Moreover, river fortresses greatly aid efforts to monitor, facilitate, or block riverine traffic, depending on what is desired.[19] Semna and Kumma, for example, guarded a treacherous section of the Second Cataract through which barely a single ship could pass at high water. Even on broader stretches of river, however, twinned fortresses meant that ships had less chance of evading imperial authorities by sailing past at a fast clip on the far side of the Nile. A similar effect could be obtained by situating fortresses on islands, as in the cases of Elephantine, Askut, Uronarti, and possibly Senmet. With the river bifurcated, a garrison situated on an island had a relatively easy time monitoring traffic and intercepting it when necessary. Moreover, nestled inside its own naturally exaggerated moat, an island fortress had the virtue of being eminently defensible.

Land routes also needed to be placed under surveillance, as these were potentially favored not only by those who wished to avoid the ship-wrecking cataracts but also by fugitives, smugglers, hostile Nubians, and any other categories of people who sought to bypass the thicket of pharaonic fortresses by traveling along the desert's edge under the cover of night. The clustering or twinning of fortresses in this case provided coverage along both banks. A series of dispatches found at Thebes but relating to the fortress at Semna demonstrate how this system of surveillance worked. Scouts were sent out each morning from a fortress to scour the desert for tracks of illicit passers-by. Once such tracks were found and reported, word was sent—presumably by river to enhance speed—to the fortresses that lay ahead of the travelers so that authorities at these fortresses could be alerted in advance and thus have a better chance of intercepting the fugitives.[20] In this manner, the system of fortresses worked very much like the chain of forts arrayed in the New Kingdom along the eastern flank of the Nile Delta and the northern Sinai land bridge to Canaan. These later military installations, which are discussed in Chapter 8, served as checkpoints to monitor passage in or out of the country and also as important nodes of communication.

What is particularly surprising about the Middle Kingdom fortresses of Nubia, as opposed to the aforementioned New Kingdom road fortresses, is that many were enormous. Mirgissa's enclosure walls, for example, encompassed 101,850 m^2.[21] Even when the Middle Kingdom installations were relatively modest in size, however—as they tended to be in the Second Cataract region especially—the external walls were elaborately defended. All fortresses had some combination of enclosure walls, citadels, multi-chambered gates, ramparts, glacis, parapets, bastions, towers, spur walls, and/or stone-lined subterranean river stairs. Indeed, the quantity of mud brick and timber required to construct even one such fortress is breathtaking. It is estimated, for instance, that at least 10 million bricks would have been necessary to construct Buhen. Meanwhile, just upstream lay Mirgissa, which was even larger and would have consumed far more bricks in its construction as well as an estimated 3,700 trees![22] Given that Egyptian records demonstrate that by the reign of Senusret III there were 17 such fortresses in evidence, the cumulative effect of this deforestation must have devastated the natural environment—a result that Egypt's military architects no doubt anticipated.

It has been a longstanding subject of speculation as to why Middle Kingdom pharaohs went to such expense constructing, staffing, and supplying the Nubian fortresses. Were the C-Group pastoralists more formidable warriors than has been previously supposed? Or were the extreme defensive measures directed primarily toward safeguarding Egyptian-held Nubia from Kerman soldiers, who were more plausibly versed in sophisticated siege tactics? Alternatively, it has been suggested that the fortresses were intentionally hypertrophic, serving as visual symbols of the awe-inspiring and unassailable power of the Egyptian state (see Figure 3.4).

Along these lines, it is possible that the Middle Kingdom fortresses were *intentionally* wasteful in their consumption of manpower. Certainly, it may

Figure 3.4 The seemingly hypertrophic fortifications of the Middle Kingdom fortress at Aniba (drawing by Franck Monnier © 2017).

have been a savvy political move for pharaohs to employ legions of young men—who might otherwise have been at the service of regional aggrandizers or otherwise agitating—in a massive, ideologically charged building project on Egypt's southern frontier.[23] As Wendy Brown has argued in *Walled States, Waning Sovereignty*, the building of massive border fortifications rarely succeeds in keeping those determined to cross a border from crossing it. What they *are* often successful at, however, is bolstering the popularity of a ruler who, by virtue of initiating or furthering such projects, is perceived to be active in both unifying and protecting his people against an outside threat. The construction of walls, she maintains, is part of an elaborate pageantry of power.

Taken together, the Middle Kingdom fortresses erected in Nubia's Nile Valley accomplished a number of imperial goals simultaneously. They not only safeguarded the entrances to quarries (e.g. Elephantine and Aniba) and mining areas (e.g. Kubban, Aniba, Serra, Buhen, and the Second Cataract fortresses), but they also kept watch over the most fertile and densely populated areas of Lower Nubia (e.g. Ikkur, Aniba, and Faras). Additionally, they secured the southern frontier and no doubt also aided authorized travel through the ever-perilous cataract zone (especially the southernmost cluster of fortresses of Askut, Uronarti, Shelfak, Semna, Kumma, and Semna South). All housed troops and granaries, though the disproportionate size of the granary at Askut and the nature of the associated sealings suggest that this fortress served to supply southern expeditions undertaken for trade or war.[24] The latter, it appears, were primarily (and not coincidentally) undertaken at the point at which Egypt's army could be assured that a secure cordon of fortresses would offer it refuge in the event of a quick retreat.

Aside from Askut, the most functionally specialized of the Middle Kingdom fortresses may have been Mirgissa, which was explicitly stated in a stele erected by Senusret III to have been the sole locale north of Semna to which Upper Nubians were authorized to travel for trading purposes.[25] Situated some 50 km north of the southern border, Mirgissa was sandwiched between Buhen and the southernmost cluster of Second Cataract fortresses, no doubt because the Egyptians believed that they would have the best chance for a favorable exchange rate if their trading partners were fully surrounded and thus rendered vulnerable. Relations with the kingdom of Kush at Kerma occasionally involved the exchange of diplomatic gifts (*inw*), but given that relations could and did turn intermittently hostile, such precautions may have been especially prudent.[26]

Nubian expeditions to Mirgissa must have been reserved strictly for high-level trade, for the Semna dispatches demonstrate that officials at Semna routinely received unspecified goods from southern Nubians in exchange for payment and a hospitality offering of bread and beer. The details of such transactions evidently did not merit recording, suggesting that the items were not particularly valuable or perhaps that the specifics were not deemed germane to a daybook that dealt primarily with surveillance issues. In their recent reassessment of the Semna Dispatches, Bryan Kraemer and Kate Liszka have mounted a convincing argument that the two all-female delegations of Nubians—who came and, unlike their male counterparts, spent the night at the fortress—likely engaged in prostitution.[27] Given that the desert was at that time reportedly "dying of hunger," it would not be surprising if the women requested their compensation in sacks of grain. Paid relations between soldiers and local women are hardly improbable and are certainly attested in the Eastern Desert in the Roman period.[28] Yet another probable occurrence is addressed in Chapter 8.

Control Outside the Fortresses

As the Semna dispatches demonstrate, the Egyptians on occasion employed the services of semi-nomadic Medjay tribesmen from the Eastern Desert. These peoples seem to have been closely linked neither to the C-Group of Lower Nubia nor to the powers at Kerma, though no doubt they interacted with both populations regularly. Like the Sheikh Muftah, the Medjay may have been especially valuable to the Egyptians for their skill as desert travelers and trackers. It is also possible that they enjoyed an adversarial relationship with the C-Group, rather similar to the longstanding enmity between the structurally similar Nuer and Dinka tribes who were to inhabit the Sudan in more modern times. Empires often exploit pre-existing hostilities for their own benefit and gain collaborators from the longstanding enemies of their

enemies. In the end, an alliance with the Medjay may also have been pragmatic. Desert nomads are notoriously difficult to subdue, and so many states
that have bordered or incorporated their territories have chosen to employ
them as allies, rather than to expose their citizens and caravans to seemingly
ceaseless depredations.

To aid the imperial project of surveillance, regular patrols and allied scouts
occupied numerous hilltop watch-towers—similar to those in Dakhla that
were discussed in the previous chapter. Taken together, these signaling stations
no doubt formed a single elaborate early warning system, such as those erected
by the armies of ancient Rome, to cite just one example.[29] In addition, the
Egyptians erected walls along important tracks at which goods may have been
unloaded for transhipment. A Middle Kingdom wall skirted the far side of the
path that connected Semna South with Semna, while another that may well
date to the same period extended for several kilometers from the region of
Shellal (near the likely site of ancient Senmut) to Elephantine.[30] Designed to be
both high and thick, such walls protected caravans when they were most
vulnerable. A successful raid on a major state-sponsored trading venture, after
all, would represent a significant blow to the king's treasury and a vast infusion
of capital to the hijackers.

Virtually the only other examples of state-built infrastructure in Lower
Nubia were a series of labor camps (ḫnrwt). In Egypt, these institutions
served as places of incarceration for individuals who had attempted to evade
corvée duty, for the families of fugitives, and for others who had offended
the state. While some of the inmates of the labor camps in Lower Nubia may
have come from the law-violators and oath-breakers in Egypt, who were
often destined to have their noses cut off and to be sent to Nubia, it is likely
that the majority of inhabitants were those Nubians who dared disobey
imperial dictates by traveling where they wished, by declining to participate
in corvée labor, or perhaps by acting aggressively toward Egyptians or
Egyptian interests. The incarceration and temporary enslavement of such state-
declared criminals would not only serve as an example to other disaffected
Nubians, but the labor these individuals provided would no doubt have been
well utilized given the continual construction and refurbishment of imperial
infrastructure as well as the quarrying of granite and diorite and the extraction
and processing of gold and other precious minerals. Certainly we know of
an official of Senusret I's who forced two Nubian leaders to wash gold under
his watch, presumably as a punitive measure.[31] Gold-washing equipment and
weights have been discovered in association with numerous fortresses, and
many of these same fortresses appear also to have had their own associated
labor camp.[32]

Such installations must have been resented intensely by the local population, and it is possible that Nubians took up arms in opposition to their
construction. An official named Intefiqer, who served under Amenemhet I

and Senusret I (c. 1956–1911), boasted in a rock inscription near the fortress of Aniba,

> One has been engaged in building this stronghold (*ḥnrt*). Then the Nubians of the entire remaining part of Wawat were slaughtered. Thereupon I sailed victoriously upstream, slaughtering the Nubian on his river-bank[s] and then I sailed downstream plucking corn and cutting down their remaining trees. I[?] put fire into their houses, as one has to act against him who rebelled against the King.[33]

While Intefiqer does not mention incarcerating prisoners in the very *ḥnrt* they opposed, the incineration of dwellings, the felling of trees, and the confiscation of crops may have been an attempt to rid the surrounding area of hostile communities and to divest it of its resources. As Josef Wegner has argued, Intefiqer's *ḥnrt* should likely be identified as the Middle Kingdom walled enclosure at Areika. Significantly, officials at this site routinely employed a seal that bore an image of an Egyptian soldier (*ꜥḥꜣwty*) dominating a fettered captive.[34]

As Intefiqer's inscription and many others demonstrate, the Egyptians did not hesitate to wield the stick as an imperial tool, and at least four punitive campaigns are known from the reigns of Amenemhet I and Senusret I.[35] Whereas Early Dynastic rulers had chosen to drive the indigenous A-Group off their land in order to claim it for themselves, however, Middle Kingdom rulers evidently deemed this same tactic impractical, impossible, or perhaps undesirable. Egypt's main imperial goals were evidently to secure access to valuable natural resources, to ensure safe passage for trade caravans, and to protect their territory from armed incursions by the Kermans.

Just why the Twelfth-Dynasty pharaohs abandoned the strategy of indirect rule, initiated by Mentuhotep II, is unclear. Perhaps the reorganization took place as a punitive reaction to Nubian rebellions against the Egyptians and perhaps also against those C-Group rulers viewed as collaborators. Additionally or alternatively, the government may have found that the relatively egalitarian and predominantly pastoral structure of C-Group society did not lend itself to imperial extraction. While Intefiqer's inscription indicates that the C-Group cultivated crops, ethno-archaeological evidence suggests that societal wealth would have been measured in cattle, not grain.[36] Likewise, judging from Harkhuf's inscriptions, C-Group leadership in Lower Nubia appears to have been highly unstable. Disputes between or within distinct C-Group tribes may well have caused leaders to cycle as political reconfigurations occurred, but there are other explanations as well. As in many egalitarian societies under threat, leaders may have arisen as needed in times of war, with the communal understanding that such power was situational and would be relinquished once peace had been restored. Certainly, as numerous ethnographies attest, leadership in such societies tends to be charismatic rather than hereditary.

Although it is dangerous to make too close a comparison between ancient and more recent inhabitants of a given region, the C-Group seems to have shared a number of structural similarities with the Nuer groups that British imperialists encountered when they assumed effective control of southern Sudan during the first part of the last century. These British officials found themselves attempting to govern a pastoral population whose leaders accumulated political and religious capital rather than personal riches. Moreover, given that the leaders exercised no coercive force over their followers, their careers as leaders rose and fell solely according to the respect they enjoyed among those within their group, a respect that could dissipate quickly.[37]

It is certainly remarkable in the case of the Early and Middle C-Group that the graves of leaders do not appear to have differed substantively from those of their followers in terms of size or wealth. While there were some small variations between tumuli in C-Group cemeteries, generally speaking—and quite unlike the situation in contemporary Kerma—no one tumulus stood out in a singular fashion. Given that Nubians throughout antiquity had a reputation for being exceptionally powerful magicians,[38] it is interesting that among the different genres of Nuer leader, the British recognized *kujur* prophets—that is, men whose power stemmed from their ability to serve as a vessel for spirits, to control rain, and even to shapeshift—as being particularly effective at mobilizing their people.[39] The material ways in which these men distinguished themselves from their followers in life and death were for the most part purposefully subtle, but the fact that they lacked the material trappings of power meant little (or perhaps, from another perspective, meant everything). According to official reports, *kujur* prophets on multiple occasions gained enough indigenous backing to pose a substantial threat to imperial rule.

The British government desired to create a stable indigenous leadership that would rule their people in a manner acceptable to imperial interests. Because the *kujur* prophets lacked pliability and even at times encouraged rebellion among their followers, the British moved to repress them and instead to promote other Nuer as leaders. As the British official Percy Coriat lamented, however, those who put themselves forward to the British as potential leaders or collaborators were either

> ...old and decrepit or of the type of tribesman to be found loitering around a Government Post for what he can pick up. In every section there was, if not an actual Chief, a man with some influence over his particular camp but for some reason these were not forthcoming in dealings with Government.[40]

In the Nuer political economy, wealth and status resided not so much in what one owned (with the exception of cattle) but in personal character and spiritual capital, both assets that might abruptly dissolve if a leader was seen as a tool of the British. Thus, collaborators—while perhaps not difficult to find and eager to assume leadership (as well as the pay that went with it)—mostly lacked legitimacy and thus any real ability to influence their communities.[41] The Twelfth-Dynasty government also appears to have failed in any efforts to identify viable local partners, ending up, as is typical in such situations, essentially placing the conquered region and its people under direct management in a system modeled after their own bureaucracy. Administration of the C-Group population in the Twelfth Dynasty, then, was to become the province of Egyptian officials designated as overseers of districts of Nubians (*imy-r w^{c}rwt n styw*).[42]

The C-Group, like the Nuer, practiced a subsistence economy from which little could be skimmed or extracted, and so although the Egyptians, like the British, levied traditional taxes and a labor tax,[43] the imperial coffers were not particularly enriched by their effort. In British Sudan, the tax on cattle was minimal, just enough to remind the Nuer that it was the British who were ultimately in charge, and the widely loathed labor tax consisted primarily of road construction. The value of the territory to the British, then, had virtually nothing to do with the income that could be gained from exploiting the local population. It is similarly remarkable that there are so few attestations of tax collection in Egyptian-held Nubia during the Middle Kingdom. While this is to some degree an argument from silence, sufficient seal impressions and other material were salvaged from the Lower Nubian forts that some records pertinent to the collection of revenue, if this was indeed a regular and important practice, should be expected.[44] Certainly, there is no evidence that either Egyptian soldiers or C-Group Nubians were engaged in farming on any significant scale, so grain to support the resident soldiers—perhaps numbering around 4,000 to 5,000 in total—as well as any other imperial needs, would necessarily have been imported.[45]

For the Egyptians, as for the British nearly four millennia later, any wealth and power to be gained in Nubia would not be because of its resident population but rather in spite of it. What was important to the British was that internal fighting between different Nuer subgroups and between the Nuer and their archenemies, the Dinka, be suppressed. When intractable conflicts persisted and threatened to undermine British authority, the government response was to settle the pastoralists such that the populations could be more easily controlled. To this end they adopted a policy with respect to the indigenous population of "settlement backed by armed assistance."[46] Such resettlement allowed the population to be more easily monitored, and it gave the British clearer guidelines for distinguishing "friendly" (i.e. settled) Nubians from hostile ones (i.e. those still insisting on freedom of movement). Local leaders could no longer slip beyond government reach when it suited them to do so, only to return later when administrators and their troops had vacated the region.[47] Whether such a policy was enacted in Egyptian-held Nubia is unclear, due primarily to the poor preservation of settlements, but it would appear likely that attempts were made to isolate Lower Nubians from their "free" counterparts in the south and to separate troublemakers by settling them in easily monitored communities. Certainly the Semna dispatches make it clear that once the Egyptians had claimed control of Lower Nubia, unauthorized roaming was not to be tolerated.

Settling pastoralists, however, is no easy matter. Peasants—rooted like their crops to one specific patch of soil—serve as the traditional foil of pastoralists, and adopting this lifeway in earnest is thus entirely antithetical to their self-definition. For example, the little bit of cultivation that the Nuer engaged in of their own volition was patently women's work, the only men deigning to engage in it being elderly and infirm. No male could plant or grind without doing violence to his own manhood, and it was even believed (or at least stated) that a man who ground grain would lose the use of both his arms.[48] Indeed, Coriat noted in one of his official reports that

> [t]he Nuer is entirely pastoral and cultivation does not appeal to him and it is doubtful whether there will be any inducement to encourage him to farming on a large scale. Cattle are the beginning and end of all things.[49]

The distaste of the Nuer for farming was highly problematic for the British, who attempted to create a native impetus to farm by encouraging among the local population a thirst for goods only the imperial government could provide. Coriat stated,

> In my opinion economic progress in the Nuer country can only be attained in one way; by creating a demand for some luxury which will eventually become a necessity as they develop a civilisation in our meaning of the word and by compelling the Nuer to supply a commodity required by civilisation and in return for which they will be given the wherewithal enabling them to obtain that for which we have inculcated a demand.... In the Western Nuer we gave the people cotton seed to grow in order that they should supply that which we required and to enable them to purchase something we could supply.... In exchange for the cotton thrust on him we have attempted to create a demand in the Western Nuer for cloth, sugar, tea, iron, beads and other trade goods but in 8 years the amount purchased in proportion to the population is infinitesimal.[50]

The Nuer's emphatic rejection of imperial lures—gifts proffered disingenuously in order to create damaging levels of dependency—may thus be seen as a survival strategy. If one cannot beat an occupying force, the expression might run, at the very least one does not have to join them.

For both the British and the Egyptians, it was imperial policy to keep a relatively modest number of officials and troops on the ground at any given time. Troops were recruited from the homeland and returned there after their tour of duty.[51] In the British case, and likely in the Egyptian as well—as suggested by parallels to Fourth-Dynasty administration and also to the practice of governance in the northern territories in the Eighteenth Dynasty (see Chapter 7)—officials rotated frequently between posts, presumably to prevent potentially subversive ties from forming between governors and those they governed. Such frequent transfers, however, necessarily impair the ability of imperial officers to develop a nuanced understanding of local complexities.[52]

The Nuer's rejection of imperial products and projects was misinterpreted by one such British official who possessed little to no understanding of the local language or cultural practice. In his report, this man stated that the Nuer were "[l]azy to a degree, indifferent to the outer world and any suggestion of progress,"[53] which is, of course, a typically imperialist response to a dynamic not fully grasped. The lack of political integration among various components of egalitarian tribal groups typically makes it difficult for such peoples to fight effectively against the juggernaut of imperial armies.[54] Ironically, however, the resistance such peoples are capable of mounting following their surrender is often far more effective. Writing on the difficulties that outside powers have encountered in effectively exploiting the labor-potential of tribal peoples, Morton Fried stated,

> Because the basic institutions of stateship are lacking in the invaded societies, there is no means by which the intruder can obtain the compulsive holds it requires. The natives are described as lazy and shiftless, disorganized, undisciplined and uncooperative.[55]

Coriat, who was more curious, perceptive, and fluent than the vast majority of his colleagues, would likely have interpreted this purported Nuer "indifference" for what it was: defiance. Peter Wells has observed in his meditation on dynamics that occurred within Rome's empire that

> ...peoples in colonial contexts express their resistance to the dominating imperial forces through a number of means besides outright armed rebellion. One is more or less subtle forms of noncooperation—arriving late for work projects, working slowly and perhaps sloppily, and creating uncomplimentary stories and songs about representatives of authority.[56]

Such peoples, Wells goes on to state, are by no means indifferent to imperial culture—they actively oppose it.

Rejection and Resistance

One of the most fascinating features of Egypto-Nubian relations in Lower Nubia during the Twelfth Dynasty is the fact that C-Group and Egyptian material cultures remained emphatically distinct from one another. Such separation stands in stark contrast to the situation in the First and Second Intermediate periods—which together bookended the Middle Kingdom. During these times C-Group peoples evinced a strong interest in pharaonic material culture and not infrequently included Egyptian pottery and other imports and imitations in their grave assemblages. In the Middle Kingdom, however, when Lower Nubians lived cheek by jowl with Egyptian soldiers and administrators, Egyptian goods appear to have been almost completely absent from Nubian contexts. Likewise, within the vast majority of the fortresses, C-Group pottery rarely appears. Significantly, the largest quantity of indigenous ceramic found in colonial contexts belonged to the repertoire of the "Pangrave people," an archaeologically attested culture that can, at least on occasion, be ascribed to Egypt's Medjay collaborators.[57]

Two primary models present themselves as explanations for the curious dearth of Nubian material culture inside Egyptian forts and, conversely, of Egyptian goods within Nubian settlements and cemeteries. On the one hand, there is a top-down explanation according to which the lack of intermixing was symptomatic both of Egypt's cultural disdain for the C-Group and of a policy that discouraged the formation of personal ties between occupier and occupied. The other model places the agency for this cultural separation in the hands of the Nubians and sees the separation as a conscious rejection of all things Egyptian and a refusal by the C-Group to act in partnership with those that occupied their land.[58] The two models, of course, are not mutually exclusive, and a negative view of the conquered by the conqueror would undoubtedly fuel pre-existing resentments.

Official rhetoric levied against the Nubians was indeed harsh and exclusionary. On a border stele at Semna, Senusret III insulted his Nubian opponents stating, "They are not people one respects. They are wretches, craven-hearted."[59] While such sentiments were undoubtedly directed at his Kerman opponents, other evidence suggests this view encompassed his Lower Nubian subjects as well. On a rock graffito etched near Areika, for example, an Egyptian soldier claims to have done his duty patrolling the roads "without placing a Nubian in my heart."[60] It would appear, then, that Nubians represented a population to be exploited when labor was needed but not to be treated as equals or allies. As Senusret I stated, "Every Nubian who pays his duties and works as a servant and who behaves in accordance with the might of the God, his people will last in eternity."[61] The flip side, of course, was that a refusal to pay off the Egyptian pharaoh or to work for him as a servant or to behave as if he were a god would incur death or imprisonment for the offender and "his people" in a *ḫnrt* labor camp.

In order to help ensure compliance with imperial dictates, the Egyptian government may have demilitarized the indigenous population, for it is notable that although walled settlements and weapons interred with corpses are found in C-Group contexts both before and after the Middle Kingdom, they are not found during.[62] The presence of both weapons and walls at Kerma in the Middle Kingdom, however, proves that their lack was not simply a trend of the times.[63] Disarming the inhabitants of a newly conquered region is practical advice and is often advocated by the political strategists of governments determined to exert their authority over those who would rather not be ruled.[64]

Clearly, then, the Egyptians had an investment in making sure that the lines between the conquerors (armed and victorious) and those conquered (defanged and domesticated) in Lower Nubia were well-defined and that their soldiers and officials did not blur those lines by placing the local inhabitants in their hearts. To this end, as is not infrequent in occupied countries, the government may well have discouraged fraternization between their own representatives and the dominated local population.[65] John Stuart Mill, familiar with such dynamics, stated,

> Now, if there be a fact to which all experience testifies, it is that when a country holds another in subjection, the individuals of the ruling people ... think the people of the country mere dirt under their feet.[66]

Certainly, populations that one keeps at arm's length, assiduously avoiding the cultivation of shared bonds of affection or trust, are much easier to exploit, as no apologies are necessary.

Horvath's model of "equilibrium imperialism"—occupation without colonization—incorporates an archaeological expectation of indigenous cultural maintenance. This particular model, typical of the Anglo-Sudan and a great many other European imperial projects in Africa and elsewhere, appears in some respects to fit the Middle Kingdom situation well, as Stuart Tyson Smith has argued.[67] The lack of cultural mixing observed in the archaeology of occupied Nubia, then, may well have been the result of such a policy—at least partially. In the tumultuous dance of imperial relations, however, it takes two to tango.

Although Maigret was in general a great proponent of the utility of fortresses, he did admit that

> Citadels built against the subject are the bane of that love and confidence they ought to place in their sovereign, and instead thereof beget perpetual fears and jealousies lest the sovereign should make use of them as instruments for their oppression.... [Many places have] celebrated the demolition-day of their citadels as the second birth-day of their liberties.[68]

The C-Group Nubians very quickly in the Twelfth Dynasty found their freedom of movement radically curtailed and their territory studded with impenetrable fortresses. Nubians reacted to this situation, no doubt, with anger, and, as in the case of the Nuer, it would not be surprising if this anger led them to emphatically reject imperial lifeways. Certainly, history provides numerous examples, both ancient and modern, of conquered peoples who actively maintained their cultural boundaries as a form of nonviolent resistance.[69]

Although they may have been forbidden by the Egyptians to build physical walls around their settlements, the C-Group seem to have walled off those elements of their culture that mattered most. Throughout the period of their occupation, they continued to cook their own food in their own pots, to dress in leather (not linen), and to bury their loved ones in tumuli. Indeed, the C-Group give the impression of attempting, inasmuch as it was possible, to live their lives as if the Egyptians had never come, thereby signaling their allegiance to their traditional lifeways and their opposition to the outside order imposed upon them.[70] In such dogged cultural maintenance, the C-Group defied the expectation, fulfilled in other times and places, that a tribal group with a low population density would have little chance of retaining its traditional culture in the face of a substantial military occupation.[71] In fact, as will be seen in the following chapter, the C-Group would only begin again to experiment with the adoption of elements of Egyptian material culture once such objects and architecture had been absolved of their association with political oppression.

Notes

1 Edwards 2004, 88.
2 Clayton et al. 2008.
3 Kendall 1997, 39; Török 2009, 59, 72–3.
4 Török 2009, 58.
5 Chaix 2004, 89.
6 O'Connor 1993, 36; Bonnet 2004, 79.
7 Sun Tzu, *Art of War*, chapter VIII, 11.
8 Giddy 1987, 53–4.
9 Wegner *forthcoming*.
10 Hayes 1953, 220.
11 Simpson 2003, 219.
12 Machiavelli, *Prince*, ch. XX, 86.
13 Simpson 2003, 156, 158.
14 Seidlmayer 2003, 120–1.
15 Arnold 1991, 5–14; Vogel 2003.
16 For recent in-depth studies of these installations, see Vogel 2004 and Monnier 2010.

17 The seemingly analogous arrangement of the fortified gold-mining camps at El Hisnein West and East was likely due primarily to the proximity of mineral deposits rather than to defensive concerns. Recent archaeological investigations of Middle Kingdom fortified mining camps at Wadi el-Hudi, El Hisnein West and East, and Dihmit North and South should shed light both on the Egyptian government's methods of extraction and on its efforts to mobilize the labor of Nubians. C-Group masonry techniques, pottery, and other material traces may indicate partnership (in an Eleventh-Dynasty context perhaps) or forced labor (Harrell and Mittelstaedt 2015 and Liszka 2017). Renewed work at Uronarti by the Uronarti Regional Archaeological Project—and perhaps eventually also at Semna and Shalfak—is similarly exciting (Knoblauch and Bestock 2013).

18 Maigret 1747, 15–17. See also Luttwak 1979, 134.

19 Maigret 1747, 70–1, 78, 109.

20 Smither 1945; Kraemer and Liszka 2016. Seal impressions confirm that letters were frequently sent between Lower Nubian fortresses (Smith 1990, 204).

21 Dunham 1967, 143.

22 Dunham 1967, 157; Williams 1999, 448, n 46.

23 Adams 1977, 187–8; Kemp 1997, 130.

24 Smith 1990, 212–13; Smith 1995, 46–7.

25 Breasted 1906a, 293.

26 Lichtheim 1988, 138.

27 Kraemer and Liszka 2016, 14–15, 23, 45–8.

28 Maxfield 2003, 164.

29 Smith 1972, 56–8; Emery et al. 1979, 100; Luttwak 1979, 66–7.

30 Kemp 1989, 176; Jaritz 1993, 107–8, 113–14.

31 Breasted 1906a, 274.

32 Smith 1997, 72; Török 2009, 85. For a discussion of the institution of the *ḫnrt* labor camp, see Wegner 1995, 153–4.

33 Žaba 1974, 99.

34 Wegner 1995, 144–8, 154–6.

35 Török 2009, 84–5.

36 Hafsaas 2006.

37 Evans-Prichard 1940, 5–6, 172–6; Johnson 1993, 77.

38 Compare the text of the letter in which Amenhotep II warns his Nubian viceroy, "Do not be lenient towards the Nubians, no indeed not! Beware of their people and their magicians" (Cumming 1982, 45) with the famous dueling magicians in the Roman-period story "The Adventures of Setna and Si-Osire" (Simpson 2003, 476–89).

39 Johnson 1993, xxxii, xxxix, li, lv, 34–5, 111, 198.

40 Johnson 1993, 111; see also li.

41 Johnson 1993, xxxix, 77, 187–8.

42 Török 2009, 95.

43 Säve-Söderbergh 1989, 4; Johnson 1993, xlviii–xlix, 91.

44 Smith 1990, 211.

45 Williams 1999, 436, n. 5.

46 Johnson 1993, 123.

47 Johnson 1993, 91, 128–9.

48 Johnson 1993, 24, 33.

49 Johnson 1993, 175.

50 Johnson 1993, 186.

51 The notion that garrisons rotated during the Middle Kingdom is based partly on the barracks-style housing within the fortresses, partly on the scarcity of Egyptian graves from this period, and partly on the great leap in the numbers of commemorative stele from the Twelfth Dynasty to the Second Intermediate period (Säve-Söderbergh 1941, 98–102; Smith 1976, 66–9).

52 Johnson 1993, xxxiii–xxxiv.

53 Johnson 1993, xlvii.

54 Doyle 1986, 132–3.

55 Fried 1967, 241.

56 Wells 1999, 196.

57 O'Connor 1974, 29–30; Smith 1976, 67–8; Säve-Söderbergh 1989, 4, 9; Smith 2003, 114.

58 Junker 1925, 11, 43–4; Säve-Söderbergh 1941, 41, 102, 130–1; Säve-Söderbergh 1989, 9.

59 Lichtheim 1975, 119.

60 Wegner 1995, 150.

61 Säve-Söderbergh 1989, 4.

62 Säve-Söderbergh 1989, 9–10; Török 2009, 98.

63 O'Connor 1993, 30–1.

64 Machiavelli, *Prince*, ch. XX.

65 Horvath 1972, 50.

66 Mill 1910, 386.

67 Horvath's 1972, 48; Bartel 1980, 16–17; Smith 1991, 83–4.

68 Maigret 1747, 29–30.

69 Cromer 1910, 82–3; Lightfoot and Martinez 1995, 485–6; Patterson 1991, 105–6; Wells 1999, 170, 193–4.

70 For discussions of C-Group cultural resistance, see Smith 1995, 49; van Pelt 2013, 527.

71 Elton 1996, 25.

4

Transculturation, Collaboration, Colonization (c. 1773–1295)

As discussed in the previous chapter, Egyptian soldiers and many C-Group individuals lived side-by-side in the Middle Kingdom, and yet the material culture of each group reveals remarkably little admixture. Both sides clearly preferred to keep to their own communities. In contrast, by the mid-Eighteenth Dynasty the cultural footprint of Egyptians and Nubians was so similar that archaeologists often find it impossible to distinguish whether a house or a grave belonged to one or the other. Indeed, they freely acknowledge that the owner may well have identified as both Egyptian *and* Nubian (or as Egypto-Nubian), thanks to the seemingly prevalent practice of intermarriage.

The aim of this chapter, then, is to bridge the gap between these two periods by discussing the changes in cultural relations that started in Egypt's Thirteenth Dynasty as a result of the permanent settlement of many soldiers in Nubia. Areas of special concern are the roles of women in the formation of this newly integrated society, the shifting sociopolitical alliances that occurred in the aftermath of the breakdown of the Egyptian state, and the impact of the Eighteenth-Dynasty policy of recruiting indigenous collaborators. A consideration of the heterogeneity in cultural response both within and among communities to the imposition of Egypt's empire rounds out the chapter.

To begin, then, it is important to set the historical scene. After the death of the last pharaoh of the Twelfth Dynasty (c. 1773), Egypt no longer had a powerful ruling family, and a succession of mostly unrelated kings reigned for short periods during the subsequent dynasty. Although the government was able to maintain a high degree of functionality during the first 50 years or so of the Thirteenth Dynasty, its finances and sphere of effective power dwindled steadily. Kings who ruled after the reign of Neferhotep (c. 1740–1729) represent a jumble of names that can be neither ordered nor connected with substantial deeds or monuments. By this point, the real powerbrokers in the north of Egypt were the Syro-Palestinian "Hyksos" (known to the Egyptians as *ḥḳ3-ḫ3swt*, "rulers of foreign countries") who occupied Tell el-Dab'a and numerous other sites along the eastern fringe of the Nile Delta.

Ancient Egyptian Imperialism, First Edition. Ellen Morris.
© 2018 Ellen Morris. Published 2018 by John Wiley & Sons Ltd.

As the state coffers dwindled in the Thirteenth Dynasty, the Middle Kingdom system of garrisoning Lower Nubia was no longer sustainable, and costs desperately needed to be cut. As evidence discussed in the prior chapter makes clear, the expense of provisioning, maintaining, and staffing such an elaborate fortress system must have been exorbitant. The governmental policy of rotating thousands of troops through these fortresses may also have become politically unpopular. No standing army existed in the Middle Kingdom, and so levied men essentially served out a particularly arduous form of corvée labor. Thus, as the Thirteenth Dynasty wore on, its rulers may have come to the conclusion that the majority of their soldiers were better utilized up north to bolster the power of the weakening state.

Whatever the prime motivation behind these changes, the upshot seems to have been that in the Thirteenth Dynasty the fortress system still functioned, but instead of being staffed by a population that was essentially passing through the region on a tour of duty, the installations became the permanent residences of soldiers, officials, and their families. The numbers of the men who manned the fortresses, then, were replenished not with the arrival of fresh troops but with the physical maturation of their sons. For roughly half a century it seems that this resident body of troops maintained most of the regular military, administrative, and perhaps also economic functions of the Middle Kingdom fortress personnel. The percentage of military titles and administrative sealings, however, eventually did decline along with the fortunes of the dynasty itself.[1]

This change can be ascertained archaeologically in the contrast between the dearth of cemeteries and commemorative stelae in the Twelfth Dynasty and their relative abundance in the Thirteenth Dynasty. For example, commemorative stelae datable to the Twelfth Dynasty at Buhen number only four, as opposed to the 41 such stelae erected in the Thirteenth Dynasty and later Second Intermediate period. This disparity exists despite the popularity of stelae in Twelfth-Dynasty Egypt and despite the fact that the Twelfth Dynasty and the Second Intermediate period were of approximately equal length.[2] Quite likely, the paucity of stelae in the Twelfth Dynasty stems from the fact that very few Egyptians were buried in Nubia during this time. Certainly, the late Old Kingdom biographies of Sabni and Pepinakht describe the elaborate lengths that Egyptians went to in order to ransom the bodies of fallen comrades who had died in foreign lands. Likewise, one of the most famous works of Middle Kingdom literature is a story about an Egyptian official who had lived in Syria-Palestine for much of his life, growing both rich and powerful and siring many sons. The central theme of the story, however, is how important it became to this individual to return home to Egypt in order to have a proper Egyptian burial with all of its rites and wrappings.[3] Judging from the scarcity of Egyptian graves in Twelfth-Dynasty Nubia, it would appear that the inhabitants of the fortresses were granted the right to be shipped home for burial if they perished while on active duty.

In many empires, military fortresses evolved into what were essentially civilian settlements once the intensity of threats and/or the imperial budget diminished. Of the Roman empire, Edward Luttwak writes,

> ...in the course of the fourth century, the full-time troops that had guarded the borders using mobile and offensive tactics gave way to part-time peasant-soldiers (*limitanei*) who farmed their own assigned lands and provided a purely local and static defense.... [M]en who have their own families and possessions to protect *in situ* should make capable defenders. In modern times, military-agricultural colonies have proved to be useful and economical agents of border defense in places and times as diverse as the Transylvania of the eighteenth century, the Volga steppe of the nineteenth, and the Israeli Negev of today. In each case, self-reliant farmer-soldiers could be counted upon to deal independently with localized infiltration and other low intensity threats, while being ready to provide *points d'appui* for mobile field armies of regular full-time troops in the event of large-scale war.[4]

Just how this change occurred in Egyptian-held Nubia is not known. It may have been that the orders to return home either never arrived or were simply so slow in coming that the resident garrison gradually settled down for good. It is also possible, however, that Nile Valley residents were recruited for resettlement or else resettled against their wishes. The names of many Second Intermediate period residents of Buhen were compounded with that of the god Sobek, and Sobek of Sumenu was mentioned frequently in their inscriptions. This led Jean Vercoutter to suggest that the inhabitants came mainly from Er-Rizeiqat, just south of Thebes and across the river from Gebelein. A sizable population of Nubian mercenaries had been settled at Gebelein in the First Intermediate period, and it is possible that some of their Egyptianized descendants numbered among the military colonists. There was also a fair amount of theophoric names at Buhen that perhaps indicated a connection to Thebes.[5] Regardless, the fact that the fortress still employed an overseer of interpreters in the early Thirteenth Dynasty implies that the majority of its inhabitants were indeed immigrants.[6]

Although the settling of permanent military colonists in Nubia was a new innovation, it was not without precedent. In the Instructions for Merikare,[7] a text purportedly written by one First Intermediate period king to his son and successor, the elder statesman advised constructing fortresses and equipping them with frontier patrols. In addition, however, he also advocated the construction of towns "filled with people, of the best in the whole land, to repel attacks against them." Such towns offered protection in numbers, which was important, the king warned, because "the Asiatic is a crocodile on its shore; it snatches from a lonely road, it cannot seize from a populous town." The king provided an example of one such town, boasting, "It is the defense against the Bowmen. Its walls are warlike, its soldiers many. Its serfs know how to bear arms, apart from the free men within." In Nubia, at the start of yet another "intermediate period," then, the Egyptian government adopted much the same philosophy. They secured their southern border with fortresses settled by a robust resident population that would raise families there and in so doing have a particularly strong stake in protecting these installations against attack.

Settling a permanent population in the Nubian fortresses may also have solved another problem for the Egyptian government, namely how to provision the fortresses on a limited budget. The C-Group were not primarily agriculturalists, and there is little sign that they adopted agriculture on a large scale during the Twelfth Dynasty, although they may have been forced to do so to a certain extent if the new restrictions on movement negatively affected their pastoral economy. Citizen-soldiers, however, would presumably have gained rights to farm the three fertile swathes of land around Kubban, Aniba, and Faras (see Figure 4.1). Prior to the construction of the Aswan Dam, Lower Nubia typically supported a population of 50,000 or so people, and it is estimated that much less than half of this number occupied the area in pharaonic times.[8] Thus, the citizen-soldiers may well have been able to produce enough grain to provision not only themselves but also the smaller garrisons in the Second Cataract region, especially if the central government exacted no additional taxes.

Crumbling Barriers

While certain of Buhen's inhabitants, especially in the early Thirteenth Dynasty, continued to bear titles such as "commander" and "overseer of interpreters," which suggested a tie to Egypt and to the original mission of the fortresses, it is notable that many of the defensive features of this and other fortresses were allowed to fall into ruin.[9] The dry ditch at Buhen, for instance, filled entirely with sand, while more than a meter of debris accumulated on the rampart. While one might attribute this neglect to a lack of state funding during this time, it is difficult to believe that the residents would have permitted this erosion in the effectiveness of their defenses if they felt imperiled.

Such neglect is particularly surprising, then, given that C-Group and Kerman polities appear from archaeological investigations far more formidable than they had been at any time previously. Kerma during the Second Intermediate period was at the height of its power and is justly famous for its sprawling city plan, highly developed industry, massive mudbrick temples, and elite tumuli. Indeed, some of the latter extend up to 90 m in diameter and show evidence of hundreds of sacrificed retainers who accompanied their lord in death. Comparable evidence for widespread retainer sacrifice in Egypt exists from the

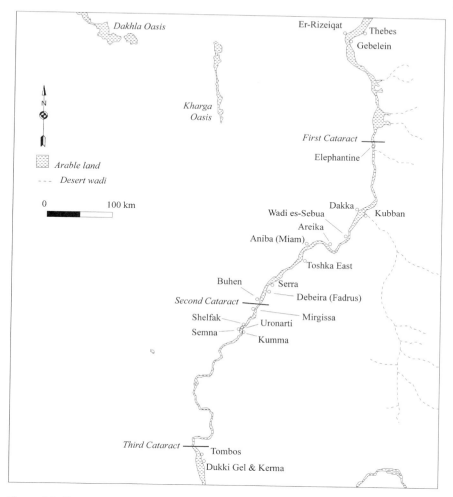

Figure 4.1 Sites mentioned in the chapter.

period of state formation in the First Dynasty, and it is extremely likely that Kerman kings were engaged in a similar process of state-building at this time.

The C-Group too, however, enjoyed a cultural florescence during the Second Intermediate period. During this era, C-Group settlements grew in size, number, wealth, and complexity. In some cases, as at Areika, the local population seems to have occupied military installations abandoned by the Egyptians. Other sites, such as Wadi es-Sebua, were newly established and fortified. The presence of walled communities and also of weapons in C-Group burials suggests that the Nubians, who had perhaps been deprived of the right to bear arms and to defend their own settlements under the pharaohs of the Twelfth Dynasty, eagerly embraced their increased political autonomy and perhaps again competed among themselves for regional authority. Certainly, an interest in self-aggrandizement among certain segments of the population seems to be evident, for at this time tumuli 16 m in diameter are in evidence— an order of magnitude at least four times greater than had ever occurred under Middle Kingdom rule. Some tumuli were likewise provided with mortuary chapels and with attendant displays of bucrania, presumably memorializing the lavish feast(s) that marked the passing of a particularly prestigious individual.[10]

Clearly then, in the Second Intermediate period, the C-Group chose leaders whom they viewed as legitimate and desired to follow. Such a renewed society-wide attention to the mortuary cult is similar to that which took place in Egypt both in the late Predynastic period and in the First Intermediate period. Under the Old Kingdom, a strong state had essentially enforced a rigid system of social stratification that had discouraged movement and mixing between the classes. Cross-culturally, showy display-oriented celebrations of rites of passage tend to occur in periods when the boundaries between the classes become porous and social movement is feasible. Otherwise, such elaborate displays are rarely deemed worth the resources expended.[11] Without the armed strata of the military dictating their position to them, Lower Nubians of the Second Intermediate period were free to structure their society as they saw fit.

Although the C-Group had rigorously defended and maintained its cultural boundaries during the Twelfth Dynasty, it is remarkable that once Egypt released its grip on Nubia, the prohibition on adopting and adapting aspects of Egypt's material culture eased significantly. Thus, Egyptian pottery and artifacts once again appeared in C-Group graves in significant numbers, while mudbrick became increasingly adopted for houses, mortuary chapels, and defensive architecture. Perhaps, just as the Kerman kings selected, borrowed, and transformed items of Egyptian iconography to signal the idea of awe-inspiring political sovereignty, the C-Group too may have looked toward Egyptian material culture to broadcast their own prosperity and authority. Egypt was clearly not their only model, however, as the C-Group also emulated the methods by which Kerman elite traditionally advertised their power, namely by expanding their tumulus mounds, augmenting bucrania displays, and embracing the custom of bed burials. Overall, this period is marked by a remarkable hybridity between C-Group, Kerman, Egyptian, and pan-grave cultures in Lower Nubia.[12]

It is important to note the reciprocal nature of this cultural interchange. At the same time that the C-Group largely dropped its barriers, the inhabitants of the fortress towns became much more open to meaningful cultural interaction with Nubians and Nubian material culture. Indeed, it may have been the Egyptians who made the first conciliatory moves, for once the soldiers lost their supply trains and settled down to became colonists, they likely realized that it was far more advantageous to form bonds with the locals economically and personally than it was to shut them out and gain them as enemies. Indeed, two of the sites with the largest and most impressive C-Group tumuli were Aniba and Dakka, both sites located in quite close proximity to the Egyptian fortresses of Aniba (Miam) and Ikkur, respectively.[13] If the Egyptian colonists entered into hostilities with such powerful neighbors, it is highly unlikely that they could have ever hoped to support themselves agriculturally. The benefits of cultivating both good relations and good crops, however, were many.

Economically, if the C-Group still maintained herds and the Egyptians took up farming, then the two communities could form a mutually beneficial alliance in which each supplemented the economy of the other. In such a scenario it is probable that individuals on both sides would make an effort to learn the language of the other and that personal relationships would form. Percy Coriat, the British officer stationed among the Nuer and discussed in the previous chapter, enjoyed an unprecedentedly close relationship with the Nuer in his district because he was willing to speak their language, both literally and figuratively. Coriat had Nuer friends with whom he would share jokes and stroll hand in hand in the local fashion. He went through a ceremony and received an "ox" name of the type all Nuer men possessed, and he took a local woman from a respected Nuer family as his companion, providing her parents with bridewealth in cattle as would a Nuer suitor.[14] Although he was a representative of the imperial government, Coriat was an unusually successful administrator because he approached his Nuer contacts with respect and a willingness to engage on their own terms as well as his.

Becoming Kin

Whether the Egyptian men who first settled permanently in Nubia took Egyptian wives is unknown. Harry Smith, who compiled the genealogies of a number of families resident at the Egyptian fortress of Buhen in the Second Intermediate period, found that all of the names, male and female, were Egyptian. It would not be surprising if Nubian women took Egyptian names in addition to their own when marrying into an Egyptian family, but there is no reason to assume that this was the case. The males in the two major families that were studied tended to hold high-ranking titles, and so it may have been that these men in particular had the clout and means to import their brides from Egypt.[15]

For the vast majority of the men who settled in the fortresses, however, and certainly for their progeny who grew up knowing no other home than Nubia, it would have made much more sense for them to have sought out local wives. Such marriages would not only have been more convenient (and thus presumably less expensive), but intermarriage is a classic way for groups to cement friendly ties to one another. If the Egyptian fortress-dwellers were no longer bent on shutting their Nubian neighbors out, then they may have been looking for ways to forge closer relationships with them. That said, the impetus might also have come from the Nubians. There are, after all, documented cases in colonial situations in which the lead in arranging such cross-cultural marriages came from the fathers of the brides-to-be so that local leaders could form kin relations with colonists that would in turn facilitate all sorts of joint economic, political, and social endeavors.[16]

Regardless of which side may have initiated intermarriages between the Egyptian expatriates and C-Group Nubians, the result for both would have been a blurring of the lines that separated them—a process of transculturation in which new cultural constructs were created out of an admixture of the two traditions. Stuart Tyson Smith, who has studied the material remains of several fortresses and New Kingdom settlements in depth, has found a number of archaeological indications that suggest that such intermarriages were not anomalous. At the fortress of Askut, he found that Nubian pottery jumped almost fourfold in the Second Intermediate period, and Nubian cookpots in particular rose from a minor component of the ceramic cooking assemblage to fully 65% in the Second Intermediate period. Moreover, when Smith had residue analysis performed on the pottery, results showed that the food prepared in Nubian-style cookpots differed from that cooked in their Egyptian-style counterparts. Thus, though the material culture of the fortresses was still predominantly Egyptian, food production—an area that fell firmly within the female sphere—became increasingly Nubian.[17] While it could be argued that such cookpots betray the presence of Nubian cooks rather than Nubian wives, other lines of evidence also suggest intermarriage.

The percentage of Nubian jewelry at Askut, for one, rose from less than 15% of the assemblage in the Middle Kingdom to almost a third of it in the New Kingdom. Moreover, some of the Nubian jewelry appeared to have been fashioned at the fortress, presumably both by and for Nubians.[18] Even more intriguing, however, is the presence of a C-Group-style female figurine that was found in association with a domestic shrine in the largest house at Askut. The altar, which fell out of use in the mid-to-late Eighteenth Dynasty, centered on the funerary stele of an individual named Meryka, who had lived in the Second Intermediate period. Given that the shrine was continuously utilized for roughly 300 years, the stele and associated fertility figurine evidently were perceived as efficacious in securing blessings for the household.[19] The combination, then, of Nubian fertility figurines, cookware, and personal adornments found throughout the fortress in domestic assemblages of the Second Intermediate period strongly suggests that Egyptian men and Nubian women were forming families and raising successive generations of individuals who may have identified as both Egyptian *and* Nubian in heritage. Indeed, it is surely significant that physical anthropologists looking at New Kingdom populations buried in the cemeteries of the fortresses and in traditionally Nubian cemeteries could find no significant physical differences between them.[20]

Intermarriage is a classic path to the creation of culturally mixed societies in which elements of native and colonial traditions are modified and creatively incorporated into a new hybrid culture that bears resemblance to the parent cultures but is essentially a new creation.[21] A priest known as Fulcher of Chartres, for instance, left a telling reflection of life in the Levant in 1127 CE, barely three decades after he had arrived with the armies of the First Crusade. While many of his companions had returned to Europe following the conquest, others chose to stay. These individuals, it appears, transformed in tandem with the communities into which they settled.

> For we who were Occidentals have now become Orientals. He who was a Roman or a Frank has in this land been made into a Galilean or a Palestinean.... We have already forgotten the places of our birth; already these are unknown to many of us or not mentioned any more.... Some have taken wives not only of their own people but Syrians or Armenians or even Saracens who have obtained the grace of baptism.... Words of different languages have become common property known to each nationality.... He who was born a stranger is now as one born here.[22]

The brave new world that Fulcher of Chartres describes was forged after only three decades of residence and intermarriage. One can only imagine, then, how intertwined the various populations of Lower Nubia must have become during the two centuries or so that separated the start of Egypt's Thirteenth Dynasty from the close of its Seventeenth (c. 1773–1550).

Archaeologists have long noted that relationships between settlers and local women in colonial and post-colonial contexts often produce broadly similar patterning in the material record. Excavations in sixteenth- through eighteenth-century contexts in the Caribbean, Florida, Mexico, and the Rio de la Plata region, for instance, consistently revealed that domestic aspects of the households—such as food processing paraphernalia and cookpots—were primarily indigenous or mixed in style, while the socially visible aspects of the material world—such as architecture, clothing, and serving ware—conformed to the norm of the colonial society. Uruk enclaves from the fourth millennium BCE in Anatolia follow this pattern, as does Askut.[23] Indeed, Smith observed that the percentage of Nubian fineware dwindled to its lowest point in the Nubian subassemblage precisely as Nubian cookpots came to overwhelmingly dominate the corpus of cooking vessels. These trends suggest that while the bloodlines of an Egypto-Nubian couple were likely to have been thoroughly mixed by the advent of the New Kingdom, their claimed cultural heritage was more variable, as encapsulated by their apparent practice of serving up traditionally Nubian food on Egyptian fineware.[24] Significantly, excavations of cemeteries from Lower Nubian fortress communities dating to the late Middle Kingdom and Second Intermediate period suggest that Egyptian identities appear to have been strongly asserted at death.[25]

The power of intermarriage to integrate discrete communities is so profound that some imperialists—Alexander the Great and Queen Isabella among them—have actively encouraged it so as to create a society in which, as Isabella put it, "both parties can communicate and teach each other, and the Indians become men and women of reason."[26] World history provides scores of examples where the acculturation of conquered societies, when these were not deemed *too* different from the culture of the military victors, was actively encouraged.[27] Smith has suggested that intermarriage in the colonial settlements of New Kingdom Nubia was not just convenient but that it was indeed part of "a deliberate imperial policy of acculturation."[28] Given that the C-Group Nubians had already in the Second Intermediate period intermarried with Egyptians and adopted select aspects of Egyptian material culture, pharaonic officials who (re)conquered the country in the early Eighteenth Dynasty would indeed have encountered a Nubia that qualified as "not-*too*-different." The evident implications of this assessment will be addressed later in this chapter and in Chapter 9.

Altering Alliances

The other agent that often aids in the melding of disparate cultures is the army.[29] In Egypt's Second Intermediate period, as in its First, regional rulers vying for power actively recruited Nubian mercenaries. Medjay soldiers appear in Egyptian inscriptions as auxiliary units in Theban armies, while pan-graves, which are commonly assigned to the Medjay culture, are found on the fringes of numerous Middle and Upper Egyptian cemeteries.[30] The mixed assemblages typical of pan-graves suggest that such men adopted at least some Egyptian lifeways as a result of their time in the army. One example is particularly illuminating. Pan-grave burial assemblages occasionally contained skulls of horned animals that had been adorned with painted geometric designs. One bovine skull discovered in association with Mostagedda Tomb 3252, however, was unusual in that its design was figural, apparently a portrait of one specific pan-grave soldier (see Figure 4.2a). This individual was depicted with black skin wearing Nubian garb, but his portrait conformed entirely to Egyptian artistic conventions. Likewise, while his name was Nubian, it was spelled out in Egyptian hieroglyphs. Clearly this Medjay soldier, concerned though he was with signaling his ethnic identity, did not hesitate to adopt those elements of Egyptian culture that he found particularly compelling.[31]

 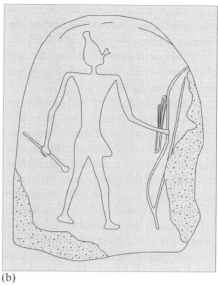

(a)   (b)

Figure 4.2 Monuments celebrating two Nubians from the Second Intermediate period. (a) Bovine skull depicting a Nubian found in a pan-grave tomb in Mostagedda (redrawn by Severin Fowles from Brunton 1937, LXXVI, no. 3252); (b) Stele depicting the king of Kerma (redrawn from Smith 1976, plate 3, figure 2, courtesy of the Egypt Exploration Society).

C-Group veterans are more difficult to identify in the archaeological record, and this may be in part due to the fact that C-Group and pan-grave material culture is often confused.[32] It is tempting to suggest as candidates for inclusion in this group, however, two individuals in the Second Intermediate period who were outfitted with Egyptian-style stelae despite being buried in traditionally Nubian cemeteries at Serra East and Aniba. The stele from Serra East honored Osiris of Busiris, while reference was made on the other stele to its dedicant "coming [from?] the deserts."[33] The man who owned the latter stele, despite being buried in typically Nubian circumstances, bore the Egyptian name Intef and made the classic claim to be "[one beloved] of his brothers and sisters." Issues of identity in the course of the Second Intermediate period, then, had obviously become quite complex.

A somewhat analogous situation to that of Lower Nubia can likewise be found in temperate Europe during the period of the early Roman empire. Just prior to Roman military incursions into the region and shortly thereafter, men from conquered and unconquered areas were actively recruited as auxiliary soldiers. During their span of service, which could last from 20 to 25 years, these foreign soldiers were enmeshed in a Roman institution that replicated features of Roman life wherever the army settled for any period of time. During their careers, auxiliaries and legionnaires no doubt formed relationships, and the auxiliaries would certainly have inhabited and visited many typically "Roman" fortresses and cities, experiencing first-hand Roman religious rites, foodways, and cultural ideas. Like Nubian soldiers, they must have returned to their homelands with a whole new worldview and set of ideas, at least some of which coded positively.[34]

A second major factor in temperate Europe that aided in the integration and eventual fusion of local and "Roman" cultures was the communities of soldiers and veterans of the Roman army who settled in the region either permanently or for extended periods of time in close proximity to indigenous communities. Paralleling the situation in Thirteenth-Dynasty Lower Nubia, discussed above, economic relationships seem to have been mutually beneficial, families quickly became mixed, and enough transculturation occurred that the loyalties of local populations could no longer be taken for granted.[35] Certainly, while the military ethos of the fortress-dwellers in Lower Nubia survived the collapse of the pharaonic state, their loyalties did not.

Leadership of Buhen appears to have been held by a single family throughout much, if not all, of the Second Intermediate period. It is thus of particular interest that one of these men, a commandant of Buhen (*ṯsw n bḥny*) named Sopedhor, boasted in a stele erected at the fortress,

> I was a valiant commandant of Buhen, and never did any commandant do what I did; I built the temple of Horus, Lord of Buhen, to the satisfaction of the ruler of Kush.[36]

The rhetoric here is hardly remarkable in an Egyptian context—just another instance of an official carrying out the command of his lord. In this case, however, the lord was not the Egyptian pharaoh; it was the pharaoh's foremost enemy! For his part, Sopedhor's brother, the noble (*sr*) Ka, boasted of a diplomatic visit to Kush, stating,

> I was a valiant servant of the ruler of Kush; I washed (my) feet in the waters of Kush in the suite of the ruler *Ndḥ*, and I returned safe and sound (to my) family.[37]

While this turn toward Kush is shocking, it is important to remember that by the time the family's monuments were dedicated in the temple of Horus, they had lived in Nubia for five generations. While no Nubian names appear among their relatives, these men would no doubt have spoken Nubian and have developed strong relationships with Kermans, C-Group Nubians, and Egypto-Nubians, if they were not indeed members of the latter category themselves. Their loyalties to the Nubians they knew and interacted with regularly, therefore, may well have been greater than their loyalty to struggling pharaohs far in the north who never in living memory had taken an interest in their land. Along these lines, it is also very possible that they recognized the Kerman king as the more immediate threat to their own safety and acted quickly to ensure peaceful relations.

Whether the transfer of this family's loyalty from Egypt to Kush was undertaken freely or under duress remains unclear. A destruction layer was indeed discovered at Buhen, but there is some disagreement as to whether it occurred before or during the Kerman occupation.[38] The fact that the Kerman king, who was depicted wearing an Upper Egyptian crown in a stele at Buhen (see Figure 4.2b), had spared the lives of the Egyptians and that they not only maintained their positions but bragged about their service to their new overlord suggests that culturally it was not much of a stretch for them to reorient their loyalties southward.

Perhaps the Kerman king retained these men in their positions because he valued them for their literacy, experience with mining, military expertise, and personal connections. By offering the fortress's inhabitants clemency in return for their submission, however, the Kerman king may also have avoided the drain of a long siege, for even with the degradation of some of its defensive architecture, Buhen must still have remained a formidable installation. Finally, based on the unexpectedly low percentage of Kerman ware discovered at the fort of Askut, it has also been suggested that the Kerman king preferred to rule indirectly, subcontracting the maintenance of his control of Lower Nubia to vassals in exchange for loyalty and its attendant obligations.[39] If so, he may have been grateful for the *in situ* presence of capable administrators at Buhen who were willing to reorient their loyalties and to wash their feet in his waters.

When the Theban ruler Kamose (c. 1555–1550) reconquered Buhen in the late Seventeenth Dynasty, he cared little for continuity—at least at the upper echelons of expatriate society. Sopedhor and Ka lost their jobs, certainly, and possibly also their lives.[40] Perhaps the first family of Buhen had been a little too valiant in their service of the ruler of Kush and had taken part in raids against Upper Egypt, such as are attested in Sobeknakht's tomb at El Kab.[41] Perhaps they had forced the Egyptians to lay siege to Buhen in order to win it. Or perhaps Kamose simply wished to reward his own loyalists with the prestigious title of commander of Buhen. Regardless, with the reconquest of Lower Nubia, a new era began and, with it, an entirely new set of cultural dynamics.

A New Kingdom; A Revised Strategy

The motivations behind Egypt's reconquest of Lower Nubia and its conquest of Upper Nubia will be addressed in the following chapter. Of interest here is the change in the dominant philosophy of governance in the New Kingdom, which represents a radical departure from Middle Kingdom models but an interesting evolution of the process that may have occurred naturally in the Thirteenth Dynasty as an accidental casualty of the diminishing imperial budget. It would not have been surprising if the New Kingdom pharaohs upon reconquering Nubia refurbished the Middle Kingdom fortresses of Lower Nubia, built new military masterpieces in Upper Nubia, and filled both old and new edifices with enlisted men. Instead, however, the New Kingdom rulers, despite their deep pockets, encouraged the growth of the largely civilian fortress towns of Lower Nubia and established counterparts in Upper Nubia. The latter will be discussed in depth in Chapter 9.

The fortress towns in Lower Nubia were not entirely demilitarized, but the emphasis in these settlements in the New Kingdom was no longer on soldiers, barracks, and armories. For instance, the outer brickwork of some Middle Kingdom fortresses was given summary repairs, but these appear to have been cosmetic and limited primarily to sites destined to serve as regional administrative centers (e.g. Kubban, Aniba, Serra, and Buhen). Elaborate defensive features constructed in the Middle Kingdom remained in ruin.[42] Likewise, while inscriptional evidence suggests that many of the southernmost fortresses seem to have housed military officials (e.g. Buhen, Mirgissa, Shelfak, Uronarti, Kumma, and Semna), the sex ratios in the cemeteries at most fortresses were equal. Thus, it would appear that even some active military men took wives and settled down with their families. Moreover, while these structures continued to be termed *mnnw* (a traditional term for "fortress"), on at least one occasion the writing of the word employed the generic determinative for "town."[43] As a sign of the times, the *tsw*-commander that replaced Sopedhor at Buhen—the very last man to hold this title—took up residence there together with his family. For the remainder of the New Kingdom, the top officials at Buhen were *ḥȝty-ʿ*-mayors, and this was true in other fortress towns as well. New Kingdom Nubia was thus not only annexed to Egypt: it was reorganized to mirror it.[44] Indigenous rulers, as will be discussed shortly, would have a place in the new order as well, but only if they followed suit, refashioning themselves according to an Egyptian model.

In Lower Nubia, most of the government-sponsored construction within the fortresses was focused not on repairing or expanding defensive elements but on refurbishing old temples and constructing new. This was the case even at the Second Cataract installations, whose resident populations were much smaller than their northern counterparts. These new or newly revamped Lower Nubian temples primarily honored the deified founders of the fortresses—Senusret I and Senusret III—and Horus gods (especially those of Buhen, Aniba [i.e. Miam], and Kubban).[45] Given that the Horus manifestations were essentially also cults of the divinized king, patronage of this suite of deities did important work for the pharaohs, as had been the case in the Middle Kingdom as well.

In Upper Nubia, where the Egyptian occupation was entirely new and the pharaonic government had a chance to erect their imperial infrastructure from scratch, it is remarkable that the pharaohs chose to replicate the "accidental" pattern that had emerged in Lower Nubia during the Second Intermediate period. A series of towns were founded in the region extending from the Second Cataract to just upstream of the Third Cataract, and another was located at the Fourth. These centers of civilian settlement lacked elaborate defenses, were overseen by mayors, and were provisioned with temples dedicated sometimes to their divinized founder and virtually always to the god Amun, who in the New Kingdom was even more closely associated with divine kingship than Horus. Amun was the patron of the Theban Seventeenth- and Eighteenth-Dynasty kings; he was anthropomorphic and possessed a face that was easily sculpted to mirror that of the ruling monarch (or vice versa). He was also relatively unencumbered with mythological baggage, having never been raped by his uncle or jeered at by other gods—as had in fact happened to Horus.[46] Already at the very beginning of Egypt's Eighteenth Dynasty, Amun and the king shared a wife, and Amun received the largest share of booty from the king's victories.

The pharaonic government established the worship of Amun as the cultic centerpiece of new settlements in Upper Nubia because of this god's intimate association with Egyptian kingship. According to Elizabeth Brumfiel, imperial religion is intended "to sanctify the ruler in the eyes of his subjects so that those subjects accept his authority."[47] Equally important, however, may have been the fact that Amun's cult animal was the ram, for Kermans also honored the ram in religious contexts. The Egyptians, then, may have made a special effort to convince the Nubians, who now counted among their subjects, that Amun and the Kerman ram were two aspects of the same deity. Certainly, Amun was most often portrayed with the head of a ram in Nubia, while north of the First Cataract iconographic representations of the god remained predominantly anthropomorphic.[48] Attempts at religious conversion—or, perhaps more fittingly, conversion via religion—will be dealt with in Chapter 9, so for the moment it is sufficient to state the obvious, namely that promoting shared religious beliefs in an empire often helps integrate diverse groups, just as the creation of new religious institutions covertly facilitates the centralization of resources and the naturalization of imperial ideology.

Collaboration

Identifying and enhancing common ground in religious traditions in order to integrate communities of the conquered with those of their conquerors is a common imperial ploy, as is the recruitment and remuneration of local collaborators willing to publicly support the imperial cause. In the last chapter, the marked absence of identifiable local leaders during the Twelfth Dynasty was noted, and it was suggested that the legitimate C-Group leaders might well have refused to collaborate with the Egyptians, whom they and their communities no doubt viewed as oppressors. Such a situation perhaps encouraged the Egyptians to adopt what Owen Lattimore has described as "the old Chinese principle of 'leave them alone if they don't want to be Chinese, as long as they aren't hostile.'"[49]

The situation at the dawn of the New Kingdom, however, was much different. As discussed previously, during the two and a half centuries since the end of the Twelfth Dynasty, Egyptian expatriate communities had settled in Lower Nubia and had evidently formed extremely close bonds with their Nubian neighbors. Egyptians and Nubians intermarried, traded, and no doubt fought beside one another, whether as paid soldiers in Egyptian militias or (later) as valiant soldiers of the king of Kush. After a few generations, the categories of "us" and "them" that had been so rigidly maintained throughout the Twelfth Dynasty may have been blurred substantially.

When the Eighteenth-Dynasty pharaohs assumed control of Nubia, they modeled its government after that of Egypt, with an official called the king's son of Kush taking the role of the resident head of state and the deputies of Kush and Wawat functioning analogously to the viziers of Upper and Lower Egypt. Mayors and bureaucrats represented Egypt's interests in the fortresses and in more recently established walled settlements. Newly included in the administrative schema, however, were Nubian leaders, who held jurisdiction over the largely native communities that inhabited Nubia's numerous villages.

In a justly famous presentation scene depicted in the tomb of the king's son of Kush in the reign of Tutankhamun, it is possible to identify three subject rulers of Lower Nubia (in the top register to the right of Figure 4.3) and six of Upper Nubia (at the right of the lower two registers). While the breakdown of these polities is not certain, it is likely that each of the three fertile pockets in Lower Nubia would have possessed its own ruler and that the remaining six leaders would have presided over parts of Upper Nubia.[50] One of these local rulers, no doubt, would have been situated in the settlement of Dukki Gel, which the Egyptians intended to replace Kerma as the most important (largely) indigenous urban center of Upper Nubia. Interestingly, an inscription describing a rebellion that occurred in the reign of Thutmose II states that Upper Nubia had been divided into five spheres of authority at the time of the insurrection. Following the rebellion, however, it would have made sense for the Egyptians to further subdivide Upper Nubia's territorial units so as to lessen the power that any individual leader might accrue.[51]

About the indigenous rulers of Upper Nubia little is known. Their Lower Nubian counterparts, however, fit the classic profile of collaborators. Instead of the "old Chinese principle" that had perhaps by necessity characterized Egypt's relations with the C-Group in the Middle Kingdom, Lattimore would no doubt have recognized the pharaonic government's successful switch to "the old Inner Asian rule: 'recruit the elite of the subordinate people into the elite of the dominant people.'" According to Lattimore,

Figure 4.3 Facsimile of a painting of a Nubian delegation in the tomb of the king's son of Kush, Huy, by Charles K. Wilkinson. Metropolitan Museum of Art 30.4.21. Rogers Fund, 1930. *Source:* http://www.metmuseum.org/art/collection/search/548571

This system has the advantage that those who want to plod along in the old ways as far as economic and administrative policies will let them, can do so. Energy is not wasted on dragooning such people into 'becoming Chinese' or 'becoming Russian.' But obviously, the more … ambitious the individual, the more clearly he can see for himself that the road to elite status … is through the … 'big' languages…. The elite thus recruits itself.[52]

While the rulers of the fertile zone in the environs of Kubban remain unattested, a good deal of information can be obtained about their counterparts in the vicinities of Aniba and Faras. A wall painting in the tomb of the late Eighteenth-Dynasty king's son of Kush, Huy, discussed above, depicts the three Lower Nubian rulers in the act of delivering tribute and paying homage. Among the three, the leader of Miam (near Aniba) was singled out specifically. This man bore the name Hekanefer, which translates as (The)-Ruler-is-Good and is exactly the type of loyalist moniker that Egyptian officials typically bestowed on foreign prisoners of war and slaves that fell under their purview. Hekanefer, however, was the son of a Nubian deputy, and thus it is likely that he bore his strongly loyalist name from birth, perhaps in addition to a Nubian name that remains unknown.

As the son of an important Nubian, Hekanefer was brought to court by his father at a young age to be a "child of the palace" (*ḥrd n k3p*), raised and educated among the children of Egyptian elites, of foreign vassals, and even of the royal family.[53] During his time in Egypt, Hekanefer would have spoken and learned to write Egyptian, formed valuable connections with his future peers in the Egyptian administration, and most likely internalized the values of an Egyptian noble. Thus, when the court returned him to Nubia to take up leadership in Miam, they must have hoped that he would act in Egypt's interests and promote its ideology among his people. Parallels to this practice do not stop, of course, with inner Asia. Of similar policies in ancient Rome, Peter Wells writes that the Romans integrated different groups by advancing indigenous elites into the Roman imperial aristocracy.

> ...[T]he indigenous elites became the focal points of the new order in the provinces. They became in effect "Romans" and faithful to Rome, but at the same time remained leaders in the local social systems. They thus served as bridges between the cultural traditions, while playing dual roles themselves.[54]

Such dual roles are indeed very apparent in the careers of Nubian leaders such as Hekanefer.

Huy's wall painting shows that Hekanefer continued this cycle by bringing his own progeny to court, as was in fact mandated by the crown (see Chapter 6). Arrayed behind this ruler and his Lower Nubian colleagues, the artist depicted their sons and daughters. One of the latter, judging from her elaborate headdress and ox-driven chariot, was likely destined to enter the royal household as a minor wife. Interestingly, in contrast to their fathers, who are depicted in traditional feathered headgear and native garb, the young people are dressed in the classic clean white linen worn by Egyptian nobility. Only the most minor of accessories provide a hint as to their origin. Hekanefer's own unabashedly exotic outfit, then, should likely be viewed as traditional formal wear, donned for ceremonial occasions such as those intended to showcase the pharaoh's far reach and world-encompassing power (see the Epilogue for an in-depth discussion of an analagous court ceremony).

On the basis of his *own* self-presentation in his Egyptian-style tomb at Toshka East, Hekanefer may well have looked every bit as Egyptian as the officials who accepted his tribute (see Figure 4.4a). In this tomb, which he equipped with personalized ushabtis and other quintessentially Egyptian-style grave goods, Hekanefer followed Egyptian norms in addressing his prayers to Osiris, Re-Horakhty, Amun-Re, Hathor, and Anubis. Likewise, in his portraits, he wore linen, and his skin tone seems to have conformed to the same brownish-red hue that typically distinguished Egyptian males in art. The same man whom the state showcased as a kneeling, likely ebony-skinned foreigner, then, evidently preferred to present himself as an admirably upright Egyptian-style noble—an insider, fluent in pharaonic culture.[55]

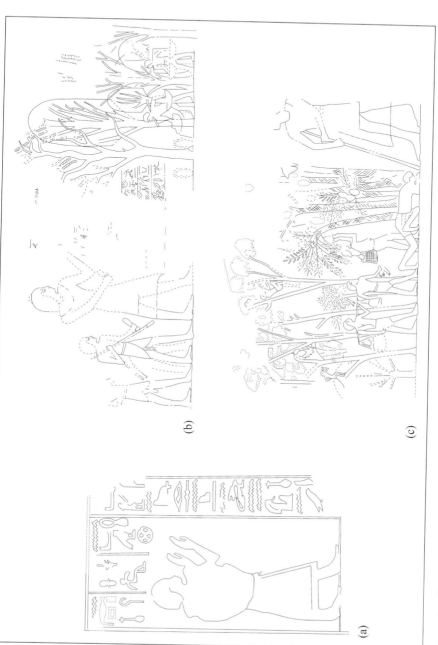

Figure 4.4 The self-presentations of two New Kingdom Nubian rulers in their own tombs. (a) Hekanefer, from the entrance of his tomb in Toshka East (redrawn from Simpson 1963, 9, figure 7). *Source*: Courtesy of Penn Museum; (b and c) Djehutyhotep, from his tomb at Debeira (redrawn from Säve-Söderbergh 1960, 39 figure 10, and 41, figure 11). *Source*: Reproduced with permission of National Corporation for Antiquities and Museums.

What is fascinating is that by the late Eighteenth Dynasty, Hekanefer's evident desire to obscure the differences between Nubian and Egyptian ethnicities may have been rooted not only in ideology but also in biological and cultural realities. Certainly, at the point at which Hekanefer served as leader of his people, the material culture of Lower Nubia and Upper Nubian centers north of the Dongola Reach was overwhelmingly "Egyptian" in character. By and large, Nubians inhabited Egyptian-style rectangular mud brick houses, utilized Egyptian-style pottery and other artifacts, and interred their dead in an extended position in Egyptian-style graves. Indeed, Egyptian-style material culture was so ubiquitous that in the early days of archaeology some scholars suggested that the Nubians had in fact been largely driven out of their land—or perhaps had left of their own volition—and were replaced by Egyptian set- tlers.[56] Numerous studies of traditionally Nubian cemeteries have since debunked this notion and demonstrated that cultural transformations of mate- rial culture often occurred over the course of only a couple of generations.[57]

The ruling family of Tekhet, the Nubian polity situated roughly between Faras and Buhen, encapsulates in its history one of the more explicit examples of this cultural shift. In the elite cemeteries of Debeira—located a few kilometers from the fortress of Serra—were the Egyptian-style burial monuments of two rulers (*wr*) of Tekhet, both brothers. The grandfather of these men ruled in the early Eighteenth Dynasty and bore an Egyptian name (Tety) along with his Nubian name (Djaiwia), while his wife's appellation was Egyptian. The tomb most likely to have been his was intermediate between the fully Egyptian-style tombs at Debeira and the largest terminal C-Group tumuli, being Egyptian in style but lacking the pyramidion that characterized later tombs.[58] This man had two sons. One, who bore the Egyptian name Senmose, was buried in Aswan and likely served with Egyptian officials in the administration of this border zone. The other—known by a Nubian name (Ruiu), as was his wife— ascended to his father's position as the ruler of Tekhet. Despite Ruiu's loyalty to his Nubian name, he bore the title "scribe," indicating that, like Hekanefer, he too was likely schooled in Egypt.

Ruiu's eldest, who ruled in the time of Hatshepsut, bore the Nubian name Pa-itsy and the Egyptian name Djehutyhotep and seems to have followed his father's career path closely. Djehutyhotep served not only as a valiant agent for the Lady of the Two Lands (perhaps during his time in Egypt) but also as scribe of the Southland. His tomb, which is quintessentially Egyptian in style, invoked the usual assemblage of Egyptian gods and also Horus Lord of Buhen. The Horus temple at Buhen would presumably have been the most significant Egypto-Nubian cult in close proximity. The tomb was otherwise decorated in good Egyptian fashion with depictions of Djehutyhotep on his chariot or supervising the work of dependents on his estate (see Figure 4.4b and c). His skin tone and that of his wife conform to Egyptian norms. The fact that his workers were generally dark-skinned, however, gestures toward a Nubian setting, as does a scene of men scaling trees to gather dates, which seemingly stood in for stock images of farmers plowing and harvesting. Little else in the tomb's design or décor would render it out of place in Thebes.

Leadership of Tekhet eventually passed to Djehutyhotep's younger brother, Amenemhet, after which the trail runs cold. One wonders whether by this point the Nubian rulers had in fact worked so hard to pass as Egyptian nobles and had served so long as Egyptian administrators that they for all intents and purposes became indistinguishable from their models. Certainly, Amenemhet's tomb and personal monuments were entirely Egyptian in style, and if he and his wife possessed Nubian names, they seem not to have memorialized them. Again, such an attitude is not unusual in imperial contexts. Regarding the Roman empire, Wells writes,

> As indigenous elites acquired status in the imperial aristocracy, they may have come to identify themselves first as members of the Roman nobility, and second as members of their local societies.[59]

Inculcated with the perspectives of the conqueror at a young age, it would be little surprise if at least some Nubian elites accepted them as their own.

Nubians capable of reading and drafting administrative documents in Egyptian, such as Amenemhet and his extended family, must have been extremely important in the new order. Nubian leaders appear to have been involved at a supervisory level in the requisitioning of taxes,[60] perhaps both because it was practically convenient for a literate bilingual person to hold this job and also because it was thought that Nubians might respond better to the requisitioning of their surplus if the request were made in their own language. One wonders, however, just how true this would remain if the Nubian making such requests could hardly be distinguished from his Egyptian colleagues.

If the authorities responsible for collecting Nubian taxes in the New Kingdom differed from their earlier equivalents, so too did the taxes. In addition to claiming a share of cattle and of prestige goods that passed through Lower Nubian territory from regions farther south, the state also gleaned proceeds from grain harvests, suggesting that the C-Group adopted more than the material trappings of Egyptian civilization (see Chapters 5 and 9). One must imagine, however, that the cultural changes that took place as the Eighteenth Dynasty progressed provoked widespread societal dialogue, much of it heated.

Discrepant Experiences of Empire

The shift in material culture from the mixed assemblage of the Second Intermediate period to the overwhelmingly Egyptian-style artifacts and architecture characteristic of Nubia north of the Third Cataract from the mid-Eighteenth Dynasty onward occurred over the course of a century or so (c. 1550–1450). Yet little was predictable about the process. Choices made by individuals and communities as to which elements of their traditional culture to curate, to abandon, or to creatively meld with aspects of the newly prevalent non-native culture varied significantly. Torgny Säve-Söderbergh, who examined numerous C-Group villages and cemeteries from this period, confessed bewilderment at their heterogeneity. In the end, he concluded that the difference could not be ascribed to chronology, "but rather indicates a division of the C-Group population into tribes and/or social groups who reacted to the advancing Egyptian civilization in individually different ways."[61] More recent studies have bolstered this view.[62]

This seeming cultural confusion, rather than being idiosyncratic in nature, is witnessed in other imperial contexts as well. For instance, an analogous phenomenon can be observed in many areas of temperate Europe in the centuries following the Roman conquest. Of the diversity that characterized the engagements of native peoples with Roman culture, Wells writes,

> In many cases, individuals re-created the traditional practices of their Iron Age forebearers, in others they combined indigenous elements with new ones adopted from Roman tradition, and in others they created new patterns without obvious reference to their native practices. The range of variation is vast, and every cemetery, every individual grave is different and needs to be examined and interpreted separately.[63]

Drawing from studies such as Wells's, David Mattingly has argued that the all-encompassing model of "Romanization" should be abandoned, as this term emphasizes conformity and "presents cultural change as a unilateral and hierarchical process, involving the passing down of Roman culture and ideas about identity to grateful provincials."[64] To his mind, cultural change in Roman provinces over the course of the empire should be viewed in terms of Edward Said's theoretical framework of discrepant experience. This paradigm recognizes that imperial structures affected local actors differently according to a suite of variables including their status, wealth, location, employment, gender, and religious practices.[65] Disparate communities and individuals reacted to the experience of empire in a variety of ways, some choosing to collaborate in the process, others to resist it, and still others to try to tailor the experience to their own benefit. As will be discussed in Chapters 7 and 8, evidence of discrepant experiences is not difficult to discover in Egypt's northern empire, where urban and rural communities responded to Egyptian rule quite differently, as did highland and lowland settlements and others located either near or far from imperial priorities such as natural resources, harbors, or highways.

Clearly, Egyptian material culture was attractive to certain Nubians for many different reasons, judging from the frequent appearance of Egyptian artifacts in Second Intermediate period burial assemblages. The reasons for adopting many of the material trappings of another culture are perhaps fewer and even more compelling in colonial contexts than outside of them, at least for those who stood to benefit. Elite males and town dwellers, for instance, tend to be among the first to fully appreciate (and benefit from) the link between a wholehearted embrace of imperial culture and vastly expanded avenues for promotion.[66] As ambitious scions of a ruling family located in close proximity to an imperial administrative center, Djehutyhotep and Amenemhet provide excellent examples of men who voluntarily adopted the trappings of a new political order—with the active encouragement of the pharaonic state—in order to thrive within it.

The situation in New Kingdom Nubia may be somewhat comparable to that which took place in Egypt following the establishment of Ptolemaic rule. Under the newly imposed Macedonian dynasty, Egyptians outside the priestly realm who had any ambitions to rise through the ranks were required to learn Greek and to Hellenize, and so they did. Like the products of mixed marriages, which they often were, ambitious Egyptians frequently bore two names signaling the two sides of their identities, one Egyptian and the other Greek. Others, who shed their Egyptian names altogether and adopted Greek lifeways, quickly become unrecognizable as Egyptians (which was, no doubt, the point). In contrast, however, the great bulk of Egyptians who had no chance of rising through the ranks maintained their Egyptian names and traditional lifeways.

In discussions of cultural shifts, there is yet another factor to consider, namely the potentially transformative effect of workshop-based mass production on a society that had previously relied on household production and part-time craft specialists. Lindsey Weglarz, in her re-evaluation of New Kingdom cemeteries in Lower Nubia, noted a "massive increase" in Egyptian pottery in the mid-Eighteenth Dynasty that she attributes to the presence of state-sponsored workshops in pharaonic administrative centers.[67] Given that C-Group Nubians had previously hand-fashioned their ceramics, this new glut of wheel-made pottery, produced *en masse* by specialists, undoubtedly saved labor. For many Nubians, then, maintaining certain cultural signatures may have seemed more time-consuming than worthwhile, especially if—as is likely—many such items were distributed gratis by governmental or temple authorities.[68]

While the excavators of the largely unplundered cemetery of Fadrus—which was situated well within the territory of Tehket—reported from their analysis a sharp plummet in prosperity from the early to mid-Eighteenth Dynasty, Weglarz in her re-evaluation noted the opposite. The size and wealth of graves in the mid-Eighteenth Dynasty evidently rose significantly, before declining steeply a generation or two later.[69] Thus, it would appear that the adoption of many elements of Egypt's material culture may initially have seemed to corre-late with a rise in personal and collective fortunes. Rather than being passively "acculturated" or "Egyptianized," then, Nubians made their own choices to take advantage of a technological advance (just as in the Middle Kingdom they had chosen to reject this particular innovation and all that came with it). Interestingly, the ubiquity of mass-produced Egyptian-style pottery was such that even those inhabitants of Lower Nubia that chose to adhere to traditional lifeways the longest generally placed more pottery that was Egyptian in style than traditionally C-Group in the graves of their dead.[70]

As the first century following Egypt's conquest of Nubia moved toward its close, the ratios of those who privileged Nubian traditional culture over Egyptian declined precipitously. By the sole reign of Thutmose III, traditional C-Group graves could be found in a handful of predominantly Nubian-style cemeteries as well as scattered within Egyptian-style burial grounds, but in Lower Nubia at least they constitute exceptions to the rule.[71] William Adams was interested in this persistence of native culture—however anomalous—and envisioned perhaps two populations of Nubians living side-by-side, one largely accepting of Egyptian influence and the other resistant. On the basis of parallels with Native American and African colonial milieus, Adams speculated that an adoption of colonial lifeways correlated to a participation by these peoples in a newly reorganized economic system. In contrast, he suggested that the culturally conservative groups were permitted to retain crucial elements of their pastoralist economy.[72]

While this model may hold true for predominantly Nubian-style cemeteries, the Nubian-style burials discovered embedded within largely pharaonic-style cemeteries likely require a different explanation. According to Weglarz, the anomalous retention of Nubian mortuary culture in pharaonic-style cemeter-ies did not correlate with gender.[73] Social status, however, may well have come into play. Graves that bore Nubian signatures, Weglarz noted, generally exhib-ited remarkably few signs of prosperity.[74] As in Ptolemaic Egypt, such adher-ence to tradition among the lower social tiers was undoubtedly due to a complex interplay of causes. Opportunities afforded the elite were likely not extended to those lower down the social ladder, and evident inequalities as well as other perceived abuses may have led some to resent colonial culture and resist the adoption of it. Over time, however, such entrenched traditionalists seem increasingly to have elected to leave the area altogether.

One destination for the disaffected and/or disenfranchised may have been the Dongola Reach—that long stretch of river between the Third and Fourth Cataracts.[75] Robert Morkot has argued persuasively that the Egyptians granted indigenous communities in this region political independence and refrained from encroaching on their land, just so long as a respectable tribute was sent each year and Egyptian activities in Kawa and Napata—the two polities that bookended the region—suffered no interference.[76] Bestowing a comparatively greater autonomy on areas deemed both potentially troublesome and devoid of big-ticket resources is a strategy the Egyptians adopted in their northern empire, as will be seen in subsequent chapters. Not surprisingly, given its agreeable ratio between costs and benefits, this strategy is in fact commonly deployed in imperial management.

In a particularly fascinating recent discovery, Stuart Tyson Smith identified evidence for intermarriage between culturally distinct Egyptians and Nubians at Tombos, an Egyptian outpost at the Third Cataract that marked the border between Egyptian-held Upper Nubia and the zone that maintained a quasi-independent status.[77] Given that by the late Eighteenth Dynasty Egyptian or Egyptianized women would not be difficult to find at Tombos, it is extremely likely that the culturally identifiable Nubian women buried in two otherwise purely Egyptian-style contexts arrived in the settlement via diplomatic marriages that cemented peaceful relations between the neighboring communities.

While C-Group material has not been found in abundance in the Dongola Reach, or many other parts of Upper Nubia outside of the temples and fortress towns, it does seem that there would have been opportunities for C-Group traditionalists to opt out of an increasingly "Egyptian" material and political culture either by leaving their homeland and emigrating elsewhere or else by retreating to the margins and preying upon it. Certainly pharaonic inscriptions throughout the remainder of the New Kingdom demonstrate persistent issues with Nubians who rustled their cattle, harassed their miners, and fomented rebellion.[78] Like many colonized people, Nubians were likely divided as to whether they chose to participate in, to leave, or to explicitly act against the sovereign state.

Notes

1 Smith 1976, 82–3; Smith 2003, 113; Knoblauch and Bestock 2017, 53–7.
2 Smith 1976, 67–9.
3 Breasted 1906a, 161–9; Simpson 2003, 54–66.
4 Luttwak 1979, 171.
5 Vercoutter 1957, 66–9; Smith 1976, 79.
6 Smith 1976, 72.
7 Lichtheim 1975, 99–107.
8 Smith 2003, 75.
9 Smith 1976, 82.
10 O'Connor 1993, 39–41; Anderson 1996, 66–8.
11 Morris 2006a.
12 Bietak 1987, 121; Säve-Söderbergh 1989, 10; Anderson 1996, 67–8; Török 2009, 116.

13 O'Connor 1993, 40.
14 Johnson 1993, xxvi–xxviii, xlviii.
15 Smith 1976, 72–6.
16 Lightfoot and Martinez 1995, 484.
17 Smith 2003, 114, 116–19.
18 Smith 2003, 106–10.
19 Smith 2003, 131–3.
20 Adams 1977, 236; Säve-Söderbergh 1991a, 10.
21 Lightfoot and Martinez 1995, 482; Webster 2001, 217–19.
22 Foucher of Chartres, *History of the Expedition*, Book 3, chapter 37, 3–5.
23 Deagan 2001, 191–3.
24 Smith 2003, 192. Nubian fineware at Askut made up 11% of the functional assemblages in the Second Intermediate period, which is not surprising. It dropped to 4.3% in the New Kingdom, which is low, but not as low as the 2% noted in Middle Kingdom contexts (Smith 2003, 118, table 5.4).
25 Knoblauch 2017, 587.
26 Quoted in Deagan 2001, 190.
27 Smith 2003, 192–3; for a variety of comparative examples, see Sowell 1998, 46–8, 56, 219–20, 226, 288–9.
28 Smith 2003, 192.
29 Wells 1999, 135, 238.
30 See the overview of scholarship on Medjay and pan-grave populations in Liszka 2012. Her caveat that the equation between the two populations is likely etic and not emic, however, is well taken.
31 Brunton 1937, 120–1, 131, plates 74, 76 (EA 63339). See Cooper and Barnard 2017 for a revised reading of the hieroglyphs, based on high-resolution color and infrared imagery.
32 Liszka 2012, 389–90.
33 Säve-Söderbergh 1949, 50–1, n. 1.
34 Wells 1999, 135–6.
35 Wells 1999, 145.
36 Säve-Söderbergh 1949, 55.
37 Save-Söderbergh 1949, 52.
38 Smith 1976, 77–8; Emery et al. 1979, 99.
39 Smith 2003, 114.
40 Smith 1976, 85.
41 Davies 2003.
42 Adams 1977, 218, 220.
43 Morris 2005, 97–8.
44 Smith 1976, 207.
45 Török 2009, 211–14.
46 Simpson 2003, 94, 99.

47 Brumfiel 2001, 283.

48 See Kendall 1997, 76–8; Török 2009, 227.

49 Lattimore 1962, 512.

50 O'Connor 1998, 262.

51 Morris 2005, 91–2.

52 Lattimore 1962, 512.

53 For Hekanefer, see Simpson 1963. The children of Medjay rulers were likewise educated at court in the Eighteenth Dynasty (Török 2009, 270).

54 Wells 1999, 132.

55 Simpson 1963, 5, 13–15. The painted scene in Hekanefer's tomb depicts four individuals processing before a seated figure. Hekanefer is likely the first man, depicted on a larger scale than the rest, whose skin tone was brownish red. There is, however, a possibility that he was instead the seated figure whose skin tone does not remain (Simpson 1963, 13). The caption "ruler of Miam" in Huy's tomb is written before three kneeling individuals. Two of these men are very dark-skinned, while one has lighter skin—likely to render him visibly distinct from the ruler beside him.

56 Reisner 1910, 342; Adams 1977, 235–40.

57 Säve-Söderbergh 1989, 11; Williams 1992, 3.

58 Säve-Söderbergh 1991b; Säve-Söderbergh 1992–1993; Török 2009, 265–70.

59 Wells 1999, 192.

60 Säve-Söderbergh 1992–1993, 264, 266.

61 Säve-Söderbergh 1963, 57. See also Török 2009, 275–80.

62 Williams 1992, 3; Smith 2013; Weglarz 2017, 208, 216, 223–4, 227–8.

63 Wells 1999, 162–3.

64 Mattingly 2011, 204.

65 Mattingly 2011, 215–17; see also Wells 1999, 193–4.

66 Lightfoot and Martinez 1995, 486; Sowell 1998, 24–5, 188–9; Wells 1999, 123–4, 266.

67 Weglarz 2017, 233.

68 Trigger 1976, 134; Adams 1977, 238; van Pelt 2013, 540.

69 Weglarz 2017, 148, in contrast to Troy 1991, 212, 249–51.

70 Weglarz 2017, 234.

71 Säve-Söderbergh 1992–1993, 259–60. It is possible, however, that the assemblages produced by traditional holdouts were more numerous than previously supposed, having been repeatedly misdated. Such confusions certainly occurred in Upper Nubia in the New Kingdom as well as in Roman-period Germany (Wells 1999, 153–4; Welsby and Welsby Sjöström 2006–2007, 384).

72 Adams 1977, 236.

73 Weglarz 2017, 207.

74 Säve-Söderbergh 1962, 94–6; Säve-Söderbergh 1991a, 13; Weglarz 2017, 187, 200, 233.

75 For a summary of numerous regional surveys, see Smith 2003, 87–94; Welsby and Welsby Sjöström 2007.

76 Morkot 1991; Grzymski 1997, 94.

77 Smith 2003, 162–6; Smith and Buzon 2017, 624–6.

78 Adams 1977, 240.

5

Motivation, Intimidation, Enticement (c. 1550–1295)

There was no reason that Egypt's New Kingdom empire should have been significantly larger than its Middle Kingdom predecessor. Yet it was. Within a century it stretched from southern Syria to present-day Sudan (see Figure 5.1). This chapter argues that the radical expansion of Egypt's empire, a feat that would become an aspiration for some rulers and an empty boast for others, occurred early on almost by accident as the plunder, glory, recognition, and revenues gained from the new conquests proved deeply exciting exhilarating. Indeed, the cultural euphoria Egypt experienced as a result of its victories was perhaps heightened given that the country had so recently undergone the humiliation of being ruled by foreigners in the north and raided by them in the south. While the first portion of this chapter concerns the motivations that prompted Egypt to expand its traditional spheres of authority, the second will discuss the role of both intimidation and enticement in the acquisition and retention of territory.

The story of Egypt's New Kingdom empire begins just prior to its formation, in the late Second Intermediate period. Kamose (c. 1555–1550), the last Theban ruler of the Seventeenth Dynasty, situated his *casus belli* in wounded national pride. In a speech that urged his council to authorize the resumption of a Theban war against the Lower Egyptian kingdom of Avaris, ruled by the descendants of Syro-Palestinian immigrants, Kamose stated,

> To what effect do I perceive it, my might, while a ruler is in Avaris and another in Kush, I sitting joined with an Asiatic and a Nubian, each man having his (own) portion of this Egypt, sharing the land with me.[1]

Certainly, there existed a strong template for a united Egypt under the rule of one (Egyptian) king. This was the situation that had persisted for roughly 800 years during the Early Dynastic period and the Old Kingdom, and then had lasted for four centuries from Mentuhotep II's reunification until the breakdown

Ancient Egyptian Imperialism, First Edition. Ellen Morris.
© 2018 Ellen Morris. Published 2018 by John Wiley & Sons Ltd.

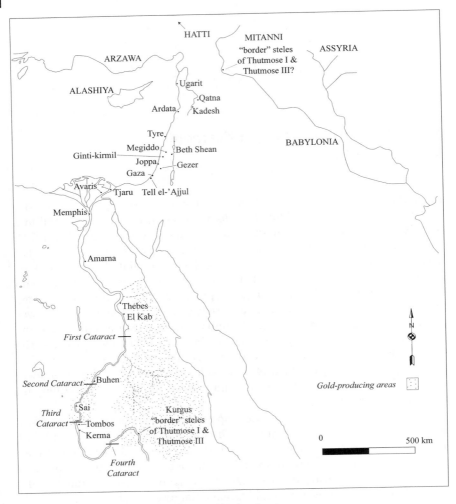

Figure 5.1 Sites and kingdoms mentioned in the chapter.

of the state in the mid-Thirteenth Dynasty. Prior to the Second Intermediate period, pharaonic Egypt had only been divided for 150 years or so, and that era, tendentiously or not, was remembered in literature as a time of chaos and widespread suffering.

Archaeological and textual sources confirm that the domain of the Syro-Palestinian rulers at Avaris (a.k.a. Tell el-Dab'a) extended significantly below Memphis, while the Kerman king appears to have raided El Kab and perhaps as far north as Asyut, if certain objects interred in Kerman graves may indeed be viewed as plunder. Before his premature death, Kamose partially delivered on his promise, reconquering Lower Nubia down to the fortress of Buhen, though his siege of Avaris did not break the city.

At the onset of the Eighteenth Dynasty, then, Egypt had less of an empire than an interest. Discussing the difference, Joseph Schumpeter writes,

> No one calls it imperialism when a state, no matter how brutally and vigorously, pursues concrete interests of its own; and when it can be expected to abandon its aggressive attitude as soon as it has attained what it was after.... For whenever the word imperialism is used, there is always the implication ... of an aggressiveness, the true reasons for which do not lie in the aims which are temporarily being pursued.[2]

Egypt's interest was to secure its newly regained traditional borders—those it had enjoyed in the Middle Kingdom—by making certain that those outsiders who had recently controlled parts of Egypt and Lower Nubia would not regroup and once more threaten its sovereignty. As Romer's rule posits, however, significant change often results from the extraordinary efforts of an entity to remain essentially the same. Thus legs, the theory states, were originally developed not to *leave* water sources but rather to find better water sources in periods of increased aridity.[3] Along these lines, it can be argued that the massive extension of Egypt's New Kingdom empire was not an original end goal. Rather, it was a by-product of a series of pre-emptive military strikes that, while designed to secure static boundaries, nonetheless whetted a renewed imperial appetite.[4]

The first task of Kamose's successor, Ahmose (c. 1550–1525), then, was to expel the northerners from Tell el-Dab'a, which he eventually did. At this point, Ahmose could have laid down his weapons, for he had re-established Egypt's hold on traditional territories from the Eastern Delta to the Second Cataract. His own father's death in battle as well as his own and his predecessor's hard-fought campaigns, however, evidently made Ahmose acutely aware of the dangers that lay just over Egypt's borders and the threat to his realm if these borders were ever again breached. Later tradition held that the Hyksos inhabitants of Tell el-Dab'a had negotiated a withdrawal from their settlement, and this scenario may explain the lack of an intensive destruction layer at the site.[5] Instead of the fiery rubble that often marks the end of a successful siege, the site seemed to have been largely abandoned, save for limited areas of uninterrupted occupation.[6] If Ahmose succeeded where Kamose had failed by offering many of the inhabitants of Tell el-Dab'a safe passage out of Egypt, then the threat to his northern border remained very real indeed.

To the south, also, Ahmose could not rest easy, for while his predecessor had wrested Lower Nubia from Kerman control, Kerma remained unconquered. Likewise, the powerful polity of Shaat, located on Sai Island, midway between the Second Cataract and Kerma, was evidently a strong supporter of its powerful southern neighbor. Ahmose thus felt it necessary to establish more control over the buffer zone between Egyptian-held Lower Nubia and Kerma. To this end, he not only conquered Shaat, but he appears to have set up camp on the site—a camp that would become a full-fledged fortress town following the definitive defeat of Kerma in the reign of Thutmose III (see Chapter 9).[7]

Ahmose followed a nearly identical blueprint in the north, turning the conquered enemy strongholds of Tell el-Dab'a and Tjaru (Tell Heboua) into Egyptian military installations. Similarly, to secure a comfortable buffer zone on his northern border, Ahmose spent three years besieging the town of Sharuhen (Tell el-'Ajjul), which was akin to Sai in its status as the nearest significant population center that had been allied with Ahmose's major opponent. Whether this siege went on for three years straight or occurred during three successive campaign seasons is not known, but the result—a completely charred and virtually depopulated city—is testament to the severity of the revenge wreaked upon this population of Hyksos collaborators.[8] As will be discussed toward the end of the chapter, Egyptian forces generally reserved such harsh treatment for their most recalcitrant foes.

Tell el-'Ajjul may not have been the only victim of an early Eighteenth-Dynasty driving desire for security and revenge, for in the century or so that separated Ahmose's reign from the sole rule of Thutmose III (c. 1479–1425), much of the area that would eventually constitute the core of Egypt's northern empire suffered widespread devastation. Over 20 sites in the Cisjordan were violently destroyed during this period, while numerous others suffered partial or complete abandonment. Indeed, less than half of the towns that flourished in Middle Bronze Age Canaan would be rebuilt in the Late Bronze Age. While it is unlikely that the Egyptians could have been responsible for all or even the majority of the destructions that marked this transitional period, their soldiers were clearly active in the region, almost assuredly engaging in some battles and taking opportunistic advantage of the aftermaths of others.

With each new conquest on the far side of Egypt's re-established boundaries, a pharaoh could claim to have made Egypt's borders ever more secure. Thutmose I (c. 1504–1492) boasted, "I made the boundaries of Egypt as far as that which the sun encircles. I made strong those who were in fear; I repelled the evil from them."[9] If, as in Romer's rule, however, Egypt's imperial legs had been developed simply to restore to themselves uncontested domination of Egypt and Lower Nubia by eradicating the threats that lay just beyond its traditional borders, what motivated pharaonic forces to dominate neighboring regions for the better part of four centuries? Further, what convinced Ahmose's own son-in-law, Thutmose I, to use these new imperial legs to keep right on marching toward the seeming limits of what the sun encircled? It is argued here that four motivations—plunder, glory, recognition, and revenue—exerted an almost irresistible allure.

Plunder

Tell el-Dab'a, Tell el-'Ajjul, and Kerma were all immensely wealthy urban centers. Although no texts have survived that record the booty reaped from their conquests, the monumental architecture, cultic buildings, elite graves, and the occasional cache of precious materials missed by plunderers at each site suggest that the rewards reaped would have been both intoxicating and addictive. Kamose's evident awe as he described the array of exotic and precious items seized from ships moored at the harbor of Avaris is illustrative:

> I have not spared a plank of the three hundred ships of new cedar filled with gold, lapis lazuli, silver, turquoise, and copper axes without number, aside from moringa oil, incense, unguents, honey, willow, *sesnedjem*-wood, *sepny*-wood, and all precious woods, and all fine products of Retenu. I took them away entirely.[10]

Military leaders generally regard the refusal of an enemy to submit as free license to pillage. Obviously, the richest cities made particularly tempting targets.

Thutmose III styled himself "a king valiant like Montu, who plunders but from whom no one can plunder."[11] Indeed, in the aftermath of his famous battle at Megiddo, in which representatives from many hundreds of Levantine cities combined forces in hopes of stopping Egypt's expansion, Thutmose III was ceded over 2,238 horses. Given that 2,041 of these horses were mares, this one battle would have secured Egypt more than enough steeds to ensure an excellent breeding population for the royal stables at a time when horses were still relatively rare in the Nile Valley.[12] Over the nearly two-decade span of time during which Thutmose III campaigned regularly, he obtained more gold and people in the wake of his victories than he did either from the benevolences regularly sent by Syro-Palestinian vassals or from the high-status trade that he engaged in with the rulers of powerful kingdoms (see Figure 5.2). Thutmose III's annals, in which these totals were assiduously logged, are crucial for understanding the structural evolution of Egypt's empire. Yet the document is in fact little more than an embellished account of various streams of imperial revenue. Its preface states,

> His Majesty commanded to have the victories his father [Amun] had given him published upon a wall of stone in the temple which His Majesty had made anew [for his father Amun, in accordance with the council] of [His Majesty him]self [in order that] 'every' campaign [be published] specifically, together with the booty that His Majesty brought from it.[13]

Such booty partially subsidized—and certainly provided much of the man-power for—the construction and ornamentation of enormous stone temples. Given that the imagery carved on the surfaces of these ideological engines invariably showcased the donor king's piety and his martial prowess, this investment yielded strong dividends. The gods evidently also found the relationship generative, for their enthusiastic oracular endorsements of proposed campaigns perpetuated the cycle.

The particular beauty of expansion and conquest from the viewpoint of the state was that it opened up entirely new avenues of income to burgeon royal coffers and temple treasuries. Further, because the requisitioned property did not belong to Egyptians, the king could augment his available funds without alienating Egypt's own subjects by raising taxes or commandeering the possessions of individuals or communities. Eventually this would change, of course, when the residents of territories outside Egypt effectively *did* become subjects entitled to certain rights. In the original honeymoon period of empire-building, however, exploitation could unabashedly walk hand-in-hand with subjugation.

Individual Egyptians also may have benefited from imperial activities, as prices for goods that prior to the empire had been difficult to obtain and expensive plunged precipitously. In the first millennium BCE, Neo-Assyrian kings boasted that because of their victories, camels and captives could be purchased by an Assyrian brewer for a jar of beer and that people could pay a price in silver as though it were copper.[14] Similarly, by the Ramesside period in Egypt, prisoners of war had so glutted the market that people of relatively modest means could afford to purchase a slave. Likewise, the ratio of copper to gold changed in the New Kingdom from 50:1 at the start of the empire to 30:1 by the time of the late Ramesside period.[15] While rampant tomb robbery and increased mining ventures within Egypt and Nubia contributed to gold's devaluation, a substantial amount of this metal likely came from campaigns like that of Amenhotep II's ninth year (c. 1418) in which he claimed to have seized 619 kg of gold and 36,400 kg of copper.[16] In 2018 prices, Amenhotep's haul in gold alone is valued at upwards of $26 million! Finally, as prisoners of war assumed a greater proportion of the grunt labor involved in mining and quarry work, ordinary citizens had the empire to thank for being relieved of some of the most onerous assignments of corvée labor.[17]

Glory

Middle Kingdom pharaohs seem to have left war to the generals who fought on their behalf. Egypt had been reunified, however, by kings who had led their troops into battle, and this idealization and valorization of the pharaoh-as-warrior persisted into the Eighteenth Dynasty. New rulers and those of somewhat shaky legitimacy have historically found war useful. As Machiavelli observed,

Without a doubt princes become great when they overcome difficulties made for them and opposition made to them. So fortune, especially when she wants to make a new prince great—since he has a greater necessity to acquire a reputation than a hereditary prince—makes enemies arise for him and makes them undertake enterprises against him, so that he has cause to overcome them and to climb higher on the ladder that his enemies have brought for him. Therefore many judge that a wise prince, when he has the opportunity for it, should astutely nourish some enmity so that when he has crushed it, his greatness emerges the more from it.[18]

To this end, it makes sense that perhaps the most militarily adventurous of Egypt's warrior pharaohs was Thutmose I, a man who married into the royal family. Certainly, this king sought to engage the most formidable contemporary foes and to travel to the farthest ends of the earth (from an ancient Egyptian perspective) in order to erect his stelae. In the course of his far-flung campaigns, he claimed to have "penetrated valleys which the (royal) ancestors knew not, which the wearers of the double diadem had not seen," and thereby to have radically extended the boundaries of Egypt.[19]

Unlike the boasts of many of his successors, Thutmose's claims seem to have been well-founded. He not only conquered the immensely powerful Kerman kingdom—shooting its ruler in the chest, according to an eyewitness account[20]—but he also traveled all the way to northern Syria to engage the king of Mitanni in battle. In the north and the south, the king traveled as far as he felt it logistically prudent. When he reached what he viewed as fitting aspirational boundaries for a new Egyptian empire, he carved his claim on rocky outcroppings adjacent to the Euphrates in the north and to the Fourth Cataract in the south. On both frontiers his judgments were sound, for subsequent kings could only match these feats, not outdo them. Further, while he had overshot the limits of where Egyptian forces could hope to exercise permanent control, his boundaries did accurately define the limits of effective Egyptian influence. Thutmose I topped off his many feats and adventures with a Syrian elephant hunt, setting a high bar for kings to come.

That these exploits were widely admired is demonstrated by the fact that Thutmose's grandson strove to match them. To this end, Thutmose III erected stelae in the same places, fought against Mitanni warriors, and boasted of shooting 120 elephants in a single hunt. Indeed, this king went further in commanding that the wonders he encountered on campaign be documented, whether these consisted of bizarre plants and animals (memorialized in the so-called Botanical Garden of Karnak Temple), a bird that laid an egg each day (noted in the annals), or a monstrous rhino (whose measurements he recorded on the Armant stele). While such feats may smack of the early days of empire, even Ramesses II burnished his reputation for bravery and martial prowess by showcasing above all other battles those in which he personally faced the greatest danger.[21]

Despite the primacy of the pharaoh in temple reliefs and stelae, the total sum of glory was not entirely consumed by the warrior kings who initiated conflicts. As early as the reign of Ahmose, the tomb inscriptions of military men detailed their many adventures and scrapes with death, the prisoners that they took, the plunder that they were allowed to keep, and the gold, land, and other rewards that were conferred upon them by the king in celebration of their valor.[22] Large gifts of land, of course, provided a very healthy income to a soldier and could place him among the local gentry, if he did not already belong to this class. As time went on, however, and the army became increasingly professionalized, the practice of awarding full-time soldiers land as a means of payment for military service became routine, and such grants could no doubt raise the status of an otherwise poor family significantly. As is typical of archaic states, the military offered its lowest classes a rare opportunity for social advancement.[23]

The army may have also exerted its traditional allure on young men, offering them an opportunity to travel the world and perform valiant deeds. Thutmose III's general Amenemhab included stories in his tomb biography that he must have recounted with great frequency while alive. There was the story, for instance, of the time in northern Syria while fighting the Mitanni that he cut off the trunk of a marauding elephant "while he was still alive, in the presence of His Majesty, while I was standing in the water between two stones."[24] Similarly dramatic was the incident when

> ...the chief of Kadesh released a mare and [it galloped] upon its legs and entered into the midst of the army; and I ran after her on foot with my sword(?) and ripped open her belly. I (thereupon) cut off her tail and presented it before His Majesty. Thanks was showered on me for it: he gave forth with rejoicing, and it filled my soul! A thrill shot through my limbs![25]

Amenemhab also claimed to have been the first of all the men in the army to penetrate the defenses of Kadesh. Such exploits no doubt aroused great admiration in listeners who had spent their uneventful, sweltering summer at home in Egypt. Yet, perhaps the most eloquent (if indirect) attestation of the lure of the new professional army is the vast production of literature that relentlessly mocked the lot of the soldier in order to promote the profession of the scribe. According to the satirists, a young soldier would indeed travel to foreign lands, but there he would stagger up steep mountain paths under heavy burdens, suffer from diarrhea, be repeatedly robbed, fear for his life at every turn, and finally trudge home a broken man.[26] While such a scenario was not entirely improbable, the frequency and virulence of this genre suggests that many potential scribes were opting not just for a job but for an adventure. Military victories abroad offered kings and able soldiers alike an opportunity to bask in adulation as they returned home, loaded with plunder, new honors, and experiences utterly unknown to those who had stayed safely in Egypt.[27]

The increasing wealth and power of the military as an institution in the New Kingdom is witnessed in the fact that its officers increasingly held lucrative positions in state temples and could afford tombs in the most elite of cemeteries.[28] Schumpeter has observed that repeated wars tend to create a military class that, in turn, is invested in creating yet more wars in order to sustain itself.[29] In this respect the cozy and extremely permeable relationship between military and religious spheres no doubt furthered the institutional interests of both. Meanwhile, for the upper echelon of society in the Eighteenth Dynasty—who memorialized within their tombs the foreign slaves that worked their estates, the chariots they drove, the exotic plants in their gardens, and the foreign envoys they introduced to the king—the rewards of empire were everywhere apparent.[30]

Recognition

For the New Kingdom pharaohs whose military ventures brought them great success, the admiration and respect that accrued to them within Egypt must have been heady. Recognition and adulation from subjects, however, is expected. What seems to have been somewhat different in the context of the Late Bronze Age is that their northern conquests earned Egypt's rulers entrance into a brotherhood of Great Kings that was jealously guarded and open only to the most powerful rulers of the ancient Near East.[31]

The embassies that Thutmose III received from the kings of Cyprus, Assyria, Babylon, and Hatti while he was on campaign indicate his acceptance into this select club. Quite likely, each of these polities had a vested interest in fostering an alliance with a proven enemy of Mitanni. In the annals, the arrival of the embassies to meet the pharaoh and his army is noted together with an inventory of the greeting gifts each bore, tokens of the donor's respect and sincerity of intention. These greeting gifts often included minerals that were difficult to obtain both for the sender and the receiver (such as lapis lazuli and silver) as well as specialties of a particular region (such as horses from Assyria and copper from Cyprus). From an analysis of the annals, it is clear that the majority of lapis lazuli and bronze entered Egypt as "gifts" sent from Great Kings or extremely high-status vassals (see Figure 5.2). The same may also be true for top-quality timber, though the quantities listed in the annals are not precise enough to tabulate.

Such embassies not only approached the kings on campaign, but they appear to have arrived with relative frequency at the Egyptian court. Certainly, mid-Eighteenth-Dynasty Theban tomb owners delighted in memorializing processions of exotically dressed foreign offering bearers arriving before the king (see Figure 6.2). A typical caption reads,

> Giving praise to the Lord of the Two Lands, making obeisance to the Good God.... They extol the victory of his majesty, their gifts (*inw*) upon their backs, namely every product of God's land: silver, gold, lapis lazuli, turquoise, and every precious stone so that the breath of life might be given to them.[32]

Because the term for voluntary greeting gifts was *inw*, which was the same term employed for the benevolences sent from vassal rulers to the king, greeting gifts could be easily passed off to an Egyptian audience as tribute, a situation that occasioned at least one diplomatic squabble (EA 1). The opportunities for internal propaganda that the arrival of foreign embassies presented, then, were obviously immense—a point that will be elaborated upon in the Epilogue. In reality, of course, the diplomats came not to pay homage but to trade and to negotiate issues concerning fugitives, caravan safety, and other fine points of international relations. The emphasis, however, judging from the contents of correspondence, was largely upon trade.

Newly established contacts with the Great Kings transformed the pharaoh into a world player such that in return for commodities that Egypt had privileged access to (especially gold, but also exotica from Nubia), he could receive the most precious items known in the ancient world in raw form or fashioned by the most skilled craftsmen that royal courts could employ. This allowed the pharaoh access to natural wonders (such as bears, elephants, and giraffes), artistic wonders, and the raw materials that together were envisioned to make up the bodies of the gods (lapis lazuli and silver chief among them). As discussed in Chapter 1, control over the production, exchange, and consumption of exotica and luxury goods constituted one of the earliest and most important sources of power in pharaonic Egypt.

As is clear from the diplomatic correspondence unearthed at Amarna, one of the major activities that Great Kings took part in was arranging diplomatic marriages among themselves. Such marriages were important for two primary reasons. First, two kings who cemented their "brotherhood" by establishing actual family ties effectively engaged in a pact of nonaggression, whether or not such an arrangement was ratified by a formal treaty. Thus, when a pharaoh incorporated a new foreign queen into his harem, along with his bride price he essentially bought himself a new (or renewed) military alliance and the security that came with such an arrangement.

The second main reason to engage in a diplomatic marriage was that the amount of gifts ordinarily exchanged between rulers exponentially increased. In correspondence between the Mitanni king Tushratta and Amenhotep III (c. 1390–1352), for example, various items of wealth that were to accompany the pharaoh's new bride were exhaustively inventoried. The value of the awe-inspiring assemblage of items fashioned for the royal couple out of precious materials remains incalculable, with one exception. Tushratta's scribes kept careful count of the gold. Thus, according to Kenneth Kitchen's tabulations, in this metal alone the king of Mitanni expended the equivalent of $106,300 on presents for Amenhotep III and $350,460 to enrich his daughter's dowry![33]

Given Egypt's vast extent and its mineral wealth, it could likely have been admitted into the club of Great Kings even without its empire in Syria-Palestine and Nubia. Having these territories, however, made the pharaoh truly a king of kings, on par with the greatest of his peers. Moreover, his southern empire allowed him much more ready access to lucrative gold mines and to the type of Nubian prestige goods craved by his correspondents. Finally, possession of Egypt's foreign territories gave the pharaoh the right to police a portion of the routes that caravans would travel, thereby greatly increasing the odds of their safe arrival. As early as the reign of Hatshepsut (c. 1473–1458), inscriptions refer to the opening of roads, and it is notable that Egyptian military bases tended to be situated particularly at harbors and along the major thoroughfares that would be utilized by caravans and merchants (see Chapters 6 and 8).[34] As Thutmose III pronounced on his Gebel Barkal stele, "I [have set] my terror in the farthest marshes of Asia, there is no one that holds back my messenger!"[35] Indeed, when Egyptians engaged seemingly low-level foes, such as Shasu Bedouin or 'Apiru, they often did so specifically because the aggressive activities of these peoples had been interfering with the passage of caravans and/or imperial functionaries.[36] As the king of Babylon admonished the pharaoh regarding an ambush of his caravan in Canaan,

> ...[I]f you do not put these men to death, they are going to kill again, be it a caravan of mine or your own messengers, and so messengers between us will thereby be cut off.[37]

Just as empire enabled high-powered trade, high-powered trade in turn necessitated the extreme security measures that empire was equipped to enable.

Revenue

In terms of reaping the financial rewards of empire, access to high-level trade is important, although each diplomatic "gift" requires another in return. Booty is also a boon to a treasury, but it is ultimately unsustainable, for the rules of war dictate that one should only plunder a hostile or a rebellious town, never a loyal vassal. Thus, if most subjects have submitted and the imperial power has already reached the limits beyond which military campaigning is not practical due to natural or political barriers, then the opportunities for plunder are severely limited. For instance, although the majority of gold, horses, and people recorded as imperial income in the annals entered Egypt as plunder during the reign of Thutmose III, very significant percentages of these came from the first campaign, when a serious rebellion was crushed and the Egyptians were entitled to extract the spoils of victory from the forces allied against them.[38] Thus, the first campaign alone accounted for 79% of the silver, 88% of the horses, and 92% of the gold that Thutmose III would acquire from plunder. This outsized percentage is surprising given that Thutmose campaigned virtually every year for the better part of the next two decades. As the comparison between the graphs in Figure 5.2 demonstrates, the importance of plunder as a revenue stream for Thutmose III appears more muted when the plunder from the first campaign is discounted.

If plunder was to some extent, then, a non-renewable resource, taxation systems were explicitly designed to be ongoing—to carefully skim off the surplus from subject societies so as to enrich the imperial government, to subsidize imperial infrastructure, and to prevent an accumulation of wealth by vassals or occupied peoples. Theorists of ancient empires and archaic states have concluded that taxation systems are typically based on a combination of wealth and staple finance. Staple finance was generally tallied in livestock and shares of harvests—especially harvests from fields worked by corvée labor. Such stores, which remained relatively close to where they were gathered, were utilized to feed armies, ambassadors, and all those who regularly or intermittently gave service to the state.[39] The key role staple finance played in Thutmose III's imperial reforms is addressed in Chapter 6.

Unlike its counterpart, wealth finance was generally collected in prestige goods. These could be consumable, such as wine or fine oil, but they might also consist of the same types of exotic or precious materials that were exchanged between rulers of equal status. For example, one of Thutmose III's officials boasted,

> I set the tax quota for [Upper] Retenu [in silver, gold], lapis, various gemstones, chariots and horses without number.... I set the tax quota for the chiefs of the land of Nubia in electrum in ore-form, in gold, ivory and ebony, and numerous ships of dom-palm wood, as a tax-quota of each year, like dependents of his palace.[40]

Not coincidentally, in the annals it is precisely these items that appear most often among the benevolences (*inw*) sent by the vassal rulers to Thutmose III, though bronze, copper, cattle, incense, wine, oil, and (especially) people were delivered with some regularity as well.

Such expected "gifts" resembled those presented on ceremonial occasions to the pharaoh by his own mayors and high-level staff.[41] Given the easy opportunities enjoyed by both mayors and vassals for exploiting their own subjects, it is

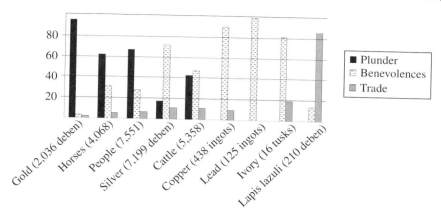

(a) Percentages of items obtained by plunder, benevolences, and high-status trade in Thutmose III's annals. Numbers given are the surviving totals from the annals. The final numbers would have been significantly higher.

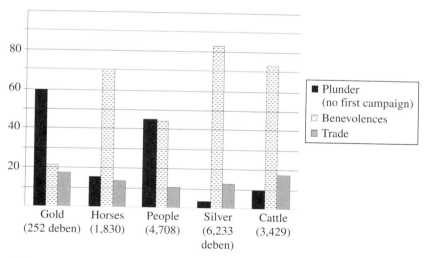

(b) Percentages of desired items according to method of attainment in Thutmose III's annals, without taking into account the plunder from the first campaign. Numbers given are the surviving totals from the annals. The final numbers would have been significantly higher.

Figure 5.2 Information on imperial revenues as recorded in Thutmose III's annals.

tempting to look upon the gifts not only as tokens of esteem but also, perhaps more cynically, as kickbacks. Such gift-giving ceremonies, however, are characteristic of the relations between monarchs and magnates. As Machiavelli put it,

> It is customary most of the time for those who desire to acquire favor with a Prince to come to meet him with things that they care most for among their own or with things that they see please him most. Thus, one sees them many times being presented with horses, arms, cloth of gold, precious stones and similar ornaments worthy of their greatness.[42]

Benevolences could also be supplemented by property or people that were requisitioned as needed at any given time for royal festivals or even for no stated reason at all, such as timber, glass, or beautiful women.[43] A model letter purportedly written by the king's son of Kush, which could just as easily be addressed to a local ruler as to a high official, reads, "When my letter reaches you, prepare the *inw* in every respect." A list of desired items is then issued, which includes cattle, desert animals, gold, Nubian exotica, minerals, gems, and people. The viceroy concludes his instructions by stating, "Exceed your obligations every year.... Think about the day when the *inw* is sent, and you are brought into the presence (of the king)."[44] Similarly, in the Amarna archive of diplomatic letters, northern vassals might refer to filling the king's orders (EA 239, 242, 247) or to "...p[*reparing*] the tribute of the Sun, in accordance with the comma[nd] of the king" (EA 325, similarly EA 254).[45]

There is no question that the gold mines in Upper and (especially) Lower Nubia enriched Egypt tremendously. The 10,000 or so ounces of raw gold that arrived annually (on average) from Nubia in Thutmose III's reign, for example, is equivalent in 2018 prices to over \$13 million, and a single delivery might require as many as 150 men to transport it into the pharaoh's presence. Even Amun's cut of such tribute was equivalent to the annual salary of roughly 17,000 laborers.[46] All things considered, then, the Assyrian king's statement to his Egyptian counterpart that "[g]old in your country is dirt; one simply gathers it up"[47] seems but a minor exaggeration when viewed from a comparative perspective. To sweeten the pot yet further, with only the slight nuisance of portaging around a cataract or two, Nubian gold could be easily transported by water. Thus, exorbitant transport costs did not reduce profits.

In terms of producing freely exploitable minerals and manpower, then, Egypt's empire generated wealth, but numerous scholars have questioned how ultimately lucrative it was.[48] Egypt's own gold mines in the Wadi Hammamat and in Lower Nubia would have provided more than enough gold to attract the admiration of other Great Kings and to purchase any amount of slaves, good quality timber, and foreign prestige goods. Once ideology is set aside, then, a real question remains as to whether Egypt's imperial expenditures in Syria-Palestine and Upper Nubia outweighed the income extracted. The resources of

Upper Nubia (mainly cattle and manpower) reduplicated those found in Egypt, and the timber, oil, incense, and wine produced in Canaan and delivered to the pharaoh can no longer be viewed as income if the opposite end of the balance sheet included the maintenance of a standing army. Gil Stein has observed with respect to Mesopotamia that "…it was far easier, cheaper, and safer to have individuals and groups outside the palace sector assume the risks and costs of international exchange"[49] than it was to compel the delivery of such products through the maintenance of an empire.

Why, then, would the Egyptians have maintained their hold on the lands they conquered for the first time early in the Eighteenth Dynasty once the initial influx of profits from plunder declined? In pondering this question, it is tempting to come back to Schumpeter's statement that a society

> values conquest not so much on account of the immediate advantages— advantages that more often than not are more than dubious, or that are heedlessly cast away with the same frequency—as because it *is* conquest, success, action.[50]

Ideology, as Barry Kemp and José Galán have emphasized, is a powerful engine.[51] Once the expectation arose that a successful pharaoh was a victorious pharaoh, actively involved in extending Egypt's boundaries and in domesticating the foreign, even pragmatic attempts, such as Akhenaten's (c. 1352–1336), to scale back imperial investitures were met with disapproval and derision. Ramesses III (c. 1184–1153), though his own northern borders had shrunk substantially even from Akhenaten's day, received less posthumous shame, in part because while he may not have fought against Amurru and the Hittites, he at least had the good sense to pretend on the walls of his mortuary temple that he had. And, indeed, one imagines that even a half-hearted imperialist like Akhenaten must have experienced the thrill of empire when carefully choreographed celebrations—like that which occurred in his 12th year—placed him elevated on his throne at the center of the world stage with Syro-Palestinians, Libyans, and Nubians bowed in obeisance before him (see the Epilogue).

Coercion and Enticement in Imperial Attainment

Although subtle distinctions are easily overlooked in the aftermath of battle, empire-builders differ from polities that regularly engage in predatory raiding because it is their goal to eventually incorporate their victims into the larger imperial enterprise. In order to convince their newly subjugated foes to remain subservient even in the absence of campaign armies, empires have typically utilized both coercion and enticement. The remainder of this chapter, therefore, focuses on whips and then on lures.

In an implicit endorsement of terror tactics in empire-building, Napoleon once observed that "...war must be made as intense and awful as possible in order to make it short, and thus to diminish its horrors."[52] The Assyrians and Aztecs evidently operated according to this principle, as many grisly archaeological finds and contemporary reports attest. While seemingly not especially creative in their methods of intimidation, the Egyptians nonetheless did make it completely clear that any polity that resisted incorporation into their empire would be brutally crushed and economically devastated. Concerning his treatment of Mitanni cities, Thutmose III boasted,

> I houghed his cities and his towns and set them on fire. My Majesty turned them into ruins which shall never be re-founded. I plundered all their inhabitants, who were taken away as prisoners-of-war along with their numberless cattle and their goods likewise. I took away from them their provisions and uprooted their grain, and chopped down all their trees (even) all their fruit trees. (And so) their districts, they belonged to (anyone) who would make an appropriation for himself(?), after My Majesty destroyed them; for they have turned into burnt dust on which plants will never grow again.[53]

Here, neatly catalogued, are the punishments that Egypt typically meted out to those opponents—especially in siege situations—who did not have the sense to surrender.

The fact that Egypt's harvest fell before that of Syria-Palestine undoubtedly facilitated the attainment of its northern empire. Pharaohs assembled armies in early April, when Egypt's farmers were free but when the crops of the Levant were still ripening. As a result, any northern city-state that defied the Egyptian army risked the loss of a year's harvest—either to feed the Egyptian army during its siege or else in a punitive torching. Records and reliefs also depict the large-scale destructions of orchards, again for purposes both punitive and practical. At Megiddo, for instance, Thutmose III's armies constructed a surrounding wall that was built of all the city's fruit trees. Moreover, a few campaigns later, the annals reported,

> ...His Majesty sacked the town of Ardata with its grain, and all its fruit trees were cut down. Now [His Majesty] found [the harvest(?) of] Djahy at its fullest, and their trees laden with their fruit; their wine was found lying in their vats like flowing water and their grain on the threshing floors (ready for) threshing. More plenteous was it than the sand of the sea-shore! And the army wallowed in their substance ... in their cups and anointed with oil every day, just as though at festival time in Egypt![54]

Given the several-year lag between the planting of a tree and the time when it bears fruit, the destruction of orchards represented a potentially devastating long-term loss of income. Assuredly, this economic factor alone encouraged many Syro-Palestinian cities to throw open their gates to Egyptian conquerors. Ironically, the same concern for lucrative renewable resources may have induced the Egyptians, as future tax-masters, to accept surrenders graciously.

If the Egyptians had to force entrance into a besieged city, the sacking and pillaging afterward served not only to reward the patience of the army but also as an object lesson to all other cities considering barring their gates. The same harsh treatment would, moreover, be meted out to a rebel. Pharaonic policy, parroted back to the king by the ruler of Tyre, stated that a loyal vassal had nothing to fear, but "[i]f he does not heed the word of the king, his lord, his city is destroyed, his house is destroyed, never (again) does his name exist in all the land" (EA 147).[55] When a settlement was strategically valuable—such as Tell el-'Ajjul, Gaza, Jaffa, Beth Shan, Sai, or Tombos—conquest might mean a permanent loss of even a nominal independence. In such cases the local leadership would be deposed and the city transformed into an Egyptian base. The town's population generally dwindled, and the economy would be reoriented to further imperial aims. Even the settlement's name was often changed to signal its new status as a directly owned royal center, becoming known as The-ruler-seized-it, Ramesses-is-strong, Ramessesburg, or the like.[56]

The fate that awaited the inhabitants of a conquered city or army was also to be feared. Soldiers killed in battle were mutilated, ostensibly in the service of proper imperial accounting. In order to tabulate the dead and to reward individual soldiers who had made kills, the Egyptians typically severed either the hand of a circumcised foe or the phallus of an uncircumcised one.[57] Merneptah referred to the brimming receptacles of uncircumcised phalli and hands as being transported on donkeys "like fish by the basketful."[58] Any individuals who witnessed the bloody aftermath of such a slaughter would no doubt think twice about incurring imperial wrath.

The corpses of enemy leaders were not infrequently exhibited as trophies. Thutmose I hung a slain Nubian leader head downward off the prow of his ship to advertise his victory and to intimidate all Nubians he passed on his northward journey.[59] Likewise, Amenhotep II sailed home from battles in Syria with the corpses of seven rebellious enemy leaders, dangling head downward like a hunter's catch, from his prow. According to his stele,

> Thereupon six men from among the foe were hung in front of the rampart of Thebes and the hands likewise. The other enemy was then transported south to Nubia and hung on the rampart of Napata in order that men should see the victories of his Majesty forever and ever....[60]

Such dramatic displays of necroviolence no doubt intimidated would-be internal plotters as well as foreign vassals. If the king could root out rebellions at the far ends of his empire, no doubt he could sniff out sedition considerably closer to home.

The treatment of vanquished populations varied according to whether their polity voluntarily surrendered (in which case they would "suffer no loss") or had to be conquered (in which case they were destined to become "like ones who had not been"), as Amenhotep I (c. 1525–1504) stated explicitly in an inscription detailing his Nubian campaign.[61] Prisoners of war were generally either transformed from free individuals into slaves and then parceled out among royal, temple, and private estates or were transformed from enemy combatants into auxiliary soldiers. The inhabitants of rebellious polities, however, were treated much more harshly. The third time that Ahmose was forced to campaign in Nubia due to rebellions, the troublemakers were uniformly executed. Similarly, Thutmose II (c. 1492–1479) claimed to have quelled an insurrection led by a Nubian ruler and sons of the former king of Kerma by killing all the males of the population. The total disappearance from historical records of any subsequent mention of descendants of Kerman royalty or even of the Kerman kingdom as an entity testifies to the effectiveness of this tactic.[62]

The ability to wield the formidable martial forces of a state against the militias of small communities and city-states played a primary role in Egypt's success in forging its empire, but coercive diplomacy was not utilized exclusively. As the author of *The Art of War* advises, "...to fight and conquer in all your battles is not supreme excellence; supreme excellence consists in breaking the enemy's resistance without fighting."[63] In this respect, the Incas were master negotiators. While they assuredly summoned the specter of violence, they simultaneously sweetened the taste of surrender with a variety of incentives. Of the Inca it is said that

> [c]ustomarily, an army that was mobilized in the agricultural off-season approached a targeted *sceñarío* with overwhelming force. Messages sent by the Inca commander would offer favorable terms of surrender: compliant subject elites received gifts and could expect to retain or enhance their status, while communities were allowed to keep many of their resources.... The newly subject populace would have to pledge loyalty to the *Sapa Inca*, agree to supply labor service, and pay homage to the sun.... The general principle was to be generous with those who capitulated, and to punish those who resisted harshly.[64]

Ironically, the Requerimiento, drawn up by the Spanish Crown in 1513, ensured that a very similar set of options would be offered to the Inca, as well as to other peoples of the New World, just before any armed encounters with conquistadors.[65]

Although we have no way to access the discussions that took place between Egyptian envoys and the rulers of foreign polities, it would appear that the pharaohs too proposed an offer that many of their adversaries would have found difficult to refuse. Thutmose III, for instance, recorded his acceptance of the surrender of the kings that had held out against him at Megiddo:

> My Majesty besieged them for a period of seven months before they emerged outside, begging My Majesty as follows: "Give us thy breath! Our lord! The people of Retenu will never again rebel!" Then that doomed one together with the chiefs who were with him made all their children come forth to My Majesty, bearing many gifts.... So My Majesty had them take the oath as follows: "We will not again act evilly against Menkheperre, living forever! our lord, in our lifetime; since we have witnessed his power, and he has given us breath as he pleased." ... Then My Majesty let them go back to their cities, and all of them rode off on donkeys, for I had confiscated their horses.[66]

Had these kings not kept up their siege for seven months, the terms of surrender would no doubt have been even more generous. As it was, however, in return for their surrender, their oaths, and their payment, the kings kept their positions, and neither Megiddo nor their own cities were destroyed.

A study of greeting formulas employed in diplomatic letters suggests that terms were especially favorable for polities located in areas that bordered other Great Powers (i.e. any polity from Kadesh north) or were located in areas that would be extremely difficult for the Egyptians to conquer (such as the mountainous regions of Lebanon and Canaan). In contrast to the majority of other Syro-Palestinian vassals, these rulers were allowed to employ much more dignified greeting formulas in their letters to the pharaoh. Instead of professing to fall at the feet of the king seven times and seven times (or, god forbid, to then roll from back to belly before him), the northernmost rulers and those in the mountains generally fell before the king between one and seven times only (see Figure 5.3).

As discussed in the Epilogue, the nature of such imagined prostrations almost certainly equated to the actual genuflections that the vassal or his ambassador would perform in person on their visits to Egypt.[67] Thus, the king could offer a potential vassal the promise of being publicly acknowledged as more important than many of his peers—a deal that might not be offered by a rival Great King. In the Hittite empire, certainly, similar arrangements were made to accommodate the pride of particularly prized vassals. Thus, while the king of Kizzuwatna was required to periodically come before the Hittite king, the treaty stipulated, "As soon as he comes before His Majesty, the noblemen of His Majesty < will rise > from their seats. No one will remain seated above him."[68]

The other enticement that pharaohs no doubt offered highly-sought after vassals was the waiving of all but the most symbolic tax payments. Likewise, after a favored vassal had paid whatever taxes had been assessed, any further goods requested by the pharaoh would be remunerated. Thus, Amenhotep III paid the ruler of Gezer the equivalent of 1,600 shekels of silver for 40 beautiful

(a)

(b)

Figure 5.3 Genuflections were a regular part of diplomatic relations. (a) 'Abdi- Aširta of Amurru claims in this letter to fall at the feet of the king seven times, both on his stomach and on his back (EA 64; British Museum E29816 © The Trustees of the British Museum); (b) Foreign envoys from Libya and the Near East bow and scrape before Horemheb, Memphite tomb of Horemheb (redrawn from Martin 1991, 77, figure 49).

female cupbearers (EA 369). Especially prized vassals also had the right to make special requests of the pharaoh. The king of Ugarit, for instance, asked for two Nubian palace attendants and a physician (EA 49), while the ruler of Qatna requested a sack of gold to replace or refurbish a statue of the sun god that had originally been gifted to Qatna by an earlier pharaoh (EA 55).

Like their domestic counterparts, dutiful vassals might also be publically rewarded for exemplary performance. For instance, the official Khaemhat reported that the stewards of the estates of the pharaoh were gathered together with "the chiefs of the South and North, from this land of Kush the wretched, as far as the boundary of Naharin (*a.k.a. Mitanni*)" and that both sets of individuals were rewarded "after the statement of the overseer of the granary concerning them, 'they have increased the harvest of year 30.'"[69] Finally, it is notable that it appears to have been regular policy for kings on campaign to punish rebels and to give rewards to rulers who had proved themselves loyal.[70] In Nubia, apparently, the king's son of Kush also distributed gifts on behalf of the pharaoh.[71]

While the nature of these royal rewards is not stated in the inscriptions, we have record in the Amarna letters of the pharaoh bestowing upon the ruler of Ginti-kirmil a gold goblet and 12 sets of linen garments (EA 265). Precious statues—like that originally gifted to Qatna—were also likely distributed in this manner.[72] Finally, as will be discussed in the following chapter, loyal vassals were typically allowed access to imperial storehouses if they acted administratively on behalf of the empire. For those vassals granted privileged access to imperial wealth, the benefits of collaboration were clear. (Attendant drawbacks, however, will be discussed in Chapter 7.)

By relying on a judicious employment of coercion and persuasion, the Egyptians were able to operate their empire at relatively low cost for much of the New Kingdom. Edward Luttwak, writing about Rome's Judeo-Claudian empire, has observed,

> All else being equal, the efficiency of such systems [i.e. empires] must be inversely proportional to the degree of reliance on force, since the force generated will require a proportional input of human and material resources. In fact, the efficiency of the systems will reflect their "economy of force."[73]

In the early Eighteenth Dynasty, when Egypt's interventions abroad, particularly in the north, were mostly limited to hit-and-run military attacks, the application of force was key. The notion of rewarding those who remained loyal to the pharaoh, however, was a concept generated in the mid-Eighteenth Dynasty, when the rulers were attempting to transform an informal empire into a functioning and relatively self-sustaining system. The success of their efforts, discussed in the next chapter, is evident in the fact that—with the exception of campaigns mounted by a few post-Amarna "warrior pharaohs"— it became exceedingly rare that Egypt unleashed the full brunt of its military might on the citizens of its imperial territories.

Notes

1 Simpson 2003, 346.
2 Schumpeter 1966, 5.
3 Romer's rule was formulated by palaeontologist Alfred Sherwood Romer. Carla Sinopoli has likewise observed that imperial trajectories often consist of improvised responses to a series of challenges and that assuming the presence of a grand strategy from the start may in fact be wrongheaded (Sinopoli 2001, 196).
4 Redford 1979, 274; Weinstein 1981, 7.
5 Bietak 1996, 67.
6 Bietak 2010, 164.
7 Budka 2014, 70–1.
8 Weinstein 1991, 106, 111, note 2.
9 Breasted 1906b, 40.
10 Simpson 2003, 349.
11 Cumming 1982, 2.
12 Redford 2003, 34.
13 Redford 2003, 60.
14 Saggs 1984, 174; Kuhrt 1995, 519.
15 Smith 1995, 168.
16 Cumming 1982, 35.
17 For example, Syro-Palestinian and Nubian names appear with great frequency on work records relating to the construction of Thutmose III's temple at Deir el-Bahari. In one list Syro-Palestinian workers made up three-quarters of the force, with Egyptians constituting the remaining fourth (Hayes 1960, 41, 44–5).
18 Machiavelli, *Prince*, ch. XX, 85.
19 Breasted 1906b, 31.
20 Lichtheim 1976, 14.
21 Kemp (1978, 20, 29–33, 56) has also emphasized the pursuit of glory as a driving mechanism behind Egyptian imperialism.
22 For the plunder soldiers were allowed to keep, see Lichtheim 1976, 13–14; Redford 2003, 95; Morris 2014, 365–77.
23 See Trigger 1993, 61, 72; Weber 1992, 23.
24 Redford 2003, 169.
25 Redford 2003, 169.
26 Caminos 1954, 92, 95–6, 317–18, 401–2; Wente 1990, 106–9.
27 The value of such experiences is aptly expressed by one Spanish father, who approached a general in 1690 with the request, "Compadre, I entreat you to do me the favour of taking my son Antonio among your troops, that when he is old, he may have a tale to tell" (Fulano de Escobedo, quoted in the opening epigraph of Weber 1992).
28 Kadry 1982, 21–2, 38.

29 Schumpeter 1966, 25.

30 Morris 2014.

31 By way of example, the ruler of Assyria initiated correspondence with Egypt (EA 15), but he did not refer to the Egyptian king as a brother until his letter received a favorable reply (EA 16). Egypt's acceptance of this relationship caused the king of Babylon to issue a formal complaint (EA 9).

32 Schulman 1988, 57.

33 Moran 1992, 51–7, 72–81; Kitchen 1998, 259. Kitchen's figures, relevant to 1993, have been adjusted for inflation.

34 Allen 2002, 4; Morris 2005.

35 Redford 2003, 114.

36 Murnane 1990, 40–2; Kitchen 1993, 12–13.

37 EA 8; Moran 1992, 16.

38 The annals have suffered damage in various places, so the totals presented are in some cases minimum numbers.

39 D'Altroy and Earle 1985, 188; Smith 1997, 80.

40 Redford 2003, 173.

41 Bleiberg 1996, 114.

42 Machiavelli, *Prince*, 3.

43 Redford 2003, 173, 248; EA 64, 148, 160.

44 Smith 1997, 78; Caminos 1954, 438.

45 Moran 1992, 353.

46 Hayes 1973, 350; Smith 2003, 72.

47 EA 16; Moran 1992, 39.

48 Ahituv 1978; Kemp 1978, 19.

49 Stein 2005b, 144.

50 Schumpeter 1966, 6.

51 Kemp 1978, 8–15, 20; Kemp 1997, 128–30; Galán 1995.

52 Quoted in Sloane 1894, 814.

53 Redford 2003, 106.

54 Redford 2003, 63–4.

55 Moran 1992, 233. See similarly EA 162 in which the pharaoh asked a wayward vassal, "But if you perform your service for the king, your lord, what is there that the king will not do for you? If for any reason whatsoever you prefer to do evil, and if you plot evil, treacherous things, then you, together with your entire family, shall die by the axe of the king" (Moran 1992, 249).

56 Morris 2005, 56, n. 102.

57 Galán 2002, 449.

58 Kitchen 2003, 6.

59 Breasted 1906b, 34.

60 Cumming 1982, 27.

61 Lorton 1974, 112.

62 Lichtheim 1976, 13; Breasted 1906b, 49–50.
63 Sun Tzu, *Art of War*, chapter III, 2.
64 D'Altroy 2003, 207.
65 Weber 1992, 22.
66 Redford 2003, 109–10.
67 Morris 2006b.
68 Beckman 1996, 15.
69 Breasted 1906b, 350–1.
70 Breasted 1906b, 31; Cumming 1982, 9, 30.
71 Morkot 2001, 239.
72 Morris 2015a.
73 Luttwak 1979, 196. See similarly Doyle 1986, 42.

6

Organization and Infrastructure (c. 1458–1295)

Chapter 5 suggested that the radical expansion of Egypt's empire in the New Kingdom was to a certain extent unanticipated, being prompted at the beginning by a desire simply to safeguard Egypt's traditional borders so that the country would not again be occupied and ruled by foreigners. In the view of Donald Redford and numerous other scholars, Egypt's first incursions outward were essentially punitive and predatory razzias.[1] The infusion of wealth and the great acclaim that accompanied reconquest in Lower Nubia and new conquests in Upper Nubia and in Syria-Palestine, however, encouraged pharaohs, nobles, soldiers, and priests to work together to extend Egypt's borders, as royal inscriptions put it, and to engage wholeheartedly in the project of empire building. Like other complex constructions of great magnitude and durability, however, empires require organization and infrastructure—two essentials that this chapter takes for its focus.

The initial attainment of territory relied on brute force. In the south armies were levied against the king of Kerma, who appears to have been able to marshal a great deal of manpower on his own behalf. The king of Mitanni was likewise a powerful enemy with considerable resources, though the fact that his power base in northern Syria lay so far from Egypt meant that the two countries never did more than threaten one another's hinterlands. In the area that would become the heart of Egypt's empire (Canaan, Lebanon, the Transjordan, and parts of southern Syria), however, Egypt marshaled the professional army of a powerful kingdom against individual city-states and settlements. This would hardly have been a fair fight in any case, but archaeology has demonstrated that those polities that were not destroyed during the extended transition from the end of the Middle Bronze Age to the beginning of the Late Bronze Age emerged from it radically diminished. According to Rivka Gonen, only 12% of settlements exceeded 25 acres in area in the early and mid-Eighteenth Dynasty, down from 28% in the Middle Bronze Age. Indeed the balance had shifted such that the number of settlements 2.5 acres and smaller

Ancient Egyptian Imperialism, First Edition. Ellen Morris.
© 2018 Ellen Morris. Published 2018 by John Wiley & Sons Ltd.

was roughly three times what it had been previously, and the culture could no longer be characterized as predominantly urban.[2]

Certain scholars have quite rightly downplayed the achievements of the early Eighteenth-Dynasty rulers in Canaan, and particularly the much-valorized king Thutmose III (c. 1479–1425), pointing out that the territory that he conquered with such fanfare happened to be "weakened, partly desolated and ruined"[3] prior to his arrival and thus constituted easy pickings. Such criticisms parallel those levied against Genghis Khan. As Owen Lattimore writes,

> It is customary to attribute the astonishing conquests of Chingis Khan simply to his military genius, but it would be more rational to point out that his genius was given its opportunity by the coincidence that at the turn from the twelfth to the thirteenth century all the great civilized states from China to the Near East were simultaneously in that phase of the cyclical rise and fall of dynasties which made them weak on their frontiers and open to nomad incursions.[4]

If Thutmose III and Genghis Khan are perhaps given more credit than is warranted for their military conquests, in which they took advantage of the weakness of their neighbors, what separated these men from the other armed predators that preceded them was a knack for imperial organization. As Genghis Khan's own advisor famously warned him, "you can conquer an empire on horseback, but cannot administer it from there."[5] Thus, while previous rulers seemed to operate as armed thugs writ large—specializing in smash-and-grab operations and extortion, as well as what Karen Spalding has termed with reference to the early Spanish empire in the Americas a "plunder economy"[6]—the administration of these reformist rulers imposed a recognizable order and thereby transformed an exploited periphery into an imperial territory.

This chapter examines the guiding principles that governed the infrastructure of Egypt's empire—particularly, though not exclusively, its northern empire—as it existed in the mid- and late Eighteenth Dynasty (see Figure 6.1). While not all of the innovations observable at this period can be attributed to Thutmose III, a good number can, and it seems to be typical of successful empires that many of the dictates that governed their organization were conscious reforms issued under the reign of a specific military leader with a flair for the imposition of order and the erection of infrastructure.[7] Rules issued on behalf of Genghis Khan, Shaka Zulu, Qin Shi Huang, Pachacuti, Augustus, Thutmose III, and other imperial innovators helped forge and/or consolidate empires and provided models to be followed by their successors. Admittedly, many of the structuring principles required amendment over time as subject peoples reacted to them and as situations changed, but in each case the dictates provided the empire with a solid foundation upon which to build.

Figure 6.1 Sites mentioned in the chapter.

Campaign Regularly in Order to Naturalize Rule and Assess Resources

Thutmose III's decision to campaign on a nearly annual basis was one of the most pivotal with regard to the solidification of Egypt's northern empire, though it was also a reform that did not outlast his reign. Following his victory against 300 or so allied Syro-Palestinian polities at Megiddo in his first year as sole ruler, he returned to the region together with a campaign army practically every year, whether there was a specific rebellion that needed quelling or not. Indeed, while some of his campaigns solidified Egypt's hold over key harbor bases or struck inland to engage Mitanni armies, others seemed more akin to the type of royal progress known from countless regimes. The regular repetition of visits to subject territories affords a ruler the opportunity to receive obeisance from regional elites and to renew oaths, to give and receive gifts, to impress those of his or her subjects who would never journey to court, to encourage the prompt payment of taxes, to settle high-level disputes, and to achieve a first-hand understanding of a region's exploitable resources and the potential risks posed by the ambitions of local rulers.[8]

In Chapter 1 it was posited that the Following of Horus procession, undertaken biennially throughout Egypt in the First Dynasty, may have borne certain similarities to the annual campaigns of Thutmose III. In both cases the central court must have hoped that by virtue of repeated exposure to the awe-inspiring pomp, instantiated ideology, and implied military might of the royal progress, pharaonic rule—relatively recently imposed—would become naturalized. Certainly, it is no doubt significant that in both cases this elaborate and costly ritual seems to have been abandoned as a regular practice only when the concept of a pharaonic overlord was no longer abstract and when the system of tax collection had became routinized.[9]

Thutmose III's impressive military achievements have led numerous writers to refer to him as "the Napoleon of Egypt."[10] The feature that makes this comparison particularly compelling, however, is the fact that on his otherwise uneventful third campaign, Thutmose III seems to have devoted his energies to collecting samples of

> ...[p]lants which his majesty found in the land of Retenu: all plants that [grow], all flowers that are in God's-Land [which were found by] his majesty when his majesty proceeded to Upper Retenu.[11]

Many animals as well as plants from this and perhaps other campaigns were memorialized in the king's Festival Hall at Karnak temple with near scientific accuracy (even if certain of the samples appear to have been wilted by the time the artists had access to them).[12] A similar desire to explore, to exploit, and to celebrate the resources of a newly acquired territory prompted Napoleon to include a whole cadre of artists, epigraphers, and scientists in his entourage when he came to conquer Egypt. In both cases, not only were all marvels documented, but the region's potentially valuable natural resources had no doubt also been exhaustively inventoried.

Underwrite the Costs of Empire Locally

Empires, however lucrative they might be, do not come cheap. The economic and social costs of extracting a host of men from their occupations and families on an annual basis would have been formidable, not to mention the astronomical costs of feeding and equipping these men during a four- or five-month campaign. As the author of the Chinese military treatise *The Art of War* cautioned:

> Raising a host of a hundred thousand men and marching them great distances entails heavy loss on the people and a drain on the resources of the State. The daily expenditure will amount to a thousand ounces of silver. There will be commotion at home and abroad, and men will drop down exhausted on the highways.... [T]he husbandry of 700,000 families would be affected.[13]

Thutmose III was probably marching only 5,000–10,000 men northward each year, but the general principle remained the same. The entire process if poorly managed could easily backfire, incurring a deep resentment against the Egyptian government on the part of the soldiers, if they felt that their needs went unmet. Egypt would likewise incur the wrath of its vassals if the soldiers on campaign arrogantly requisitioned food and livestock from those they passed by. Such armed extortion had been a worry since the mustering of the first state armies, as is illustrated by a late Sixth-Dynasty official *cum* military leader's proud boast that because of his rectitude "...no one attacked his fellow, ... no one seized a loaf or sandals from a traveller, ... no one took a cloth from any town, ... no one took a goat from anyone."[14] Thutmose III had spent time in the military prior to assuming sole control of the governance of the state, and thus he must have been particularly attuned to the consequences of mismanagement and desirous to ensure that his army would not only be well provisioned for each year's campaign but that the costs incurred would not cripple the economy.

The first step in ensuring the supply of such provisions seems to have been to requisition enough land within Syria-Palestine that the profits could serve to feed an army (literally), as well as to provision garrison troops, government functionaries, and local Canaanite collaborators. The pretext for doing so came conveniently enough during the siege of Megiddo, when, according to the report in the annals,

> ...the arable land was made into fields and entrusted to controllers of the king's house, life, prosperity, and health, to reap their harvest. Tally of the harvest which His Majesty took from the fields of Megiddo: wheat 207,300(+ x) khar-measures, not to mention what was cut in foraging by His Majesty's army.[15]

Extrapolating from profits typically extracted from directly held land in Egypt, scholars have calculated that the requisitioned fields would likely have amounted to some 12,355 acres or roughly an eighth of the entire Jezreel Valley.[16]

Now, while it could be argued that the harvest was intended to supply the Egyptians during the siege and that the fields were returned to their original owners after the surrender of the coalition at Megiddo, there is strong evidence that the fields remained crown property. Certainly, the annals record the regular receipt of expected deliveries of grain by the king's seventh campaign. A letter found at Taanach, likely dating from late in the reign of Thutmose III, suggests that fields in the Jezreel Valley were being farmed by corvée labor on behalf of the Egyptians and that the ruler of Rehob supervised the work of contingents of laborers sent by nearby polities. Further, diplomatic correspondence discovered at Amarna indicates that a century or so later (c. 1362–1332) it was the ruler of Megiddo who oversaw labor on Egyptian-owned fields located in the city's vicinity, though he complained that many of the surrounding cities had been negligent in furnishing corvée laborers (EA 365).[17] Thus, it would seem that among the terms of surrender at Megiddo was the stipulation that Egypt now had rights to the land that it had harvested during the seven-month siege and that the defeated rulers would agree to supply the manpower to work that land in perpetuity.

By his seventh campaign, Thutmose III had devised a system whereby the grain and other agricultural products cultivated on Egyptian-owned fields or requisitioned as tax were to be transported to a series of harbor depots. The annals for this campaign proudly state:

> Now every harbor His Majesty came to was supplied with fine bread, various breads, oil, incense, wine, honey, [various fine] fr[uits of this foreign land, and … c. 80 cm… Now all this…] was more numerous than anything, beyond the comprehension of His Majesty's army—and that's no exaggeration!—and they remain (on record) in the day-book of the king's house—life, prosperity, and health. The tally of them is not given in this inscription so as not to increase the text and so as to accommodate them properly in the place [where] th[ey are done into writing…. Now] report was made of the harvest of the land of Retenu consisting of much grain, wheat, barley, incense, fresh oil, wine, fruit and all the sweet products of the foreign land. They may be consulted at the treasury, just like the census of the labor.[18]

This practice of warehousing agricultural products at harbor storehouses is also noted in the 13th, 14th and 17th campaigns, though the phrase "according to their agreement of every year"[19] suggests that the arrangement was ongoing. Just where the storehouses were located is not specified, but based on evidence from the Amarna letters and other sources it is likely that at various points in the Eighteenth Dynasty such installations were to be found at Gaza, Joppa, Yarimuta, Byblos, Sumur, and Ullaza.[20] The specifically Egyptian nature of the harbor granaries is attested by the fact that in the Amarna letters they are individually referred to as *šu-nu-ti*, a transliterated version of the term for granary (*šnwt*) used in Egypt.[21] From the Amarna letters, we know that in addition to the grain and foodstuffs listed above, such installations could also contain clothing and stores of silver (EA 82, 287).

The source(s) of the grain for the harbor depots located in Lebanon is never specified, but potentially prohibitive transport costs might suggest that the storehouses were filled by the produce of fields situated north of the Jezreel Valley, as they were to be in the Amarna period. In this regard it is notable that the annals specify that part of the booty that fell to Thutmose III after the battle of Megiddo were three northern towns: Yeno'am, Nugsa, and Harenkaru—towns that previously had belonged to the king of Kadesh, one of the major instigators behind the uprising at Megiddo. Following Thutmose III's victory, these towns were charged with providing *bȝkw* taxes—the same type of tax that supplied the harbor depots. Nominal ownership of this income stream fell to the god Amun.[22]

While this divine dedication may suggest that the products of the three towns were shipped back to Amun temples in Thebes, the bulk of the produce may well have been stored locally. It is known, for instance, that Minmose, one of Thutmose III's high officials, was involved not only in taxing northern rulers but also in sponsoring construction at two temples—one to Hathor of Byblos; another dedicated to Amun, which seems to have been located farther north. Egypt's utilization of foreign temples as financial agents is a subject addressed in Chapter 8. For now, suffice it to say that on parallel with the Baalat (a.k.a. "Hathor") temple at Byblos, Minmose's Amun temple almost assuredly belonged in fact to a local deity and would have been situated in close proximity to an Egyptian harbor depot.[23]

Some Syro-Palestinian grain does seem to have been sent to Egypt, especially as contributions for special occasions, such as the Sed-festival of Amenhotep III (c. 1390–1352), where the garnering of contributions from the entire realm was symbolically important.[24] What is fascinating, however, is that records of such imports in late New Kingdom temples show that generally only token amounts of grain—200 liters or so at a time—were transported.[25] These paltry quantities should come as little surprise, however, for Egypt had no need of Syro-Palestinian grain. In later years, after all, the Nile Valley would feed not only its own population but also that of the teeming city of Rome. The same held true for the cattle, sheep, and goats that the Egyptians collected as taxes. While these staple goods would not add significant wealth to Egypt, they could be put to excellent use in Syria-Palestine subventing the costs of military occupation.

In his annals, Thutmose III reported,

> Now all the harbors were stocked with every good thing, in accordance with their yearly custom (for) both northward and [southward] journeys and (with) [the *bȝkw* of Lebano]n likewise, and the harvest of Djahy, consisting of grain, incense, fresh oil, sweet [oil] and wi[ne].[26]

Thus, soldiers traveling along the Via Maris coastal highway or arriving by boat could be supplied at regular intervals and resident imperial functionaries could be supported year-round. Controlling the harbors was, of course, a vital strategic move, as seafaring boats in the Late Bronze Age sailed close to the coast, anchoring frequently to refresh their supplies, trade, or seek shelter.[27] Harbor bases were ideally situated, then, for levying tariffs, enforcing embargos, and guarding against unauthorized entry.[28]

Institute a System of Staple Finance

The system that Thutmose III developed in his northern empire of storing produce from state-owned farms in state-owned storehouses is one originally developed as a part of Egypt's own internal colonization, as discussed in Chapter 1. Because of its efficiency, however, imperial governments virtually always adopted some version of the same schema. According to the logic of staple finance—which complemented the system of wealth finance, discussed in the last chapter—agricultural products and other subsistence goods are collected as harvest taxes and also, often, from directly owned land worked with corvée labor. These foodstuffs and other items, which are typically bulky and expensive to transport, remain in the provinces in which they were collected in order to supply the needs of imperial troops and functionaries.[29]

When Inca troops conquered a region, for example, they typically divided the fields such that one third belonged to the state. These lands, worked by corvée laborers, were devoted to the cultivation of crops useful to the empire, such as maize and coca. These would be delivered to storehouses, which were typically located at 20-km intervals from one another—a comfortable day's travel—along major transport routes and the coast. One Spanish conquistador described the system as follows:

> ...in the more than 1,200 leagues of coast they governed, they had ... great storehouses full of necessary things, which were for provisioning the soldiers. Because in one of them, there were lances, and in others darts, and in others sandals, and in others the remaining arms they had. Moreover, some storehouses were filled with rich clothing, and others with more goods and others with food and all manner of supplies. In this manner, once the lord was lodged in his housing, and his soldiers nearby, not a thing, from the most trivial to the greatest, was lacking, because it could be provided.[30]

Because these stores were specifically intended to supply the needs of army personnel, the Inca king issued an edict stating that soldiers who pillaged the property of locals would be put to death.[31] The Hittites issued a very similar law once they had constructed their network of more than 100 imperial storehouses.³² Thus, in both of these cases, organized extraction was apparently passed off as a paternalistic and protective measure. Given these virtues of simultaneously strengthening the occupier, weakening the occupied, and purportedly safeguarding the inhabitants of their empire from governmental abuse, it is little wonder that the most enthusiastic imperialists of the ancient world embraced it.³³

Co-opt, Don't Construct

Despite the sophistication of Thutmose III's system of storehouses, these installations have steadfastly eluded detection in the archaeological record, along with most other traces of imperial activity in the Eighteenth Dynasty. The fact that the Egyptian empire is so difficult to *see* at this time has led many scholars to downplay its intensity, especially in contrast to the situation in the Nineteenth Dynasty. The visibility of Egypt's later imperial installations is taken to betray a fundamental restructuring and intensification of imperial rule.³⁴ While there is undoubtedly truth in this assessment, a close reading of the archaeological and textual evidence of both periods adds a more nuanced perspective.

Taking into account Egyptian textual sources for the reign of Thutmose III alone, for example, it is evident that in addition to the harbor depots quite a number of installations should theoretically be recoverable on the ground. Thutmose III erected at least two known fortresses: one in Lebanon (dubbed Menkheperre-is-Conqueror-of-the-Vagabonds) and another immediately east of Megiddo.³⁵ Thutmose III also possessed one or more campaign palaces. According to the boast of one of his heralds,

> Every palace situated in a foreign land was assessed for [supplies] and I travelled before the elite corps at the head of the army; and (by the time) my lord came safely to me I had provisioned it. I supplied it with all good and desirable things (available) abroad, better than an Egyptian palace, purified, cleansed, with privacy and security for their apartments, and the pantry staffed by its attendants.³⁶

Garrisons occupied the towns of Tell el-'Ajjul (Sharuhen) and Ullaza, while the city of Gaza likely served as Egypt's headquarters in the southern Levant.³⁷ In addition, as discussed above, one of Thutmose III's officials directed construction at a temple of "Hathor" in Byblos and as well as at a temple of "Amun" located somewhere to the north.³⁸ These Egyptian installations—many of which are only attested in private inscriptions—assuredly represent only a fraction of the total.

Contemporary texts, thus, clearly demonstrate that Egyptians were not only present in the Levant in significant numbers during the mid-Eighteenth Dynasty but also that they were engaged in provisioning the empire with fortresses, storage depots, administrative buildings, and temples at a rate which equaled—if not exceeded—their textually documented counterparts in the Nineteenth Dynasty. A similar situation is observable for the late Eighteenth Dynasty, where archaeological evidence north of the Negev is scanty and limited mostly to highly portable objects such as scarabs and plaques. According to information contained in the Amarna archive, however, within a period of 30 years the Egyptian government stationed garrisons at the towns of Ullaza, Byblos, Gaza, Akko, Kumidi, Jerusalem, Gezer, Megiddo, Tell el-Hesi, Lachish, Joppa, Yarimuta, and Sumur. Officials stationed at the last three headquarters on this list likewise administered harbor depots that stored grain, oil, silver, clothing, as well as sundry other items for the use of imperial functionaries.[39] So why is this situation so poorly reflected in the archaeological record?

A partial answer may be that empires tend to increase their investment in conquered territories over time, as security and control over a given region increase. Thus, at the onset of their domination, many imperial governments adopt a very pragmatic attitude and refrain from building when it is possible to billet. This tactic has two main advantages. First, in post-conquest situations, feelings of vulnerability may cause governments to hesitate before investing heavily in an installation that might be wrested from them in short order. Second, when resources—human and material—are available locally and can be co-opted, this serves both to weaken local governments, which would otherwise have had such resources available for themselves, and to substantially cut costs for the occupying government. Such tactics are often characteristic of hegemonic imperial systems, where the bulk of the territory is ruled indirectly through local leaders who govern much as they always had but who now provide military support and taxes to the imperial government. As Sue Alcock has formulated it, the general rule is that

> [i]f the pre-existent organization of the conquered territory is judged efficient and acceptable by the imperial power, it is left virtually intact.... Expansionist powers tend to turn an existing framework to their advantage whenever they can.[40]

Along these lines, then, it is important to note that the only imperial infrastructure dating to the mid- to late Eighteenth Dynasty that remains visible in Egypt's northern empire lies along the Ways of Horus military highway across the Sinai Peninsula (namely at Tell Heboua I and II, Tell el-Borg, Bir el-'Abd, Haruba site A-345, and perhaps also Deir el-Balah) as well as at the site of Tell el-'Ajjul. While the latter base did occupy space within a Canaanite town, Tell el-'Ajjul had been sacked and burned so thoroughly by Ahmose's army in the early Eighteenth Dynasty (c. 1550) that the Egyptians were essentially forced to build their base from scratch. Thus, in each of these places, no pre-existing architecture was available to co-opt.[41]

Significantly, pottery made according to Egyptian style and technique may complement texts in revealing otherwise invisible military occupation at Eighteenth-Dynasty bases. Tell el-ʿAjjul, Joppa, and Deir el-Balah—three visible bases that the Egyptians ruled directly—all exhibited substantial assemblages of Egyptian-style pottery in the Eighteenth Dynasty.[42] It is surely significant, then, that the six other sites at which appreciable quantities of this ceramic have been identified hosted key Egyptian bases in the Ramesside period (Tel Seraʿ, Beth-Shean, Tell el-Farʿah South, Tel Mor, Aphek, and Tell es-Saʿidiyeh).[43] While Ramesside levels at these sites yielded far greater quantities of Egyptian-style pottery, as will be discussed in Chapter 8, the early presence of this predominantly open-form and utilitarian ceramic is revealing. Ceramicists are confident in equating these particular pots with people, since they are unlikely to have arrived via trade.

Indeed, the only seeming exceptions to the rule that the Eighteenth-Dynasty Egyptians preferred to co-opt existing structures rather than to construct new ones are the stone blocks inscribed with Thutmose III's cartouche excavated at Byblos from the temple precinct of Baalat, a goddess whom the Egyptians identified with Hathor. But here too the pattern is in fact consistent. The construction that Thutmose III commissioned at the temple to "Hathor" at Byblos was not new work at an "Egyptian" temple at all but rather took the form of relatively minor additions to a pre-existing local temple whose divine occupant the Egyptians felt comfortable equating with a deity of their own.

While the Egyptians generally did not boast in their monumental inscriptions of co-opting local buildings, billeting their own troops, and commandeering the troops of their vassals, information from the more mundane cuneiform documents discovered in Egypt and Canaan provides confirmation that the pharaonic administration in fact engaged in all of these practices. For example, the ruler of Gezer complained in a letter to Akhenaten,

> I built a house ... to make preparations before the arrival of the archers of the king, my lord, and Maya has just taken it away from me and placed his commissioner in it. Enjoin Reanap, my commissioner, to restore my village to me, as I am making preparations before the arrival of the archers of the king, my lord.[44]

A similar complaint was levied by the ruler of Jerusalem, who reported to the king that the king's commissioner

> ...se[nt] a *military [force]* here, *[and it has not vac]ated* the house *[that I w]ant....* And *as for [the garrison] that belongs [to Adday]a*, the

commissioner of the king, [I] want their house. So may the ki[ng] provide [f]or them.[45]

And finally, one can bring to bear the statements of Aziru, the ruler of Amurru,
who had—ostensibly for its own protection—overrun Sumur, the Egyptian
base that is described in diplomatic correspondence as the king's "garrison-
city" and contained "the palace" and "my lord's court and [h]is bedchamber"[46]
(EA 76, 62, 84). In a letter to Akhenaten, Aziru defended himself from the
king's accusation that he had purposefully not rebuilt Sumer:

> ...[T]he kings of Nukha[šše] have been at war with [me], and so I have
> not built Sumur.... O king, do not listen to the treacherous men that
> [de]nounce me be[for]e the king, my lord.... [N]o[w you are going to
> hear t]hat I am buil[ding *the city of* the king].[47]

These three passages in the Amarna letters provide a fitting explanation for
why the ruins of Eighteenth-Dynasty military bases are so difficult to find
north of the Negev: namely, because the buildings were generally either local
structures that had been co-opted by Egyptian officials or else they had been
built by local rulers for the Egyptians at the command of the Egyptian
government. It would appear very likely that the same was true of Thutmose
III's storehouses and other installations. The herald of the king, discussed
above, after all, had simply boasted of *preparing* palaces for the king—he made
no claim to have erected them. Likewise, there is Thutmose III's boast that he
incarcerated northern captives in a prison (*ḫnrt*) that they themselves had
built. While this statement may simply refer metaphorically to the siege at
Megiddo, it might alternately point toward a policy of forcing Canaanites to
erect the infrastructure used for their own subjugation.[48] A pharaonic policy of
utilizing indigenous labor and co-opting existing resources to meet the needs
of Egypt's imperial infrastructure would have freed the bulk of the army for the
ever-pressing task of subduing new and rebel territories.

Egyptian soldiers and administrators not only made it a habit to commandeer
locally built installations in the Eighteenth Dynasty, but their foodstuffs too
came from the surrounding region. The system that Thutmose III instituted of
storehouses stocked with local produce has been discussed above. The annals
also record that during the siege of Megiddo local rulers came to the king "carrying grain, wine, beef, and wild game to His Majesty's army."[49] The Amarna
Letters confirm that not only did the system of storehouses persist in the late
Eighteenth Dynasty, but troops could also be expected to be provisioned by
local rulers while they marched, just so long as these rulers were provided with
enough warning that they could begin to stockpile the "food, strong drink, oil,
grain, oxen, sheep and goats"[50] ahead of time. So if Egyptian troops stayed in
locally constructed buildings and were supplied with locally procured food

delivered in Canaanite vessels, it is no wonder that Egypt's empire in the Eighteenth Dynasty is so difficult to discern in the archaeological record.

Fight Canaanites with Canaanites

This issue of visibility is yet further exacerbated by the fact that many of the "Egyptian" troops were in fact not Egyptian at all. Supplying soldiers to fight on behalf of Egyptian interests ranked among the most important of the duties of Egypt's vassals. In the time of Thutmose III, an Egyptian official designated as Amanhatapa (quite probably the king's son and heir Amenhotep) dispatched a missive to the ruler of Taanach ordering him to send warriors, horses, chariots, and captives to him at Megiddo.[51] This tactic of "using barbarians to fight barbarians," if not always efficient, lessens strain on the empire's own forces and weakens its subjects and enemies.[52] Vassal responsiveness to such commands, however, was often far from ideal (for more on this theme, see Chapter 7). Thus, in a subsequent letter the Egyptian berated his correspondent for the fact that not only had he failed to appear before him at Gaza, but neither had he sent his brother or supplied troops to the garrison. This last point was an especially serious offense, as a campaign was at that time being readied.[53] Despite such issues, this same system was operative in the late Eighteenth Dynasty. The Amarna letters reveal that vassals were routinely expected to provide soldiers to guard Egyptian storehouses and also auxiliary troops to fight on behalf of the pharaoh and to man military bases such as Sumur and Beth Shan.[54]

In addition to contributing troops to Egyptian armies and to garrisoning Egyptian bases, vassals were frequently called upon to quell internecine disputes in which the Egyptians had no desire to intervene directly. The ruler of Byblos, for example, wrote the pharaoh,

> Moreover, it was a gracious deed of the king, my lord, that the king [wr]ote to the king of Beirut, to the king of Sidon, and to the king of T[y]re, [*sa*]*ying*, "Rib-Hadda will be writing you for an auxiliary force, and all of [y]ou are to go." This *pl*[*eased*] *me*, [and so] I sent my messenger, but they have [no]t come, and *they* [*have*] not *s*[*en*]*t* their messenger(s) to *gre*[*et*] us.[55]

As stated, issues concerning the reliability of hiring others to fight one's own battles and the subtle and not-so-subtle ways that Egypt's vassals subverted its authority will be the subject of the following chapter. What is emphasized here is the fact that Egypt's cost-saving measures—requiring vassals to supply the buildings, food, and sometimes even the troops who manned their bases and fought their wars—left only the barest of archaeological traces.

Comparable situations are not unusual in imperial contexts. At Sardis, for example, the Persians utilized the country's pre-existing infrastructure and so, as a specialist put it, "Apart from a few portable artifacts, excavations at Sardis have yielded very little that betrays Persian presence."[56] Without outside historical sources, archaeologists would never have suspected that Sardis was controlled by Persia and was absolutely key to its strategic interests in the West. Indirect rule through client kings can be difficult to detect, and it would be a mistake to judge, as have many scholars, the intensity of Egyptian activity in the region by the lightness of Egypt's material footprint.

Gain Leverage Over Current and Future Leaders

One of the ways that Thutmose III endeavored to maintain control over his empire with a minimum use of force was through a cross-frontier policy that he articulated in the entry for his sixth victorious campaign in year 30:

> Now the children of the chiefs and their brothers were brought to be detainees in Egypt; and whenever any of these chiefs died, His Majesty would have his [son] go to assume his position.[57]

As discussed in Chapter 4, evidence that Lower Nubia's elites quite quickly adopted Egyptian cultural signatures strongly suggests that this practice originated in the early Eighteenth Dynasty, though it is most abundantly chronicled in mid-Eighteenth Dynasty tomb paintings (see Figure 6.2). In contrast, rulers north of Kadesh or south of Tombos appear to have sent their sons only after an unsuccessful rebellion.[58] Not normally being required to do so was presumably a perk of their position.

Amenhotep III boasted of this practice,[59] and it does appear to have been embraced by other late Eighteenth Dynasty rulers as well. Evidence from the tomb of Tutankhamun's viceroy, Huy, has been discussed in Chapter 4, and the seemingly routine importation of heirs is also attested in the Amarna archive. A vassal named Yakhtiru, for example, made explicit reference to his time in Egypt, stating,

> May the king, my lord, inquire of Yankhamu, his commissioner. When I was young, he brought me into Egypt. I served the king, my lord, and I stood at the city gate of the king, my lord.[60]

Likewise, the ruler of Jerusalem assured the pharaoh that "...as far as I am concerned, neither my father nor my mother put me in this place, but the strong arm of the king brought me into my father's house."[61] This last was just the sort of sentiment that Egypt's administrators would no doubt have hoped to hear.

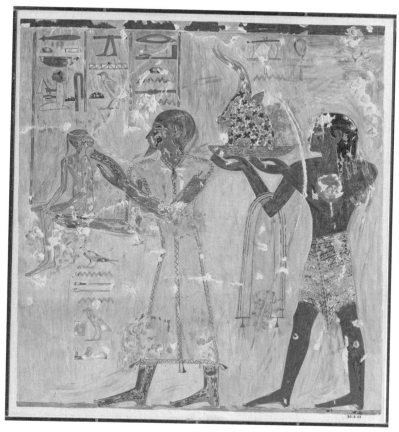

Figure 6.2 Facsimile of a painting depicting a ruler of Tunip bringing his son to court, by Nina de Garis Davies. Metropolitan Museum of Art 30.4.55. Rogers Fund, 1930. *Source:* http://www.metmuseum.org/art/collection/search/544600

These foreign vassals, who had been sent by their fathers to Egypt, in turn sent their own sons, perpetuating the cycle. In one of his very first letters to the pharaoh, Aziru of Amurru wrote,

> Now as to a(ny) request the Sun, my lord, makes, I am [yo]ur servant forever, and my sons are your servants. I herewith give [*my*] sons as *2 att*[*endants*], and they are to do what *the k*[*ing, my lord*], orders.[62]

Recalcitrant vassals, however, may have needed some coaxing to deliver their heirs. The ruler of Gezer, for instance, reported that an Egyptian official confronted him with the ultimatum, "Hand ov[er] your wife and your sons, or I will kill (you)."[63]

This policy of "safeguarding" heirs was one of the most ingenious in Egypt's imperial repertoire, for at the same time that it accomplished two very important objectives, it could be presented as an act of solicitous statesmanship. Ostensibly, the Egyptians were offering the vassals a valuable service. Court intrigues and coups in virtually any premodern state placed a ruler's heir in very real danger—and numerous letters in the Amarna archive report on the assassination or attempted assassination of various rulers (e.g. EA 75, 81–2, 89, 139–40). By sending a designated successor to the Egyptian court, however, the vassal not only placed his heir out of danger from relatives and other rivals, but he also ensured that the heir would have Egypt's backing should his right to the throne be contested. Objectively, then, the Egyptians could present themselves as operating for the sole benefit of the vassal. Whether or not the vassal actually desired such a service, it purportedly existed for his own good.

At the same time that the imperial government claimed altruism, however, it secured for itself the single most valuable hostage in the realm, and all parties must have understood that a son was unlikely to survive the disloyalty of his father. In certain cases, however, when facing vassal sedition, it might actually have been advantageous for the Egyptians to kill the father and to replace him with his son, for a secondary goal of the hostage policy appears to have been to indoctrinate the heir with Egyptian values, to impress him with Egypt's might, and to create bonds between him and the pharaoh's own heir. Thus, it would appear that foreign princes were raised at court together with the sons of Egypt's own regional and high officials. These "children of the *k3p*" (the palace's private interior) were evidently educated together with the royal children and thereby became well schooled in the ideology promoted by Egypt's elite.[64]

The caretaking and education of vassals at court is yet another well-worn imperial tactic. Under Inca rule, the sons of provincial nobles were required to be raised at court and to attend four years of school so that they might become fluent in Quechua and in Inca administrative methods.[65] Likewise, according to Suetonius, Augustus "also brought up many of their children [*i.e., those of client kings*] with his own, and gave them the same education."[66] The Assyrians, the Han, and many other regimes likewise groomed heirs whom they hoped would eventually function as puppets or surrogate rulers. The only problem, of course, is that provincial populations have always been quick to reject rulers who, after too long a stint at the core of the empire, are no longer recognizably *of* the region that they intend to govern.[67]

Create Family Ties

Amenhotep III's zeal for contracting diplomatic marriages is well known. Over the course of his reign he negotiated two such unions with Mitanni, two with Babylon, and one with Arzawa. Ramesses II's two diplomatic marriages to

Hittite princesses are equally well known (c. 1245 and another at a later date). What is less often discussed, however, is the pharaonic practice of requisitioning the daughters of vassals to serve as wives of subordinate status. Whether this was a practice started by Thutmose III is not known, but it is notable that on his second campaign, his scribes recorded the delivery of "a daughter of a ruler" together with 30 of her slaves, as well as gold and lapis jewelry. The horses and chariots also listed as among the ruler's "benevolences" may well have served to fill out her dowry.[68]

As is demonstrated by the receipt of diplomatic gifts from the rulers of Assyria, Babylon, and Hatti, Thutmose III's scribes were only interested in recording for posterity income coming in, not the value of the reciprocal gifts given at such occasions. Yet, despite this bias, it would seem that the Egyptian king had the power simply to command a vassal to offer up his daughter as a bride. For example, in a letter to the ruler of Ammiya, Amenhotep III commands him,

> Prepare your daughter for the king, your lord, and prepa < re > the contributions: [2]0 first-class slaves, silver, chariots, first-class horses. And so let the king, your lord, say to you, "This is excellent," what you have given as contributions to the king to accompany your daughter.[69]

In this case, at least, it seems that a satisfied remark issuing from the pharaoh was intended as ample compensation. The ruler of Einshasi also sent his daughter to the king, though who and what accompanied her is not specified (EA 187), while the dowry for a Lebanese vassal princess might be partially preserved in EA 120. A comparable situation is likely memorialized in the aforementioned tomb of Tutankhamun's viceroy of Kush, as the daughter of a Lower Nubian ruler is depicted arriving at court wearing an elaborate headdress in a chariot pulled by a team of oxen (see Figure 4.3).

Just as the collection of taxes deprives a community of wealth that would ordinarily be theirs, so the requisitioning of daughters deprived vassals of at least one accepted means of forging mutually beneficial relationships with political peers. As with the "safeguarding" of sons, however, such an arrangement may not have been entirely without benefit to the vassal. The group tomb of three West Semitic wives of Thutmose III demonstrates that in certain cases even minor wives buried in undecorated tombs could be lavishly outfitted with jewelry, toiletries, and other items from Egypt's royal workshops that indicate that they enjoyed a sumptuous style of life.[70] Thus, a vassal might rest assured that his daughter would be honored in her new position. Likewise, if she found special favor with the pharaoh, the match would no doubt have been even more advantageous in that the vassal would now potentially have an especially intimate intercessor with his overlord, and one imagines that a sentimental attachment to a vassal's daughter would bode well for the political fortunes of her father. Likewise, any children born to a vassal's daughter—as children of the king—would occupy the highest strata of Egyptian society, even if it was decidedly unlikely that a vassal's grandson would ever ascend the throne.

This manner of filling out a royal harem and forging family ties between vassals and the king is, of course, commonplace in imperial contexts. Assyrian kings on campaign, for example, also demanded that in addition to their taxes vassals offer up their daughters (together with their dowries).[71] Where the Egyptians departed most radically from other imperial governments, however, was in their refusal to provide vassals (or even Great Kings) with daughters. Neither did they utilize royal sons as governors, as did the Hittites, for example, although there is ample evidence for the involvement of crown princes in the army during the Thutmosid and Ramesside periods.[72] This follows a general practice within Egypt and its territories, however, of not awarding royal princes positions from which they could accumulate a potentially dangerous regional power base. The office of the viceroy of Nubia, known as the king's son of Kush, for instance, was never filled by an actual son of the king, lest a prince's ambitions assume a royal scale. As will be explored below, a number of important parallels existed between the management of Egypt's state and its empire.

Convert Kings into Mayors

The system adopted by the Egyptians in Syria-Palestine was hegemonic, such that—with the exception of a few directly held bases and properties—the Egyptian government superimposed itself on pre-existing governing structures and primarily focused its attention on securing routes that connected strategic places and valuable resources. The administration of day-to-day civic affairs remained in the hands of local rulers.[73] The Egyptians evidently believed, as Machiavelli would articulate a couple of millennia later, that "a city used to living free may be held more easily by means of its own citizens than in any other mode, if one wants to preserve it."[74] Therefore, taxes were collected in much the same way as before (if not in the same amounts or for the same purposes), and the people of the governed region still dealt with their local rulers, rather than with Egyptian appointees.

For the rulers, however, the shift from independence to subordination brought profound changes. Thus, while they maintained their political positions, vassals were (officially at least) no longer free to forge their own political agendas. Likewise, when corresponding with the pharaoh, these men shed their status as kings (*šarru*) for that of mayors (*ḫazānūtu*), and the Egyptians seem to have endeavored to treat them as such.[75] This system mirrored that of large Near Eastern kingdoms, like Hatti or Ugarit, but it also shared fundamental similarities to the administrative structure of Egypt.[76]

As early as the late Middle Kingdom (c. 1870–1831), pharaohs had moved within Egypt to abolish the system of regional governors so as to ensure that each mayor dealt directly with the central government, rather than with an intermediary who might develop outsized ambitions. This same system was operative in Syria-Palestine, where the Egyptians were justifiably concerned that if their vassals were united into larger political units, they might present more formidable opposition. Like many other empires, Egypt appears to have found a low level of discord among its vassals reassuring. As Tacitus put it,

> Long, I pray, may foreign nations persist, if not in loving us, at least in hating one another; for destiny is driving our empire upon its appointed path, and fortunes can bestow on us no better gift than discord among our foes.[77]

Thus, each Canaanite "mayor" dealt directly with the king and also with his deputy—the district commissioner, an official who will be considered in greater depth in the following chapter. Likewise, if two neighboring regions had difficulties, they were directed to address their concerns to the pharaoh rather than to form coalitions against one another and to take up arms. Whether Egypt's vassals followed such directives, however, is another matter and one that will also be taken up in the next chapter.

Like Egyptian mayors, Syro-Palestinian rulers were expected to travel to the court for major state events or whenever the pharaoh saw fit to summon them with a letter stating "Enter and pay me homage."[78] If urgent business made it difficult for a vassal to attend personally, he was entitled to send a representative—ideally a brother. This was not the case, however, if a vassal's loyalty was suspect. Then, the pharaoh might compel him under force of arms to "visit" the Egyptian court and to stay as long as his presence was desired. Such was the case for the double-dealing ruler of Amurru, Aziru, as will be discussed in the subsequent chapter (EA 169, 170).

Even the responsibility of Egypt's vassals to provision traveling imperial functionaries seems to mirror a system that Thutmose III had implemented in Egypt proper. Following the Amarna period, the pharaoh Horemheb issued an edict intended to quell unrest by enacting a series of administrative reforms designed to curb abuses that had purportedly been allowed to run rampant in times past. The blame for most of the problems that Horemheb sought to reform was laid at the feet of Akhenaten and his successors, but there was one notable exception. Horemheb twice explicitly accused Thutmose III of instituting an "instance of dishonesty [about which] one [hears] in the land." According to the edict, royal agents had long made it a practice to "go after the local mayors, oppressing them and searching for [material] for the progress northwards and southwards [*lit.* downstream and upstream]." According to Horemheb,

> ...the [agents] of the royal quarters would approach the mayors saying, "Give [the] material for the journey which is lacking" ... [everything]

> which [*should be* at] the quay [*under the authority of the agents*] of the royal quarters; and one goes after [the] material [belonging to the mayors] and has them prepared by force.... This is [an instance of cravenness]![79]

The supplies stored by mayors for state business at Egypt's quays sound very much like the royal provisioning system envisioned by Thutmose III for Syria-Palestine and described above, whereby

> ...all the harbors were stocked with every good thing in accordance with their yearly custom (for) both [northward] and southward journeys, (with) the *bꜣkw* of Lebanon likewise, and the harvest of Djahy, consisting of grain, fresh oil, incense [wine and honey].[80]

Given that Thutmose III enjoyed a very positive posthumous reputation in Horemheb's day, it is unlikely that the system was unfairly attributed to him.

Other vassal *cum* mayoral duties have been discussed earlier in this chapter. These include supplying soldiers for pharaonic campaigns; for even though the army was on its way to being professionalized in the Eighteenth Dynasty, it still relied heavily on local levies managed by regional rulers.[81] As discussed above, the Syro-Palestinian vassals were also responsible for organizing contingents of laborers to serve on state building or farming projects, as were their Nile Valley counterparts.[82] Likewise, both mayors and vassals were responsible for ensuring the payment of taxes as well as for offering the pharaoh benevolences (*inw*). The deliveries of *inw* gifts catalogued for Syro-Palestinian vassals in the annals are paralleled by the delivery of special items by mayors and other high Egyptian officials on special occasions.[83] Given the degree to which vassal and mayoral offices overlapped in function, one might speculate that the lack of formal treaties between the pharaoh and his vassals was due to the fact that in Egypt oral oaths were deemed entirely sufficient to bind the king and his mayors. Syria-Palestine was *not* Egypt, however, and this inconvenient fact led to many of the problems that will be explored in the next two chapters.

Imperial Overview

The system that Thutmose III institutionalized and that his Eighteenth-Dynasty successors perpetuated was one that combined a variety of strategies. In its core territories, the empire was ruled indirectly through the co-option of local elites. Heirs to vassal thrones spent time at court during their formative years, while their sisters (and eventually daughters) were married to the king and incorporated into his harem. Once they ascended to positions of authority, these men officially foreswore any rights to act as independent agents and instead assumed the same basic functions as those of Egyptian mayors, meaning that they administered their territory, arranged for the payment of taxes, and subordinated their own political agendas to that of the pharaoh (at least in theory). That said, as was the policy of the Hittites, the Persians, the early Romans, the colonial English, and countless other imperial systems intent upon holding sway over large areas with small investments of manpower, the Egyptians abided by the philosophy that so long as a vassal acknowledged his submission and fulfilled his duties, he was free to govern his territory as he saw fit.[84]

Vassal compliance was overseen by Egyptian commissioners, who were generally situated in directly administered Egyptian military bases. These men will be discussed at greater length in the next chapter. The *real* guarantee of vassal compliance, however, was almost certainly the fact that during the campaign season the Egyptian army could reach these territories in a matter of weeks. Further, given the fact that the Egyptians seem to have forbidden conquered or newly settled cities from (re)erecting the type of elaborate fortifications typical of the region in the Middle Bronze Age,[85] an individual polity had very little chance of mounting an effective resistance against a campaign army of the size that Egypt was capable of mustering. Thus, so long as Canaanite vassals did not combine forces, as they had at Megiddo, and so long as the armies of another nation-state did not march southward, Egyptian dominance in the core of its empire faced no serious challenges.

Further to the north, in what is today southern Syria, Lebanon, and northern Israel, the Egyptians ruled with the help of client polities, namely city-states and small kingdoms that allied themselves with Egyptian interests and sent benevolences rather than regular taxes. Their independence from the crown meant that they by and large provided for their own security and in so doing buffered Egypt from having to guard fixed borders directly adjacent to the land of another Great King. As was the case also in Upper Nubia, these political clients were for the most part not obligated to send children to court or to supervise corvée labor—though they might agree to host an Egyptian garrison if they felt it advantageous.[86] While one cannot properly talk of Egyptian "control" in these regions, pharaonic armies could still potentially reach such polities either to help them or to harm them. Thus, as Edward Luttwak asserted with regard to the Roman empire, "Client-states and client tribes [*obeyed according to*] their perceptions of Roman military power and their fear of retaliation."[87] In that they were difficult to conquer and often located on the peripheries of other powerful kingdoms, clients had options. And if they chose to ally themselves with Egypt's enemies, instead of with Egypt, this represented a heavy blow.

Because of this potential freedom of movement, the rulers of client states served as political players in a way that Egypt's nearer neighbors did not. Thus, the Egyptians often found themselves adopting a much more conciliatory stance than they no doubt preferred, for fear of driving these clients to embrace the patronage of rival empires. The political machinations and routine subversions of authority practiced by Egypt's more coddled clients will be discussed in the following chapter. What is important to understand here is that in its early stages, Egypt's empire in Syria-Palestine relied on an economy of force. Thus, once Thutmose III's army had marched through the region enough times, the point no longer had to be made. Syro-Palestinian rulers assumed the costs and fuss of governance, while simultaneously extracting taxes for their overlords. Egyptian bases were co-opted from, supplied by, and even largely staffed with locals. As many early empires have discovered, such a system of "hegemonic," "indirect," or "parasitic" rule is arguably more cost-effective than it is truly effective. But that, again, is a discussion best saved for the following chapter.

Notes

1 Redford 1979, 273–4; see most recently Höflmayer 2015.
2 Gonen 1984, 63, 66, 68–9; Weinstein 1991.
3 Na'aman 1994, 183. For similar assessments, see Weinstein 1981, 2–5; Gonen 1992a, 216–17.
4 Lattimore 1962, 486.
5 Quoted in Baumer 2008, 84.
6 Spalding 1984, 109.
7 Flannery 1999.
8 See, for example, Beattie 1971, 138–9; Kuhrt 1995, 483; Trigger 2003, 109.
9 Galán 1994, 101 argues that troops continued to go forth each season and that this is not recorded because without the king's participation it was a routine matter and not a glorious one. The Amarna letters suggest, however, that by the late Eighteenth Dynasty large-scale troop movements occurred much more sporadically.
10 See, for example, the Ancient History Encyclopedia. https://www.ancient.eu/ Thutmose_III/, accessed January 7, 2018.
11 Breasted 1906b, 193.
12 Beaux 1990.
13 Sun Tzu, *Art of War*, chapter XIII, 1.
14 Lichtheim 1975, 20.
15 Redford 2003, 42.
16 Na'aman 1988, 182–3; Redford 2003, 43.
17 Na'aman 1981, 179.
18 Redford 2003, 72–3.
19 Redford 2003, 75, 89, 91, 96.
20 See Morris 2005, 138–9.
21 EA 294; Moran 1992, 337, n. 2.
22 Redford 2003, 121, 139.
23 See Morris 2015a, 171–82.

24 Davies 1994, 26.

25 Ahituv 1978, 96.

26 Redford 2003, 91; see similarly 75, 80, 89, 96.

27 Karmon 1956, 35–6.

28 Rib-Hadda of Byblos, for instance, advised the pharaoh to "[p]ut a man in each city and let him not allow a ship from the land of Amurru (to enter)" (EA 101; Moran 1992, 174).

29 D'Altroy and Earle 1985, 188; Smith 1991, 92–3.

30 Pedro de Cieza de León writing in 1551, quoted in D'Altroy 2003, 280.

31 D'Altroy 2003, 224.

32 Beckman 1995, 539.

33 Grayson 1995, 962; Kuhrt 1995, 690–1.

34 Weinstein 1998, 229.

35 Redford 2003, 31, 115.

36 Redford 2003, 180–1.

37 Morris 2005, 116, 137–8, 155–7.

38 Cumming 1984, 140; Morris 2015a, 175–81.

39 Morris 2005, 140–2, 269–72.

40 Alcock 1989, 92.

41 Morris 2005, 177–9, 293–310. If Killebrew et al. (2006) are correct in their redating of Deir el-Balah's stratum 9 to the Nineteenth Dynasty, the list of archaeologically attested Egyptian bases shrinks further.

42 Burke and Lords 2010, 14, 19, 25–6; Martin 2011, 265, 273. As noted, the dating of Deir el-Balah is disputed.

43 Martin 2011, 243–6, 265–6, 273.

44 EA 292; Moran 1992, 335.

45 EA 285; Moran 1992, 325.

46 Moran 1992, 147, 133, 155.

47 EA 160; Moran 1992, 246.

48 Morris 2005, 274.

49 Redford 2003, 34.

50 EA 324; Moran 1992, 352. See also EA 55, 226, 337, 367. Similar, if far more extravagant, directives were issued to Egyptian officials in preparation for a visit from the pharaoh within the Nile Valley (Caminos 1954, 198–201).

51 Albright 1944, 23–4.

52 Barfield 2001, 27.

53 Albright 1944, 24–5.

54 EA 96, 103, 289, 294; Horowitz 1996, 214–15.

55 EA 92; Moran 1992, 166. See also EA 100 where the pharaoh commanded the people of Irqata to win back territory conquered by the rulers of Amurru.

56 Sancisi-Weerdenburg 1995, 1046.

57 Redford 2003, 68–9.

58 Breasted 1906b, 50, 206.

59 Davies 1992, 4.

60 EA 296; Moran 1992, 338.

61 EA 286; Moran 1992, 326.

62 EA 156; Moran 1992, 242. In EA 59 the citizens of Tunip beg the pharaoh to send them the son of Aki-Teššup—a personage who was, presumably, the hostage-heir of the former ruler.

63 EA 270; Moran 1992, 316–17.

64 Bresciani 1997, 231–2.

65 Patterson 1991, 78–9.

66 Suetonius, *Divus Augustus*, no. 48.

67 Peden 1994, 13; Hölbl 2001, 213–14.

68 Redford 2003, 52.

69 EA 99; Moran 1992, 171.

70 Lilyquist 2003.

71 Kuhrt 1995, 485.

72 Gurney 1990, 16, 59–60.

73 The early Neo-Assyrian rulers devised a similar strategy (Bedford 2010, 42).

74 Machiavelli, *Prince*, ch. V, 20.

75 Redford 1990, 28–9; Higginbotham 2000, 18.

76 Gurney 1990, 61; Vita 1999, 474, 484.

77 Tacitus, *Germania*, 33. For a discussion of dividing and ruling, see Sinopoli 2001, 196, 198.

78 EA 283; Moran 1992, 323.

79 Murnane 1995, 237–8.

80 Redford 2003, 89.

81 Redford 1992, 215.

82 Redford 1990, 40.

83 Gordon 1983, 6–7, 174–6, 238, 330–1, 339; Redford 1990, 40–1; Morris 2005, 458–60; Bryan 2006, 99–100.

84 See Cromer 1910, 84–6; Goetze 1969, 211; Sancisi-Weerdenburg 1995, 1040; Elton 1996, 27.

85 Gonen 1992a, 218. For the strategic utility of demolishing the fortifications of a subdued foe, see Maigret 1747, 231–2.

86 Cumming, 1982, 34; Morris 2015a, 179–81.

87 Luttwak 1979, 19.

7

Outwitting the State (c. 1362–1332)

While the previous chapter focused on the establishment of Egypt's imperial infrastructure, this chapter regards the empire from the perspective of a variety of its northern subjects. Specifically, the chapter argues that although the city-states and semi-nomadic peoples of Syria-Palestine were unable to mount a successful military defense against Egypt's armies following their defeat at Megiddo, they nonetheless subverted and sabotaged imperial authority on a regular basis. As discussed below, strategies such as relocating to areas beyond the effective control of pharaonic forces, engaging in assassinations and acts of insurrection, enriching themselves at Egypt's expense, threatening defection, and employing disinformation so as to redirect imperial aggression to their own advantage proved remarkably effective. Political anthropologists refer to such tactics as "outwitting the state."[1]

Although identifying subversive activity in the distant past is difficult, three decades of political machinations and intrigue in Egypt's northern empire are brilliantly illuminated thanks to an archive of diplomatic correspondence discovered at the royal city of Amarna. Roughly 270 of these letters were written by or to Egypt's vassals during the latter portion of Amenhotep III's reign until the very beginning of Tutankhamun's (c. 1362–1332). Because different writers describe many of the same events, vassals can be caught in artful dissimulations and resident Egyptian officials in instances of corruption and incompetence. While the richness of this archive permits detailed insight into the strategies employed by disaffected subject populations over the course of three decades, these tactics were no doubt wielded throughout the four centuries of Egypt's rule and are, in fact, still practiced throughout the world today. Empires remain, after all, far easier to outwit than to oust.

Ancient Egyptian Imperialism, First Edition. Ellen Morris.
© 2018 Ellen Morris. Published 2018 by John Wiley & Sons Ltd.

Head for the Hills

Archaeological and textual evidence complement one another in suggesting that the Canaanite peasantry in the late Eighteenth Dynasty may have been stretched thin. Regional surveys indicate that Late Bronze Age Canaan never fully recovered from the series of catastrophic destructions that marked the end of the Middle Bronze Age. In the aftermath of this chaotic period, the number of settlements plummeted by 60–70%, and the archaeologically observable population dove from an estimated 140,000 or so people to only 60,000–70,000. Although Canaan exhibited limited signs of recovery by the late Eighteenth Dynasty, only 5% of its settlements exceeded 25 acres, while 37% occupied an area a tenth of that size or less[2] (see Figure 7.1).

In proportion to its mostly modest settlements, Canaan's tax burden may have been outsized. Thutmose III's annals (c. 1457–1425) regularly recorded the receipt of thousands of jars of oil (olive and moringa), thousands of jars of wine, hundreds of jars of incense, and hundreds of head of cattle, not to mention heaps of grain and tremendous quantities of wood. If such items continued to be regularly requisitioned in the late Eighteenth Dynasty, as seems certain, this would no doubt have had a profound effect on the local economy, whereby production would likely have been intensified to meet imperial demand. Yet, because a large percentage of the yield would simply be taken, not bought, the local people would see little return for their labor. The regular loss of hundreds of male and female "slaves" that Egypt requisitioned on an annual basis would also have had a profound impact on Canaan's labor supply and on its social fabric.[3]

Forced to support not only their own traditional palace-based elite but also to fill imperial storehouses in order to finance their own subjugation, Canaan's peasantry worked hard for little in return. Further, the Amarna letters reveal that Canaanite farmers were expected to tend their fields amidst armed attacks from neighboring polities and to surrender yet more of their surplus to help finance the seemingly unceasing series of low-level internecine wars fomented by their leaders. It is little wonder, then, that many of them appear to have decided to opt out.

The stresses placed on the peasantry at this time are illuminated in the letters of Rib-Hadda, the ruler of Byblos. Rib-Hadda claimed that incessant raids by the neighboring polity of Amurru—a political entity located in the mountains of Lebanon that will be discussed a great deal in this chapter—had dangerously depleted his grain supply. Because of the worsening food situation, Rib-Hadda anticipated an insurrection, telling an Egyptian general, "I am afraid the peasa[ntry] will strike m[e] down."[4]

According to his letters, the inhabitants of Byblos were angry at the lack of provisions and furious that their sons and daughters and even the furnishings of their houses had been sold to the Egyptians stationed at the base of Yarimuta to pay for the few provisions they did receive. The Byblites voiced

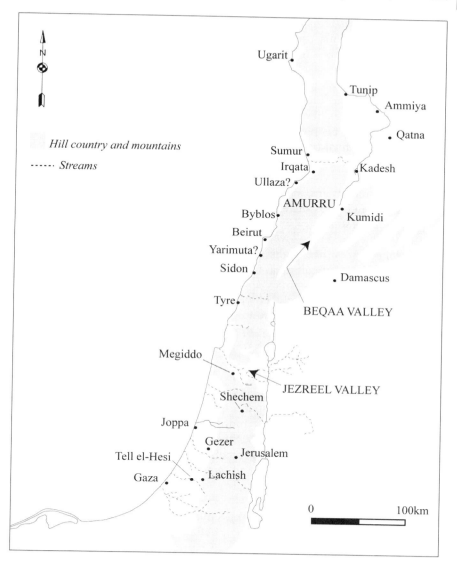

Figure 7.1 Sites mentioned in the chapter.

their complaints to their leader, saying "*Our* money is completely gone for the war."[5] Rib-Hadda then passed their concerns on to the pharaoh and flatly stated that because of this war, the attendant food shortage, and the heavy burden of taxes, the peasantry was no longer under his control, and many had "...gone off to towns where there is grain for their food."[6]

Oppression and attempts to escape oppression bear no geographic or temporal constraints. Thus, the words of a modern school teacher from Myanmar could likely have echoed those of a beleaguered Canaanite peasant in the Late Bronze Age:

> Along the road ... down in the plains, there used to be many villages, but the big villages have become small and the small villages have become forest. Many people have gone to the [other] towns or come up here [to the mountains] because the SPDC [military government] demands so many taxes from them and forces them to do all kinds of labor.[7]

Flight to the mountains was, evidently, also an option preferred by a great many resident in Byblos and elsewhere in Syria-Palestine who sought to escape the poverty, food shortages, armed attacks, and endless exploitative extractions they were subject to in the lowlands under pharaonic rule.

Mountains and other regions characterized by inimical terrain that is typically both very difficult for a state to penetrate and relatively bereft of easily appropriated natural resources and/or wealth have been variously termed nonstate spaces, zones of refuge, regions of resistance, outlaw corridors, and shatter zones—all terms designed to convey their utility to populations intent on evading state control. In the mountainous region of Southeastern Asia known as Zomia, a bewildering variety of individuals have found refuge. As James Scott describes it,

> Many of the people in the hills were, in all likelihood, valley peoples who long ago had fled state space. Others, however, were "state-making" valley peoples ... who lost to more powerful states and who scattered or moved together to the hills. Still others ... were the shards of valley states: deserting conscripts, rebels, defeated armies, ruined peasants, villagers fleeing epidemics and famine, escaped serfs and slaves, royal pretenders and their entourages, and religious dissidents.[8]

In the Late Bronze Age, the term for a similarly disparate assemblage of people—united not by ethnicity but by a defiant rootlessness that made their labor no doubt purposefully difficult to harness—was 'Apiru. Significantly, according to Rib-Hadda, those of his peasantry who did not flee to other towns deserted instead to the mountains that loomed just east of Byblos in order to join the 'Apiru and lend their might to the predatory polity of Amurru (EA 118).

The 'Apiru seem to have fallen into a category that still frustrates state administrators—that of having no fixed abode. Instead of tilling the soil or residing as long-term citizens of a particular city, the 'Apiru were freebooters, individuals who traveled wherever they could support themselves—sometimes by practicing a trade but most often as soldiers of fortune or as brigands.[9] The latter choice of livelihood makes sense given that bandits, like 'Apiru, tend to frequent mountainous regions and consist of opportunistic assemblages of young herdsmen, landless laborers, and ex-soldiers.[10]

Not surprisingly, the 'Apiru were distrusted by their settled counterparts, and to term someone an 'Apiru, or to accuse him of having consorted with them, was an insult. At the same time, however, the term often appeared as a mere descriptor. In the Amarna letters, for example, the ruler of Damascus responded to a command for auxiliaries from the pharaoh by stating,

> I am indeed, together with my troops and chariots, together with my brothers, my 'Apiru and my Suteans, at the disposition of the archers, wheresoever the king, my lord, shall order (me to go).[11]

Thus, the 'Apiru comprised a recognized, if oft-maligned, category of people. Their numbers, however, seem to have swelled during the Late Bronze Age as the life of a landless pariah in the employ of regional rulers—especially those who, like Aziru of Amurru, lived far beyond the easy reach of pharaonic forces—struck many as preferable to the lot they left behind.

Bled dry and furious, the people of Byblos, according to Rib-Hadda,

> ...moved against me, but I killed them. They said "How long can you go on killing us? Where will you get people to live in the city?" So I wrote to the palace for troops, but no troops were given < to > me. Then the city said, "Abandon him. Let's join Aziru!"[12]

The association of the 'Apiru with mountain warlords—men whose wealth and power came primarily through feats of arms rather than bountiful harvests or natural resources—was not limited to Amurru. The rulers of Shechem, too, drew upon 'Apiru to augment the troops they used to aggress their neighbors (EA 246, 254, 287, 289). Moreover, similar situations exist today. In the mountainous regions of Afghanistan, for example, clan-based polities still regularly boost their militias with refugees from recent wars against hated regimes.[13]

Heading to the hills on the part of the populace falls under a technique for outwitting the state termed simply "avoidance."[14] It should be stated, however, that vassals too could attempt this tactic. Aziru of Amurru took a literal approach, finding a convenient pretext for being away just as an irritated Egyptian ambassador came to visit (EA 161). Examples of evasive noncompliance, however, are far better attested. The rulers of Beirut and Sidon, for example, simply ignored requests by Egypt to throw their weight against Amurru—neither refusing to help nor actually helping. Rib-Hadda reported with indignation, "...the [mag]nate keeps writing [t]o them, but they pay n[o] attention to him."[15] As will be addressed shortly, however, Rib-Hadda himself was by far the most accomplished practitioner of yet a third evasive technique, the artful and endless excuse.

Kill Your Lords

Rib-Hadda not only saw much of his peasantry desert to the mountains to join the 'Apiru in the service of his enemies in Amurru, but he also accused the ruler of Amurru and his 'Apiru of taking their anti-imperialist stance further by directly fomenting rebellion against Egypt's vassals. Rib-Hadda reported that Aziru's father, 'Abdi-Aširta,

> ...said to the men of Ammiya, "Kill your *leader* and then you will be like us and at peace." They were won over, following his message, and they are like the 'Apiru.[16]

This turn of events, not surprisingly, greatly alarmed Egypt's vassals. Rib-Hadda reports in a different letter, "Accordingly, the mayors say, 'He will do the same thing to us, and all the lands will be joined to the 'Apiru.'"[17] Later he reported that 'Abdi-Aširta even incited rebellion among the men of Byblos, stating,

> "[Ki]ll your lord and be join[ed] to the 'Apiru like Amm[iya]." [And so] they became trait < ors > to me. A man with a bronze dagger [at]tacked m[e], but I ki[ll]ed him.... I was struck [9 ti]mes. [According]ly I f[ear for] my life."[18]

Thus, by modeling freedom by means of their escape to the hills, the 'Apiru managed to inspire egalitarian revolts against the empire and its vassals—even among those committed to remaining in the lowlands.

Play Imperial Powers off One Another

The earliest letters in the Amarna archive had been composed at a time when Egypt and the northern Syrian kingdom of Mitanni constituted each other's closest allies. Within a decade, however, the Hittite king Suppiluliuma II had begun a series of campaigns destined to destroy the kingdom of Mitanni and to devour much of its empire. In the face of these aggressive campaigns, many of Mitanni's vassals appealed to diplomatic ties with Egypt that had been established during Thutmose III's campaigns in the region roughly a century before (EA 47, 51, 55, 59). Following the peace established in the reign of Thutmose

III's son between Egypt and Mitanni (c. 1420), some of these vassals split their loyalties between the two allies, while others allowed their ties to Egypt to go dormant. Once these born-again vassals and would-be vassals—such as Ugarit, Qatna, Nukhasse, Tunip, and Kadesh—had a chance to contrast the strength and determination of the Hittite army with Egypt's own muted response, however, they swiftly allied themselves with Suppiluliuma.

Such abrupt changes of overlord were fully within the rights of vassals and could be announced with the simple statement "We were voluntary subjects. Now we are no longer your subjects."[19] Many of Egypt's Syrian vassals seem simply to have ceased sending messengers. The disloyalty of these polities was duly reported to the king by others (e.g. EA 98, 165), but in the meantime, as the Hittites might put it, the cattle had chosen their stable.[20] Some enterprising rulers, however, appear to have attempted to utilize their borderland status to their own advantage.

Perhaps the most egregious example of this tactic is witnessed in a letter from the ruler of Qatna which reported that the Hittite king had raided his territory, sending settlements up in flames. Then, directly following this alarming report, the vassal stated that the Hittite king had also captured a divine statue. Ostensibly because of this theft, the ruler of Qatna requested that the Egyptians send him "a *sack* of gold, just as much as is needed"[21] so that the statue could be refashioned. The amount of gold needed for this project had more to do, no doubt, with the price of Qatna's continued loyalty than it did with the size or composition of the statue. Given that on the same raid or a different one, the ruler of Kadesh had invited the ruler of Qatna to join the Hittite king (EA 53), the Egyptians would have known that in the face of their own inaction such offers would have become increasingly inviting and difficult to refuse.

The city of Irqata, whose leader had recently been assassinated by the 'Apiru agents of 'Abdi-Aširta (EA 75), was similarly poised to be drawn into the Hittite orbit. In view of the fact that the city had options when it came to overlords, the elders of Irqata felt free to request a gift from Egypt, stating, "May the king, our lord, heed the words of his loyal servants. May he grant a gift to his servant(s) so our enemies will see this and eat dirt."[22] Finally, a shipment of gold and silver that Aziru of Amurru received from Akhenaten may also have been a gift intended to secure the mountain warlord's loyalty, for it seems to have been confiscated by an Egyptian official following charges that Aziru had not only attacked the Egyptian base of Sumur under false pretenses (about which, more below) but that he had also entertained Hittite messengers in a much more sumptuous manner than he had received Egypt's envoys (EA 161).

The ambivalent loyalties of frontier peoples, who often profited from their liminal status and formed bonds with trading partners and confederates on both sides of a fractious political boundary, is well attested. For example, regarding the long period of Anglo-Scottish feuding, Thomas Sowell writes,

[T]he contested borderlands were not simply a region of battles between opposing armies during intermittent warfare, they were a continuously lawless frontier where feuding clans, marauders, vigilantes, and "protection" racket extortionists flourished. In short, these were not loyal followers of either English or Scottish kings, but freebooters who were said to be "Scottish when they will, and English at their pleasure."[23]

Such men had much in common with the inhabitants of the Lebanese mountains in the Late Bronze Age. When the inhabitants of a frontier zone organized into a state that served as a buffer between two polities, their position was further strengthened as, in the words of Edward Luttwak, "...[a] buffer state cannot be freely disciplined by one side or the other without provoking the intervention of the rival greater power."[24] Such an arrangement certainly worked to the advantage of the rulers of Amurru and explains the unusual latitude these rulers were given, even in the face of seemingly shocking acts against Egyptian property and personnel. What is known of Amurru perfectly illustrates Luttwak's point.

The Ambiguous Loyalties of the Buffer State of Amurru

As a mountain polity located at the far reaches of the Egyptian, Mitanni, and Hittite empires, Amurru was well positioned to play one imperial power off of another—and, indeed, it seems to have had a long tradition of doing so. ʿAbdi-Aširta, the ruler of Amurru at the time that the Amarna archives open, professed loyalty to both Egypt and Mitanni. Given that the two powers were officially allied and that the letters exchanged between their kings positively dripped with professions of fraternal love, this would not necessarily have been an issue. What lurked behind these officially expressed sentiments of brotherhood, however, may have been a good deal darker.

ʿAbdi-Aširta at one point attacked Egypt's base at Sumur, protesting after the fact that he had only intervened at the invitation of the base's inhabitants, as it was undefended and under threat by the troops of Sekhlal (EA 62). Sumur was vital to Egypt's strategic interests in the region, as it was not only a harbor town but also situated at the mouth of a pass inland toward Kadesh, features no doubt attractive to Mitanni as well. Certainly, Rib-Hadda of Byblos reported that the king of Mitanni had visited the base and had even intended to push south to Byblos (EA 85, 95). As Sumur and Byblos were both firmly "Egyptian" territories, the visit from the king of Mitanni—apparently unannounced in the monarch's honey-tongued letters to the pharaoh—was viewed by Rib-Hadda as a potentially aggressive gesture (EA 85, 95). ʿAbdi-Aširta's attack on Sumur, then, may well have had the implicit backing of Mitanni, especially as it seems that Mitanni forces had been attacking the settlements of other Egyptian vassals (EA 60).

Not surprisingly, the Egyptians were furious about the attack on Sumur, and yet they did not want to alienate the ruler of Amurru, driving him firmly into Mitanni's embrace. Relations between Mitanni and Amurru, however, were evidently also not easy. An incident in which 'Abdi-Aširta withheld tribute from Mitanni seems to have resulted in a punitive campaign (EA 86), his removal to the Mitanni capital (EA 90), and later, perhaps, even his death at the hands of Mitanni or of men from Amurru acting on Mitanni's behalf (EA 101, 124). It is telling, however, that the evidence for his death is seemingly conflicting, as different passages from the Amarna letters can be used to argue that it occurred due to an illness or even at the hands of the Egyptians, who seem at Rib-Hadda's urging to have finally sent an expedition to bring him back to Egypt for questioning (EA 108, 117). Finally, there are also suspicions that 'Abdi-Aširta, at the very end, may have collaborated with the Hittites, for this was the time that Suppiluliuma initiated the First Syrian War and quickly proved himself the region's most dangerous and dynamic ruler.[25] "Do not you yourself know that the land of Amurru follows the stronger party?"[26] Rib-Hadda once asked an Egyptian official. The question, of course, was rhetorical.

The fact that 'Abdi-Aširta cultivated such a complex web of relations seems incomprehensible, yet cross-culturally it is common. The mountainous region of Zomia serves as a comparative example:

> Many hill peoples and petty chieftaincies strategically manipulated the situation of dual sovereignty, quietly sending tributary missions to two overlords and representing themselves to their own tributaries as independent. Calculations of tribute were not an all or nothing affair, and the endless strategic choices of what to send, when to send it, when to delay, when to withhold manpower and supplies were at the very center of this petty statecraft…. [S]mall kingdoms were often identified as "under two lords" or "under three lords" in the Thai language.[27]

Powerful warlords in Afghanistan have frequently found themselves in similar situations, being courted separately by the Afghan central government, the Americans, and al-Qaeda—all suitors with deep pockets.[28] While this competing constellation of relationships brought headaches, it also, assuredly, could be quite lucrative. Thus, while the ruler of Amurru may have paid tribute to multiple overlords, the fact that his territory was difficult to conquer and control, yet extremely strategic, meant he also no doubt received subsidies in excess of whatever he paid out. This issue of subsidies will be returned to below.

Certainly, despite the evident dangers of playing such a high-stakes double (or triple) game, 'Abdi-Aširta's son Aziru continued in his father's footsteps. On the surface, he was the most dutiful of Egyptian vassals, sending regular letters and disbursements of tribute (see EA 157–8, 160–1). Behind the scenes, however, he and his brothers also attacked and conquered the Egyptian bases of Sumur and Ullaza as well as the towns of Egypt's vassals along the coast, in the Biqa' valley, and in southern Syria. These aggressive activities may have been undertaken at the urging of Suppiluliuma (EA 126). Indeed, the Hittite king had won over the ruler of Kadesh, who—despite paying lip-service to loyalty—had been lobbying the ruler of Qatna to throw in his forces with the Hittites (EA 53, 189). The ruler of Kadesh was also in close contact with Aziru, such that Akhenaten wrote angrily,

> Now the king has heard as follows "You are at peace with the ruler of Qidša. The two of you take food and strong drink together." And it is true. Why do you act so? Why are you at peace with a ruler with whom the king is fighting? And even if you did act loyally, you considered your own judgment, and his judgment did not count. You have paid no attention to the things you did earlier. What happened to you among them that you are not on the side of the king, your lord? Con[sider] the people that are [tr]aining you for their own advantage. They want to throw you into the fire. *They have lit (the fire)*, and (still) you love everything so very much!"[29]

From this letter, it appears that Aziru had been brought to the Hittite court, just as a few years later he would be hauled to Egypt for questioning. Tellingly, however, Aziru seems to have agreed to go to Egypt only after the government paid a sum of gold to his sons (EA 161, 169)! Likewise, despite being fully aware of the pharaoh's growing displeasure, Aziru felt secure enough to issue thinly veiled threats of his own. For instance, in one missive he followed an elaborate assertion of loyalty with this rhetorical question: "[*But i*]*f* the king, my lord, does not love me and rejects me, then what a[m] I to s[a]y?"[30]

As it turned out, Aziru did eventually pick a side and, as Suppiluliuma phrased it, "came from the gate of Egyptian territory, and knelt [down at the feet of My Majesty]."[31] Although both Aziru and his son and successor stayed loyal to the Hittites, the treaty with the latter included a personalized clause that read:

> You shall not turn your eyes to another. Your ancestors paid tribute to Egypt, [but] you [shall not pay it....] [If] you commit [...], and while the King of Egypt [is hostile to My Majesty you] secretly [send] your messenger to him, [or you become hostile] to the King of Hatti [and cast] off the authority of the King of Hatti, becoming a subject of the King of Egypt, you, Tuppi-Teshshup, will transgress the oath.[32]

While the Hittites did not need to worry about Tuppi-Teshshup's loyalty, this ruler's grandson would renounce Hittite sovereignty to defect to the Egyptians, only to come running back after a defeat in battle and the promise of a pardon.[33] Thus, for those vassals who could play one overlord against another, this constituted a significant source of power—just so long as their overlords abided by the same principle as Rome—namely, that when it came to strategically located, hard-to-discipline vassals, forsworn transgressions were best forgiven.[34]

Engage in Creative Fundraising

For a polity such as Amurru, which was located in mountainous terrain that was relatively resource-poor and largely inhabited by people who had abandoned or rejected the life of the farmer, agriculture could not be relied upon to provide a comfortable standard of living, let alone enough funds to pay tribute to multiple "overlords," even if this tribute was relatively modest.[35] The rulers of Amurru and their counterparts elsewhere in Egypt's empire, however, appear to have been masters at the art of creative fundraising. Some of their more important sources of income included plunder, subsidies, banditry, and ransom.

During the three decades or so covered by the Amarna archive, the rulers of Amurru were engaged in aggression against a whole series of polities including Irqata, Ardata, Ammiya, Shigata, Bit-Arha, Batruna, Eldata, Ullaza, Sumur, Tunip, Damascus, Qatna, Amki, and Niy (see EA 55, 59, 73–6, 79, 81, 83, 87–91, 100, 102–5, 109, 139–40, 151, 161, 197). Further, they seem to have leveraged these victories to make advantageous alliances with Beirut, Sidon, Tyre, Arwada, Ampi, Ibirta, Wahliya, Ugarit, and eventually even Amurru's traditional arch-enemy Byblos (see EA 67, 83, 85, 98, 102–6, 118). Although the location of some of these polities is unknown, a great many were situated along the Lebanese coast. Conquering Egypt's harbor depots and garrisons at Sumur and Ullaza, although necessitating the manufacture of creative excuses, provided Amurru with access to Egyptian grain stores and supply depots. Further, these and other conquests secured Amurru the funds to pay tribute to Egypt. As Rib-Hadda's successor in Byblos would caution the pharaoh,

> The king is to take < n > o account of whatever Aziru sends him. *Where* were the things that he sends *coveted*? It is property belonging to a royal mayor whom he has killed that he sends to you.[36]

Perhaps not coincidentally, the similarly seditious and belligerent rulers of the mountain-based polities of Shechem and Jerusalem were also especially diligent in supplying Egypt with tribute (EA 254, 287–8).

In addition to stockpiling stores of grain, harbors typically benefited from the lively eastern Mediterranean trade circuit, and so attacks on harbors would likely net Amurru exotic items as well as access to local specialties such as incense, wine, and oil that had been stored for trade. Likewise, as the new overlord of these towns, Amurru would almost assuredly be in a position to demand a cut of harbor fees and taxes. Finally, a domination of harbor towns gave the rulers of Amurru access to sea power, such that during the reign of Aziru, Amurru could rely on the ships of Arwada to provide a blockade of Sumur (EA 98, 105). By commanding both land and sea, Amurru made itself such a formidable force that Rib-Hadda compared the scope of Amurrite ambitions to those of the Great Kings of Mitanni, Hatti, and Babylon (EA 104, 116).

Plunder and steady revenue from conquered and subject territories no doubt netted the rulers of Amurru a healthy income with which to support their followers and enhance their prestige. A plea sent by Rib-Hadda to Amenhotep III, after ʿAbdi-Aširta's attacks had divested him of all his dependent cities and the good will of his peasantry, sheds light on yet another source of income. Rib-Hadda wrote that ʿAbdi-Aširta

> ...has attacked me (and) my orchards.... I have been plundered of my [grain]. [May] you pay a thousand (*shekels of*) silver and 100 (*shekels* of) gold, so he will go away [fr]om me.[37]

Now, if the Egyptians took Rib-Hadda up on his suggestion, then by doing nothing more than *stopping* their attacks, the Amurrites would have netted themselves over a third of the yearly tribute that they would later owe the Hittites. And opportunities for raising revenue did not end there. Ironically, once ʿAbdi-Aširta's son Aziru did manage to help engineer the coup that deprived Rib-Hadda of his control over Byblos, the former ruler seems to have written to Aziru with the message, "Take me to yourself and get me into my city,"[38] a plea that no doubt implied the payment of a substantial reward for services rendered.

The payment of subsidies in order to dissuade chronic raiders—men who like the soldiers of Amurru often were highly mobile, relatively poor, and inhabited regions that were difficult to conquer—is a solution that even the most powerful empires adopted in order to resolve an otherwise intractable problem. As Thomas Barfield puts it,

> ...frontier warfare was economically more disruptive for the Chinese than for the nomads. It drained the treasury and strained the peasantry with ever increasing demands for taxes and for soldiers. For the nomads war was cheap. Steppe households were always prepared to provide horses, weapons, and supplies on short notice, and the loot collected in China repaid this investment many times over.... [A]ggressive military campaigns ... were far more expensive than simply paying the nomads to stay away.[39]

The Persians and the Romans too did not balk at paying subsidies to nomadic groups and tribes that they preferred not to fight on a continual basis.[40] Thus, it is likely that Egypt's vassals often did resort to paying protection money or asking Egypt to do so. Not surprisingly, such expenses would not have been bragged about in any official inscriptions, but the "gifts" received would no doubt have fattened the coffers of predatory polities.[41]

Amurru may have practiced similar types of extortion with regard to ensuring safe passage along various mountain corridors, as these were notorious sites for ambushes. At its height, Amurru would have been in a position to dominate both the pass that led from Sumur to Kadesh and the Beqaa Valley corridor through which many royal caravans likely passed. Letters sent by the king of Babylon to Akhenaten indicate that caravan raiding certainly did occur (EA 7–8). Likewise, an incomplete letter from an unknown vassal reported that 13 merchants of Egypt were "struck down in the attack of the 'Apiru."[42] Given the lavish inventories of gifts that accompanied diplomatic correspondence, the regular caravans of vassal tribute, and the cargo of merchants, one can imagine that polities such as Amurru may have netted a healthy income from banditry, from "protecting" others from bandits, and from the installation of highway checkpoints and tolls.

While other strategies no doubt deserve discussion, the final fundraising scheme to be considered here is the kidnapping of enemy soldiers, travelers, and other vulnerable individuals. The ruler of Qatna, for example, wrote to Akhenaten stating that

> ...Aziru took men of Qatna, my servants, and has le[d] *them away* out of the country of my lord. They now d[wel]l outside the country of my lord. If it ple[ases] him, may my lord send [(*the ransom) money*] for the men of Qatna, and may my lord ransom them.[43]

Not surprisingly, citizens of Byblos were also kidnapped and held for ransom. Given that the going rate was 50 shekels of silver per individual, enterprising kidnappers could make a fortune. Rib-Hadda, for instance, reported that some Byblite families had been financially ruined, "...having paid ransom money, some twice, some three times."[44] Likewise, even if ransom went unpaid, the victim could be sold into slavery up north in the land of Subaru (EA 108–9, 114). The Amurrite penchant for kidnapping seems indeed to have been so well known that when the Hittites did finally draft a treaty with Aziru, they took care to insert a clause that made their new vassal personally responsible for ransoming any Hittite citizen kidnapped in his realm.[45] Entering into this relationship with eyes wide open, the Hittites evidently had no wish to foot the bill for any of Aziru's extra-curricular revenue-raising activities.

Employ Disinformation

The leeway that vassals enjoyed in Late Bronze Age Syria-Palestine to hoodwink the imperial government was possible in large part because the Egyptians preferred indirect rule. They did, of course, have islands of direct control, bases like Gaza and Joppa that they placed under the authority of pharaonic officials. Nowhere in their northern empire during the Eighteenth Dynasty, however, did they import Egyptian colonists or even keep a suite of high officials who resided at the base permanently and thus might have some sense of the subtleties of local power dynamics. Likewise, as discussed in the last chapter, the troops that the Egyptians employed to garrison their bases were in many cases Syro-Palestinian, a heritage these soldiers often shared with their commanding officers, judging from the names of these men and/or those of their parents. While all of these officers were "Egyptian" in that they worked *for* Egypt, the imperial government was nonetheless reliant for its understanding of the dynamics operative in their empire on the reports given by individuals who may well have had vested interests in practicing disinformation.

Because the letters cached in the Amarna archive involved so many different correspondents, they offer a unique opportunity to access cases in which the words of a vassal did not match up to his deeds. The rulers of Amurru, of course, raised specters of Hurrian or Hittite aggression at the same time as they were actively in league with these kingdoms (EA 60, 157, 164–7). Likewise, it is no doubt telling that they repeatedly peppered their letters with statements urging the king and his officials to ignore the words of treacherous men who spread lies about their activities (EA 62, 158–61, 165). Of all the "treacherous men," Rib-Hadda of Byblos no doubt figured most prominently, given his enthusiasm for copiously detailing the misdeeds of his rivals. What is less recognized, however, is the degree to which Rib-Hadda himself enthusiastically engaged in the art of disinformation.

Rib-Hadda of Byblos, the self-proclaimed blameless and ever-imperiled victim of wrongdoing, wrote more than 60 letters to the pharaoh and pharaonic officials, a number that even the pharaoh found excessive (EA 106, 117, 124). This was, from what we can tell, six times the quantity sent by the second most prolific letter writer. Rib-Hadda's missives are crammed with information concerning the supposedly nefarious activities of those vassals he considered enemies or competitors. On the surface, there was nothing wrong with this seemingly endless torrent of letters. One of the duties of a faithful vassal was to "[w]rite whatever you hear to the king,"[46] in order to keep him informed about potentially seditious activities of neighbors and rival Great Kings. Further, although the Egyptians seem not to have drafted the same type of detailed treaties favored by the Hittites, it was understood by Egypt's vassals that their overlord had an obligation to assist them if they found themselves aggressed. Rib-Hadda, for example, bluntly stated to an Egyptian general named Amanappa, who had formerly operated out of Sumur, "the (legal) violence done to me is your responsibility, if you neglect me."[47]

Where Rib-Hadda's good faith becomes suspect, however, is that in the 62 letters that survive in a reasonably well-preserved state, Rib-Hadda makes approximately 27 requests for personnel and goods from the Egyptians and a further 37 requests for troops. On the other hand, he sent goods or military aid to the Egyptians only four times and offered 11 excuses for why he could not fulfill requests that were made of him. This is in contrast to his enemies in Amurru, who, as stated earlier, seem to have been much more conscientious about providing the Egyptians with "gifts." According to Rib-Hadda, the aggression of Amurru prevented him from providing boxwood (EA 126). He could not give Egypt copper or sinnu, since he'd already paid his stores to the ruler of Tyre for his protection (EA 77), and for a whole host of reasons he could neither help defend the beleaguered Egyptian base at Sumur (EA 96, 102, 104–7, 109) nor could he harbor its refugees (EA 106).

Rib-Hadda's correspondence with the general Amanappa is telling for it reveals that Rib-Hadda *had* options. The ruler of Byblos writes,

> You ordered me again and again, "Send your man to me at the palace, and as soon as the request arrives, I will send him along with an auxiliary force, until the archers come out, to protect your life." But I told you, "I am unable to send < him>".... You ordered me again and again, "Send a ship to the land of Yarimuta so silver and clothing *can get out* to you from them." All the men whom you gave me have run off.[48]

So, by his own admission, Rib-Hadda had indeed received help and offers of more help. Yet from the Egyptian point of view their assistance was neither properly taken advantage of, nor properly acknowledged. Nor was it reciprocated. In two other letters, no doubt further weakening his credibility, Rib-Hadda sought to convince the Egyptians that even though Yankhamu—the Egyptian official stationed at the pharaonic base of Yarimuta—swore that he had given Rib-Hadda grain, he actually hadn't (EA 85–6).

It was likewise telling that while Rib-Hadda complained constantly about the dire state of his finances, once a palace coup removed him from office, he urged the pharaoh to send troops to conquer Byblos—adding, by way of enticement, "Note, there is much silver and gold in it, and much is the property belonging to its temples."[49] He likewise tempted the Egyptians with the great riches of Tyre in order to convince them to interfere in the affairs of a ruler he did not approve of (EA 89). Moreover, the virulence of Rib-Hadda's accusations against the ruler of Beirut was also suspicious, as it is likely that it had more to do with a lawsuit in which the two men were embroiled than with any treasonous activity that might or might not have transpired (EA 83, 85, 105, 113, 116–17, 119–20).

Despite the fact that the ruler of Byblos cautioned the pharaoh that he "... must not inquire about me from my enemies"[50] (who apparently included his own countrymen, other vassals, Egyptian officials, and Egyptian soldiers), this advice was ignored. Thus, Rib-Hadda was forced to defend himself from charges that he had led the Egyptians into a trap (EA 94) and also that he had sold their soldiers into slavery in Subaru (EA 108–9). Notably, Rib-Hadda's refusal to allow refugees from Sumur into Byblos was met with a strong rebuke from an Egyptian general, who saw fit to wonder what the pharaoh would think upon hearing of it (EA 96). Such speculation is unnecessary, however, with respect to yet another of his letters, the contents of which prompted the pharaoh to ask Rib-Hadda how it was that he could be responsible for such treacherous words (EA 117).

By Rib-Hadda's own admission, not a soul came forth to attest to his loyalty before the pharaoh (EA 119). Thus, the conclusion appears inescapable that although Rib-Hadda presented himself in his correspondence as the most victimized of vassals, in reality he was a skilled manipulator. Like the Afghan warlord who utilized the cell phone given to him by the Americans to report as al-Qaeda agents all those with whom he had personal feuds,[51] Rib-Hadda habitually and enthusiastically attempted to employ the might of the empire to his own ends. That said—his fellow vassals, no doubt, did much the same.

Influence, Impugn, or Assassinate Imperial Functionaries

The Egyptian government knew that it was in the best interests of their vassals to amplify threats they faced, to slander their rivals, to present seditious activity as being in reality undertaken for the good of the empire, etc.[52] To help wade through this morass of disinformation, the government relied on a class of functionary designated in the Amarna letters as commissioners (*rabisu*, literally a watcher or an observer[53]). These men, who typically held the position of troop commander (*ḫry pḏt*), were not generally permanent governors stationed at specific bases. Instead, they and their troops typically resided at bases located along the coast and associated with imperial storehouses, such as Gaza, Joppa, Yarimuta, and Sumur. From these headquarters, however, commissioners could be sent out to nearby towns (such as Kumidu, Lachish, Gezer, Megiddo, Tell el-Hesi, or even Jerusalem) on an as-needed basis.[54] Some commissioners seemed to specialize in certain regions (typically southern Canaan and the hill country or else southern Syria and Lebanon), while others, like Yankhamu and Pawuru, were transferred between regions. The many postings, the relatively short periods in residence at bases, and the frequent trips back to court were likely devices designed by the imperial government to help guard against the formation of "comfortable arrangements" between their watchers and their vassals.

Certainly, there would have been an extremely strong incentive for vassals to attempt to exercise undue influence on their local commissioner through bribes or threats, just as there would have been a strong incentive for the commissioners to accept these bribes, to capitulate before the threats, and/or to practice their own brand of extortion. Akhenaten, for example, bragged that he was

> ...laying [a charge on...] ...[the custodians (?)] of copper [and] genuine [...], the commanders of hosts, cavalry commanders, king's scribe<s>, commanders of the army, commanders of all the troops of every foreign country.... Pharaoh ... ordains that all the officials and the chief men of the entire land be obliged to give him silver, gold, [cattle], clothing and copper vessels—they being imposed ... like taxes.[55]

Thus, it was not only vassals that felt the pressure to squeeze their subjects for income to send to the crown. Commissioners too needed to extract funds on a regular basis.

Such pressure may have driven representatives of the empire to unorthodox methods of fundraising. The ruler of Gezer, for instance, accused the commissioner Yankhamu of shaking him down for 2,000 shekels of silver (EA 270). Another ruler of Gezer was harassed by Peya son of Gulatu—a man with an Egyptian name, though his father's name was Semitic—who may well have been an Egyptian official stationed at Joppa. Peya is accused not only of requisitioning men that the ruler of Gezer had sent to guard the granary at Joppa (EA 294) but also of holding men and demanding ransom at exorbitant rates. Indeed, the ruler complained that "[p]eople are ransomed from the mountains for 30 shekels of silver, but from Peya for 100 shekels."[56] Other corrupt or rogue Egyptian officials may perhaps be visible in the instances in which Egypt's enemies bore Egyptian names (EA 62, 186).

An examination of the history of the commissioners stationed at the everimperiled base of Sumur, as gleaned primarily through the intensely biased letters of the rulers of Amurru and Byblos, will serve to illustrate the complications of relying on such men to serve as the counterparts to vassals. In the reign of Amenhotep III, the former commissioner of Sumur, a general named Amanappa, resided in Egypt, though he still corresponded with Rib-Hadda, who continued to ask for his military aid and his help intervening with the king (EA 73–4, 82, 86–7, 93), a tactic that on occasion did work (EA 79, 108–9, 117). At the opening of the archive, however, the base at Sumur was the seat of a commissioner named Pakhamnate. 'Abdi-Aširta attacked the base (ostensibly for its own protection) during a period when the commissioner and much of the garrison appear to have been temporarily off base, perhaps investigating recent Hittite incursions (EA 60, 62).

According to 'Abdi-Aširta, he and Pakhamnate had previously enjoyed an amicable, cooperative relationship (EA 60), indirectly indicated also by Rib-Hadda's intense dislike of the commissioner (EA 131–32). But when Pakhamnate returned to find the base in ruins—25 of its remaining inhabitants dead and the other four fled—he was furious and sent a scathing letter to ʿAbdi-Aširta accusing him of being an enemy of Egypt (EA 62). This event seems to have spurred Sumur's former general and commissioner Amanappa to make a special trip to Amurru in order to capture ʿAbdi-Aširta and bring him to Egypt, where he could account for his actions. Pakhamnate then regained control of Sumur (EA 68), although he held the base for only a short time and may even have been murdered when ʿAbdi-Aširta's sons attempted to reconquer it (EA 106).

Pakhamnate's successor was his son, a man named Haʾip, who if he wasn't raised at Sumur probably spent a good amount of time there. Given his first-hand experience with Amurru's might, he found it advisable to collaborate closely with the sons of ʿAbdi-Aširta, a decision that, not surprisingly, infuriated Rib-Hadda. On this basis, Rib-Hadda strongly suggested that Haʾip should be brought to Egypt for questioning, which it appears he may have been (EA 107). While Haʾip was in Egypt, however, he was replaced by a commissioner named Pawuru. This man had been transferred from Gaza, where he had been deeply embroiled in the small wars plaguing the hill country—thus he would presumably have been familiar with the independent agendas of mountain warlords and their ʿApiru (EA 263, 287, 289). Pawuru should have kept the dangers of crossing such men in mind, however, for he appears not to have collaborated with ʿAbdi-Aširta's son Aziru, despite the latter's initial hopes that he would prove pliable (EA 171). Faced with a potentially hostile government agent in what he considered to be his territory, Aziru took matters into his own hands and had Pawuru assassinated. Further, in order to send a strong message to the imperialists who dared interfere in his affairs, Aziru purportedly engaged in an act of terrorism specifically tailored to play upon Egyptian anxieties concerning the afterlife. Pawuru's corpse was cast out to the elements without embalming, prayers, or funerary rites (EA 124, 129, 131). Perhaps it is no surprise, then, that upon being reinstated at Sumur, Haʾip promptly surrendered the base to Aziru to manage as he saw fit (EA 132, 149).

The murder of uncooperative governors is an extreme tactic but perhaps worth the risk for vassals, such as the rulers of Amurru, who felt secure enough in their zones of refuge and in their relationships with competing overlords to send such strong messages. Aziru, for instance, does not appear to have been sanctioned after the murder of Pawuru, despite the brazenness of this attack. So, given the prompt surrender of Haʾip, the assassination seems to have had its intended effect. Other warlords have tried this technique as well. Padsha Khan Zadran of Afghanistan, for example, refused to recognize governors sent by the central government to provinces he considered under his control. Like the rulers of Amurru, he occupied government buildings himself, although he did for a time allow a governor to situate himself in his guesthouse. About this man, however, he scoffed, "He sits in a room and is afraid to come out. He is not acting as governor. All matters are controlled by me." Zadran regarded president

Hamid Karzai, the nominal ruler of Afghanistan, with similar disdain, stating, "He appoints one governor in the morning and another in the evening. I wish he would come fight me. He can find me in my barracks."[57] The mysterious death of one governor, who perhaps refused to sit quietly in a guesthouse, suggests that if intimidation alone failed, Zadran, like Aziru, did not hesitate to assassinate those governors that would presume to govern him.[58] Considering the anti-government stance of Aziru and Zadran, it is perhaps ironic that part of the goal in assassinating their governors may have been to take over their duties (and the perks that came therewith).

Collaborate for Cash

It is seemingly counterintuitive that, while most vassals desired the freedom to act in their own interests, many nonetheless implored the imperial government to send them a commissioner and/or troops. The motivation for requesting troops is obvious, as it brought state muscle to bear on local contests. A vassal that requested and was granted troops could flaunt his favor before his rivals. Moreover, all would appreciate that consequences for attacks on his town had just skyrocketed, for dead Egyptians were far more likely to occasion a significant armed reprisal than Canaanite casualties.

Perhaps as important as the presence of troops, however, was the store of supplies granted to vassals who hosted Egyptian garrisons. ʿAbdi-Aširta and Aziru both appear to have lobbied for and received Egyptian troops and to have had, therefore, access to Egyptian grain as well as to payments of silver and gold (EA 70, 82, 122, 126, 161). Such arrangements resemble those offered by the Americans to Afghan warlords, which generally involved the disbursement of a great deal of money to the warlord and to his followers. The Afghans have even formulated an adage concerning their proven willingness to fight for those that pay and to switch their loyalties if a better offer arises: "No one can own us," they say. "They can only hire us."[59]

References in the Amarna archive indicate that horses, chariots, oil, clothing, and other provisions were likewise granted to mayors who allowed Egyptian garrisons on their territory and provided auxiliaries for their army (EA 70, 74, 76, 79, 85–6, 100, 112, 125–6, 130, 137–8, 152, 161, 263, 287). Rib-Hadda liked to remind the pharaoh that "…in the days of my ancestors, there was a garrison of the king with them and property of the king was at their disposal."[60] The mayor of Byblos desperately wanted to resume this arrangement during the decades that he wrote to the pharaoh with such pleas as "May [yo]u put me in Yankhamu's charge so he will give me grain to eat th < at > I may guard for him the king's city."[61] But such requests seem not to have been granted, and any grain Rib-Hadda received from Yankhamu, he had to pay for (EA 85). While one could, like ʿAbdi-Aširta, simply seize a pharaonic granary, the state would not then refill it, and the vassal would be in danger. If the vassal guarded the granary on *behalf* of the king, however, the grain became a renewable resource. It is thus quite likely that Aziru arranged with Ha'ip to serve as the administratively authorized guardian of the Egyptian storehouse in return for a promise not to hand the entire base over to the Hittites.

The rulers of Amurru, like other privileged vassals, were already experienced at acting as proxies for the commissioners when the latter were away on business. Indeed, one of Rib-Hadda's main bones of contention was that when Yankhamu, the commissioner stationed (mostly) at Yarimuta, was away from base, it was the ruler of Beirut who both dispensed pharaonic grain supplies and collected payment from vassals like Rib-Hadda who did not receive it for free (EA 85). When the ruler of Beirut then turned actively hostile toward Rib-Hadda, this proved extremely unfortunate. Indeed, the ruler of Byblos was then in a very bad position, because the surrogate for the commissioner at Sumur (the other store of Egyptian grain located in close proximity to Byblos) was none other than his arch-enemy 'Abdi-Aširta. The latter wrote to the king,

> [*Look*], there is [Pa]khanate, [my] commissioner. May the king, the [Su]n, ask him if I do not guard Sumur and Ullassa. When my commissioner is on a mission of the king, the Sun, then I am the one who guards the harvest of the grain of Sumur and all the lands for the king, my Sun, my lord.[62]

This clearly was Rib-Hadda's worst nightmare.

One way of outwitting the state, then, was to play an important role in it. If a vassal had the ear of the king and the support (however it may have been gained) of the nearby commissioner, then he was effectively placed on Egypt's payroll and granted pharaonic tools with which to intimidate his rivals and gain more power for himself. So long as a vassal kept his commissioner happy (or at least quiet), so long as he used some of his booty to provide Egypt with tribute, and so long as his loyalty remained strictly optional due to the presence of other nearby powers, it seems that imperial tolerance ran much higher than one would expect. Not all of Egypt's vassals were so lucky, but indirect rule afforded local leaders a good deal of room to play the system and to use it to their own advantage. The ruler of Akko, for example, received more attention from the pharaoh than did Rib-Hadda (EA 88), yet he was accused both of attacking caravans (EA 8) and of accepting a (no doubt exorbitant) ransom for a prisoner rather than delivering him to the Egyptians, as he was supposed to do (EA 245). Thus, if both crime and collaboration paid, how much more lucrative was it to engage in the two together? Given all this, it may be no accident that some of the richest burials, palaces, and temples of the Late Bronze Age occurred at precisely this period and precisely in those areas deemed most crucial to the Egyptian government.[63]

Notes

1 Skalník 1989.
2 Gonen 1984, 63–8; Finkelstein 1988, 341.
3 Ahituv 1978; Na'aman 1981; Redford 1990, 40–51.
4 EA 77; Moran 1992, 148; see similarly EA 130.
5 EA 138; Moran 1992, 222; see also EA 74–5, 81, 85.
6 EA 125; Moran 1992, 204–5.
7 Quoted in Scott 2009, 94–5.
8 Scott 2009, 144.
9 Greenberg 1955.
10 Hobsbawm 2000, 39.
11 EA 195; Moran 1992, 273.
12 EA 138; Moran 1992, 222.
13 Morris 2010b.
14 Skalník 1989, 11.
15 EA 103; Moran 1992, 176.
16 EA 74; Moran 1992, 143.
17 EA 73; Moran 1992, 141–2; see similarly EA 74.
18 EA 81; Moran 1992, 150.
19 Beckman 1996, 99.
20 Gurney 1990, 64.
21 EA 55; Moran 1992, 128.
22 EA 100; Moran 1992, 172.
23 Sowell 1998, 52, 54–5.
24 Luttwak 1979, 116.
25 Altman 1979; Schulman 1988, 60–1, 78, n. 119.
26 EA 73; Moran 1992, 141.
27 Scott 2009, 60–1.
28 Morris 2010b, 424–5.
29 EA 162; Moran 1992, 249.
30 EA 158; Moran 1992, 244.
31 Beckman 1996, 33.
32 Beckman 1996, 56.
33 Beckman 1996, 95–8.
34 Luttwak 1979, 30.
35 When Aziru finally committed to Hatti, Amurru's tribute was 300 shekels of gold annually. This was not a huge sum, as tributes go, but as there was no gold in the hills, revenues still had to be raised (Beckman 1996, 33).
36 EA 139; Moran 1992, 225.
37 EA 91; Moran 1992, 165.
38 EA 162; Moran 1992, 248.
39 Barfield 2001, 17.

40 Luttwak 1979, 33, 37, 115–16; Kuhrt 1995, 689–90; Wells 1999, 229.

41 Lattimore 1979, 38–9 points out that the Chinese disguised the true nature of their payments as "gifts" given in return for (much less valuable) "tribute."

42 EA 313; Moran 1992, 346.

43 EA 55; Moran 1992, 127.

44 EA 116; Moran 1992, 191.

45 Beckman 1996, 34.

46 EA 149; Moran 1992, 236; see similarly EA 151.

47 EA 82; Moran 1992, 152. In a similar vein, the ruler of Tyre states, "Since I gua[rd the ci]ty of the king, [my] lo[rd], *m*[*y*] *s*[*afety*] is the king's *responsibility*" (EA 153; Moran 1992, 240).

48 EA 82; Moran 1992, 152.

49 EA 137; Moran 1992, 218.

50 EA 102; Moran 1992, 175.

51 Seierstad 2004, 244–5.

52 The relative scarcity of destruction levels in cities of this era is one indication that the magnitude of the threats may have been exaggerated for effect (Several 1972, 128).

53 Goetze 1980, 2.

54 Morris 2005, 254–6.

55 Murnane 1995, 193.

56 EA 292; Moran 1992, 335.

57 Both quotes are found in Bearak 2002.

58 Morris 2010b, 426.

59 Bearack 2002; Seierstad 2004, 246.

60 EA 122; Moran 1992, 201; see similarly, EA 125–6, 130.

61 EA 83; Moran 1992, 153.

62 EA 60; Moran 1992, 132.

63 Bienkowski 1989.

8

Conversions and Contractions in Egypt's Northern Empire (c. 1295–1136)

Long-lived empires go through many stages, regularly reconfiguring their policies and tactics in response to shifting internal priorities and to changes in the political structure and outlook of those they govern. These last two chapters will trace the twin themes of conversion and contraction with respect to Egypt's northern and southern empires in the Nineteenth and Twentieth Dynasties. As shall be seen, over the course of the last two centuries of Egypt's empire, the dialogic relationship between imperial policies and local response transformed the character of these two dominated regions until they bore little resemblance to the places they'd been during the empire's infancy.

Specifically, this chapter looks at the manner in which post-Amarna pharaohs attempted to reform their empire in order to more aggressively assert their control over its core and to solve some of the problems that Egypt's former policy of minimal investment had occasioned for the proper functioning of government. As will be seen, Egypt invested in its cross-desert highways so as to improve the flow of people and information between the government and its subject territories. The imperial administration also increased its investment in bases, bringing more and more under direct rule, in apparent recognition of the fact that such installations served a wide variety of functions. This chapter addresses Egypt's efforts to intensify its material investment in the heart of its northern empire, and it explores the divergent manner in which Canaanites reacted to Egyptian occupation. On a related theme of conversion, it also examines Egypt's attempt—via its promotion of the cults of Amun and the divine king—to reshape Canaan's ideology and economy to more closely approximate its own. A brief consideration of increasing contractual agreements with foreign troops as well as the complex constellation of factors that led to the contraction of Egypt's empire by the end of the reign of Ramesses VI (c. 1136) brings the chapter to a close.

Just as the nature of the expansionism of the early Eighteenth Dynasty cannot be understood without a glance backward at the Second Intermediate period, so it is crucial to take the recent trauma of the Amarna era into account

Ancient Egyptian Imperialism, First Edition. Ellen Morris.
© 2018 Ellen Morris. Published 2018 by John Wiley & Sons Ltd.

when seeking to understand the foreign policy of the Nineteenth-Dynasty pharaohs. In Egypt the Amarna period saw Akhenaten (c. 1352–1336) proscribe the old gods and elevate to primacy a formerly obscure version of the Sun God. As discussed in the previous chapter, under Akhenaten's watch Amurru, Kadesh, and areas further north were lost to the newly voracious Hittite empire. This contraction of Egypt's northern frontier is almost always blamed on Akhenaten's preoccupation with his internal religious revolution. While this critique has much to support it, Akhenaten may also have decided— as have rulers of a great many empires well past their first expansionistic flush—to sacrifice areas that were difficult and expensive to control in favor of strengthening the empire's core.[1]

Realistically, Kadesh had never been firmly in Egypt's control, even when the full resources of the state were expended to this end. Thutmose III (c. 1479–1425) devoted at least two campaigns to the capture of the city, and it would appear that his ultimate conquest and claiming of Kadesh only held firm because under the peace with Mitanni Egypt's authority went unchallenged. Moreover, following its defection to the Hittites, the Nineteenth-Dynasty rulers would once again crash massive campaign armies against the city's gates, only to meet with fleeting success or—famously, in the case of Ramesses II's Battle of Kadesh (c. 1274)—none at all. Perhaps anticipating the prodigious resources that would have to be expended on recapturing Kadesh, as well as the slim chances of success regardless, Akhenaten decided that negotiating trade agreements and rights of passage with the ruler of Kadesh would be more practical than trying to win a notoriously untrustworthy vassal back by force of arms. His decision not to contest the city's secession, then, makes a great deal of sense, and the same is true, of course, with respect to polities located even farther north. Imperial policy, however, does not always make rational sense, especially when national pride is deeply invested in the idea of empire.[2]

After the Amarna revolution had been repudiated and the royal family had petered out, a general named Horemheb ascended the throne (c. 1323–1295). This man, in turn, bequeathed his office to a general named Ramesses (c. 1295–1294), in whose family kingship continued throughout the Nineteenth Dynasty. For these rulers, who were not of ancient royal blood, their chief claim to kingship was their martial strength and the ideological power they derived from emphatically *not* resembling Akhenaten. Thus, their approach to empire appears both reactionary and highly militaristic. Rather than sacrificing the beleaguered extremities of their empire in order to strengthen its core, they would return to an expansionistic policy—leading armies in person, combating worthy enemies, and returning to Egypt with captives in tow.

In writing on much more recent political events, Chalmers Johnson has argued that the onset of militarism in a society is marked by three broad indicators: the emergence of a professional military class, a preponderance of military officers in high government positions, and a devotion to policies in which military preparedness becomes the highest priority of the state.[3] Under Thutmose III, military men had assumed an unprecedented role in the state, but their fortunes dipped once peace with Mitanni had been established. In the Amarna period soldiers became increasingly visible in their role as enforcers of the new order. It would not be until the ascension of the generals Horemheb, Ramesses I, and the latter's successors, however, that the wealth and political power of the military would skyrocket, radically increasing the internal differentiation and profession-alization of the army as well as the political power of its highest officials.[4]

Investments in Infrastructure and in the Information Superhighway

In order to simultaneously work toward augmenting their empire and safe-guarding their own borders, the Nineteenth-Dynasty kings Seti I (c. 1294–1279) and Ramesses II (c. 1279–1213) enhanced the fortifications of the primary entrance points to the Delta (e.g. Tell Heboua, Tell el-Retaba, and numerous sites along the edge of the western Delta)[5] and militarized the coastal highways that approached these points (see Figure 8.1). The substantial size of the for-tress towns at the borders acted as a deterrent to would-be attackers, while the securing of all available water sources with troops and/or fortified structures ensured that the desert would serve as its own defense.

As with the Middle Kingdom Nubian fortresses, such intense militarization of a border zone likely helped keep disaffected members of its own populace *in* fully as much as it kept the uninvited out. Surveillance along the desert highways east and west of the Delta was accomplished in part by desert scouts stationed in the fortresses in order to identify and track those who attempted to travel safely under cover of night.[6] Model letters that were (or purported to be) missives sent by fortress officials to their colleagues stationed at road forts, for example, reported on the flight of fugitives and the progress made in tracking them.[7]

Seti I seems to have erected the series of fortresses along the Ways of Horus in part because the in-fighting of Bedouin groups interfered with Egyptian use of this route.[8] Whether then, as today, the Sinai represented a region of refuge for those united primarily by their opposition to the state and their desire to be both beyond its clutches and within striking distance of its resources is unclear. Prior to Seti's reign we know of only two installations, one of which (Haruba A-345) was entirely unfortified. Seti's system, illustrated with pride on the outer wall of the temple at Karnak, depicted 10 road forts, located along the 220-km stretch of desert between Tjaru and Gaza. Each fort was labeled with a name that glorified the king and was depicted together with its water source (see Figure 8.1a).

Archaeology has supplemented the Karnak relief in demonstrating that such forts were also equipped with granaries that could provision officially authorized

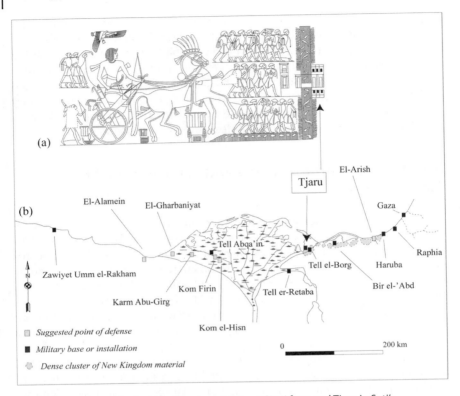

Figure 8.1 Highways in the New Kingdom. (a) Three Sinai forts and Tjaru in Seti's (directionally reversed) depiction of the Ways of Horus military highway (redrawn from Gardiner 1920, pl. XI); (b) major border installations and highway forts to the west and east of the Nile Delta. Deir el-Balah and Tell el-'Ajjul are omitted between Raphia and Gaza (partially redrawn from Oren 1987, 79, figure 4).

travelers, troops, and resident personnel, especially if, as is likely, they were most often spaced at intervals of roughly a day's travel for an army (c. 15–20 km).[9] Information technology in the ancient world essentially depended on how fast an individual could travel, and messengers unburdened by all the food and water necessary for a long journey across an arid landscape could travel with maximum speed and efficiency. Records kept at road forts detailing the arrival of various couriers, what they carried, and where they were going demonstrate that trans-Sinai traffic was indeed heavy at the time these forts were operative.[10] Such forts also, of course, facilitated the travel of Egypt's own army, so that errant vassals and enemies might be disciplined as quickly and efficiently as possible.

While the Sinai road forts were admirably suited to guarding vital resources of food and water from raiders, they would likely have served as little more than speed bumps for an invading army. The dimensions of the excavated forts at Bir el-'Abd and Haruba site A-289—1,600 and 2,500 m^2 respectively—suggest that such installations were small in size. Thus, a large contingent of troops could have easily overwhelmed their defenses and thereby gained access to the stores of food and water within. As Edward Luttwak writes of comparable forts erected by Roman authorities,

> In order to secure safe passage for gathering concentrations of imperial troops and supply trains as well as for civilian traffic, while denying unimpeded use of the roads to enemy bands, road forts were built at intervals along the highways. Road forts manned by small detachments could not effectively oppose the passage of large enemy forces, but they could at least intercept stray groups and foraging parties or impose time-consuming detours.[11]

Perhaps in recognition of their futility against sizable armies, the Sinai forts appear to have been purposefully decommissioned just in advance of a probable invasion from the east during the reign of Ramesses III (c. 1184–1153). If the fortified granaries were emptied and the wells were hidden or sabotaged, the government may have felt that the arid stretch of desert wasteland would prove a much more formidable obstacle than the string of installations that had formerly punctuated it. Certainly this was to be the case in the first millennium BCE, when invaders often failed to make the crossing or only barely made it, even with the help of camels and allied desert tribes.[12]

Interestingly, although inscriptions and archaeology confirm that the fortresses Ramesses II constructed along the Libyan highway were also strongly associated with wells, these installations were designed much differently. The only fully excavated fortress, Zawiyet Umm el-Rakham, for instance, was 19,600 m^2 and possessed a glacis, a feature never found along the Sinai route. Presumably, then, they were intended to ward off a greater threat than Seti had expected from the east. This makes sense given that Libyan tribes had been penetrating Egypt's borders in increasing numbers during Ramesses II's reign, presumably in order "to seek the necessities of their mouths," as would be the case in the reign of his son Merneptah (c. 1213–1203).[13] Increasing aridity in the Nineteenth Dynasty hit those living in the most marginal environments the hardest. In consequence, large populations appear to have been on the move within Libya, displacing other groups and ultimately occasioning a large-scale immigration into the fertile Nile Delta. In order to stanch this flow, Ramesses II sponsored the construction, wherever carrying capacity would allow, of much larger and more intensively fortified installations than his father had built along the Sinai highway. These fortresses, theoretically at least, had a far greater chance of holding their own against invaders, though it is significant that Zawiyet Umm el-Rakham, at least, seems not to have outlasted Ramesses' reign.

Conversions in the Imperial Footprint

Egypt's project to revamp its imperial infrastructure did not stop along its desert highways at the eastern end of the Sinai (see Figure 8.1b). In the Nineteenth and Twentieth Dynasties, Egyptian-style buildings (see Figure 8.3) littered with simple, utilitarian Egyptian-style pottery became commonplace in the core of Egypt's northern empire. Archaeological traces of at least twelve such installations are easily identified in Canaan from the Ramesside period, and more certainly existed. The nature of this evidence has been the subject of numerous studies[14] and cannot be done justice within the scope of this chapter. Suffice it to say that archaeologists have found buildings constructed with

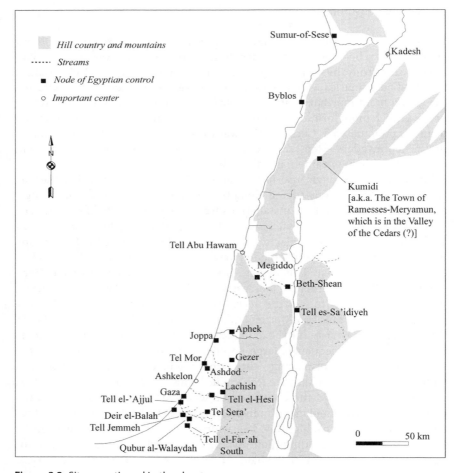

Figure 8.2 Sites mentioned in the chapter.

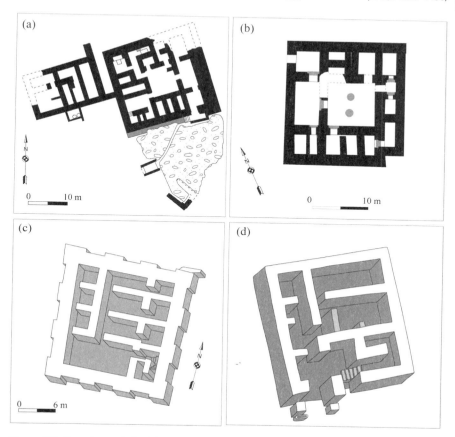

Figure 8.3 Egyptian-style buildings in Canaan. (a) Tell el-Far'ah South (redrawn from Starkey and Harding 1932, pl. 69); (b) Building 1500 at Beth-Shean, level 6 (redrawn from Mazar 2009, 16, figure 1.5, courtesy of the Institute of Archaeology, The Hebrew University of Jerusalem; (c) Tel Mor (redrawn from Dothan 1993, 1073); (d) Aphek (redrawn from Kochavi 1990, xiii, courtesy of the Israel Museum).

Egyptian masonry techniques and/or on a more or less Egyptian plan from Ramesside levels at Deir el-Balah, Tell el-Far'ah South, Tell el-'Ajjul, Qubur el-Walaydah, Tel Sera', Tell el-Hesi, Ashdod, Tel Mor, Aphek, Beth-Shean, Tell es-Sa'idiyeh, Joppa, and Lachish.[15] Egyptian-type wall paintings have been discovered in association with these buildings and settlements at Beth-Shean, Aphek, and Lachish,[16] while hieroglyphic inscriptions intended for display on gateways or official buildings have been excavated at Joppa, Gezer, Beth-Shean, Byblos, Ashdod, and perhaps also Lachish.[17] Many other similarly indicative categories of material culture associated with these bases will be addressed below (see Figure 8.4).

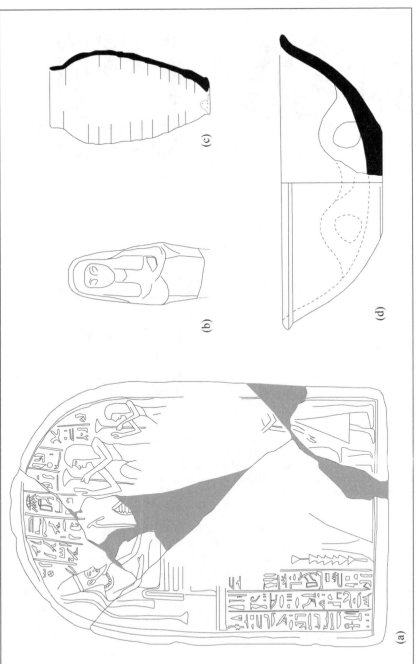

Figure 8.4 Egyptian-style material culture found in Canaan (not to scale). (a) Stele dedicated to the god Mekal, Lord of Beth-Shean, by the son of an Egyptian architect (redrawn from Levy 2016, 111); (b) clay shabti from Deir el-Balah (redrawn from Dothan and Brandl 2010, 202, figure 17.7, courtesy of the Institute of Archaeology, The Hebrew University of Jerusalem); (c) beer bottle from Deir el-Balah (redrawn from Dothan and Brandl 2010, 33, figure 2.5, courtesy of the Institute of Archaeology, The Hebrew University of Jerusalem); (d) spinning bowl from Deir el-Balah (redrawn

Most scholars suggest that this sudden visibility corresponded to a radical increase in the intensity of Egypt's presence in Canaan, and this may well be true, although there is little evidence for change in the nature of inscriptional evidence relating to garrisons and bases between the Eighteenth and the Nineteenth Dynasties. Likewise, in regions north of the Jezreel Valley, it is rare to find Egyptian investment, though the doorjambs emblazoned with the cartouches of Ramesses II at Byblos demonstrate that there were exceptions to this rule. Otherwise, the relative dearth of Egyptian-type pottery and utilitarian material culture at sites like Tell Kazel (a.k.a. "Sumur-of-Sese") and Kamid el-Loz (likely christened "the town of Ramesses-Meryamun, which is in the Valley of the Cedars" or, perhaps, "the town of Ramesses in Upe") suggests that the style of rule at the outer zone of Egypt's empire continued to resemble Eighteenth-Dynasty precedents.[18]

Any change in policy, then, occurred at the heart of the empire, where it appears that Egypt not only ramped up its imperial presence but also decided to own it—perhaps literally as well as figuratively. If so, this late intensification would conform to a pattern witnessed in numerous other imperial contexts in which an original preference for indirect rule faded as client kings rebelled, safety decreased, or revenues plummeted.[19] Certainly, the Roman and British empires aged, subject territories were increasingly annexed, and, consequently, the imperial presence was asserted more forcefully. The Inca too exhibited a similar trajectory. Terence D'Altroy writes,

> As the empire matured, the Incas moved from expansion to more stable dominion. Governance shifted from a low intensity, low control approach in most areas to a high intensity, high control strategy.... Broadly speaking, the goals of military policy shifted from acquisition towards pacification and securing frontier areas.[20]

To this end, the Inca—like the Egyptians and the Romans before them—proceeded to broadcast their permanent presence at bases and storage depots established along key transit corridors and near high-value resources over which they desired to establish tighter control.

Base Aspirations

No other nation has, or likely has ever had, more military bases than the United States in the early 21st century. Many of these installations, which number 700 to 1,000 according to conservative estimates, were won in the aftermath of wars and "armed interventions," just as may have been the case for Gaza (named "Town-of-the-Ruler's-Seizure"), Joppa (according to a Nineteenth-Dynasty tale in which a historically attested Egyptian general took the city via the same stratagem that was to be more famously employed by both Odysseus and Ali Baba), and Beth-Shean (the acropolis of which was entirely redesigned along Egyptian lines following its involvement in an insurrection at the beginning of the Nineteenth Dynasty—see Figure 8.5).[21] Other American bases, as was likely the case with Egyptian bases as well, were established in conjunction with trade or treaty agreements, or with the consent of allies who, while perhaps desirous of protection from their enemies, also likely felt deeply pressured to set aside land for a base if requested to do so by a dominant superpower.

In his discussion of America's seeming obsession with the acquisition and staffing of military bases throughout the world, Johnson enumerates nine roles

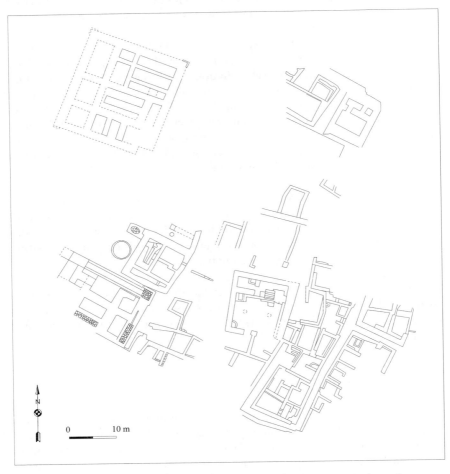

Figure 8.5 The Egyptian base of Beth-Shean in the Nineteenth Dynasty (redrawn from Mazar 2009, 6, figure 1.2).

that such bases play in America's grand strategy to further its own political and economic interests internationally.[22] Eight of these roles are useful to consider with respect to the utilization of military bases in Canaan during the Nineteenth and Twentieth Dynasties.

To Project Military Power into Areas of Concern

As discussed in Chapter 5, Canaan was nowhere near as fertile as Egypt, nor as rich in mineral resources as Nubia, and thus some have argued—perhaps a bit dramatically—that Canaan was valued primarily for the routes that ran through it toward the richer regions of the north.[23] While this view under-plays Canaan's military value as a buffer zone and its ideological value as a dominated territory, it is certainly true that Egyptian bases punctuated Canaan's main transit routes. In the Nineteenth Dynasty, the Egyptians set up or augmented administrative headquarters at regular intervals along the Via Maris—the main coastal highway that picked up where the trans-Sinai route left off and traveled northward to a point south of Acco (namely, Gaza, Ashdod, Gezer, and Aphek). Bases were also situated at harbors slightly off the coastal highway (Tel Mor and Joppa), along other major highways such as the Transjordan (Beth-Shean, which also guarded an important ford in the Jordan River, and, in the Twentieth Dynasty, Tell es-Sa'idiyeh), and along wadis that served as thoroughfares across the Negev (Tell el-Far'ah South, Tel Sera', Tell el-Hesi, and in the Twentieth Dynasty Qubur el-Walaydah and per-haps also Tell Jemmeh).

Already in the early Eighteenth Dynasty, Hatshepsut (c. 1473–1458) had boasted, "The roads that were formerly blocked up, are now (well) trod."[24] Her nephew and co-regent, Thutmose III (1479–1425), likewise claimed to have "[set] my terror in the farthest marshes of Asia, there is no one that holds back my messenger!"[25] Letters in the Amarna archive demonstrate that travel was occasionally made difficult in Canaan due to the numerous internecine battles waged between various polities. Thus, the late New Kingdom system of bases seems to have been designed at least in part to solve this problem by securing transit corridors and harbors. With assurance that the major trunk routes were safe, armies and officials could travel with ease and rulers could dispatch cara-vans, secure in the expectation that their "gifts" and taxes would reach their destination unmolested.

To Eavesdrop on the Communications of Citizens, Allies, and Enemies Alike

The movement of information was nearly as important to imperial mainte-nance as was the movement of goods and people. These bases, placed along major transit corridors, could keep track of the movements of individuals traveling throughout Canaan. The importance of intelligence gathering is, of course, repeatedly stressed in the Amarna archive, and a great many of the vassal letters included briefings not only on activity directly relevant to the writer but also on activities occurring in the general vicinity. As discussed in the previous chapter, however, it was often in the interests of vassals to engage in deliberate campaigns of disinformation, and thus the reports provided by Egyptian officials stationed in the region provided an invaluable counter-narrative.

Indeed, Ramesses II castigated three categories of subordinates—garrison commanders, governors of foreign territories, and vassal rulers—in the course of the disastrous ambush at the Battle of Kadesh for failing to warn him that the Hittite army, instead of being hundreds of kilometers to the north, was in actuality already lying in wait at the city.[26] The garrison commanders stationed in Syria-Palestine in the Nineteenth Dynasty likely resembled their predecessors—men such as Amenmose of the mid-Eighteenth Dynasty, who simultaneously held the titles of troop commander, overseer of northern foreign lands, and eyes and ears of the king in the foreign land of Retenu (i.e. Syria-Palestine).[27] Rather than reforming their intelligence system, the Nineteenth-Dynasty policy makers may simply have hoped that by increasing the numbers of their ears and eyes and—perhaps more importantly—by keeping those ears and eyes on the ground longer, both the quality and the quantity of their intelligence would be enhanced.

The Egyptians were also interested, however, in intercepting information that was being exchanged covertly between foreign powers and the pharaoh's vassals or between the vassals themselves. Such covert correspondence was, no doubt, exchanged regularly. For instance, according to a commemorative stele, Amenhotep II (c. 1427–1400) had been "travelling south in the plain of Sharon when he found a messenger belonging to the chieftain of Naharin carrying a letter which was sealed with clay about his neck."[28] The description of this letter seems very similar to one uncovered at Beth-Shean that had been written on a small, pierced clay cylinder, 24 mm in length and 40 mm in circumference. The absurdly small size of this document makes little sense unless it was designed to escape detection if its bearer were searched. Indeed, given that the cylinder seems to have been sent by Tagi of Ginti-kirmil (whose troops were occupying Beth-Shean) to Lab'aya of Shechem (a ruler who often acted against Egypt's interests) so that Lab'aya would be informed of Tagi's most recent communication with the pharaoh, something shady was indeed likely afoot.[29]

A great many Egyptian bases undoubtedly remain undiscovered, as most are unattested in inscriptions and are known only through excavation. Even judging solely from the bases presently known, however, it appears that the vast majority would have been less than a day's travel from at least two other bases (roughly 25–30 km). Given this proximity, the government assured itself that any information gathered could be transmitted and acted upon as quickly as possible.[30] Indeed, as Jeffrey Blakely has observed, both the horse-based postal systems developed by the Persian empire and the American Pony Express deemed a 24-km distance between relay stations optimal. Likewise he notes that the Islamic Imperial Post placed their postal stops along routes that closely approximated those favored by the Egyptians.[31] Thus, Egypt's administrative headquarters may perhaps be viewed as key nodes along an extremely early version of the information superhighway.

To Maintain Absolute Military Preponderance and Ensure via Policing that no Part of the Empire Slips its Leash

If the American military is famous for anything, it is for overkill. Bringing disproportionate power to bear on any given negotiation or encounter almost always ensures victory, at least in the short term. In the case of a newly martial Egypt, which appears to have been wagering its national pride in part on the restoration of its northern empire, levying such force on dominated territory just across its borders was not difficult. Without any strong intercity leagues in Canaan, the power that Egypt brought to bear was that of a nation-state against a city-state (or even a town or a group of Bedouin). Further, as many scholars have noted, in the Nineteenth Dynasty there seems to have been a greater will to intervene with significant force in affairs of seemingly local scope than ever before, presumably to prove the point that the state was in control and ever-vigilant.[32]

If the bases that lined Canaan's major trunk routes and cross-desert wadi routes at regular intervals also served as checkpoints, their preponderance in southern Canaan and the Negev may have served a psychological purpose as well as a practical one. Certainly checkpoints are a major source of dissatisfaction for Palestinians in the present day and constitute one of their most strident complaints against the Israeli military. Said Zeedani writes of the checkpoints,

> They make it extremely difficult for Palestinians even to move from one city to another and from one village to another within the same area or region…. [They] have transformed each and every Palestinian city, village and refugee camp into an island separate unto itself, or, as some would say, into a large prison.[33]

Now, the 50 or so present-day checkpoints in Israel-Palestine no doubt far exceed their Late Bronze Age equivalents, but those individuals stopped in ancient times would likely have felt a similar mixture of irritation, humiliation, and anger at being detained and questioned by foreigners in their own territory, if, indeed, as the material culture suggests, many of the soldiers in the garrisons at this time were Egyptian.

To Function as Symbols of Power

The apparent overkill in the emplacement of bases at such close intervals in Canaan was likely related, then as now, less to the practicalities of power than to the aggressive performance of it. In Egypt's case, this new desire to advertise its imperial control resulted in the construction of purpose-built administrative precincts, often emblazoned with hieroglyphic inscriptions carved on stone (i.e. at Joppa, Gezer, Ashdod, Byblos, Beth-Shean, and perhaps Tell Delhamiya). Such inscriptions obviously weren't meant to be read for their content. At a less literal level, however, the message chiseled onto these monumental jambs and lintels would have been easily decipherable.

With the exception of major centers like Joppa and Beth-Shean, the bases, although numerous, were on the whole remarkably small. Many consisted of only a handful of buildings—the largest of which might cover a floor plan of barely 625 m². Although the thick walls of the most important buildings likely betray the presence of a visually impressive second story, the power that the bases projected had little to do with the numbers or fearsomeness of the soldiers stationed within. It was rooted, rather, in the fact that the bases stood as symbols of Egyptian authority and of the overwhelming force that the government could summon and wield—at lightning speed—if its property were encroached upon or its orders disobeyed.

To Serve as Tripwires that would Allow the Imperial Power an Excuse to Attack Should a Base be Harmed

The vast majority of Egypt's bases were relatively isolated and unfortified. If they proudly advertised their imperial presence in a way that they never had previously, and if such buildings occupied the landscape in a denser fashion than ever before, they must have made tempting targets for those who opposed Egypt's rule. The visibility of bases and their propensity to be targeted, however, may have been less a side effect of "owning" one's empire than a key part of a developing imperial strategy.

Military interventions can be profitable ventures, but—as discussed in Chapter 5—they are perhaps most lucrative at first blush, when the property of defeated foes can be requisitioned as spoils of victory. Within an already incorporated area, however, such moves are no longer legitimate, as the operative ideological fiction—that the empire is benevolent and protects its inhabitants—must be at least somewhat respected. The economy of plunder and of requisitioning, however, need not be entirely abandoned. If bases are viewed as the declared property of an imperial country, attacks on them are *de facto* attacks on the empire itself and may be avenged with impunity. Further, each righteous retaliation provides an opportunity to accrue the empire more wealth and directly owned property as well as to tighten its grip on dominated regions.

The role that smaller American bases and embassies play as tripwires is therefore an extremely important, if understandably untrumpeted, aspect of American foreign policy.[34] Whether such considerations also played a role in Egypt's foreign policy is not known, but it is a possibility worth considering.

To Control Natural Resources and Industries

In many imperial contexts, intensification in the core of the empire meant an increasingly direct co-option of industry. Concerning the Inca, D'Altroy observes that "early plundering was augmented by demands for tribute and then replaced by the seizure of productive resources."[35] In Canaan, productive resources ripe for seizure were relatively few, save those related to copper mining or agriculture. The Egyptians do appear to have assumed a prominent role in the mines at Timna during the Nineteenth and Twentieth Dynasties, even investing in the construction of a small shrine to the goddess Hathor for the spiritual benefit of their own personnel.[36] Given that Timna was an industrial site rather than a base, however, it is only tangentially related to the discussion at hand.

At least two of Egypt's bases were directly associated with installations devoted to the production of wine. Wine was one of the four products of Canaan that particularly attracted the Egyptians, along with olive oil, moringa oil, and pistacia incense. Thutmose III received jars of wine as taxes and benevolences (*b3kw* and *inw*) on a yearly basis. According to the records archived in his annals, the numbers of transport jars could tally into the thousands (e.g. 5th campaign: 6,428; 10th campaign: 3,909; 14th campaign, 1,405), equating on a particularly heavy year to an extraction of as much as 95,000 liters![37] Much of this wine, according to the annals, was destined for storage at harbor depots within Canaan to be consumed by imperial personnel and passing troops. Given the paucity of evidence for imported wine in Egypt, this tradition may well have continued throughout the New Kingdom.[38] Such levies were high, regardless of where they were destined, however, and one wonders whether they eventually had such a depressing effect on the wine industry that the Egyptians were forced to step up and organize production themselves. Alternatively, perhaps the industry was simply so lucrative that the Egyptian government desired to acquire direct control over the country's best vineyards in order to bolster its coffers.

Certainly, it is telling that several meters from the Egyptian base in the Nineteenth Dynasty at Aphek were two wine presses, each of which had tanks capable of holding 3,500 liters of wine. Given that the most convenient area for locating a wine press was on the outskirts of a vineyard, the close proximity of the presses to the residency suggests that the Egyptians either owned the vineyard and oversaw work on it directly, or that they simply had a monopoly on the means of production and took a lord's cut of the profits—profits that may have been particularly large as the vineyard seems to have specialized in white wine! Fragments of Canaanite storage jars like those observed shattered in the vicinity of the presses were also discovered in the residency's storage magazine.[39] As will be discussed below, yet another vineyard was situated just outside the base at Joppa. The fact that its workers fell under Egypt's legal protection suggests that here too the Egyptians assumed authority over vineyards in the vicinity of their bases.[40]

After the Egyptian administrative headquarters at Aphek came under attack sometime in the late Nineteenth Dynasty and was subsequently abandoned, the center of Egyptian wine production may have relocated to Tell es-Sa'idiyeh in the Transjordan. Here it was not the wine presses that were discovered but rather an elaborate installation incorporating two interconnected vaulted cisterns as well as a thickly plastered pool that drew upon an underground spring as a cooling device. The remains of 50 to 60 Egyptian-type storage jars, identical to those discovered in the administrative headquarters itself, were excavated in association with this installation.[41] Archaeologists also discovered 45 large wine jars in a storeroom in the contemporary Egyptian headquarters at Tell el-Far'ah South, although, judging from the Canaanite deity stamped on some of the jars' stoppers, this wine had likely been requisitioned the old-fashioned way.[42]

Whether the Egyptians directly controlled the production of incense or oils—the other industries that Canaan's climate and lack of an inundation rendered superior to Nile Valley equivalents—is not known. Recent analyses of Canaanite storage jars discovered in Egypt, however, suggest that Egyptians were intimately involved in the production of oils, incense, wine, and honey—often making notations in hieratic on the storage jars that were so precise that they could only reasonably have been made at the point that these jars had been filled. Industries producing incense (i.e., pistacia resin) and honey seem to have been centered at Abu Hawam and regions east and south, while olive oil production took place at Ugarit and along the Lebanese coast.[43] Although Ugarit was firmly in Hittite territory, Egyptians were resident at the site in substantial numbers after the forging of the Egypto-Hittite peace treaty in the reign of Ramesses II. Indeed, an Egyptian steward of a royal estate dedicated a stele to Ba'al Saphon at one of Ugarit's most important temples, suggesting that the estate may have belonged to the temple's landholdings and have been leased to the Egyptian government in a mutually beneficial arrangement.[44]

Thus, the Egyptians may well have preferred in the Nineteenth and Twentieth Dynasties to play an active part in the production of highly desired goods such as wine, oil, and incense. In the case of wine, at least, its production appears to have been overseen by administrators in nearby Egyptian bases. Similar suggestions have also been made with respect to the involvement of the Egyptians in promoting the cultivation of flax in the vicinity of Beth-Shean and Aphek as well as, perhaps, the cultivation of papyrus in the marshes near Aphek.[45]

To Provide Work and Income for the Military Industrial Complex

There is not enough evidence at present to expand at length on the notion that the elaboration of Egypt's system of bases served to feed and sustain a war machine that had been initiated by the ramping up of militarism from the reign of Horemheb until the reign of Merneptah, but it is an idea worth some attention. Certainly, many of the bases were so similar in design and in building technique—even down to the composition of the foundation deposits—that it almost looks as if teams of military architects had at various points been sent from one base to another in order to initiate construction on official buildings.

In modern times, contracts for building and overseeing maintenance work at foreign bases have been extremely lucrative, as have contracts for producing weapons to be utilized by troops and for furnishing the modern-day equivalents to horses and chariots. At the Egyptian capital of Pi-Ramesses (modern Qantir), archaeologists have discovered tethering points for 460 horses, and one would suspect that it would have been far more economical to send chariot teams beyond Egypt's borders to intimidate Canaanites and to eat their fodder than it would be to keep them idle and consuming local resources. The same might be said with regard to the soldiers, military scribes, and other personnel, many of whom seem to have been employed year around as professionals. While campaigns lasted only a few months, bases would need to be staffed throughout the year.

Others too may have profited from finding work in Egyptian installations abroad. In Papyrus Anastasi I, a satirical letter purportedly sent by a military official to his colleague, the writer describes how helpful it would be if his correspondent, in an imagined scenario, could only enter Joppa—a privilege denied to him due to an act of indiscretion with a local woman, as will be discussed further below. Because of his (imagined) poor choices, the correspondent could not access the carpenters and leatherworkers who

> would do all that you desire. They would take care of your chariot so that it would cease to be inoperative.... You would then go quickly forth to fight on the battlefield.[46]

Thus, the Egyptians seem to have located at their base in Joppa a full-service repair shop where, according to the text, craftsmen could mend chariots, horse tackle, and even horsewhips! While such technical workers may, of course, have been Canaanite, Egypt did employ its own craftsmen at bases in the Nineteenth and Twentieth Dynasties.

A substantial portion of the pottery excavated at Egyptian bases had been manufactured with local clays but according to Egyptian style and techniques. These strong technological similarities suggest that the Egyptians brought their own potters to the region, just as they had in the Protodynastic period, when Egyptian traders resided in the southern coastal plain, as discussed in Chapter 1.[47] An Egyptian background has also been suggested for the craftsmen and artisans who painted the walls of various administrative centers, temples, and houses in the Nineteenth and Twentieth Dynasties, for those who carved and decorated the stone architectural features mentioned above, and for those who fashioned the personal stelae discovered at Beth-Shean (see Figure 8.4a) and Deir el-Balah.[48] Faience and glass manufacture at Beth-Shean was likely under the oversight of Egyptians,[49] while the extensive artisan's quarter at Deir el-Balah produced numerous items that were Egyptian in style and technique, including anthropoid clay coffins, female figurines, shabtis, linen, and jewelry (see Figure 8.4b).[50] It is both curious and important to note, however, that, unlike their counterparts at Joppa, the craftsmen at Deir el-Balah concerned themselves far less with the repair and manufacture of implements of war than with the production of funerary items, capable of ensuring that those buried in the adjacent cemetery could be sent off in good Egyptian style.

To Ensure that Members of the Military and Their Families Live Comfortably and are Entertained While Serving Abroad

The presence of Egyptian-type pottery at Egyptian bases in Canaan is extremely interesting, for Egyptians resident in the region had been largely content to employ local pottery for two and a half centuries.[51] In the Nineteenth Dynasty, however, to a much greater degree than ever before, the personnel stationed at Egyptian bases ate out of Egyptian bowls, manufactured and drank beer using Egyptian vessels, and wore linen clothes that had been locally fashioned by individuals who utilized Egyptian-type spinning bowls (see Figure 8.4c and d).[52] There are two primary reasons why one might imagine that an imperial government would prefer to invest in the on-site production of their own ceramics rather than to utilize local wares. The first would be to aid in accounting. The same scribe in P. Anastasi I who taunted his correspondent with alarming imagined scenarios also presented him with a mathematical word problem in which he would be responsible for dividing (insufficient) rations among numerous different contingents of troops.[53] Meting out standardized rations in standardized containers, as all good quartermasters know, eases both logistics and accounting significantly.

Krystal Lords Pierce has recently argued that Egyptian-style simple bowls—a type ubiquitous on Egyptian bases—held 0.87 liters of grain on average, comparable to the typical rations provided to workers according to Egyptian documents. The largest of the bowls, moreover, averaged 9.17 liters, roughly equal to a week's rations for unskilled laborers.[54] While an imperial power might, of course, commission local potters to produce what they needed, they would presumably have had to pay for that production, and it may have been felt that it was better to support their own personnel than to advance local industry.

Pierce's analysis of Egyptian-type ceramic at Joppa has also led her to conclude that the necessities of manufacturing, storing, and serving "Egyptian" beer very likely accounted for nearly all of the Egyptian and Egyptian-type pottery that had been imported and manufactured on site.[55] As a staple of the Egyptian diet and a standard element in ration allotments, beer would have played a vital role in provisioning personnel with both comforts and calories. On American bases abroad, it is not unusual for soldiers to binge drink in order to cope with boredom and stress, two seemingly contradictory emotions that garrison soldiers regularly experience.[56] It is unknown whether Egyptian military men indulged in a similar manner, but sources suggest so. According to a Ramesside tale concerning the fall of Joppa, for example, the drunkenness of soldiers facilitated the success of the aforementioned sly stratagem employed by Thutmose III's general![57] Perhaps more trustworthy is evidence from Thutmose III's own annals, in which it is stated that the army celebrated a festival on one occasion and got drunk—just as they would have done at a festival—on another.[58] Ramesses II's Hittite Marriage Stele likewise makes reference to mass celebratory drinking by soldiers in order to mark a momentous occasion.[59]

A second important reason for commissioning Egyptian-type pottery in preference to Canaanite volumetric equivalents would have been psychological. In the New Kingdom, it seems, soldiers could be stationed in Canaan for up to five or six years at a stretch,[60] and thus it may have been deemed prudent to provide such men with at least some of the comforts of home. American bases, like their Egyptian equivalents, are often set apart from local population centers in securable locations. Thus, their planners take care to equip the soldiers stationed in such strongholds with familiar fast-food franchises as well as—at many of the larger forward operating bases—gyms, swimming pools, shopping malls, movie theaters, and the like. The more these bases are capable of simulating life in America, the more open soldiers, officers, and family members of long-term operatives would be—theoretically at least—to the prospect of extended deployments.[61]

Archaeologists have yet to uncover entertainment centers associated with pharaonic bases in Canaan; however, the Egyptians did strive to fashion familiar environments for their personnel. The son of an architect at Beth-Shean dedicated a stele in memory of his father, who must have been resident at the site right about the time that it was entirely redesigned along Egyptian lines (see Figure 8.4a).[62] The stele thus suggests both that Egyptian architects designed the base and that they designed it with families as well as single soldiers in mind. Other evidence too supports the notion that posts at such bases were becoming increasingly hereditary.[63]

If the government deemed it important that their operatives feel at home in the spaces they inhabited, they may perhaps also have made it a priority to provide their personnel with the taste of home as well. The possibility that

Egyptian beer was made on site has been discussed above. Likewise, faunal remains indicate that expatriates stationed at Beth-Shean, Lachish, and Megiddo in the Ramesside period consumed large quantities of perch, among other Nilotic species imported from Egypt. While the presence of Nile perch at Canaanite sites does not necessarily indicate the presence of Egyptians, faunal analysts at Beth-Shean do suggest that the fish had likely been imported so far inland in order to cater to the tastes of Egyptian personnel.[64] An Egyptian appetite for geese too could explain the sharp spike in goose consumption in levels coeval with the Twentieth Dynasty at Lachish.[65]

At sites like Beth-Shean and Deir el-Balah, Egyptian-type pottery made up roughly half of the assemblage, and recent excavations at Joppa suggest that fully three-quarters of the ceramic may have been Egyptian in style![66] Meanwhile, at many other bases where the share of Egyptian-type pottery in the assemblages could be assessed—such as at Aphek, Ashkelon, and Tel Sera'—the share of Egyptian-type pottery ranged from 25–40%.[67] Significantly, the division between the predominantly Egyptian-type serving vessels and the overwhelmingly Canaanite-style cooking and baking implements strongly suggests that Egyptian men may have settled down at Beth-Shean and other bases with local women, a dynamic encountered during the latter stages of Egypt's Middle Kingdom domination of Nubia, as discussed in Chapter 4.[68] While some Egyptian-type spinning bowls and one Egyptian-type oven were admittedly present at Beth-Shean, the vast majority of the typically female-dominated technologies related to food preparation and clothing manufacture here, as at other Egyptian bases, were Canaanite in character.[69]

If the Egyptian government strove to secure a comfortable life for its service personnel abroad, so too, it seems, they increasingly offered another amenity: a familiar and comforting death. Evidence from physical anthropology suggests that those buried at Deir el-Balah bore more affinities to Egyptian than to Canaanite populations. Moreover, here as at Tell el-Far'ah South and Tell es-Sa'idiyeh, burials of women and children complemented those of males.[70] At Tell el-Far'ah South, Beth-Shean, Deir el-Balah, and Lachish, archaeologists discovered the type of anthropoid clay coffin frequently associated with military bases in Egypt as well as Nubia. At Tell es-Sa'idiyeh, on the other hand, some bodies had been wrapped in linen and treated with bitumen in what certainly seems like a gesture toward mummification. Significantly, the richest burials at this Transjordanian site occurred in graves that were lined with mudbrick, oriented east–west, and provided with Egyptian-type grave gifts such as pottery, jewelry, scarabs, amulets, carved ivory implements, and bronze items that were very often wrapped in linen.[71]

Increasingly, then, Egyptian men or men of Egypto-Canaanite heritage stationed in Canaan could enjoy the pleasures of raising a family, of occupying buildings that were familiar in structure and decoration, of eating Egyptian-style food out of Egyptian-style vessels, of offering at a temple in which the architecture and material finds were not too discordant with equivalents in Egypt (more about this below), and even of rounding out their mortal existence with a funeral and subsequent burial rites that resembled those in Egypt and were presided over by relatives, descendants, and close comrades.

Divergent Reactions to Intensified Occupation

As is often the case in imperial situations, the population of Canaan appears to have been divided between those who agreed to collaborate with the dominant power and those who actively or passively resisted. Collaboration, of course, had its benefits. Numerous studies have demonstrated that many of the wealthiest polities in New Kingdom Canaan, and especially in the Ramesside period, were those that were located along the main transit routes and that served as military and administrative nodes of control (e.g. Tell el-Far'ah South, Beth-Shean, Megiddo, Ashdod, or Lachish).[72] This pattern—in which wealth accrued to sites situated along the highways frequented by an imperial power and, conversely, stayed static or decreased elsewhere—is also observable in the Roman empire. There, too, certain centers housed a disproportionate share of wealthy collaborators willing to cater to imperial desires and to emulate aspects of the dominant political culture.[73]

As Rivka Gonen has argued, communities located in lowland Canaan along the Via Maris, the Jordan Valley, and the Jezreel Valley, especially, not only profited from increased imperial investment but also proved most amenable to emulating aspects of Egyptian material culture. This is especially evident in the widespread adoption of individual pit burials in these areas during the Ramesside period.[74] While some of those interred in pit burials were no doubt Egyptian, especially in cemeteries situated in close proximity to Egyptian bases, this subgroup was likely small and some may well have been of mixed heritage. Indeed, even at Egyptian bases like Tell es-Sa'idiyeh and Tell el-Far'ah South, scholars studying cemetery remains have largely abandoned attempts to discern Egyptians who adopted aspects of Canaanite culture from Canaanites who adopted elements of Egyptian culture.[75] Clearly the context was one of intensive transculturation, no doubt abetted by the practice of intermarriage. Thus, while the Egyptian presence in Canaan was never intense enough to affect widespread cultural transformation, a distinct conversion in ways of life, ways of death, and the manner in which indigenous (lowland) elites advertised their own status and power is observable.

If pit burials became the preferred method of inhumation along the main Levantine highways during the Ramesside period, this was emphatically not the case in the more mountainous regions of Canaan. In the highlands, multiple internments in caves remained the most popular method of burial, as had been the case since the Middle Bronze Age.[76] Largely devoid of imports, the assemblages of cave burials have struck archaeologists as impoverished, at least in comparison with the cosmopolitan grave-goods typically evident in burials within Egypt's more intensive spheres of influence. Likewise, the communities in which these burials were situated, with some urban exceptions, were also those that exhibited the fewest evident signs of prosperity. Intriguingly, the richest cave burials were often associated with weapons, though whether such weapons served Egyptians, hindered them, aided in extortion, or operated in a separate sphere, is unfortunately unknown.[77]

This patterning, one suspects, may have been due to a progressive marginalization of those areas of little interest to Egypt, though one imagines that they also attracted at least some Canaanites who deeply resented Egyptian control of their produce, travel, and trade. Here again, at the risk of anachronism, it is interesting to gain insight into the dark view of imperial bases often held by the inhabitants of the areas in which they are situated. Johnson writes,

> Only slowly did I come to understand that Okinawa was typical, not unique. The conditions there—expropriation of the island's most valuable land for bases, extraterritorial status for American troops who committed crimes against local civilians, bars and brothels, crowding around the main gates of bases, endless accidents, noise, sexual violence, drunk driving crashes, drug use, and environmental pollution—are replicated anywhere there are American garrisons.[78]

It is impossible to ascertain whether a substantial portion of Canaanites shared this view of Egyptian bases, though one suspects that they may have. As discussed above, for instance, beer jars constituted a substantial portion of the refuse at these bases, as did vessels that seem to have been utilized for beer brewing.[79] Given that sexual assaults by soldiers against locals are often correlated with intoxication on American bases, it's interesting to return to an incident in P. Anastasi I, alluded to earlier in the chapter, which sheds a little light on problematic relations between Egyptians and Canaanites who lived in the vicinity of Egyptian bases.

In the text, the writer imagines his correspondent finally reaching Joppa after having been frightened by Bedouin and alarmed by unfamiliar and unsafe environments throughout his travels. He continues the narrative.

> You have now entered Joppa and find the meadowland verdant in its season. You force your way in because of appetite and encounter the beautiful maiden who is tending the vineyards. She allures you to herself to be a partner (in love) and surrenders to you the flesh of her bosom. You are recognized as soon as you have uttered advice (i.e., sexual advice in the throes of the act).[80]

Mutually desired spontaneous sexual acts between unacquainted men and women, however, rarely occur in traditional societies except in fantasy. Thus, it is likely that any encounter in real life would either have been preceded by a financial transaction or would be better classified as rape. In either case, the effects on the surrounding community would have been deleterious. If the transaction was financial, this would fit with a general pattern found in military contexts that bases and brothels are commonly twinned. On the other hand, if the act was rape, it is worthy of note that the scribe's punishment consisted of being denied access to the base. No mention is made of a physical punishment or of the victim receiving any legal or financial recompense.

While archaeologists have not observed evidence of increased settlement in the hill country during the Eighteenth and Nineteenth Dynasties, as one might expect if Egypt's occupation were deeply resented, such factors are difficult to gauge with respect to refugees. There is a possibility, however, that the hill country populations were in fact substantially reduced during the latter portion of Egypt's empire due to active Egyptian intervention. Akhenaten and Ramesses II, after all, made it a practice to resettle troublesome northerners elsewhere in their empire. In Akhenaten's case, he transplanted groups of 'Apiru in Nubia, commanding his vassal in Damascus, "Send me the 'Apiru of the pastureland (?).... I will settle them in the cities of the land of Kush to dwell in, inasmuch as I have plundered them."[81] Indeed, the god Reshef, who is attested in several Nubian stelae and who appears in a late Eighteenth-Dynasty cultic graffito at Gebel Agg alongside the deified Senwoseret III and Horus, Lord of Miam (a.k.a. Aniba), may well have arrived in the south along with his worshipers as a result of similar resettlement efforts.[82]

Ramesses II may have dealt with similar foes in a similar fashion, as he bragged that he made it a practice to settle northerners in the south (and vice versa).[83] Given that he also claimed to have settled easterners in the west, it is significant that a cultic pillar resembling a Canaanite *massebah*—a type of standing stone shrine often associated with highland locales—was discovered in the enigmatic Southern Building at Ramesses II's fortress at Zawiyet Umm el-Rakham. Whether this monument served as a cultic center for a foreign garrison is unclear, but the fact that it was surrounded with votive pottery is suggestive.[84] If it did serve this purpose, those soldiers who worshiped there had likely been recruited from amidst a population of prisoners of war that the Egyptians had regarded as particularly formidable fighters.

Resettlement has always been and continues to be a powerful tool for empires and nation-states, as extracting a people from their homeland deprives them in one fell swoop of their livelihoods, their natural and built defenses, and their established alliances and social support. The Incan, like the Assyrian and many other empires, utilized resettlement routinely in their imperial maintenance, resettling fully a quarter to a third of newly conquered populations.[85] The chronicler Sarmiento de Gamboa reported that the Inca emperor Pachacuti

> ...began to level the fortresses he wished, and moved those inhabitants to lower land. And he moved those of the plains to the heights and mountains, each so far from the others and so from their natural [land] that they could not return to it.[86]

Whether the Egyptians made it a point of policy to root out hostile populations in the hill country is not known, but in the case of repeat offenders, this would certainly have served their interests.[87]

While the feelings of local communities subjected to Egyptian rule remains a source of speculation, the fate that many of these bases suffered at the end of the Nineteenth Dynasty is quite clear. Four of the bases located in the heart of Egypt's empire (Ashdod, Tel Mor, Aphek, and Tell el-Hesi) came under attack and were put to flame in the turbulent decades between c. 1213 and 1190, when the instability and chaos that marked the end of the Late Bronze Age was first felt in earnest. During this time Merneptah apparently faced rebellions from Ashkelon, Gezer, Yeno'am, and even a tribe by the name of Israel, making its debut in extra-biblical historical sources. Whether the damage to Egyptian bases at roughly this period resulted from this or other insurrections is not known. A fierce burning event in an administrative building at Beth-Shean, however, may indicate that the disturbance even reached this stalwart bastion of Egyptian power. Certainly, the arrowheads embedded in the walls of the residency at Aphek provide vivid testimony of the pitched battles that must have raged at this time.[88]

In his discussion of the role bases play and have played in American foreign policy, Johnson traces a seemingly inexorable trajectory of ever-accelerating base-building but notes one exception. Taking advantage of a perceived weakness in American power following the defeat in Vietnam, the population surrounding many bases worldwide attempted to evict the Americans, and some ultimately succeeded.[89] A similar situation may well have occurred in the reign of Merneptah (when this king faced large-scale invasions from the west and rebellions in the heart of his northern and southern empire) as well as in subsequent years (when succession troubles greatly weakened Egypt's central government). These instances of insurrection and instability would have been ideal times for locals to attempt to rid themselves of their occupiers. The destructions that occurred at this period are, for chronological purposes, taken to mark the transition between the Late Bronze and Iron Ages. A second wave of destructions that was to follow shortly after the advent of the Twentieth Dynasty, however, should be seen as part of the same extended period of upheaval.[90]

Twentieth-Dynasty Canaan: A Site of Religio-Political Conversion

In the eighth year of Ramesses III's reign (c. 1176), a heterogeneous assemblage of armed refugees from the Aegean and from Anatolia invaded Egypt and Egyptian-occupied Canaan by land and by sea. Multiple lines of evidence suggest that these people were fleeing an interrelated combination of famine conditions and large-scale regional warfare. Trouble had been brewing already since the late Eighteenth Dynasty, when the pharaoh accused the ruler of Cyprus of sponsoring or condoning piracy. Denying involvement, the latter complained of the suffering of his own people at the hands of the Lukki, a specific subgroup of the so-called "Sea People."[91] Moreover, by the Nineteenth Dynasty, armed raiders managed to penetrate Egypt's Delta on at least two occasions. In retrospect, however, these appear to be but predatory preludes to the main event.

The war reports that Ramesses III carved on the walls of his temple at Medinet Habu serve as the primary historical source for this conflict, which is, of course, problematic. Notably short on specifics, the accounts may well conflate multiple small battles into two large ones and exaggerate the fearsomeness of Ramesses' foes in order to add luster to his victory.[92] Judging from outside textual and archaeological evidence, however, the scale and devastation of a rash of attacks in the Levant and on the borders of Egypt at this time were indeed cataclysmic. Not all of these destructions are attributable to the Sea Peoples, but all seem to have been related to a maelstrom of unrest and opportunistic hostility that characterized a 20–50-year period at the beginning of the 12th century BCE.[93]

Some of the Egyptian bases that suffered attack in this chaotic period never recovered. With respect to those that survived the first decade of Ramesses III's reign (Deir el-Balah, Tell el-Far'ah South, Gaza, Tel Mor, Tel Sera', Tell el-Hesi, and Beth-Shean) or were newly established (Tell es-Sa'idiyeh, Qubur el-Walaydah, as well as, perhaps, Lachish, Megiddo, and Tell Jemmeh), however, pharaonic investment intensified, as often occurs following episodes of intense disorder and rebellion in imperial situations.[94] In tightening his grip, Ramesses III seems to have followed Thutmose III's lead in requisitioning great swaths of land for Amun. Papyrus Harris I, which served as a compilation of the king's great deeds and pious donations, credits him with establishing temple estates for Amun in nine Syro-Palestinian and Nubian cities as well as 56 Egyptian towns. Likewise, in the Medinet Habu Festival Calendar, Ramesses III claimed to have built *bekhen*-structures in Amun's name in Egypt, Nubia, and Syria-Palestine.[95]

The nature of *bekhen*-structures is not well understood, but available evidence suggests that they often constituted fortified country residences or farms that might be dedicated to producing *bȝkw* taxes for the temple of a god

(Amun, Seth, or Re),[96] but could also belong to a king.[97] Such temple-owned farms may have controlled fields, gardens, and herds and have been worked in part with unfree labor, as royal boasts and a hieratic ostracon found at Qubur el-Walaydah might suggest.[98] If so, the term may well have designated many of the more isolated residencies or bases discussed above. The fact that such structures were operative in Nubia and Egypt as well suggests that Egypt's administration of Canaan had never resembled its own self-governance more closely than it did in the final decades of its existence.

While *bekhen*-structures in the northern Negev would have been useful for all the reasons enumerated above, and perhaps also for monitoring access to potable perennial water sources, they likely could not have provided much in the way of agricultural surplus on their own. Indeed, Blakely, who has excavated at Tell el-Hesi for decades, has observed that the region is far better suited to ranching than agriculture. The excavation of a branding iron just outside the early Eighteenth-Dynasty Egyptian residency at Tell el-'Ajjul may provide support for this thesis, and in this respect it is especially significant that the mark left by the brand took the form of one of Amun's animal avatars—a goose![99] If the bases truly could provide little in the way of an agricultural surplus, the ability of the Egyptians to maintain a permanent presence in such an environmentally marginal region must have been contingent on securing a steady stream of staple produce from regions just to the north.

Hieratic inscriptions on shallow bowls that have been discovered at Lachish, Tel Sera', Tell el-Far'ah South, Deir el-Balah, Qubur el-Walaydah, and perhaps also at Tell el-Hesi and Tel Haror support the theory that Egypt's administration was substantially reworked in the Twentieth Dynasty. The inscriptions deal in the main with deliveries of harvest tax ($šmw$) submitted by local rulers and the occasional Egyptian official. In some cases, the quantities delivered could range as high as 150,000 liters of grain—enough to support the annual wages of 12,500 unskilled workmen (or garrisoned soldiers).

Simple bowls such as those that the hieratic tax receipts were written on are often found in association with temples in which a high percentage of Egyptian and Egyptian-type goods were dedicated, such as those discovered at the Egyptian bases of Beth-Shean, Tel Sera', and Lachish.[100] Indeed, the presence of sherds from similar bowls in the thick layer of grain on the floor of the Mound Temple at Lachish strongly suggests that in the Twentieth Dynasty those delivering taxes to the Egyptian administration took them to a temple or its affiliated administrative structure and there had an Egyptian scribe write the amount delivered on a bowl into which a sample of the grain was placed. The bowl may then have been taken inside the temple or chapel and presented before the statue of the god. Analogous practices are certainly known from Egypt.[101]

As discussed in Chapter 6, Egypt had invested in the temples of foreign allies and in those established near its bases since at least the reign of Thutmose III.

In the vast majority of cases the Egyptians either practiced syncretism—whereby they identified (or continued to identify) a local deity with an orthodox Egyptian counterpart (e.g. Hathor at Byblos or Amun at a locale north of Byblos)—or else they promoted the worship of cross-over deities revered in Egypt as well as Canaan (e.g. Ba'al Saphon at Ugarit as well as Anat at Gaza and Beth-Shean).[102] The promotion of deities that appealed to imperial functionaries as well as to local constituencies was, of course, a characteristic feature of Rome's governance over imperial provinces.[103] Egyptians also on occasion patronized wholly Canaanite deities such as Mekal at Beth-Shean (see Figure 8.4a).

In the Twentieth Dynasty, however, evidence for the worship of quintessentially Egyptian deities is more frequently observed. At Beth-Shean, for example, architectural inscriptions praise the Nile god Hapy and the pharaoh.[104] More intriguingly, Ramesses III actively promoted the composite cult of the divine king and Amun, long, attested in Egypt and Nubia.[105] Certainly at the Egyptian base at Gaza, which hosted a temple of Anat, Ramesses III claimed to have constructed a temple that he named "the temple of Ramesses, Ruler of Heliopolis, life, prosperity, and health, in Pa-Canaan (i.e., Gaza)." Concerning the temple, he boasted to Amun,

> I fashioned your great statue that it might rest in its interior, Amun of Ramesses, Ruler of Heliopolis, life, prosperity, and health. The foreigners of Retenu [*i.e., Syria-Palestine*] come to it bearing their *inw*-gifts to its face according to its divinity. I ushered in the land, assembled for you, bearing their *b3kw*-taxes in order to send them to Thebes.[106]

This inscription may find a material counterpart in a life-size statue of Ramesses III—likely fused with the god Amun—that was discovered out of its original context in a later level of Beth-Shean's temple.[107] While no hieratic tax receipts are known from Beth-Shean, archaeologists discovered bowls similar to those on which receipts were typically written in association with the recently remodeled and highly Egyptianized temple (along with other Egyptian-type vessels, cultic items, and even a life-sized limestone Horus falcon wearing a crown of Upper and Lower Egypt).[108] The base of a smaller royal statue, this time of Ramesses VI (c. 1143–1136), was discovered at Megiddo and may well have originally stood in that town's temple.[109] This royal god perhaps also owned land and received the tax "offerings" of his subjects, but, if so, he would have been the last.[110] No indication of Egyptian rule in Canaan postdates his reign.

This practice of inserting the divine king into the center of religious life in Canaan and forcing Canaanites to bring their taxes before him appears to have been a newly imposed policy. Presumably the aim would have been to enact and enshrine the "proper" relationship between subject and divine king through ritual. As Michael Given has observed,

> The ceremonial of taxation ... helped to legitimize it. Invocations of a deity and the display of religious symbols made taxation seem divinely ordained, as natural as the agricultural cycle of which it was an integral part. In spite of their oppression, people could be drawn into the pageantry of the occasion and so be incorporated into the state.[111]

Such, at least, was the hope. One suspects, however, that this policy of promoting a pharaonic ruler cult may have been deeply resented. If taxes had been paid at temples in the past, as there is some evidence to suggest,[112] the donor who presented his "offerings" to a local deity could still maintain the inward hope that the deity would appreciate these offerings and perhaps use them to effect a greater good (such as, for example, sending the Egyptians back to Egypt)! The chances that taxes delivered to the statue of a divinized pharaoh erected at a temple or within a chapel at a strategically located *bekhen*-building would answer such prayers, however, must have felt far more remote. Indeed, the reality—that any goods delivered would only help prolong Canaan's subjugation before the pharaoh—must have been rendered depressingly (or perhaps maddeningly) transparent.

The Contraction of Mercenaries

On the subject of contraction, it is worthwhile briefly addressing the controversy as to whether—following their pyrrhic victory over the Sea Peoples—the Egyptians increasingly contracted with members of the invading population that now resided in Canaan as well as with prisoners-of-war-turned-soldiers to help staff their bases. As noted above, Egyptians stationed at certain Ramesside bases in Canaan employed clay coffins, as have also been found at military bases and assorted other sites in Egypt and Nubia. These coffins emulate the style of sarcophagi fashioned out of other materials in Egypt. In Twentieth-Dynasty Canaan, however, a new type of highly stylized (often termed "grotesque") coffins appeared alongside their Egyptian equivalents at Deir el-Balah, Tell el-Far'ah South, and Beth-Shean. The similarity of five of the headdresses that ornamented highly stylized anthropoid clay coffins found in two tombs at Beth-Shean to those worn by some members of the Sea Peoples is extremely suggestive. Moreover, the extreme stylization of their faces is made somewhat more explicable when the imagery is placed into dialogue with Mycenaean gold masks (see Figure 8.6). In this context, it is relevant to note that a sheet of gold foil had been discovered in the mouth of an additional individual buried in a clay coffin at Beth-Shean![113]

While the arguments for and against Egypt's employment of Sea People garrison troops in their Canaanite bases are summarized elsewhere,[114] it is worthwhile stating that the scarcity of Aegean-style ceramic at Beth-Shean

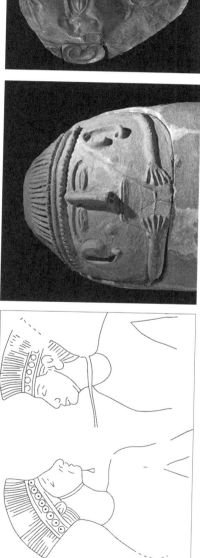

Figure 8.6 Depictions of Aegean individuals. (left) Sea People prisoners from Medinet Habu (redrawn from The Epigraphic Survey 1930, pl. 41); (middle) anthropoid clay coffin from Beth-Shean (Collection of The Israel Museum, Jerusalem; Photo © The Israel Museum, Jerusalem); (right) gold funerary mask from Mycenae (Scala/Art Resource, NY).

should not be taken as damning. Ramesses III had boasted on the walls of Medinet Habu that Sea People recruits were settled "in strongholds, bound in my name. Their military classes were plentiful, like hundred thousands. I apportioned them all with clothing (and) grain from the treasuries (and) granaries each year."[115] One would imagine, therefore, that any Sea People mercenaries who took up posts at a distance from the settlements their people had established along Canaan's coasts would be supplied with the pottery obtainable at Egypt's bases.

The recruitment of these northern invaders and pirates as soldiers in the New Kingdom is reminiscent of the eager embrace of raiders and professional mercenaries from the same general regions in the Saite and Persian periods. In both cases, their advanced maritime technology and military prowess made these men highly sought after in the armies of the major powers of the day, some of whom hired them for pay and others of whom offered them land to settle and a permanent place in their armies. Thus, in both eras, Mediterranean mercenaries in Egypt's hire found themselves battling counterparts fighting on behalf of Near Eastern rulers.[116]

Whether the Egyptians in the Twentieth Dynasty came to encounter the same frequent frustrations as later Egyptians (and also as leaders such as Frederick the Great and Napoleon)[117] with their foreign troops switching sides as soon as a better opportunity arose is not noted, though it is perhaps probable. Despite their uncertain loyalties, however, mercenaries are often increasingly relied upon the longer an imperial project lasts. As Lord Cromer pointed out in 1910, the British, like their Roman predecessors, utilized auxiliaries from the countries they conquered "owing to the paucity of their own numbers compared to the extent of their dominions, and to the unpopularity of foreign service among their own troops."[118] Similar factors likely account for the fact that as of 2015 CE contractors made up half of the personnel that America maintained in Iraq and close to 70% in Afghanistan.[119] As opposition grows, as expenditures increase, and as returns diminish, the allure of empire inevitably fades—even among its core constituents.

The Contraction of Borders

The contraction of Egypt's empire back to the eastern fringes of the Nile Delta in the Twentieth Dynasty certainly began with the widespread unrest that accompanied the change from the Late Bronze to the Iron Age. This complex and multi-causal epidemic of destructions, collapses, and abandonments has been the subject of numerous books.[120] The most recent of these, Eric Cline's *1177 B.C.: The Year Civilization Collapsed*, has garnered an unusual amount of press for a book on pre-classical antiquity precisely because the stresses that brought low so many civilizations at that time mirror those faced in our modern world: disruptive climactic conditions and consequent armed migrations, dangerous levels of interdependence, increasingly "unruly" groups hostile to large states, and wars aplenty. This "perfect storm," as Cline refers to it,[121] resulted in the devastation of virtually all of the main urban centers in the lowlands of Canaan, precisely the nodes that the Egyptians relied upon and also fostered for the health of their empire. Villages that had not played a direct role in Egypt's world system by and large did not suffer a similar collapse, and, indeed, the hill country witnessed a dramatic rise in population.[122]

In the contraction of Egypt's empire, weakness at its core undoubtedly played an enormous role. In the reign of Ramesses III, alone, Egypt had fought off two large-scale invasions from Libya and one double-pronged invasion from the Sea People. The scorched gateway at Tell el-Borg, one of Egypt's eastern border fortresses, likely testifies to the seriousness of this threat.[123] As if this weren't enough, Ramesses III had to deal with rampant inflation, workers' strikes, tomb robbery, and a conspiracy that cost him his life. Indeed, it is notable that many of the prisoners of war taken following his struggles with the Libyans were recruited into his personal service as "shield bearers, charioteers, retainers, and fan-bearers in the King's retinue."[124] Thus, just as the unpopular Libyan ruler Muammar Gaddafi purportedly surrounded himself with mercenaries as his own support crumbled,[125] Ramesses III's intensive recruitment of Libyans to guard his person suggests an increasing (and increasingly well-founded) distrust of those closest to him. Further, after Ramesses III's reign, the internal political situation only deteriorated as his sons and brothers battled it out for control and the internal conditions of the country worsened. As with Rome, the potent cocktail of internal disorder, shaken and stirred with successive splashes of foreign invasions, precipitated the inglorious fall of empire.

Egypt's rule in Canaan did not outlast Ramesses III's reign by even 20 years, and archaeological evidence suggests that the end was brutal. No evidence for Egyptian control in Canaan postdates the reign of Ramesses VI, and every Egyptian base—save that at Tell el-Far'ah South, which transitioned smoothly into sole Philistine control—appears to have been torched.[126] One can imagine any number of different perpetrators attacking Egypt's bases or even a scenario in which the Egyptians themselves put their bases to the torch as they withdrew to prevent others from profiting from them. It is difficult, however, not to envision a process somewhat similar to the start of the Arab Spring in which an uprising against one base—perhaps sparked by frustration at continued extractions in the face of patently inadequate protection—succeeded. The idea may then have spread like wildfire among the populations surrounding other imperial bases until, in a very short time, the Egyptians were driven out of the country, and Canaan's inhabitants were free to govern themselves.

Notes

1 Lattimore 1979, 37–8.
2 Peter Brand (2007, 19) has termed the Nineteenth Dynasty obsession with regaining Kadesh "irrational and emotional."
3 Johnson 2004, 58, 62–3.
4 Redford 1992, 217.
5 See Habachi 1980; Morris 2005, 382–4 et passim.
6 Morris 2005, 622–3, 633–4.
7 Caminos 1954, 254–5.
8 Kitchen 1993, 7–8.
9 Oren 1993, 1388–91; for more detail on individual sites, see Oren 1987.
10 Caminos 1954, 108–9; see Morris 2005, 478–86.
11 Luttwak 1979, 133.
12 Morris 2005, 711, 743–4; Kahn and Tammuz 2008; Figueras 2000.
13 Morris 2005, 618, 621–4, 635–45.
14 See Oren 1984; Higginbotham 2000; Killebrew 2005, 58–65; Morris 2005.
15 Similarities in masonry between Qubur el-Walaydah and Tell Jemmeh may suggest that the latter should be added to this list, as Oren originally suggested (Oren 1984, 46; Lehmann et al. 2010, 142).
16 David 2009, 710–11.
17 A stone block bearing the cartouche of Ramesses IV discovered at Tell Delhamiya in the Jordan Valley is the only known evidence pointing to an Egyptian presence at this site (Bietak 1993, 295).
18 Morris 2005, 392–5.
19 For an overview of this process, see Doyle 1986, 133.
20 D'Altroy 2003, 208.
21 Redford 2003, 13; Simpson 2003, 72–4; Mazar 2009, 3.
22 Johnson 2004, 151–2.
23 Aharoni 1967, 139; Ahituv 1978, 105.
24 Redford 1992, 152.
25 Redford 2003, 114.
26 Kitchen 1996, 16.
27 Der Manuelian 1987, 121.
28 Cumming 1982, 31.
29 Horowitz 1996.
30 Singer 1988a, 3; Morris 2005, 387–8.
31 Blakely, personal communication.
32 Weinstein 1981, 17–18; Murnane 1990, 70.
33 Zeedani 2007.
34 Johnson 2004, 151.
35 D'Altroy 2003, 60.
36 Rothenberg 1988.

37 See Ahituv 1978, 99; Redford 1990, 61.

38 Redford 2003, 72, 91.

39 Gadot 2010, 56–7.

40 Wente 1990, 108.

41 Tubb 1990, 26–9.

42 Starkey and Harding 1932, 28.

43 Bavay 2015.

44 Morris 2015b, 335–7.

45 Kislev et al. 2009, 770; Gadot 2010, 58.

46 Wente 1990, 109.

47 Martin 2011, 271–4.

48 See Ward 1966; David 2009, 711.

49 Mazar 2009, 21.

50 Dothan 2008, 72–87.

51 As discussed in Chapter 6, a limited amount of Egyptian-type pottery has been discovered in Eighteenth-Dynasty contexts. Both the amount of such pottery and the sites at which it is attested increase dramatically in the Ramesside period (Martin 2011, 262–6).

52 Killebrew 2004; Pierce 2013, 556–7.

53 Wente 1990, 106.

54 Pierce 2013, 527–8.

55 Pierce 2013, 519.

56 von Zielbauer 2007.

57 Simpson 2003, 72–3.

58 Redford 2003, 13, 64.

59 Kitchen 1996, 95.

60 Caminos 1954, 24, 242.

61 See, for example, Johnson 2004, 1, 5, 7, 197; Santora 2009.

62 Mazar 2009, 7.

63 Ward 1966, 175; Morris 2005, 500–2.

64 Lernau and Golani 2004, 2458, 2467–70, 2486–7; Mazar 2009, 22; Routledge 2015, 216–25.

65 Koch 2014, 163, 166–7.

66 Killebrew 2004, 342; Mazar 2009, 18–19; Burke and Lords 2010, 27–8. Jacob Damm, who is analyzing the ceramic from the most recent excavations at Joppa, shared the figure of 75% in a personal communication.

67 Martin 2011, 267.

68 See the discussion in Mazar 2009, 19–20 and also in Martin 2004, 280. Martin notes the same pattern at other Egyptian bases and comes to the same conclusion.

69 Mazar 2009, 19–20. Yahalom-Mack and Panitz-Cohen (2009, 733) even noted that the grinding platforms discovered at Beth-Shean conformed to a Canaanite rather than an Egyptian preference.

70 Braunstein 1998, 165–7; Green 2006, 107–16; Lipton 2010, 9, 12. The age and sex of the human remains at Beth-Shean were unfortunately unrecorded.

71 Green 2013, 420–1.

72 Bienkowski 1989, 59. The degree to which the fortunes of Lachish, Tel Sera', and Megiddo markedly improved as a result of increased Egyptian intervention has been pointed out by David Ussishkin (2004, 74–5).

73 Elton 1996, 43; Wells 1999, 179.

74 Gonen 1992b, 32–4.

75 Green 2013, 419–20, 427; Braunstein 1998, 245–6.

76 Gonen 1992b, 9, 32.

77 Gonen 1992b, 14–15, 19–20, 38.

78 Johnson 2004, 8.

79 Killebrew 2004, 331–3.

80 Wente 1990, 108.

81 Redford 1992, 208.

82 Simpson 1963, 36–41.

83 Kitchen 1996, 67.

84 Snape 2004, 151, 157–8.

85 D'Altroy 2003, 248.

86 Quoted in Hyslop 1990, 150. For the Assyrians, see Oded 1979.

87 Amenhotep II claimed to have taken 3,600 'Apiru prisoner in his Memphis stele, though the totals given in this text are typically met with some skepticism (Cumming 1982, 32; Hoffmeier 1999, 113).

88 Morris 2005, 377–81, 550, 556, 560, 583; Mazar 2009, 14–15.

89 Johnson 2004, 203.

90 Hasel 1998, 1–2; Martin 2011, 20.

91 EA 38; Moran 1992, 111.

92 Cifola 1988, 303.

93 Dever 1992, 107–8; Hoffmeier *forthcoming*.

94 Singer 1988a; Morris 2005, 712, 744–72. See Killebrew et al. 2006 for a redating of the latest levels of Deir el-Balah.

95 Morris 2005, 704, 714, 729–31.

96 Haring 1997, 47, n. 2, 48–9; Morris 2005, 399–402.

97 A retainer bearing letters was said to be "of the *bekhen* of Merneptah Hotephirmaat." Interestingly, while the envoy's name was Egyptian, his father's was not (Morris 2005, 479, 484).

98 Wimmer and Lehmann 2014, 344–7; Haring 1997, 49–50.

99 Blakely, personal communication. For the goose brand, see Morris 2005, 65–6.

100 Martin 2011, 250–1.

101 On the hieratic bowls, see, for example, Goldwasser 1984; Higginbotham 2000, 59–63; Wimmer and Lehmann 2014. I thank Jeff Blakely for information on the as-yet-unpublished Tell el-Hesi sherd. Martin (2011, 250) points out that evidence for the hieratic notations were found in connection

with the administrative center at Tel Sera' rather than the temple; however, these two buildings were no doubt closely connected by the Twentieth Dynasty. While no temples are attested at some of the sites at which the hieratic bowls have been found, the limited area of exposure at most of these sites and the small size of cultic chapels mean that no argument from silence can be mounted.

102 Mazar 2009, 10, 22; Morris 2015a; Morris 2015b.
103 Wells 1999, 163–4.
104 Ward 1966, 167, 171.
105 See Habachi 1969, 21.
106 Morris 2005, 727.
107 Ben-Tor 2016, 84–5.
108 Rowe 1940, 13–21, 29; James 1966, 14–19.
109 Singer 1988b, 107, n. 12.
110 Morris 2015a, 182–3.
111 Given 2004, 93.
112 See Bleiberg 1988, 163–5; Morris 2015a.
113 Oren 1973, 138–40; Dothan and Dothan 1992, 57–73, 92–4, 204–8.
114 Bietak 1993; Morris 2005, 701–6; Yasur-Landau 2010, 207–9.
115 Morris 2005, 699.
116 Kaplan 2003; Sandars 1985, 105–37.
117 Luvaas 1999, 73; Heuser 2010, 154.
118 Cromer 1910, 35–6.
119 McFate 2015.
120 See, for example, Drews 1993; Ward and Joukowsky 1992.
121 Cline 2014, 11.
122 Langgut et al. 2013, 167–8.
123 Hoffmeier 2004, 101–2.
124 Kitchen 2008, 70.
125 See, for example, Gwin 2011.
126 Weinstein 1992, 143–5. For descriptions of each destruction, see Morris 2005.

9

Conversions and Contractions in Egypt's Southern Empire (c. 1550–1069)

Over the course of the nearly five centuries that Egypt ruled Nubia in the New Kingdom, a great many conversions occurred. Some of these—such as the conversion of soldiers into settlers, military commanders into mayors, and Nubian rulers and ambitious elites into Egyptian-style nobles—have been discussed at length in Chapter 4. In this chapter, three other types of conversion will be addressed: the conversion of the built environment (in the service, no doubt, of a continuing conversion of the social environment), the conversion of Nubia's economy into a system that mirrored Egypt's own, and the conversion of its religious landscape into one dominated by Amun, divine kings, and other "Egyptian" gods but nonetheless increasingly placed under the stewardship of Nubians.

Finally, the chapter will draw to a close with a consideration of contractions. At the end of the Twentieth Dynasty, of course, contractions occurred in the extent of Egypt's Nubian empire, the southern border of which moved progressively north until it reached the First Cataract and the empire disappeared altogether. To shamelessly stretch the metaphor, contractions also herald births. Thus, the cultural reclamation of certain traditional Nubian material signatures—apparent in Twentieth-Dynasty contexts and even more pronounced in the wake of Egypt's retreat northward—is seen to have played an important role in the ideological formation of a vibrant indigenous state centered at Napata. This new state not only dominated Egypt's former territories but would come, eventually, to dominate Egypt itself.

Considering the several chapters now that have lingered on Egypt's experience in Syria-Palestine, it is useful to begin by briefly reviewing the conquest and character of Nubia at the start of the New Kingdom. In the late Second Intermediate period, much of Upper and Lower Nubia was ruled from Kerma, an immensely powerful polity located just upstream of the Third Cataract. Egyptian expatriates located in Lower Nubia had served the Kerman king, and during this period there seems to have been intermarriage between Egyptians and Nubians as well as a lively interchange of cultural influences.

Ancient Egyptian Imperialism, First Edition. Ellen Morris.
© 2018 Ellen Morris. Published 2018 by John Wiley & Sons Ltd.

Although the reconquest of Lower Nubia was largely complete by the beginning of the Eighteenth Dynasty (c. 1550), it would take roughly a century of repeated campaigns until Kerma was definitively defeated and Upper Nubia could be counted as firmly under Egypt's control. "Conquest," as Carla Sinopoli has observed, "is rarely a single event; resistance, rebellions, and cycles of reconquest are common."[1] And so it was in Nubia during the early and mid-Eighteenth Dynasty. As discussed in Chapter 4, the Nile Valley between Kawa and Gebel Barkal may have been granted provisional independence in return for regular deliveries of tribute and a pledge of noninterference. Certainly, it is remarkable that along this substantial stretch of fertile riparian land, no pharaonic monuments or settlements have been recovered. It may have been that the Egyptians traveled between Kawa and Gebel Barkal along the now waterless Sikkat el-Maheila desert trail, but as yet there is no evidence for this.[2] Otherwise, they must have arranged with local authorities to have rights to pass through the Dongola Reach by water. This dearth of imperial architecture stood in stark contrast to the region north of Kawa, into which Egypt's authorities had crammed numerous temples and temple-towns (see Figure 9.1).

Tellingly, the zone between the First and Third Cataracts as well as the outpost of Gebel Barkal near the Fourth Cataract appear overwhelmingly Egyptian in their material culture, despite scattered evidence for Nubian-style burials and for craftsmen who manufactured typically Egyptian goods in notably Nubian ways. In Chapter 4, grassroot reasons why Nubians may have actively chosen to adopt Egyptian-style material culture were discussed. Perhaps paramount among these reasons was that along with imperial administrators and settlers came workshops that mass-produced Egyptian-style objects, many of which were no doubt subsequently widely distributed by governmental and temple authorities. Thus, it was quite likely easier, if one lived near Egyptians, to outwardly become Egyptian than it would have been to refuse the clothing, pottery, and other items offered and insist on manufacturing them oneself. Under Kerman rule, after all, Nubians had of their own volition already begun to experiment with adopting aspects of Egyptian material culture.

A second important element in the conversion of Nubia's material culture was, no doubt, the fact that access to power for an ambitious Nubian under Egyptian rule meant speaking Egypt's language, cultivating an Egyptian appearance, and adopting an Egyptian name. This new colonial power dynamic quite likely meant that the most elite, upwardly mobile individuals in a Nubian community now looked Egyptian. If such "leading citizens" were viewed as role models, it would be little wonder if others followed suit in changing suit. Convenience and increased opportunity are powerful motivators.

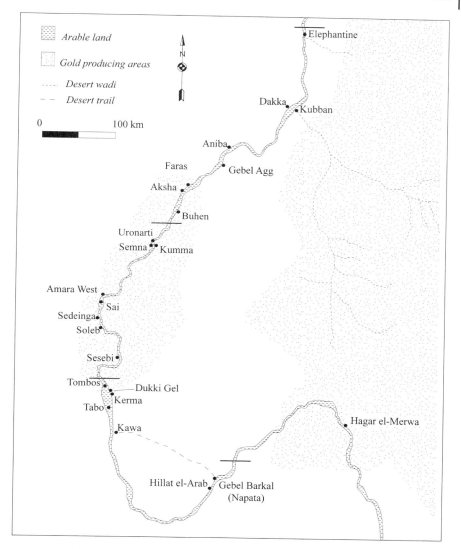

Figure 9.1 Major New Kingdom settlements and sites in Nubia.

Converting the Built Environment

While the trend in recent scholarship to resist any implication that Nubians played a passive role in their "acculturation" or "assimilation" is of vital importance, the active hand of the Egyptians in converting (or attempting to convert) former enemies into willing servants of the state must be kept in mind. Once its armies had secured control of Nubia, the Egyptian government began work to materialize its vision for a new order on its southernmost frontier. Just what this order would look like, however, was evidently not immediately apparent.

Following Thutmose I's initial conquest of Kerma, this royal capital was abandoned and the population shifted to Dukki Gel, a site located roughly a kilometer away. Given the simultaneous abandonment of one site and radical expansion of the other—right as Egypt took control of the region—it is safe to assume that the resettlement was forced. If so, the Egyptians may have intended to showcase their authority and to provide the population with a fresh start on their journey toward becoming compliant subjects of the empire. Charles Bonnet suggests that Thutmose I (c. 1502–1492) intended the heart of the settlement to serve as an Egyptian-held fortress at which Nubian cattle were kept. Such structures—referenced by Thutmose I's son[3]—should be archaeologically observable. In support, Bonnet cites the presence of a 6-m-thick fortification wall, basins for watering livestock, and hundreds of hoof prints![4] If the core of the settlement was indeed a *mnnw* fortress town, however, it is unique in its incorporation of numerous distinctively Nubian (or at least emphatically non-Egyptian) architectural elements.

Much about Dukki Gel remains unclear, as its stratigraphy is quite complex. Prior to the move, however, the site already housed two Nubian temples, whose oval shape, flamboyant use of rounded bastions, and sinuous curves dramatically differentiate them from Egypt's own sacred architecture.[5] Perhaps (rightly) realizing the fragility of his hold on this newly conquered territory, Thutmose I demolished two adjacent structures (palaces perhaps) but left the Kerman temples standing. Beside them, he constructed a sacral complex of rectilinear temples built in good Egyptian fashion. The protrusion of rounded bastions appended to all sorts of architecture throughout the early Eighteenth-Dynasty colonial center, however, and an unusual interest in rounded forms lent Dukki Gel a distinctively hybrid character.

In this new settlement, then, Egyptian architecture co-existed with Nubian architecture. Moreover, immediately to the southwest of the Egyptian complex and aligned perpendicular to the processional entrance, a new ceremonial structure was erected. This building resembled a series of densely packed hypostyle halls, but its other elements—including the two enormous rounded towers that flanked the gate and the numerous tiny rounded buttresses on the outside of its walls—marked the building as a peculiar architectural compromise between two communities with markedly disparate aesthetics.

Thus, in the beginning, it would seem that Egyptian-dominated Nubia had the potential to have evolved much differently than it did. That this awkward fusion of styles may have been unsatisfying to Nubian sensibilities, however, is perhaps indicated by the fact that once the Nubians rebelled and briefly regained their autonomy, they set the building aflame and then dismantled it down to its foundations. The Egyptians too seem to have come to a similar decision to end this experiment, for not only was the building never reconstructed, but all efforts at developing and promoting an emphatically hybrid architectural style were abruptly dropped. Although the pre-existing Nubian temples at Dukki Gel were not destroyed, upon Thutmose III's reassertion of Egyptian control of the precinct was marginalized, being pointedly excluded from a completely redesigned Egyptian-style temple precinct and no doubt excluded as well from any imperial budget for embellishment (see Figure 9.2). Significantly, Nubian architectural influences are completely absent in all other settlements established under Egyptian pharaohs from the mid-Eighteenth through the Nineteenth Dynasties.[6]

Beginning in the reign of Thutmose III (c. 1479–1425), when the Egyptians finally felt confident that Kerma would not rise again, the pharaonic government began a concerted program of establishing civilian settlements on the sites of what were likely armed camps (e.g. Tombos, Sai, Sesebi, and Amara West) and at other places located near mines, trails, or other strategic settings. Such communities appear to have been essential to Egypt's efforts to colonize a region that had never before been theirs. In Upper Nubia these settlements extended south of the Second Cataract down, eventually, to Kawa. New towns were also constructed during the New Kingdom in Lower Nubia at Faras, Aksha, and Dakka, while certain older centers—such as Aniba, Kubban, and Buhen—received refurbishments and continued to thrive.[7]

In Syria-Palestine, the Egyptians largely relied on elites located in key cities to manage their empire for them by gathering revenue and maintaining order. Governing through cities is a common imperial tactic. Indeed, so crucial were towns and cities to Rome's imperial strategy that its officials—like their counterparts in New Kingdom Nubia—took the liberty of creating such settlements where none had existed previously (or where pre-existing entities had been eradicated).[8] The Spanish in North America, who likewise attempted to extend imperial control over areas far beyond their own borders, also felt it necessary to create settlements where none existed and consciously drew upon Roman models for inspiration. The Laws of the Indies, composed in the 16th century CE, which laid out in great detail the principles that should guide the founding and establishment of a new settlement, drew upon the writings of Alberti, who was himself at least partly inspired by Vitruvius.[9] These 148 ordinances have been deemed "in terms of their widespread application and persistence, probably the most effective planning documents in the history of mankind."[10] Significantly, many of the principles outlined therein had been anticipated in New Kingdom Nubia.

From the ordinances, for example, it is clear that newly established colonial settlements were explicitly constructed with an eye toward two audiences: colonists and people from the local region. In the previous chapter, the need to

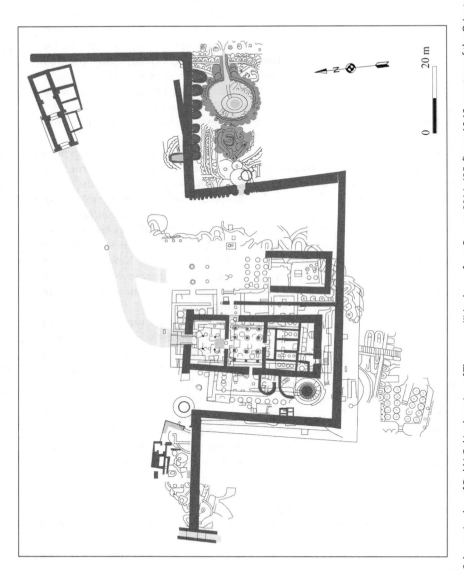

Figure 9.2 Schematic plan of Dukki Gel in the reign of Thutmose III (redrawn from Bonnet 2014, 435, figure 18.12, courtesy of the Oriental Institute of the University of Chicago).

0   20 m

make soldiers, administrators, and resident expatriates feel secure and at home in foreign lands was discussed at some length, and a similar concern must have prevailed in Nubia. Ordinance 128 of the Laws of the Indies states that the construction of a palisade or ditch for the protection of the inhabitants should be among the first tasks undertaken.[11] Egyptian-style settlements in Upper Nubia were in many cases strategically situated on islands (Tabo, Sai, and Amara West), and at least four newly created Upper Nubian towns were walled (Sai, Tombos, Sesebi, and Amara West). The nature of many other settlements that we assume existed—due to the proximity of major temples or to the existence of offices like that of "mayor"—is less clear as movements of the river or activities of later inhabitants evidently obscured their remains. In the following discussion of colonial settlements, then, it is Sai, Sesebi, and Amara West that will be the focus of interest. Fortuitously, excavations at each of these sites have recently been renewed and are already beginning to yield some of the most nuanced information available on the dynamics of town life in New Kingdom Nubia.[12] A fortified town at Tombos, recently identified by Stuart Tyson Smith, will add to our knowledge shortly. Smith's initial investigations suggest that the town—likely to be equated with Taroy—was founded during the reign of Thutmose III and would have been roughly comparable in size to Sesebi.[13]

Shortly following the reign of Thutmose III, the offices of the deputies of Kush and of Wawat appear to have been created to mirror the recent splitting of the viziership in Egypt into two regionally based subdivisions.[14] The two deputies resided in Upper and Lower Nubia, respectively, though their seat of office shifted in various reigns so as to coincide with current pharaonic projects and priorities. The construction of walled towns in the New Kingdom, then, was often associated with the establishment of a new region-wide administrative capital. Thus, in Lower Nubia, Tutankhamun founded the walled town of Faras, while Seti I founded one at Aksha. Likewise, in Upper Nubia, Thutmose III built the walled town at Sai, Akhenaten constructed Sesebi, and Seti I initiated work at Amara West.

Given the vast quantities of agricultural and mineral wealth that no doubt filled the massive storehouses situated in these government centers, the thick, bastioned walls may have been deemed a prudent precaution to protect the deputy and the goods he accumulated on behalf of the Egyptian government. Defense seems unlikely to have been the *sole* issue at stake in the creation of the walls, however, given that they possessed few of the elaborate defensive features present in Middle Kingdom fortresses. Likewise, the inhabitants of the sumptuous extramural villas at Amara West appear to have felt they had little to fear from the outside world. The unique outward focus of Amara's temple, too, suggests a desire for connectivity rather than a highly policed insularity. Perhaps, then, the walls that surrounded the capitals of Upper Nubia were primarily intended to project power as well as to aid in the surveillance of both visitors and inhabitants.

So far as can be ascertained, the majority of these Upper Nubian capital towns had been meticulously planned on an orthogonal layout, such that (originally at least) straight streets met at right angles, drains kept major thoroughfares clean, and everything was in its proper place.[15] Temples and their storehouses, for example, were generally nestled in a corner of the town together with administrative offices. The commandant's quarters—occupied in all likelihood by the deputy or the mayor—generally constituted the only other monumental structure. These administrative mansions were easily distinguished by the thickness of their walls, by their extravagant use of space, and by the employment of far more columns than was structurally necessary. Elsewhere, if Sesebi can be taken as representative, fairly uniform housing had been provided for various social classes.[16] Bakeries, workshops, and other practical amenities filled out remaining built spaces.

Communities such as Kahun and the workmen's village at Amarna demonstrate that the Egyptian government occasionally erected such orthogonal settlements within Egypt for its own citizens. Thus, one should perhaps think of these towns as constructed orthogonally in part because such architecture was comfortably familiar. Cross-culturally, colonists often attempt to recreate the built environment of their homeland down to the smallest detail in order to enhance their feeling of belonging in an alien environment. It is thus notable that over a doorway of an Egyptian-style house in Aniba someone had written the words: "When you enter into this house, may you believe yourself in Thebes and rejoice."[17]

Grid-towns have numerous other benefits from an imperial point of view, however. For instance, they enable architects to draft plans that—with their standardized measurements and right angles—allow large-scale installations to be built as quickly and efficiently as possible.[18] Moreover, as James Scott has masterfully explicated in his book *Seeing Like a State*,[19] grids have the virtue of rendering settlements legible to outside authorities. Gridded establishments are easy to police, easy to navigate, free from local signatures that might provoke anti-imperial sentiments, and free from blind alleys or other potential sites of ambush. Finally, and crucially, orthogonal settlements offer a way of instantiating the principles of order that states typically wish to promote as they extend their frontiers and work to convert the foreign into the familiar. As Aulus Gellius observed in his own day, Roman colonies were in essence copies or miniatures of Rome, designed as such in order to help transplant Roman laws and institutions in unfamiliar soil, thereby causing them to take root and flourish.[20]

In New Spain, the gaze of the native population was kept very much in mind in the process of city-planning. Ordinance 135 of the Laws of the Indies stipulated that a new town should be built as quickly as was feasible and with an eye toward the drama of its unveiling.[21] According to Ordinance 137,

...nor [should the settlers] allow the Indians to enter within the confines of the town until it is built and its defences ready and the houses built so that when the Indians see them they will be struck with admiration and will understand that the Spaniards are there to settle permanently and not temporarily. They [the Spaniards] should be so feared that they [the Indians] will not dare offend them, but they will respect them and desire their friendship.[22]

If only a handful of local elites might ever be impressed first-hand by the great cities of the imperial core, then the solution seems to have been to erect smaller replicas of these cities in dominated peripheries in hopes that they might still dazzle and seduce. Colonial towns, then, may have been constructed to simultaneously repel native peoples with hostile intentions and to attract and help convert those who might be willing to participate in the colonial project.

Once Kerma was defeated, Egypt still had enemies, even if these were increasingly limited to small-scale groups of semi-nomadic peoples, like those of Ibhet and Akuyta, who perhaps preyed like bandits upon state mining expeditions.[23] The people of Irem, a region located perhaps somewhere in the desert periphery of the Third Cataract, however, continued to pose a recurrent and formidable threat. It is significant, then, that Ramesses II decorated the western gateway into Amara West with a (somewhat improbable) scene of himself slaying a purported 2,000 Iremites and capturing 5,000 more.[24] Thus, "wild" Nubians, who actively resisted Egypt's attempts at pacification, were advertised at the very gates to an Egyptian town as fit to kill. Significantly, as a stele erected at Semna demonstrates, those doing the killing would be drawn as military levies from the inhabitants of the walled settlements of Upper and Lower Nubia, even if (or perhaps especially if) they were Nubian themselves.[25]

The Spanish in North America distinguished between native peoples who abided by the regulations of the imperial government, *indios domésticos*, and *indios bárbaros*, who could be hunted down and killed should they prove dangerous. It was widely recognized, however, that the borders between these categories were permeable and that pacification was preferable to killing. Religious conversion was an important step in "civilizing" natives, but so too was the teaching of Spanish ways of life, a process that was in many cases most efficiently accomplished by inviting native peoples into colonial settlements to live with (and like) settlers. As the full-blooded Spanish population was miniscule in comparison to the population already inhabiting the land they wished to control, the colonists recognized that the conversion of natives *into* Spaniards was absolutely essential for their own security, for the expansion of their empire, and for their continued enrichment.[26] Thus, in order to help eradicate native traditions and promote the adoption of Spanish ways of life, the Spanish crown issued a decree stating that those natives that could be enticed to settle in Spanish-style settlements were to be given new clothes, food staples, crops, livestock, technologies, and luxuries and taught new trades.[27] Like the Romans before them, the Spaniards quickly realized a side-benefit to this approach, namely that natives that had already adopted a colonial lifestyle made much more effective go-betweens to their "barbarous" counterparts than did representatives of the imperial government![28]

Once native peoples abandoned (at least in public) their former names, languages, clothes, and other obvious ethnic markers, they became harder and harder both for contemporary Spanish authorities and for modern historians to track. Those conducting censuses in the Spanish Americas originally dutifully subdivided the Indians living among them into numerous categories, depending on the ratios of their Spanish to native ancestry. In many cases, however, the census taker had to rely upon the word of an individual as to what he or she was, which resulted in an opportunity for those questioned to shift categories in whatever way seemed most advantageous. Finally, in many cases quantifying exact ethnicities seemed increasingly irrelevant. If a person possessed all the trappings of a Spaniard, lived like a Spaniard, and identified as such—and if the distribution of state funds or perquisites was not at issue— who was to say that the individual *wasn't* for all intents and purposes a Spaniard? By and large, historians writing on Spain's empire have found themselves forced to adopt a similarly pragmatic approach.[29]

Physical anthropology offers scientists an avenue through which to investigate biological backgrounds in addition to ethnic identities, and the results—though limited—have been interesting. For instance, the inhabitants of Egyptian-style tombs at Tombos included Egyptians, Nubians, and a mixed population. Strontium and oxygen isotope data further indicate that the majority of the town's population had grown up in Nubia. Perhaps not surprisingly, immigrant Egyptians peaked at roughly a third of the population in the mid-Eighteenth Dynasty, during the first blush of colonization.[30] Studies that were expanded to include Amara West suggest that similar spikes in immigration may have occurred there in the Ramesside period, perhaps also in the immediate aftermath of the initial construction of the town.[31]

Bereft of such data, archaeologists excavating New Kingdom habitation zones have struggled, and continue to struggle, with distinguishing the material signatures of Egyptians from those of the Nubians who almost certainly settled alongside them. The seemingly radical homogeneity of the material record convinced early archaeologists that they were in fact dealing with towns almost completely populated by Egyptian settlers, who must have either exterminated Nubians or excluded them from settling there. This paradigm was eventually abandoned, however, once scholars realized that the shift occurred somewhat gradually and that it occurred in traditionally Nubian villages as well. Thus, rather than abandoning their country, it seems that many

Nubians had simply begun to live in Egyptian-style houses, utilize Egyptian-type pottery, and inter their loved ones according to Egyptian norms.[32] Only within the past few decades, in conjunction with excavations at sites like Tombos and, more recently, Sai, Amara West, and Sesebi, however, have archaeologists begun to pay concentrated attention to teasing out extremely subtle clues from the material record in order to determine (so far as is feasible) the ethnic affiliation and heritage of populations at Egyptian-style settlements in Nubia (see Figure 9.3).

Sai

At all sites that have been carefully analyzed, the most prevalent traditionally Nubian-style artifacts are handmade cookpots. As discussed in Chapter 4, this type of behind-the-scenes ceramic is useful in colonial contexts as it frequently reveals a seeming cultural disjuncture between the nature of the food cooked (likely indigenous) and the style of the vessels upon which it was served (generally colonial). At Sai, the lowest ratio of Nubian cookpots to Egyptian cookpots was noted in the early Eighteenth-Dynasty armed camp (levels 5 and 6), which appears to have been intended to secure the island of Sai from reoccupation by the inhabitants of the Kerman vassal polity of Sha'at. In the camp, a large proportion of the Egyptian cookpots appear to have been imported from Egypt, most probably from the army base located at Elephantine. The large quantities of Egyptian-style firedogs—ceramic forms useful for propping up cooking pots and thus unlikely vehicles for broadcasting cultural prestige—strongly suggest that a majority of the earliest cooks at the site were Egyptian. At the same time, the presence of some Nubian cookware and smaller amounts of other Nubian pottery, including storage jars, may indicate that negotiations between the Egyptians and their former enemies had in fact begun.[33]

Once the camp at Sai was converted into a walled town in the reign of Thutmose III, imported Egyptian cookpots were never again found, and the ratio of Nubian to Egyptian-style cookpots climbed steeply. This new predominance of native cookware likely indicates that Nubians increasingly occupied the site as servants, wives, and/or settlers in their own right. Whether this pattern suggests, as on the Spanish frontier, that the local population was not invited to move into colonial towns until these entities were fully established is not known. It does suggest, however, that—as in Spanish America and numerous other colonial milieus—the imperial settlers quickly adopted the foodways of the local population.[34] The hybrid styles of at least some of the ceramic found at Sai—for example, pottery made in Egyptian style but given a typically Nubian finish or constructed with the type of clay generally favored by Nubians—suggests that at least some Nubians resident in the town took up Egyptian-style crafts, thereby directly participating in a new economic order.[35]

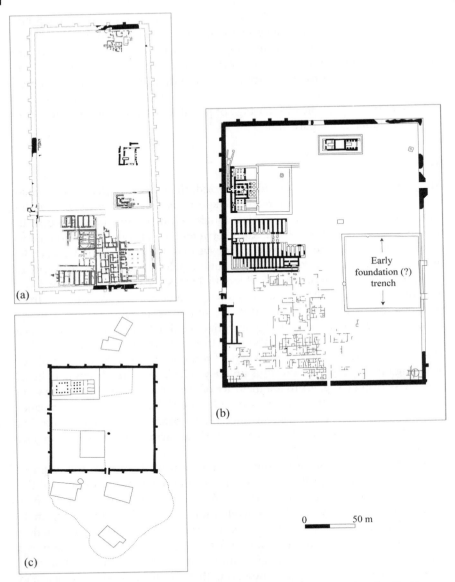

Figure 9.3 Three New Kingdom walled towns. (a) Map of the New Kingdom fortified town of Sai Island, including field work results up to 2016 (redrawn from Budka 2017, 17, fig. 3, courtesy of Julia Budka, ©AcrossBorders, Ingrid Adenstedt); (b) Sesebi (redrawn from Morkot 2012, 316, figure 182, courtesy of the Egypt Exploration Society); (c) Amara West with extramural villas (redrawn from Spencer n.d.).

Along these lines, it is interesting to note that when non-Christian native Americans began to practice Spanish trades, due to chronic labor shortages, this intensive exposure to a radically new economy is said to have done more to alter traditional native lifeways than an enforced residency at a mission ever could have.[36]

It would be a mistake for the pendulum to swing too far, however, and for it to be assumed that the nonelite social stratum at Sai was predominantly made up of Nubians who had agreed to participate in colonial culture. While Egyptian-style architecture and serving ware are too closely tied to centralized planning, distribution, and prestige to be useful for determining ethnicity, numerous mundane features in the material record showed a distinct affinity to Egyptian rather than Nubian traditions. These included quern emplacements, ovens, spinning bowls, fishing equipment, special fish platters, and even fertility figurines—though at least one typically Nubian fertility figure was also uncovered.[37] Fully two-thirds of Sai awaits excavation, and so there is much currently unknown about the town itself. The settlement boasted a mayor (*ḥȝty-ꜥ*) and likely also served as the seat of the deputy of Upper Nubia prior to the late Eighteenth Dynasty.[38] Clearly, then, if parallels with Egypt hold valid, it would have housed administrators and priests, as well as laborers, craftsmen, and farmers.

Sesebi

Virtually nothing is known of the town at Soleb, which appears to have taken over from Sai as the capital of Upper Nubia in Amenhotep III's reign. Perhaps it did not have long to develop, as almost immediately after ascending the throne Amenhotep IV moved the capital to Sesebi.[39] The walled town of Sesebi, at 270×200 m, was substantially larger than Sai (perhaps 238×120 m). Like Sai, however, excavations have revealed that the site had been occupied already in the early Eighteenth Dynasty, presumably to secure recent conquests in the region. While the nature of the earliest settlement isn't clear—as the builders of the fortress town razed it and covered it over with roughly 2 m of alluvial mud—the site possessed monumental architecture and two probable temples prior to the reign of Amenhotep IV. Pamela Rose has noted the presence of Nubian pottery (especially cookpots and Kerman fineware) alongside Egyptian ceramic types in levels dating to the early Eighteenth Dynasty.[40]

Although a greater percentage of Sesebi has been excavated than was the case at Sai, most of the excavation took place in the 1930s, and so the subtle questions of identity that are the focus of the teams working at Sai and Amara West have yet to be addressed in depth, a situation that is currently in the process of being remedied. Early excavations at Sesebi did, however, reveal much more about residential zones than had been the case at Sai and shed light on sharp class divides. According to their reports, small houses at the site possessed only a handful of rooms, while other houses, often located in closer proximity to the temple zone, resembled townhouse versions of Amarna-style villas, complete with master suites, bathrooms, and upper stories.[41]

At least some of the owners of these large villas no doubt exercised control over the resources accumulated by Sesebi's four temples (three of them contiguous), and it is quite likely that some of the same or other elite residents were in charge of overseeing mining operations. Recent excavations have found evidence for gold-working at the site, and, indeed, the entire Abri-Delgo reach from the Second to the Third Cataracts is relatively rich in auriferous quartz vein systems (see Figure 9.1).[42] Given the amount of gold required by the state on a regular basis for high-level trade and dowries, for gifts to temples and high officials, and for the ornamentation of the pharaohs and their palaces, access to these new mines would have been welcome, especially as Amenhotep IV, a radical and polarizing pharaoh, prepared to move to Middle Egypt and erect a brand new capital city (see the Epilogue for a more in-depth discussion of this particular king and his attitude toward empire).

As for the lower levels of the social strata at Sesebi—including the individuals who presumably worked the gold, tilled the soil, fashioned the pottery, and did all other types of manual labor—renewed excavations will, it is hoped, reveal new information that will help nuance our understanding of ethnic relations at the site. While one might at this point comfortably assume the presence of Egyptians, Nubians, and Egypto-Nubians, these may not have been the only ethnicities thrown into the mix. As briefly referenced in the last chapter, Akhenaten is known to have ordered his vassal in Damascus to send him 'Apiru of the pastureland, such that he might settle them in the cities of the land of Kush.[43] Considering the authorship of the letter, the likeliest candidates for the Nubian towns would be Sesebi, Dukki Gel, and (quite likely) Kawa.[44] Ramesses II similarly brought children of Retenu (i.e. Syria-Palestine) south in order to serve on the divine estates at Abu Simbel.[45] Likewise, when labor was needed for yet another of Ramesses II's vanity temples at Wadi es-Sebua, the viceroy of Kush led expeditions to capture desert dwellers so that they could serve as labor.[46] While no traces of Syro-Palestinians show up in the archaeological record—presumably due to the standard Egyptian practice of divesting prisoners of war of their belongings and provisioning them with new clothing and supplies from the state treasuries[47]—these examples serve as a reminder that the ethnic encounters that took place within these settlements were likely even more complex than is generally suspected.

Amara West

Although the archaeological situation at Sesebi remains somewhat unclear, Robert Morkot has estimated that as much as half of the walled town was taken up by temples and storehouses.[48] The trend toward an ever-dwindling ratio of domestic to official space (and especially to space occupied by temple complexes) continued in the Nineteenth Dynasty with the last two walled towns built in Nubia: Amara West and Aksha. These towns, both founded by Seti I and finished by Ramesses II, quite likely served as new seats for the deputies of Upper and Lower Nubia, respectively.[49] The size of these towns was significantly smaller than either Sai or Sesebi (Amara West measuring 108×108 m and Aksha 120×82 m), yet the temple and administrative complexes still occupied close to half the total area. Thanks to recently renewed excavations, the (former) island site of Amara West has already revealed a great deal about life in Nineteenth- and Twentieth-Dynasty Nubia, which is especially welcome as the nature of this period is both poorly understood and much debated.

Like Sai and Sesebi, an early Eighteenth-Dynasty settlement was located in the vicinity of the later town and exhibited a mixed Egypto-Nubian assemblage.[50] Seti I had constructed Amara West's town walls, but the site was occupied up until the Egyptian government ceded all claims to control at the very end of the New Kingdom. Interestingly, rather than having been rigidly planned from the start, Amara West seems, outside of the temple and administrative quarters, to have allowed its inhabitants some freedom in shaping their space as they saw fit.[51] As time progressed, significant alterations were made—both by the authorities and by individuals—and eventually habitation spilled outside its walls, creating a new and relatively upscale suburb.[52] Without the addition of the suburb, it has been estimated that Amara West could hold some 200 inhabitants, though the incorporation of industrial areas (including workshops for processing gold-bearing quartz) within the walls must have rendered the atmosphere unwholesome at times.[53]

As at Sai, the percentage of Nubian cookpots increased over time at Amara West,[54] quite likely testifying to an ever-increasing population of Nubians and Egypto-Nubians in the settlement. Hybrid forms too were present in the ceramic repertoire, and at least some of the fertility figurines most commonly found in later levels of the site conform more closely to Nubian than to Egyptian parallels.[55] The architecture of the town was, of course, typically Egyptian, though with one notable exception. In the suburbs, one of the largest of the quintessentially Egyptian-style villas encompassed within its grounds an oval mudbrick structure that looked far more Nubian than Egyptian. The purpose of the building, which contained primarily Egyptian-style material culture but seems to have been occupied only very briefly, is unknown. The suggestion, then, that it may have been set up for a festival or celebration of some sort is particularly intriguing.[56]

The fact that Nubian elements—like this outbuilding—began to reappear in prominent public settings at the end of Egypt's occupation of Upper Nubia is notable, as it coincided with an increased visibility of Nubian and hybrid elements evident in the mortuary realm at Amara West and elsewhere.[57] This subject will be taken up again at the chapter's end. Inside the villa's walls, Nubian-style cookware made up roughly 10% of the assemblage.[58] Although this percentage was fairly typical for the site as a whole, it is perhaps likely that the reason the owner of the luxurious villa constructed a Nubian-style outbuilding on his property is because he was, in fact, Nubian.

Scholars who have studied the backgrounds of the deputies of Kush and Wawat have noted that beginning in the late Eighteenth Dynasty these men seem to have been recruited from prominent Nubian families rather than from among Egypt's nobility. Given that nepotism appears to have been as endemic in Nubia as it was in Egypt,[59] it would make sense if both the deputy of Upper Nubia—resident at Amara West—and the occupant of one of the site's largest villas belonged to the same extended family. Perhaps it is no coincidence that the largest multi-chambered tomb yet discovered at Amara West (G244)—which possessed an unusually rich burial assemblage and, anomalously, a tumulus superstructure—dated to the Twentieth Dynasty.[60]

Divine Conversions

As discussed in the last chapter, the cult of Amun was not unknown to Syro-Palestinian worshipers, but it appears to have been practiced half-heartedly and abandoned quickly. In Nubia, however, the situation was much different, for when the New Kingdom ended, worship of Amun and of other Egyptian gods continued unabated or perhaps even with renewed vigor. Indeed, it might truthfully be said that Egypt had never witnessed a more pious ruler than Piankhi (c. 747–716). When the Nubian warrior-king conquered Egypt just prior to the Twenty-fifth Dynasty, he was shocked and appalled by the degenerate state of Amun-worship that he encountered, stating of the citizens of Memphis, "They do not place Amon in their hearts, nor do they know what he has commanded."[61] The cult of Amun seems to have been introduced to Gebel Barkal—the spiritual seat of the Twenty-fifth-Dynasty kings—already in the mid-Eighteenth Dynasty, and careful stewardship of the cult over several centuries had only strengthened it. Clearly the attitudes toward Egyptian gods differed starkly on the two frontiers. This contrast, then, must be accounted for.

One could perhaps point to a greater time-depth in the exposure of Nubians to Egyptian gods and temples. For instance, once cultural barriers broke down during the late Middle Kingdom, it is likely that many Nubians who had developed working relations with Egyptians or married into their families also began to adopt the Horus gods, cataract gods, and the deified Senwosret III as patrons, whose divine protection might keep their communities safe and prosperous. Indeed, even the king of Kerma, when he gained control over Lower Nubia in the Second Intermediate period, commanded the refurbishment of the cult of Horus of Buhen. Moreover, the fortuitously preserved letters penned by the scribe Djutmose to his family in the Twentieth Dynasty suggest that the cults of the Horus gods of Kubban and Aniba still functioned even in the final throes of Egyptian control. It was presumably in the courtyards of these temples that the frightened and ailing old scribe poured his libations to the resident Horus gods and to Amun of the Thrones of the Two Lands (a.k.a. Amun of Gebel Barkal) to ask that they confer blessings on his family and deliver him home safely from the wilds of Nubia.[62]

Egypt invested early and often in recrafting the religious landscape of Nubia. When the Egyptians invaded in the early Eighteenth Dynasty, they began immediately to refurbish old temples and to initiate work on new cultic structures—tasks undertaken with far more relish and regularity than the repair or construction of fortifications. In the early to mid-Eighteenth Dynasty, temples and chapels were built in old fortresses (Kubban, Aniba, Faras, Buhen, Uronarti, Semna, and Kumma), in the middle of new settlements and encampments (Dukki Gel and Sai), and even in areas in which the supporting settlement has not yet been located (Kurte, Amada, Ellesiya, Qasr Ibrim, Tabo, Gebel Dosha, Pnubs, and Napata).[63] It may well be that many of these new temples were built in the vicinity of areas thought to have been sacred to the local Nubian populations, especially in the case of seemingly out-of-the-way shrines, rock outcroppings, or caves at which a great deal of marking activity is observed (such as perhaps at Gebel Barkal, Gebel Agg, or Hagar el-Merwa). If so, the temples could be viewed as attempts by the state to co-opt and redirect the numinous energy of a particular place. Early attention to the god Dedwen, too, may also have been intended to convince Nubians that their deities had a place in Egypt's pantheon.[64]

Just as the Egyptians likely converted Nubian sacred places into typically pharaonic shrines and temples, so too they may have converted their state god Amun into a deity fit for export south of the border. As discussed briefly in Chapter 4, it appears that the new ram-headed form of Amun—dubbed Amun-Re, Lord of the Thrones of the Two Lands—promoted by the Egyptians at Gebel Barkal and at other sites in Nubia, was designed specifically to appeal to Nubians. Judging from archaeological and iconographic evidence, Kerman Nubians seem to have venerated images of rams, perhaps as animals sacred to a specific deity. Thus, in promoting a new ram-headed version of Amun, who appears relatively suddenly and without a strong character of his own, the Egyptians presumably hoped to syncretize their state god with an indigenous deity that had predated colonial rule.[65] At Kawa too, the version of Amun-Re worshiped as "the Lion over the South Country" may represent a fusion of Egypt's main deity with a local Nubian lion god.[66] Similar creations or reworkings of divine entities to resemble others that they are intended to replace is, of course, a tried-and-true tactic employed by imperial governments and missionaries alike.

Conversions in Spiritual Wealth

Just what the Nubians thought of the cult of the divine pharaoh—which seems to have been promoted as enthusiastically in Nubia (e.g. Soleb, Sedeinga, Faras, Aksha, Amara West, Abu Simbel, Derr, Wadi es-Sebua, and Gerf Hussein) as it was in numerous Egyptian temples (e.g. Karnak, Luxor, and the Ramesseum)—is not known.[67] Perhaps the long-lasting cult of Senwoseret III or the royal connotations inherent in the cults of the older Horus gods and in that of Amun would have paved the way toward a relatively easy acceptance. Additionally or alternatively, the cult of a sacred king may have felt familiar as a similar dynamic seems to have been operative in Kerma in the Second Intermediate period, judging from the hundreds of sacrificed retainers interred within royal tumuli. One suspects, however, that the primary attraction of such divine kingship cults and of the other Egyptian-style cults newly established in Nubia may have been the opportunities for enrichment that they offered to those willing to assume leading roles within their administrative hierarchy.

From a cynical perspective, the building of temples in Egyptian-occupied Nubia appears to go hand in hand with a sacral land grab. Thutmose III, the first large-scale temple builder in Nubia, boasted that he had obligated the Nubians with yearly *b3kw* taxes, just as he had obligated his own dependent laborers.[68] *B3kw* taxes, as Edward Bleiberg has demonstrated, were a type of tax well known in Egypt that was delivered by classes of people (rather than specific rich individuals) to temples (rather than to the king directly) for use in the temple and also for redistribution in the context of state projects.[69] If an alarming amount of land was transferred into the hands of temples in Nubia, however, it is vital to recognize that much the same dynamic was operative in Egypt. The amount of land transferred to temples in the New Kingdom was entirely unprecedented, with fully a third of Egypt's arable land likely under temple control by the Twentieth Dynasty. This process not only transformed the country's economy by placing so much of its land in institutional holdings, but it also served as a covert method to gain the support of local elite, who were then recruited in a managerial capacity, acting on behalf of various gods and statues of the blessed dead.[70]

If the temple estates of Nubia functioned in a similar manner to those of Egypt, however, this does not mean necessarily that the system was benign. Far from being held as commons, resources were now closely guarded by the temples for the benefit of the state. Moreover, penalties for encroaching on resources claimed by a state temple were extremely harsh and could include being beaten with 100 blows and the restitution of 100 times the value of whatever was stolen, or else bodily mutilation and the demotion to servitude for the offender and his family.[71] North of Kawa, the floodplain is generally quite narrow, so arable land in Egyptian-occupied Nubia would have been a relatively scarce resource. The fact that gigantic temple storerooms generally stood beside impressive stone temples at administrative headquarters would appear to be no accident, for the vast majority of land in Nubia was likely owned by the statues lodged within temples—whether these were of patron deities, of Egyptian royalty, or of the Egyptian gods who were absentee landlords in Nubia. Indeed, a stele that Ramesses II erected at Amara West states that the temple had been built to receive the statues of the gods that the king had brought to Nubia—statues that were, no doubt, destined to become the owners of tremendous swathes of land.[72]

The tomb of Pennut, a deputy of Lower Nubia who resided at Aniba (a.k.a. Miam), is especially revealing as to the state of land ownership at the end of the Twentieth Dynasty, for in his tomb chapel he documents his bestowal of five discrete parcels of land on a statue of Ramesses VI, which he dedicated within the temple of Horus of Miam (see Figure 9.4). These estates would serve to supply the statue with offerings in the future, though whether they came to Pennut by virtue of family wealth, personal investments, or via his office is not

Figure 9.4 The deputy of Wawat dedicates a statue of Ramesses VI to a temple in Aniba along with five fields (redrawn from Breasted 1948, 136).

known. What is fascinating, however, is that the land that bordered the donated parcels was nominally under the control of a number of different entities, including the pharaoh (namely, royal flax fields), the deputy of Lower Nubia (in one case Pennut is specified, but usually the title was generic), various statues (the statue of queen Nefertari, which resides in Miam; a statue under the charge of the first prophet Amenemopet; and a statue under the charge of the deputy of Lower Nubia, Meri), and temples (the house of Re, lord of the eastern bend; land in the district of the house of the goddess). Only a very few entities or individuals that didn't fall into one of the categories just mentioned are listed (land belonging to a herdsman; field of the Arasa).[73] Under the watch of these statues—and the mortals that fed them—then, Nubia's economy quickly changed from one that was predominantly pastoral to a plantation economy that emphasized agriculture and also perhaps the growing of cash-crops, such as flax, dates, and grapes for wine.[74]

Although land in Nubia does seem to have been assigned increasingly to temple statues, by the late Eighteenth Dynasty those who cared for the statues and benefited from the arrangement may well have been primarily Nubian. In his position of "deputy of Lower Nubia" and "steward of the temple of Horus Lord of Miam," Pennut obviously wielded a tremendous amount of power locally. Certainly, he seems to have had the authority to bestow upon his close relatives the titles of "treasurer of the Lord of the Two Lands in Miam," as well as "scribe of the treasury and mayor of Miam."[75] The enrichment of the temple of Horus Lord of Miam and the statues that were lodged within it, then, had everything to do with the simultaneous enrichment of a very important family that had evidently wielded power in Miam for at least two generations running.

Pennut was also, it should be stated, a "chief of the quarry-service," which suggests that much of the revenues amassed in the vast temple magazines remained in Nubia and were utilized in part to finance major state ventures, such as quarrying for high-quality stone, goldmining, or the like.[76] Evidence such as the Nauri Decree and P. Harris I indicates that some Egyptian temples owned land in Nubia, and thus much of the wealth excavated and amassed under their auspices assuredly flowed northward. Even in these cases, however, the management of such ventures no doubt fell in part to men who oversaw affiliated Amun-temples in Nubia. Nubian officials who acted as local power-brokers for the Egyptian state, inasmuch as they constituted crucial cogs in the imperial system, presumably profited handsomely.[77] In its delegation of increasing amounts of authority over time to local elite, Egypt is typical.[78]

Conversions in Sacred Landscapes

Throughout the Eighteenth and Nineteenth Dynasties, Egypt's construction of temples and its emphasis on the god Amun became ever more prevalent. Manifestations of the divine king began to be promoted alongside Amun in

Nubia beginning in the reign of Thutmose III, and this trend ratcheted up from the reign of Amenhotep III (c. 1390–1352) onward.[79] Likewise, as stated above, the ratios between temple vs. town size shifted in favor of the former. This trend progressed up until the reign of Ramesses II (c. 1279–1213), when this pharaoh's mania for temple construction and for self-aggrandizement appears to have surpassed all bounds of reason or common sense.

While the civilian settlements that would have supported some temples established in Eighteenth-Dynasty Nubia cannot be located, this was the norm with respect to Ramesses II's temples. The recovery of habitation at any period along the banks of the Nile is notoriously difficult, and often the only clue pointing toward a town is its cemetery. In the late New Kingdom, however, a change in burial practice throughout Egypt and Nubia rendered even this rather dubious method of identification far more difficult. In the Ramesside period not only were hundreds of corpses commonly interred in only a few reused vaults, but if these bodies possessed grave goods they would be few and generally hard to date.[80] Thus, the paradox of a land studded with temples yet seemingly devoid of habitation led one archaeologist, who surveyed extensively in Nubia, to state hyperbolically that the country had "become a sort of no man's land ruled by the gods and peopled by the ghosts of the dead."[81]

As recent work at sites like Amara West has demonstrated, theories positing a radical depopulation of Nubia are no longer viewed as tenable, though excess quantities of sand in late New Kingdom levels and other indications do show that the environment was particularly dry.[82] Even if Nubia's population was relatively stable, however, the profusion of temples in comparison to the probable size of local populations still seems disproportionate to a degree only rivaled by the numerous Greco-Roman temples established along the 120-km stretch of northern Lower Nubia known as the Dodekaschoinos (see Figure 9.5).[83] Here too the rationale behind the establishment of so many temples in a comparatively limited space is much discussed. Perhaps the most plausible suggestion is that the temples were situated in particularly advantageous locations and at intervals that would have been convenient for boats carrying administrators, soldiers, messengers, or the like to land and to be reprovisioned on journeys to the far outer edge of Egypt's authority.[84] As in New Kingdom Nubia, however, the temples certainly served as the primary sites of administration, taxation, and the promotion of the cult of the divine ruler.[85]

What is perhaps most interesting about the temples located along the Dodekaschoinos for present purposes, however, is the fact that the small temple (or large chapel) of Dendur was dedicated in part to two drowned sons of a local ruler. Considering this fact, Cyril Aldred argued quite plausibly that the temple was in fact constructed in order to gain the good graces of a Nubian ruler and that it may have been placed in his charge so that he would benefit from lands ceded to the temple and also from the relationships established

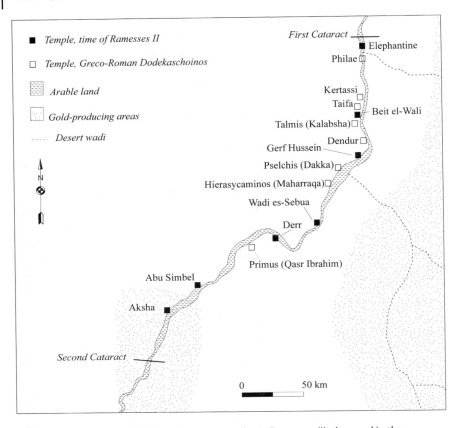

Figure 9.5 A comparison of Lower Nubian temples in Ramesses II's time and in the Greco-Roman period.

along the Dodekaschoinos between this temple and others, especially the temple of Isis at Philae.[86] For the New Kingdom, Morkot has suggested that the temple complex at Kawa, which is not known to have possessed an accompanying Egyptian-style town, served as the base for a Kushite ruler, who would presumably have profited from the temple established in his territory.[87]

Indeed, on parallel with the sacral economy of the Dodekaschoinos, it would not be surprising if mixed Egypto-Nubian priesthoods oversaw the temples at Kawa, Gebel Barkal, and those newly established under the reign of Ramesses II. In Roman times, the temple of Isis at Philae was not only revered both by Egyptians and by Nubians, but votive inscriptions suggest that cultic envoys and "agents of Isis" from Meroe cooperated in the cultic management of her temple. Likewise, in the late third century, when Diocletian grew weary of fending off incursions by hostile Nubian raiders, he apparently not only provided these tribes with financial subsidies to make peace worth their while, but he also attempted to utilize their affection for Isis in order to bind them closer to Egypt. Thus in Philae,

> ...he established certain temples and altars for the Romans [*i.e. Egyptians*] and these barbarians in common, and he settled priests of both nations in this fortress, thinking that the friendship between them would be secure by reason of their sharing the things sacred to them.[88]

Even prior to this time, however, the Romans had left long-distance trade, the integration of Egyptians and Nubians, and diplomacy primarily to the priests and personnel situated in the environs of these temples.[89] Evidence for an analogous situation occurring at late New Kingdom Gebel Barkal may perhaps be found in the elite family tombs located only 3 km south at Hillat el-Arab. Here the tombs, which were notably Nubian in certain respects but also incorporated numerous Egyptian and Egyptianizing elements, indicate a trade with Egypt that was either more robust than at earlier periods or else fell increasingly under the control of the indigenous population.[90]

Under both Ptolemaic and Roman rule, it was the case that the position of Egyptians improved over time. This was a result of indigenous revolts, a slackening of immigration (in the Greek case), and a gradual diminishment of cultural differences. For these two governing powers, the lesson to be learned was evidently that subject peoples were more easily ruled by the carrot than the stick. The Spanish government in North America came to a similar realization, after neither concentrated military campaigns nor forced conversions brought the stability or peace that they sought. Once the government adopted a policy of proffering gifts and tangible benefits to the locals, however, they began to meet with greater success. As a missionary in Florida put it succinctly, "gifts can break rocks."[91] Along the same lines, Ordinance 139 of the Laws of the Indies specified that Spaniards were to try to establish friendships with the natives,

> also giving them things in barter that will attract their interest, and not showing greediness for their things. [The Spaniards] should establish friendship and alliances with the principal lords and influentials who would be most useful in the pacification of the land.[92]

In Egyptian-held Nubia, much the same philosophy may have been operative, for it seems that by the latter half of the New Kingdom it was the principal lords in Nubia who would take the lead in both pacifying the land and in profiting from it.

In light of these considerations, it is worth returning to the question of why the cult of Amun outlasted Egypt's empire in Nubia, whereas it most certainly did not in Syria-Palestine. The most compelling answer appears to be that the Nubians assumed a much more direct leadership role in this cult over time than their northern counterparts. If, as William Adams asserted, the temple had largely taken the place of the fortress as the primary symbol of pharaonic rule in New Kingdom Nubia,[93] it is of crucial importance that the Egyptians appear to have entrusted stewardship of this vital symbol increasingly to Nubian elites. Such men—whose revenues and prestige depended in large part, then, on the health of the temple they oversaw—had a vested interest in promoting, protecting, and perpetuating these cults. Placed under such attentive care for so long, it is little wonder that the god Amun outlasted his imperial sponsors.

Contractions in Egypt's Empire Lead to the Birth of the Kushite Empire

As discussed in the last chapter, Egypt's government failed relatively quickly following the reign of Ramesses III (c. 1183–1153) due to a "perfect storm" of calamities that included an unreliable Nile, recent invasions, an assassination, succession troubles, and corruption. A significant revolt in Lower Nubia predated this storm in the reign of Merneptah (c. 1213–1203), however, and may suggest that the Nubians played an active role in resisting the imperial government and in bringing about its downfall.[94] Significantly, at the end of the Twentieth Dynasty, when Ramesses XI's feeble grasp on Upper Egypt finally failed, it was the king's son of Kush who was called upon to restore order in Thebes. This viceroy, tellingly, bore the name Panehesy, which means, literally, "the Nubian." While such names cannot be taken as a rock-solid assertion of ethnic identity, chances would appear very good that, by the end of the New Kingdom, Nubians had climbed even to the highest echelon in their country's governmental hierarchy. Moreover, Panehesy evidently had the resources to wrest control of the Theban government and even to fight his way northward to the Middle Egyptian site of Hardai in a bid, no doubt, to claim the throne.

Panehesy's main enemy in Thebes, it appears, was the high priest of Amun, a man named Amenhotep, whom he "suppressed" for the better part of a year. Panehesy had earlier claimed the title of "overseer of the granaries," and so—given the intermittent famine conditions that prevailed in Egypt at the time—it may have been that access to Amun's storehouses in Thebes was the issue. One wonders, however, given Piankhi's later emphatic devotion to the cult of Amun, whether a desire on the part of Panehesy to preside at important religious ceremonies and festivities created a clash with Amenhotep, who had already been, rather scandalously, depicting himself on the same artistic scale as the king!

When after a period of seven years or so Panehesy exhibited a reluctance to give up the control that he had asserted over Thebes (and indeed perhaps showed a desire to extend it), it became clear to the Egyptian government that he himself needed suppressing. To this end a general named Piankh was sent from the north and succeeded in driving Panehesy back to Nubia, where he seems to have spent a decade or so attempting to defeat the renegade viceroy—now known as "the enemy"—and to reassert Egyptian control. At some point, however, Piankh must have realized that he was fighting a losing battle, and if other generals took up his mission, we have no record. What is known is that Panehesy was interred with honor in a tomb at Aniba, the same site presided over a generation or so before by Pennut.

Beginning in the Third Intermediate period, then, it is valid to refer to Nubian identity as post-colonial—a stage for societies that typically involves increased experimentations with cultural identity. Thus, Nubians freed from pharaonic rule went through a process of deciding for themselves which elements of their traditional culture they wished to revive (round tumuli and beds, for example) and which elements of Egyptian material culture they wanted to either preserve (pyramid-shaped tombs, perhaps, and anthropoid coffins) or discard (orthogonal walled settlements).[95] The decisions made differed from community to community and, indeed, from grave to grave.[96] While the reassertion of traditional practices and lifestyles after the weakening or overthrow of an imperial power is a frequent phenomenon and to some extent to be expected,[97] and while Nubians seem gladly to have freed themselves from some elements of Egyptian cultural hegemony, there were also many aspects of the material culture that had been theirs throughout much of the New Kingdom that they evidently felt ownership over and desired to preserve.

This period in Nubia's social history seems to have parallels in the end of the Spanish empire in North America. Prior to the formal end of Spanish rule, it was noted that, while natives in Pueblo communities retained their own language, religion, and cultural identity, Pueblo leaders

> ...held Hispanic offices, understood how and when to appeal to Hispanic law, communicated with Hispanics in their language and on their terms, and identified themselves and their children with a Spanish surname and with Christian given names.[98]

One imagines in the late Spanish empire in the Americas and in the late Egyptian empire in Nubia that as community and governmental leaders began to look more and more similar to the people over whom they held authority, increasing elements of colonial civilization were naturalized. Today numerous native communities in the American Southwest practice a mixture of Catholic and traditional rituals and feel that both are integral to their identity and heritage. The exuberantly hybrid burials discovered in many late New Kingdom and

Third Intermediate period cemeteries in Nubia suggest that a similar process occurred there, in which, increasingly, both Egyptian and traditional Nubian practices began to be accepted as "native."

As the Third Intermediate period progressed, the main power in Nubia was to become a dynasty based at Napata, who claimed Gebel Barkal as their holy site, who buried themselves in supersized versions of typically New Kingdom pyramid-tombs, and who would eventually succeed where Panehesy had failed in conquering all of Egypt and asserting themselves as the rightful sons of Amun. Interestingly, Third Intermediate period burials at el-Kurru, the ancestral cemetery of this Kushite Dynasty, exhibited more traditionally Nubian traits than those discovered at the nearby cemetery of Hillat el-Arab.[99] As the wealth and power of this lineage and polity increased, however, the ruling elite evidently turned back to Egypt in their search for an aesthetic vocabulary of dominant authority. To this end they constructed stone temples, pyramids, and a line of such strong divine kings that they were able eventually to extend their rule over Egypt. Thus, some two centuries after the last New Kingdom pharaoh had withdrawn resources and personnel from Nubia, the Twentieth-fifth Dynasty claimed complete control of both countries. The fact that Egyptian burial customs underwent a resurgence of popularity at this time,[100] then, undoubtedly had far more to do with the general population's desire to emulate their own rulers than it did with any inclination to adopt the customs of a country now under Nubian control.

Notes

1 Sinopoli 1994, 163.
2 Welsby and Welsby Sjöström 2006–2007, 383.
3 This inscription is discussed at greater length in the Epilogue.
4 Bonnet 2017, 115–16.
5 For a plan of the town in the reign of Thutmose I, see Bonnet 2017, 118, figure 10.
6 For work at Dukki Gel, see Bonnet 2014 and 2017.
7 New Kingdom settlement is also evidenced in certain Second Cataract fortresses, probably in order to facilitate travel in this rough stretch of river (Török 2009, 185).
8 Alcock 1989, 90, 94, 99.
9 Crouch 1991, 21–2. For a discussion of the Roman use of towns to introduce a Roman way of life into conquered territories, see Wells 1999, 131–2, 171.
10 Crouch et al. 1982, 2.
11 Crouch et al. 1982, 16. The construction of defenses was also a priority of the Roman settlers, upon whose practices the Spanish modeled many of their own (Crouch 1991, 22).

12 Excavations have also recently restarted at the site of Kawa under the auspices of the Kawa Excavation Project. It is hoped that as a result of their work the nature of the New Kingdom town associated with Tutakhamun's temple will be clarified. The plethora of Kerman mortuary material, however, suggests that, like Sai, the site hosted a substantial Kerman population prior to the New Kingdom (Welsby n.d., 7).

13 Smith 2017, 31 and personal communication.

14 Morkot 2013, 924–5.

15 Fairman 1938, 152; Shinnie 1951, 6.

16 Badawy 1968, 58–9.

17 Säve-Söderbergh 1941, 189.

18 For the utility of the grid in planning new settlements with maximum efficiency, see Crouch et al. 1982, 2. Indeed, the Hippodamian grid system is thought to have originated in a colonial context in the eighth century BCE for precisely this purpose (Hansen 2006, 102).

19 Scott 1998, 53–63.

20 Aulus Gellius, *Attic Nights* 16.13.9. See also the similar sentiments expressed by Tacitus in *Agricola*, chapter 21).

21 Crouch et al. 1982, 17.

22 Crouch et al. 1982, 18.

23 The fact that by the reign of Ramesses IX gold-washing activities had been placed under the "protection" of the Akuyuta suggests that these people over time wrested a lucrative contract from the Egyptian government (Wente 1990, 38–9)! Like the 'Apiru, such groups may have been partially swelled by individuals seeking an alternative to life under Egypt's rule (Morris 2005, 323–4, 653).

24 There is reason to believe that the Iremites may have been joined by the semi-nomadic people of Akuyuta (Morris 2005, 647–8, 652–4).

25 For a discussion of this text, published on a stele at Semna, see Morris 2005, 330–3.

26 Weber 1992, 112, 213–16, 224.

27 Weber 1992, 105–6, 233.

28 Crouch 1991, 24, 29, 32.

29 Historians tend to refer to anyone who lived like the Spanish as Spanish, while acknowledging that the vast majority of such "Spaniards" were not in fact Spanish by blood (Weber 1992, 8; Kessel 1997, 50–1).

30 Smith and Buzon 2014, 432; Smith and Buzon 2017, 618–19.

31 Spencer et al. 2017, 46.

32 For a recent review of various perspectives, see van Pelt 2013.

33 Budka and Doyen 2012–2013, 196–7; Smith 2013, 92–3.

34 Budka 2014, 68; Budka and Doyen 2012–2013, 196–7. For the Spanish settlers in the American West, see Weber 1992, 316–17. As Budka and Doyen (2012–2013, 199) have pointed out, however, there is some evidence that fish

may have been specifically imported to Sai in order to please those Egyptians that had not given up their taste for this food, which may have been eschewed by Nubians.

35 Budka and Doyen 2012–2013, 188–9; Budka 2014, 68.
36 Weber 1992, 307.
37 Budka and Doyen 2012–2013, 184, 198–200.
38 Vercoutter 1958, 161.
39 Spence 2017, 449.
40 Spence et al. 2011, 37; Spence 2017, 451, 454, 456, 461–2; Rose 2017, 466, 471.
41 Blackman 1937, 149–50; Badawy 1968, 58–9.
42 Spence and Rose 2009, 24; for increasing evidence of gold-working at sites throughout the Abri-Delgo reach, see Budka 2014, 59.
43 Redford 1992, 208.
44 Török 2009, 237; Spence et al. 2011, 36.
45 Kitchen 2000, 142.
46 Kitchen 2000, 66.
47 Davies 2002, 47–8, pl. LVII. Identifying resettled foreigners in imperial contexts is notoriously difficult (D'Altroy 2003, 248–9).
48 Morkot 1987, 35.
49 Both new towns were located in close vicinity to former seats of deputies. Aksha was located only 15 km south of Faras, while Amara West lay 13 km north of Sai (Török 2009, 191; Spencer et al. n.d., 10).
50 Spencer et al. n.d., 23.
51 Spencer 2017, 338–9, 342.
52 Fairman 1948, 4–5; Spencer et al. n.d., 38–9; Spencer 2017, 350–2.
53 Fairman 1948, 4; Spencer et al. n.d., 20, 51, 54. Both Seti I and Ramesses II were concerned with finding new, reliable sources of gold (Vercoutter 1959, 135–7).
54 Spencer et al. n.d., 60.
55 Spencer et al. n.d., 62, 65; Stevens 2017, 418–19.
56 Spencer et al. n.d., 40; Spencer 2010, 23.
57 The character of mortuary remains in New Kingdom Nubia had never been strictly homogenous, as at least some traditional elements can generally be identified. Likewise, at all times it appears that deliberate choices were being made by the wealthiest social strata as to which elements of Egyptian material culture they felt were most important for their eternal well-being (Säve-Söderbergh 1967–1968, 237–40; Török 2009, 277–9). Nonetheless, this heterogeneity increases in the Twentieth Dynasty and Third Intermediate period as can be observed at sites like Hillat el-Arab (Smith 2013, 100–1; Smith 2015, 773–6).
58 Spencer 2009, 55.
59 Säve-Söderbergh 1991a, 7; Morkot 2013, 936–7.
60 Binder 2017, 599–610.

61 Simpson 2003, 380.

62 Wente 1990, 189, 191.

63 See Török 2009, 185–6.

64 Williams 2006; Török 2009, 213–16.

65 Kendall 1997, 76–8; Török 2009, 227–9.

66 Török 2009, 238.

67 Habachi 1969; Wildung 1977, 1–30.

68 Lorton 1974, 100.

69 Bleiberg 1988.

70 O'Connor 1983, 227; Haring 1997, 5–35, 389–96; Moreno García 2013, 3–5.

71 Edgerton 1947, 223–4.

72 Fairman 1939, 142. Scholars who believe that Egypt's ultimate desire was to extend Egypt's borders by re-creating its main institutions in Nubia include Kemp 1978, 31–3; Frandsen 1979, 169–74.

73 Breasted 1906c, 233–5.

74 Adams 1977, 230–1.

75 Breasted 1906c, 231. The term *pr-ḥḏ* is here translated as treasury.

76 Adams 1977, 231; Smith 1997, 80.

77 Morkot 1987, 44.

78 Howe 2002, 16.

79 Török 2009, 215. For a discussion of the cult of the divine king in Nubia, see Habachi 1969. The conscious creation of ruler cults can be found in numerous imperial contexts—for example, in the Roman and Incan empires—though it should be stated that in all cases such cults were present in the core as well as the peripheries.

80 See Török 2009, 200–1, 286–7. The situation is exacerbated by the fact that, even in Egypt, a distinctive Twentieth-Dynasty repertoire of pottery is difficult to identify (Aston 1989, 12).

81 Firth 1927, 28.

82 Shinnie 1951, 11; Woodward et al. 2017.

83 Török 2009, 387–9, 400–1, 406, 443–56.

84 Habachi 1969, 16; Hein 1991, 129–34; Török 2009, 245–6.

85 Török 2009, 405.

86 Aldred 1978, 37.

87 Morkot 1995, 234.

88 Procopius, *History of the Wars* 1.19.

89 Török 2009, 455, 457, 461–2.

90 Liverani 2004, 139–40.

91 Weber 1992, 107.

92 Crouch et al. 1982, 18–19. An emphasis on the utility of enticement and gentle persuasion, rather than force, in convincing natives to adopt Spanish ways is also the thrust of Ordinance 140.

93 Adams 1977, 220, 230.

 94 Morris 2005, 380–1, 657–8.
 95 Smith 2013; Spencer et al. n.d., 60, 74–5, 82–3; Binder 2017, 609. Evidence for settled populations between the First and Third Cataracts is difficult to discover in the Third Intermediate period, though burials at sites like Amara West continued (Spencer et al. n.d., 88). If the settled population reverted to a semi-pastoralist lifestyle once no imperial officials were there to discourage such movement, this might explain a seeming lack of settlement (Török 2009, 201).
 96 Welsby and Welsby Sjöström 2006–2007, 389.
 97 For examples pertaining to Inca and Roman provinces, see Patterson 1991, 105–6; Wells 1999, 124–5, 196–8.
 98 Weber 1992, 303.
 99 Welsby and Welsby Sjöström 2006–2007, 389.
100 Welsby and Welsby Sjöström 2006–2007, 391–2.

Epilogue

In the 12th year of Akhenaten's reign (c. 1340), the Egyptian government staged an elaborate performance of power, captured for eternity on the walls of the tomb belonging to a courtier named Meryre II at Amarna (see Figure 10.1). Although this scene has been touched upon briefly in Chapter 5—in a discussion of the many attractions of empire for those that this system most directly benefited—it is worth circling back to it as an end to this book insomuch as it serves as an efficient encapsulation of an idealized empire. Subjecting the scene to a closer read affords an opportunity to revisit foundational themes that concern the ideology and stated goals of Egypt's empire and of empires as a generic category. Moreover, due to the wide variety of complementary sources available from Akhenaten's reign (c. 1352–1336), the same scene may also be viewed from a pericentric perspective that exposes the far more complex and seamier side of empire, with all its imperial falsehoods, weaknesses, and divided loyalties.

Akhenaten's tribute ceremony, staged as a cosmogram, presented the Egyptian empire writ small, such that it could easily be appreciated by an audience of Egyptians from the comfort of their own capital city. As such it saw the king seated center stage in a raised pavilion. Above his figure, the rays of his chosen god—the Aten—extend down to touch his crown. The arms of his wife, too, caress him, though her figure is otherwise obscured behind his. Finally, the couple's six daughters stand grouped in two sets of three—forming together with their family and their chosen god an ennead. This is worth noting as in the old religious order, which Akhenaten had recently replaced, a family grouping of nine gods had set the world in motion.

Located in the next concentric ring around the figure of Akhenaten-as-emperor were the inner members of his court. At the base of the pavilion, bending low, like the rest of his dutiful subjects, were three women posed behind two men. The women almost certainly represented a much larger assemblage of subsidiary wives who were important to include due to the alliances they cemented (some undoubtedly with leaders pictured elsewhere in the scene). So too, his exclusive sexual and reproductive rights over these women provided

Ancient Egyptian Imperialism, First Edition. Ellen Morris.
© 2018 Ellen Morris. Published 2018 by John Wiley & Sons Ltd.

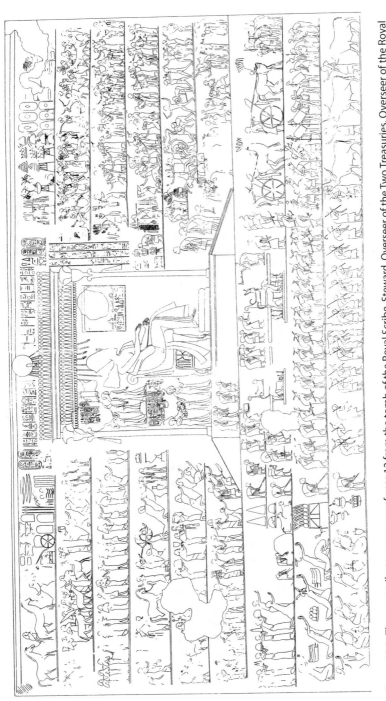

Figure 10.1 The great tribute ceremony of year 12 from the tomb of the Royal Scribe, Steward, Overseer of the Two Treasuries, Overseer of the Royal Harem of the Great Royal Wife, Nefertiti, Meryre II at Amarna (reused with permission from Silverman et al. 2006, 103, figure 90; courtesy of Penn Museum).

proof of the pharaoh's difference from all other men. High officials, priests, and fan-bearers—who saw to the administrative functioning of the state and its constitutive institutions—flanked the two ramped entrances to the pavilion. The presence of the fan-bearers is particularly interesting as these men often were stationed abroad and held high posts in Egypt's empire.[1] Finally, as if to emphasize that their king's domination over foreigners was something to celebrate, performers wrestled, clapped, and danced as they would at festival time.

The inhabitants of lands outside Egypt's official borders that had come to pay Akhenaten homage and to bring him benevolences (*inw*) occupied the outermost ring and provided the scene's primary visual interest. In his contribution to *Empires: Perspectives from Archaeology and History*, Sanjay Subrahmanyam offers a definition of empire that employs three primary criteria. First, an empire must have "an extensive geographical spread, embracing more than one cultural domain and ecozone." Second, it must be fueled by "an ideological motor that claimed extensive, at times even universal, forms of dominance." Lastly, in states headed by monarchs, the ruler must claim to be not just a king but a king over kings.[2] Subrahmanyam's admittedly "minimalist" definition is flawed in that it ignores varieties of imperialism extended over peoples who actively resisted the formation of hierarchical political structures, as well as situations in which imperial strategy dictated that rival rulers be eliminated altogether. I reference it here, however, as the ceremony currently under discussion seems specifically designed to prove to any would-be detractors— whether ancient or modern—that Egypt under Akhenaten's rule did indeed lay claim to an empire (and a dazzling one at that).

Nubians, Syro-Palestinians, Libyans, and even emissaries from the land of Punt, located in the far-off Horn of Africa, all bow before the king and offer up their goods, while a caption informs the viewer:

> His majesty appeared on the throne of the Divine and Sovereign Father, the Aten, who lives in Truth; and the chiefs of all lands brought the tribute ... praying favour at his hand (?) in order to inhale the breath of life.[3]

In this single relief, then, each of Subrahmanyam's diagnostic boxes is checked. The cultural and genetic differences between the inhabitants of lands under Egyptian suzerainty are showcased and celebrated. Likewise, the dominant size and central positioning of the king and his god make it clear that these two entities constituted the officially recognized ideological motors behind Egypt's imperialism. Indeed, the Aten's theology, as expressed in a widely promulgated hymn, is unusual in its emphasis on the god's dominion over foreigners as well as the inhabitants of Egypt.[4] Finally, with respect to Subrahmanyam's third point, the relief foregrounds individuals engaged in prostrations before the king. Ironically and importantly, it is the highest status representatives of a polity—most often the rulers themselves or a close relative—that engage in the most humbling abasements.

What renders Egyptian imperialism so attractive to investigate—in addition to its longevity, to the variety of the geographic regions and socio-political entities over which various governments claimed dominance, and to the flexibility of the tactics attempted and abandoned over time—is the wide variety of source material that can used to investigate what is elided or actively obscured in representations such as the one under discussion. There is, of course, the foundational dichotomy of "us" vs. "them" to unpack. Within Egypt proper, names and other heritage markers betray the presence of foreigners integrated into Egyptian society, which increase in the New Kingdom along with imperial activity. Indeed, in Akhenaten's day, foreigners could be found at all levels of society, ranging from slaves at the bottom of the social ladder to the northern vizier and one of Akhenaten's most important wives, who were, quite obviously, at the top of it. Similarly visible on either side of the Atenist revolution were the deities that these foreigners introduced into Egypt's pantheon. Artistic representations of foreigners in tombs, temples, and palaces; their own self-presentations in letters, on tombs, and in personal monuments; and the traces they left in the material record all demonstrate the impact of Egypt's imperial territories on its own society. Such evidence is worth a book unto itself.

For activities outside Egypt's borders, however, evidence regarding Egyptian imperialism is just as rich. In addition to royal inscriptions and accounts of campaigns, much more prosaic texts as well as excavations in countries as diverse as Lebanon, Syria, Jordan, Israel, occupied Palestine, Sudan, and the arid wastes of the Sahara provide a glimpse into more mundane aspects of life under imperial rule. Moreover, as archaeological techniques of analysis become ever more informative, the ability of material culture to address nuanced questions concerning life in Egypt's imperial territories expands exponentially. Finally, for Akhenaten's reign and a decade or so of his father's (c. 1362–1332), an archive of correspondence exchanged between the Egyptian court and kings located in the north of the empire constitutes an irreplaceable trove of information. Knowledge of the back stories gleaned from all of these sources, then, breathes extra energy into the event depicted in Meryre's tomb, illuminating both what the ceremony reveals and what it actively conceals about empire.

Part I: What Akhenaten's Ceremony Reveals About [Egypt's Eighteenth-Dynasty] Empire

The Persistence of a Prestige-Goods Economy

Of paramount importance in the depiction of this ceremony is the presentation of wealth to the king—though this wealth came in many forms. As noted in Chapter 1, the investment of elites in a prestige-goods economy is part of what prompted the initial conquests out of which the state was formed. Obtaining a dominant share or even a monopoly over rare and precious items became one of the primary means through which leaders augmented their power. Such items were valued not only for their ability to increase the awe inspired by a leader, but also because in giving gifts to his subordinates, the king wielded his power to purchase loyalty. Some such items, known as "boons which the king gives," became deeply enmeshed in what was seen as a proper and desirable preparation for the afterlife. Thus, we have the lament of the noble narrator in a text known as The Admonitions of Ipuwer, whose access to imported goods had ceased once the central government collapsed in the First Intermediate period:

> Verily, none indeed voyage north to Byblos today. What then are we to do for cedar trees for our mummies? For the priests are entombed in the wood of such trees, and the nobles … are embalmed with the oil thereof. But these things arrive (here) no longer. Gold too is no more, and the materials for all workmanship have been depleted.[5]

Thus, in a prestige-goods economy it took power to obtain such exotic and precious materials, upon which visual symbols of status and important life transitions for the elite increasingly depended. So too, however, did access to such goods and the power to dispense them become essential to exhibiting and maintaining that power.[6]

In the ceremony depicted, lions arrive from the north and leopards from the south. The association of exotic animals with Egypt's rulers in reality as well as in iconographic representations predates the state, and the fact that many had spent a great deal of time in captivity has been revealed by the work of archaeologists excavating at the precocious predynastic polity of Hierakonpolis.[7] Animal products too were important, and the scene duly depicts tusks, pelts, feathers, and tails being delivered to the king. Such exotic materials were no doubt destined to be incorporated into regalia, furniture, and fittings suitable for display or already had been fashioned into sumptuous gifts.

In the north, where Egypt's empire did not extend into zones with as rich a variety of raw materials, Egypt laid stress on requisitioning crafted items such as fine glass—or metalwork that had been or were to be transformed into items bearing social prestige. As David Warburton has observed, much of the wealth accrued via the northern empire came from Egypt's control of important trade hubs—a factor rarely considered in archaeological adaptations of world systems theory.[8] In the relief, as in reality, many such items seem to have been associated with drinking culture, suggesting—as did the early breweries discovered at Hierakonpolis and the great caches of wine in the Protodynastic and Early Dynastic tombs at Abydos—that just as power could be intoxicating, so too could it be promoted through intoxication.

As discussed throughout this book, control of trade was of central importance in Nubia, but so too were the country's vast reservoirs of gold—that untarnishable metal the Egyptians viewed as akin to the flesh of the gods. In Meryre II's depiction of this ceremony, the deliveries of gold ingots and bags that Norman de Garis Davies identifies as gold dust are prominently displayed. The presence of gold in Nubia's deserts, and the absence of any precious metals save copper in Syria-Palestine, undoubtedly accounts for Egypt's much more intensive and long-lasting attempts to control the region south of the First Cataract. Moreover, the fact that this region, like their own, was primarily confined to the floodplain of the Nile also made the process of acquiring dominance far less daunting.

As discussed in Chapter 1, Egypt's initial attempts to ensure access to Nubian resources came through eradication imperialism, in which competitors and former trade partners were defeated and the indigenous population appears to have been largely run off. Chapter 3, meanwhile, chronicled the Eleventh-Dynasty experiments with diplomacy and indirect rule as well as the Twelfth-Dynasty rejection of this tactic in favor of what looks to have been a quite severe military occupation. In Akhenaten's day, however, the Egyptians had taken a much more conciliatory approach to governing the south, endeavoring to attract—rather than necessarily to coerce—the participation of Nubians through the medium of towns and temples that had been built on an Egyptian model. The promotion of elites willing to refashion their society along class-based lines was also key to their strategy. Thus, as time went on, as in Egypt, Nubian society became increasingly bifurcated between a privileged nobility (who were co-opted into the country's administrative structure) and a laboring class. As Stuart Tyson Smith has argued, many Nubians would have served as labor—again, as Egyptians did in Egypt—on massive temple estates designed in part to underwrite the costs of mining ventures.

Nubian gold was, of course, utilized to decorate the persons and the environs of the royal family and the gods. Another employment of the metal that is duly illustrated in this relief, however, is the fashioning of the instantly recognizable collars doled out to reward the king's followers. In Akhenaten's day, particularly favored nobles received a thick collar, which was composed of linked necklaces strung with gold disk beads. Comparable in concept to the "boons which the king gave," the necklaces had the virtue of being more conspicuously consumable in life and also of advertising the perks of loyalty. In order to sell the king's agenda of shuttering the temples of the nation's most important gods, promoting to power another relatively obscure counterpart, and moving the capital to a bare stretch of riparian land in the middle of the country, one suspects that gold became particularly crucial. As might be expected, scenes of the royal reward ceremony are especially prevalent in this king's reign.

Nubian gold was useful too in buying the loyalty of elites elsewhere in the empire. Once refashioned into luxury items in Egyptian workshops, gold was sent as rewards to vassals, such as the ruler of Ginti-kirmil, who received a goblet and 12 sets of linen garments.[9] Such items were also sent in far greater quantities to the Great Kings, whose emissaries are likely pictured in the bottom left-hand register. One incomplete inventory of gifts sent by Akhenaten to the king of Babylon (EA 14) appears to include nearly every type of precious item discovered in Meryre II's relief (and a great deal more besides)! A large quantity of linen was disbursed, for example—a costly finished product for which the Egyptians were justly famous. Hailing from outside their borders were finished items of ebony and ivory, quantities of sweet oil—such as the Egyptians often requisitioned from Syria-Palestine—as well as gifts comprising silver and occasionally lapis lazuli. Most astonishing, however, was the 1,500 pounds of gold that had been incorporated into the statues, goblets, furnishings, and other gifts, a shipment equivalent in 2018 prices to over $31 million![10] Thus, one of the ironies of empire is that while the emphasis in the depiction of this ceremony is on the goods that *arrived* to Egypt by virtue of its empire, the vast expenditure that it took to maintain such far-flung relationships, to keep a standing army ready to enforce imperial will, and to render service abroad for officials and soldiers worth their while would have easily consumed these resources and have demanded more. Even an empire quite consciously designed to be run as cheaply as possible—as Chapter 6 asserts that Akhenaten's empire was—would have been hard-pressed to cover its own expenses!

An Imperial Interest in the Divestment of Human and Natural Resources

The elites of Egypt's empire were undeniably interested in exotic, rare, and precious items. As discussed in Chapter 6, however, it seems that the empire often requisitioned material—especially staple goods—from its subjects not necessarily because they needed it (having plenty of its equivalent in Egypt proper) but in order to support imperial ventures on foreign soil. Above and beyond any practical purpose, however, one suspects that Egypt may also have taxed its subjects simply to tax them. Doing so not only deprived dominated communities of resources they might otherwise have utilized for their own ends; it also served to demonstrate that Egyptians were, in fact, fully within their rights to requisition whatever they wished.

In Meryre II's tomb, for example, Nubians lead a bull before the king, which functions as a visual synecdoche for the hundreds of head of cattle requisitioned from Nubia on an annual basis according to Thutmose III's annals (c. 1457–1425).[11] Egypt had countless herds and oxen so abundantly overfed that they hobbled on deformed feet toward their own sacrifice, as is witnessed at the lower right of the scene. In comparison, the Nubian animal is but a poor offering. Interestingly, hundreds of cattle were also requisitioned from Syria-Palestine on a regular basis, yet these deliveries are unmarked in Meryre's relief. It is quite probable then that they only appear in the southern portion of the equation because cattle held a central importance in traditional Nubian society—a factor discussed at some length in Chapter 3. Thus, the levy on these animals, although roughly equivalent for both regions, bore far more symbolic weight in the south.

In the early days of Egypt's New Kingdom empire, divesting Nubians of their cattle seems to have been something of a priority. Thus, Thutmose II (c. 1492–1479) authorized a campaign to Nubia after hearing a report that

> [t]he ones who were as serf(s) of the Lord of the Two Lands are thinking of plotting. The rebels will rob the people of Egypt in order to steal the cattle from behind these fortresses, which your father ... built in his victory in order to repress the rebellious lands of the bowmen of Nubia.[12]

Three aspects of this inscription are especially important to note here. First, fortresses had been built for the purpose of repressing Nubians who would challenge Egypt's authority. Second, Nubians, in all likelihood, sought not to steal cattle but rather to reclaim their own stolen property. Third, Nubians were now viewed by the Egyptian government as serfs (*ndt*), akin to the dependent laborers who toiled on Egypt's royal estates.[13] Thus, it seems that the Egyptians, in the early days of their New Kingdom empire, were engaged in an attempt to force the Nubians to surrender what they held most dear and to transform their economy from a largely pastoral to an agro-pastoral or even a predominantly agricultural system.

Indeed, much of the logic of imperialism in Nubia seems to have been to alienate individuals from resources that might otherwise sustain them and perhaps help them mount a more effective martial and cultural resistance. Such resources included cattle but also land. As discussed in Chapter 9, increasing amounts of land in Nubia became ceded to temples as the New Kingdom progressed. Akhenaten's reign was no exception, for the king sponsored work at Sesebi, Dukki Gel, Gebel Barkal, and Soleb, as well as—circumstantial evidence suggests—Kawa (a.k.a. Gem Aten) and Buhen.[14] This trajectory of increased cultic ownership mirrored trends observed in Egypt proper. As discussed in Chapters 4 and 9, however, it does not seem to have been at odds with efforts to recruit and reward local collaborators. Thus, the faces of the officials and enforcers who came to collect taxes in Nubia likely resembled those who now toiled on large estates. Nubia's priests, too, likely were increasingly drawn from the local elite, which almost assuredly accounts for the fact that Egypt's religion far outlasted its political influence in Nubia.

As discussed in Chapter 5, one of the attractions of empire for private citizens seems also to have been the influx of foreign slaves, who may have assumed many of the more onerous tasks that ordinarily fell to Egyptians as part of the state's labor tax. Thus, it is notable that included among the property delivered to Akhenaten by peoples in both the north and the south are prisoners, who arrived shackled or led by a leash like animals. Women and children followed along behind on their way to being donated to royal estates, temple estates and workshops, or even to favored nobles. Their presence, resettled in Egypt's heartland, ensured that the population of the empire's core became increasingly heterogeneous as the New Kingdom progressed.

Some of these captives may have been netted in the campaigns led by generals in Akhenaten's army, such as the expedition sent to punish a Nubian nomadic group guilty of raiding settled communities of law-abiding Nubians—undertaken only 78 days prior to this festival[15]—or else one of the relatively minor campaigns in the north, such as that sent to re-secure Egyptian control over the base of Sumur and/or to bring in the ruler of Amurru for questioning.[16] Prisoners too, however, occasionally arrived as cuts of the booty sent by allies (EA 17) or as a form of tribute sent by vassals (EA 173, 288). As discussed in Chapter 8, for instance, Akhenaten had requested that the ruler of Damascus send him 'Apiru of the hill country for resettlement in Nubia. Thus, one suspects that in such cases, Egypt's vassals would have been motivated to deport those most opposed to collaboration with Egypt, providing a strong incentive for dissenters to either lie low or to flee to lands outside the limits of Egypt's empire. The fungible worth of human labor has been addressed in Chapter 5, but it is worth noting that documents discovered at Kahun in Akhenaten's reign record the use of slave work hours to pay personal debts![17]

An Imperial Interest in Political and Military Collaboration

Considering the vital importance of collaborators in Egypt's imperial project, the most precious gifts of all, then, may be depicted in the Syrian side of the scene: namely, the children of the rulers, who were offered to Akhenaten as guest-hostages. Nubian vassals, it is known from other sources (see, for example, Huy's tomb, Figure 4.3), offered children as well. Significantly, regardless of origin, the offspring seem to have been delivered to court in Egyptian garb, as if to signify their willingness to adopt the values and lifeways of the imperial culture. Daughters came in order to be incorporated into the king's cadre of lesser wives, while sons constituted heirs apparent, destined to ascend the thrones of their fathers (with Egyptian backing if necessary). As discussed in Chapter 6, outside evidence confirms that many of Egypt's vassals had indeed spent at least some of their formative years at court. If these princes, after a long period of absence, arrived to rule their realms with far more supporters in Egypt than they enjoyed at home, one suspects such a situation would only have furthered their dependence on their imperial backer.

The collaboration of foreigners in their own domination and in the imperial project generally is also made explicit in the depiction of Akhenaten's ceremony. Weapons of war gifted to the Egyptians by their vassals and allies, for instance, are awarded primacy of place in the top registers of the scene. The Nubians, famed for their skills as archers, fashioned bows and shields for the Egyptians, while the northern rulers gifted the highly valued compound bows, spears, swords, and—most especially—horses and chariots. If evidence from the Amarna Letters is indicative, the horses and chariots may well have been diplomatic gifts sent to Akhenaten by the kings of Babylon, Assyria, and Alashiya (as in EA 7, 9, 15, 16, 34, 37)—gifts the like of which Akhenaten would have sent in return (EA 14).

Chariots, though no longer a new technology, were still state-of-the-art in terms of military innovations, comparable to helicopter gunships in their capacity for sowing fear and confusion on the battlefield. On the flip side, however, chariots could be employed at home to impress and intimidate other Egyptians. At the lower right of the scene, for example, Akhenaten and Nefertiti's chariots, parked next to their carrying chairs, await the royal pair. Indeed, depictions in the tomb of Akhenaten's chief of police showcased the king and queen processing through their city, chariot-borne, accompanied by officers running on foot like secret-service men escorting an official motorcade. The martial nature of Akhenaten's self-presentation within his own capital city and the conspicuous police presence that is noted in art, archaeology, and textual sources have prompted Barry Kemp to point to the many structural similarities between his regime and that of many a modern dictator.[18]

If foreigners contributed arms to Egypt's arsenal, this relief and numerous outside sources make it clear that foreigners similarly constituted an important component in Egypt's army, whether as forces contributed by local leaders, as independent contractors, or as former prisoners-of-war, offered freedom in return for service. The presence of Syro-Palestinian and Nubian soldiers is referenced in the second register from the bottom, just above the fattened cattle, while by far the greatest precedence is given to a squadron of men wearing double feathers, who likely represent a contingent of Egyptianized Libyan troops. The presence of these soldiers was perhaps intended to bulk up Libya's otherwise paltry offerings of ostrich eggs and feathers. The presence of such desert dwellers among Egypt's soldiers is particularly interesting as, from an imperial perspective, nomads are by and large more trouble than they are worth to control directly. Indeed, as discussed in Chapter 2, Egypt's best option in many cases was to placate semi-nomadic peoples by offering them an incentive to cooperate with imperial efforts rather than to continually harass settled populations and caravans. It is notable as well that unpopular rulers often find foreign bodyguards and close officials particularly useful as such men owe their position of authority solely to the king's favor, rather than to independent wealth or to family connections (see Chapter 8).

Part II: What Akhenaten's Ceremony Conceals About [Egypt's Eighteenth-Dynasty] Empire

Something Rotten at the Core

Royal ritual, it is often asserted, tends to be at its most elaborate precisely when the power it projects is in question—when a ruler has the most to prove. Akhenaten, of course, was a famously ambivalent imperialist. Known campaigns that occurred under his watch were few in number, of questionable effect, small in scale, and invariably led by generals. So too would this king be blamed by later rulers for the loss of Egypt's most important and prestigious northern vassals to the Hittites. Quite purposefully, however, the staged ceremony reveals no trace of weakness or diminishment in the empire. Nor does the relief betray strains in Akhenaten's relationship to his god, his family, or his subjects.

In reality, Meryre II's tomb and another showcasing the same ceremony were to be the last monumental tombs constructed in Akhenaten's capital city. Moreover, this scene would be the last in which the royal family would be seen together in its entirety, due to untimely deaths and Nefertiti's seeming fall from favor.[19] Indeed, within five years both Akhenaten and the fundamental tenets of his exclusive religion would have died—evidently to little mourning. The rapidity with which his reforms were repealed and his monuments erased suggests a widespread repudiation of his reign.

As it turns out, Egypt's empire survived this disruption at its core. In fact, Akhenaten's perceived weakness with regard to foreign relations led to a new drive toward expansion on the part of his successors, as discussed in Chapter 8. Many empires, however, have floundered in the face of such internal upheavals. In studies of empires generally, then, events in the core and those in the periphery were intimately related and must always be placed into dialogue.

Discrepant Experiences

The parallel poses and actions of the southerners and the northerners here pictured processing and prostrating before Akhenaten are not entirely misleading. As discussed in Chapter 6, Egypt does appear in the Eighteenth Dynasty to have attempted to implement a number of cross-frontier policies with reference to taxation, the cultivation of local rulers, the "safeguarding" of their heirs, etc. Imperial dynamics, however, are always in flux. Moreover, the character they take has as much to do with the nature of the people and the place over which the government intends to exert authority as it does with the policies and goals that it strives to implement. Archaeology, textual studies, and art-historical approaches are all immensely informative in piecing together a complex and nuanced picture of the discrepant experiences of empire for those who lived within it.

If Egyptian depictions of court ceremony were the only sources available, for example, the exotically clad, feather-wearing Nubian rulers of the late Eighteenth Dynasty would seem entirely "other." In fact, however, archaeology and the self-presentations of their real-world counterparts suggest that the more obvious aspects of this alterity were indeed a performance. In their daily lives, the great ones (*wrw*) of Nubia quite consciously styled themselves as Egyptians. As discussed in Chapter 4, Egypt's policy of incentivizing collaboration ensured that already quite early in the Eighteenth Dynasty recognized Nubian leaders bore Egyptian names and Egyptian titles. When not at Egypt's court, they eschewed all but the most subtle signs of "traditional" Nubian culture. Had the Nubian rulers in Meryre II's tomb been depicted in the same outfits that they wore in their own tombs, they would have closely resembled the officials depicted receiving gold collars or—even more closely—the Egyptian mayors who offered their benevolences (often comprising, especially in the south, exotic goods) to the king in the tomb of Rekhmire.[20]

Based on statements of Indian rulers who participated in the British Durbar ceremonies wearing patently anachronistic traditional regalia, Stuart Tyson Smith has suggested that the rulers in ceremonies like that depicted in Meryre II's tomb may well have reacted with irritation at being required to present themselves at court functions wearing consciously archaizing clothing for the sole purpose of rendering the far-flung power of the imperialist ruler starkly visible to all observers. In contrast, a number of other scholars suggest that local leaders wore the costumes that harkened back to their precolonial heritage with defiant pride.[21] Here Edward Said's meditation in *Culture and Imperialism* concerning the "discrepant experiences" of empire among its quite varied participants is well taken.[22] Attitudes to this enforced adherence to national dress were almost assuredly various, depending on any given ruler's own feelings regarding his position within the empire. The views of the Nubians these men governed, too, assuredly varied according to a great many vectors. Foregrounding the variety of responses—from collaboration, to avoidance, to subversion and resistance—within and among populations under Egypt's authority is a central project of this book (see especially Chapter 7).

Pushback on Bowing, Scraping, and Disingenuous Staging

If ceremonies such as the one depicted in Meryre II's tomb depended in large part on costuming, so too did they depend on choreography, which is a topic about which those forced to go through the motions of submission and abasement would have had much to say. From the epistolary addresses of the Amarna letters, we know that genuflections before the king were far from uniform and varied according to the status of the ruler. Thus, the most prestigious vassals would simply fall at the feet of the king (e.g. EA 49, 227), while those who ranked lowest in the hierarchy threw themselves down on their bellies and their backs seven times and seven times (e.g. EA 314, 322) in a manner that was no doubt deeply humiliating.

   What the relief conceals is the great lengths that Egypt's government had to go to in order to gather so many representatives of polities together at one time. Understandably unwilling to grovel before Egypt's pharaoh in person—in front of their peers—as well as to absent themselves from their realm for many months at a time, rulers most often invented excuses for their inability to attend and sent a son, brother, or emissary in their stead. Evidence in the letters is revealing as to the degree to which foreign rulers had to be forced, or occasionally provided with financial incentives (EA 169), to attend in person. Complaints of envoys and rulers being detained in Egypt for uncomfortably long periods of time were no doubt due to a reluctance on Egypt's part to send such colorful and politically expedient illustrations of their own world dominance home.

   As in Egypt's own court functions, staging assumed a vital function in broadcasting messages concerning relative status. Relations between Egypt and Babylon, for example, were at one point threatened, because—as the king of Babylon complained in a letter—"[You] put my chariots among the chariots of the mayors. You did not *review* them *separately*. You *humiliated* them before the country *where you are*."[23] Quite clearly, then, in the staging of this particular act of political theater, the Egyptians had made it seem as if Babylon—undeniably a great kingdom and Egypt's equal in status—was in fact Egypt's underling. So too, the king protested, was it upsetting that Akhenaten's Babylonian royal wife was huddled anonymously with women culled from far less prestigious powers (EA 1). Extrapolating from these complaints, it would not be at all surprising if Babylon's diplomatic gifts (for which fully comparable gifts were expected in return) were passed off as benevolences—an easy task given the lack of distinction in the official vocabulary. This type of disingenuous performance, while infuriating to the offended kings, no doubt served the pharaoh well. Before his internal audience, he had the opportunity to cast himself as the victorious conqueror of the most famous political entities in the known world.

The Fact that Disempowerment Begins at Home

Perhaps the most telling complaint lodged in the Amarna archive was levied by the king of Assyria, who wrote to Akhenaten infuriated after the latter—perhaps during the course of this very same ceremony—had left his envoy to stand in the sun for hours awaiting the king's pleasure. Clearly outraged at his envoy's report, Ashurubalit wrote,

Why should messengers be made to stay constantly out in the sun and so die in the sun? If staying out in the sun means profit for the king, then let him (a messenger) stay out and let him die right there in the sun, (but) for the king himself there must be a profit. Or other[wi]se, why should they [d]ie in the sun?... They are made to die in the sun![24]

Kemp's comparison of Akhenaten to a modern dictator, referenced above, appears even more compelling when the Assyrian's complaint regarding his envoy's treatment is compared to reporter David Lamb's description of the lead-up to one of Muammar Gaddafi's public appearances in the 1980s:

Inside, gathered on bleachers around the parade field, the crowd was starting to grow restless. It had been rounded up off the streets by government security men and told to sit there to greet Khadafi's arrival, but that was six hours ago, and the wooden seats were hard and the heat was oppressive. "Be patient," a government man said, moving among the people, "Brother Leader will be here any minute." From the surrounding rooftops, marksmen carrying rifles with telescopic sights peered down on the crowd.[25]

Archaeologists have determined that the most likely staging ground for the year 12 ceremony was out in a stretch of open desert at a place termed the "desert altars." The discomfort shared by Assyria's envoys and by the others at Akhenaten's ceremony—with only the royal family protected under its pavilion from the direct rays of the king's chosen god—was a sensation, no doubt, routinely experienced by Egypt's own citizens at state ceremonies. Indeed, it is worth ending the book by reiterating a point that has been stressed since its initial chapter: namely that the approach that Egypt's rulers took to governing its core and to dominating its imperial territories was in all likelihood far less different than one might imagine from scenes like the one in Meryre II's tomb.

Throughout Egypt's history in both its core and its peripheries, the government operated according to a system that privileged the co-option of land into large estates whose produce would be funneled toward the state directly (via royal estates) or indirectly (through temple estates or prebend land allotments that compensated those who served the state). The system also sought to promote influential individuals willing to collaborate with state goals. In Akhenaten's reign, Egypt's own administration relied heavily both internally and externally on "mayors" rather than governors. Thus, those representatives who interfaced with the state on the behalf of their constituencies did so as isolated entities, and power differentials were rendered menacingly clear. In all cases, such men routinely sent their children to be educated at court, traveled themselves to court, abased themselves before the king, and delivered an expected contribution of some of their most prized possessions. Egyptians and the pharaoh's foreign subjects had far more in common than many, on either side, would have cared to admit.

Notes

1 Morris 2005, 258, 293, 388–9, 448–9.
2 Subrahmanyam 2001, 43.
3 Davies 1905, 38.
4 Simpson 2003, 281–2.
5 Simpson 2003, 193.
6 McGuire 1989, 49–51.
7 Van Neer et al. 2015.
8 Warburton 2001, 137.
9 EA 265; Moran 1992, 314.
10 The calculation is based on a minimum figure of 1,208 minas of gold—the amount that can be deduced from the summaries given in EA 14, lines 71–74 (Moran 1992, 31).
11 Smith 1995, 167–8.
12 Morris 2005, 89.
13 While this term appears to have evolved over the course of the New Kingdom to assume the more generic meaning of "subjects," the implications of Thutmose II's initial choice of vocabulary remain important (Lorton 1974, 115).
14 Török 2009, 236–7.
15 Darnell and Manassa 2007, 127.
16 Redford 1959, 37.
17 Campbell 1964, 18–19.
18 Kemp 1989, 264, 273–9.
19 Campbell 1964, 90.
20 Davies 2002, 32–6, pls. 29–35.
21 See Smith 2015.
22 Said 1993, 31–43.
23 EA 1; Moran 1992, 2.
24 EA 16; Moran 1992, 39.
25 Lamb 1988, 66–7.

References

Adams, B. (1996) "Elite tombs at Hierakonpolis," in *Aspects of Early Egypt* (ed., Spencer, J.), London: British Museum Press: 1–15.

Adams, B. and R. Friedman (1992) "Imports and influences in the Predynastic and Protodynastic settlement and funerary assemblages at Hierakonpolis," in *The Nile Delta in Transition: 4th–3rd Millennium B.C.: Proceedings of the Seminar Held in Cairo 21.–24. October 1990, at the Netherlands Institute of Archaeology and Arabic Studies* (ed., van den Brink, E. C. M.), Tel Aviv: E. C. M. van den Brink: 317–38.

Adams, W. Y. (1977) *Nubia, Corridor to Africa*, Princeton, NJ: Princeton University Press.

— (1984) "The first colonial empire: Egypt in Nubia, 3200–1200 B.C.," *Comparative Studies in Society and History* 26 (1): 36–71.

Adamski, B. and K. Rosińska-Balik (2014) "Brewing technology in Early Egypt. Invention of Upper or Lower Egyptians?," in *The Nile Delta as a Centre of Cultural Interactions between Upper Egypt and the Southern Levant in the 4th Millennium B.C.* (ed., Mączyńska, A.), Poznań: Poznań Archaeological Museum: 23–36.

Aharoni, Y. (1967) *The Land of the Bible: Historical Geography* (ed. and trans. Rainey, A. F.), London: Burns and Oates.

Ahituv, S. E. (1978) "Economic factors in the Egyptian conquest of Canaan," *IEJ* 28 (1/2): 93–105.

Al-Baghdādi, A. (1964) *The Eastern Key* (*Kitāb Al-Ifāda wa'l-I'tibār*) (trans., Zand, K. H., John, A., and Videan, I. E.), London: George Allen and Unwin.

Albright, W. F. (1944) "A prince of Taanach in the fifteenth century B. C.," *BASOR* 94: 12–27.

Alcock, S. E. (1989) "Archaeology and imperialism: Roman expansion and the Greek city," *Journal of Mediterranean Archaeology* 2 (1): 87–135.

Aldred, C. (1978) *The Temple of Dendur*, New York: Metropolitan Museum of Art.

Allen, J. P. (2002) "The Speos Artemidos inscription of Hatshepsut," *BES* 16: 1–17.

Ancient Egyptian Imperialism, First Edition. Ellen Morris.
© 2018 Ellen Morris. Published 2018 by John Wiley & Sons Ltd.

Altman, A. (1979) "The fate of Abdi-Ashirta," *UF* 9: 1–11.

Amiran, R. and E. C. M. van den Brink (2001) "A comparative study of the Egyptian pottery from Tel Ma'ahaz, Stratum I," in *Studies in the Archaeology of Israel and Neighboring Lands in Memory of Douglas L. Esse* (ed., Wolff, S. R.), Chicago, IL: Oriental Institute of the University of Chicago: 29–58.

Andelković, B. (1995) *The Relations Between Early Bronze Age I Canaanites and Upper Egyptians*, Belgrade: Faculty of Philosophy, Centre for Archaeological Research.

Anderson, W. (1996) "The significance of Middle Nubian C-Group mortuary variability, ca. 2200 B.C. to ca. 1500 B.C.," Dissertation, McGill University.

Arnold, D. (1991) "Amenemhat and the early Twelfth Dynasty at Thebes," *Metropolitan Museum Journal* 26: 5–48.

Aston, D. (1989) "Qantir/Piramesse-Nord — pottery report 1988," *GM* 113: 7–24.

Aulus Gellius (1927) *The Attic Nights of Aulus Gellius*, vol III (trans., Rolfe, J. C.), New York: G. P. Putnam's Sons.

Badawy, A. (1968) *A History of Egyptian Architecture: The Empire (The New Kingdom) from the Eighteenth Dynasty to the End of the Twentieth Dynasty 1580–1085 B.C.*, Berkeley, CA: University of California Press.

Bard, K. (1989) "The evolution of social complexity in Predynastic Egypt: An analysis of the Nagada cemeteries," *Journal of Mediterranean Archaeology* 2 (2): 223–48.

Barfield, T. J. (2001) "The shadow empires: Imperial state formation along the Chinese-Nomad frontier," in *Empires: Perspectives from Archaeology and History* (eds., Alcock, S. E., D'Altroy, T. N., Morrison, K. D., and Sinopoli, C. M.), Cambridge: Cambridge University Press: 10–41.

Barta, M. (2013) "Egyptian kingship during the Old Kingdom," in *Experiencing Power, Generating Authority: Cosmos, Politics and the Ideology of Kingship in Ancient Egypt and Mesopotamia* (eds., Hill, J., Jones, P., and Morales, A. J.), Philadelphia, PA: University of Pennsylvania Museum of Archaeology and Anthropology: 259–83.

Bartel, B. (1980) "Colonialism and cultural responses: Problems related to Roman provincial analysis," *World Archaeology* 12 (1): 11–26.

Baumer, C. (2008) *Traces in the Desert: Journeys of Discovery across Central Asia*, New York: I. B. Tauris.

Bavay, L. (2015) "Canaanite jars and jar sealings from Deir el-Medina: Scattered evidence of Egypt's economic relations with the Levant during the New Kingdom," in *Policies of Exchange: Political Systems and Modes of Interaction in the Aegean and the Near East in the 2nd Millennium B.C.E., Proceedings of the International Symposium at the University of Freiburg Institute for Archaeological Studies, 30th May–2nd June 2012* (eds., Eder, B. and Pruzsinszky, R.), Vienna: Austrian Academy of Sciences Press: 129–40.

Beal, R. (1995) "Hittite military organization," in *CANE I* (ed., Sasson, J. et al.), New York: Charles Scribner's Sons: 545–54.

Bearak, B. (2002) "Two Afghan paths: Warlord or Professor," *The New York Times*, May 11, http://www.nytimes.com/2002/05/11/world/two-afghan-paths-warlord-or-professor.html, accessed August 18, 2016.

Beattie, J. (1971) *The Nyoro State*, Oxford: Clarendon Press.

Beaux, N. (1990) *Le cabinet de curiousités de Thoutmosis III: Plantes et animaux du "Jardin botanique" de Karnak*, Leuven: Peeters.

Beckman, G. (1995) "Royal ideology and state administration in Hittite Anatolia," *CANE II* (ed., Sasson, J.), New York: Charles Scribner's Sons: 529–43.

— (1996) *Hittite Diplomatic Texts* (ed., Hoffner, H. A.), Atlanta, GA: Scholars Press.

Bedford, P. R. (2010) "The Neo-Assyrian Empire," in *The Dynamics of Ancient Empires: State Power from Assyria to Byzantium* (ed., Morris, I. and Scheidel, W.), New York: Oxford University Press: 30–65.

Beit-Arieh, I. and R. Gophna (1999) "The Egyptian Protodynastic (Late EBI) site at Tel Ma'ahaz: A reassessment," *TA* 26: 191–207.

Bell, B. (1971) "The Dark Ages in ancient history: I. The first Dark Age in Egypt," *AJA* 75 (1): 1–26.

Bell, L. D. (1976) "Interpreters and Egyptianized Nubians in Ancient Egyptian foreign policy: Aspects of the history of Egypt and Nubia," Dissertation, University of Pennsylvania.

Ben-Tor, A. (1991) "New light on the relations between Egypt and Southern Palestine during the Early Bronze Age," *BASOR* 281: 3–10.

Ben-Tor, D. (2016) "Statue of Ramesses III," in *Pharaoh in Canaan: The Untold Story* (ed., Ben-Tor, D.), Jerusalem: The Israel Museum: 84–85.

Bergmann, C. (2016) "A solution to the Clayton ring problem," www.carlo–bergmann.de, accessed August 5, 2016.

Bestock, L. (2017) *Violence and Power in Ancient Egypt: Image and Ideology before the New Kingdom*, New York: Routledge.

Bienkowski, P. (1989) "Prosperity and decline in LBA Canaan: A reply to Liebowitz and Knapp," *BASOR* 275: 59–63.

Bietak, M. (1987) "The C-Group and the Pan-Grave culture in Nubia," in *Nubian Culture Past and Present: Main Papers Presented at the Sixth International Conference for Nubian Studies in Uppsala. August 1986* (ed., Hägg, T.), Stockholm: Historie och Antikvitets Akademien Konferenser: 113–28.

— (2010) "From where came the Hyksos and where did they go?," in *The Second Intermediate Period (Thirteenth–Seventeenth Dynasties). Current Research, Future Prospects* (ed., Marée, M.), *Orientalia Lovaniensia* 192, Leuven: Peeters: 139–81.

— (1996) *Avaris: The Capital of the Hyksos. Recent Excavations at Tell el-Dab'a*, London: British Museum Press.

— (1993) "The Sea Peoples and the end of the Egyptian administration in Canaan," in *Biblical Archaeology Today, 1990: Proceedings of the Second International Congress on Biblical Archaeology* (eds., Biran, A. and Aviram, J.),

Jerualem: Israel Exploration Society, the Israel Academy of Sciences and Humanities: 292–306.

Binder, M. (2017) "The New Kingdom tombs at Amara West: Funerary perspectives on Nubian-Egyptian Interactions," in *Nubia in the New Kingdom: Lived Experience, Pharaonic Control and Indigenous Traditions* (eds., Spencer, D., Stevens, A., and Binder, M.), Leuven: Peeters: 591–613.

Blackman, A. M. (1937) "Preliminary report on the excavations at Sesebi, Northern Province, Anglo-Egyptian Sudan," *JEA* 23 (2): 145–51.

Bleiberg, E. (1988) "The redistributive economy in New Kingdom Egypt: An examination of BAkw(t)," *JARCE* 25: 157–68.

— (1996) *The Official Gift in Ancient Egypt.* Norman, OK: University of Oklahoma Press.

Bonnet, C. (1991) "Upper Nubia from 3000 to 1000 BC," in *Egypt and Africa: Nubia from Prehistory to Islam* (ed., Davies, W. V.), London: British Museum Press: 112–17.

— (2004) "Kerma," in *Sudan: Ancient Treasures: An Exhibition of Recent Discoveries from the Sudan National Museum* (eds., Welsby, D. A. and Anderson, J. R.), London: British Museum Press: 78–82.

— (2014) "An unusual architecture of Hatshepsut in Nubia," in *Creativity and Innovation in the Reign of Hatshepsut* (eds., Galán, J. M., Bryan, B. M., and Dorman, P. F.), Chicago, IL: University of Chicago Press: 427–35.

— (2017) "From the Nubian temples and palaces of Dokki Gel to an Egyptian *mnnw* during the beginnings of Dynasty 18," in *Nubia in the New Kingdom: Lived Experience, Pharaonic Control and Indigenous Traditions* (eds., Spencer, D., Stevens, A., and Binder, M.), Leuven: Peeters: 107–21.

Brand, P. (2007) "Ideological imperatives: Irrational factors in Egyptian-Hittite relations under Ramesses II," in *Moving Across Borders: Foreign Relations, Religion and Cultural Interactions in the Ancient Mediterranean* (eds., Kousoulis, P. and Magliveras, K.), Leuven: Peeters: 15–33.

Brandl, B. (1992) "Evidence for Egyptian colonization of the southern coastal plain and lowlands of Canaan during the Early Bronze I period," in *The Nile Delta in Transition: 4th–3rd Millennium B.C.: Proceedings of the Seminar Held in Cairo 21.–24. October 1990, at the Netherlands Institute of Archaeology and Arabic Studies* (ed., van den Brink, E. C. M.), Tel Aviv: E. C. M. van den Brink: 441–77.

Braun, E. (2003) "South Levantine encounters with Ancient Egypt at the beginning of the Third Millennium," in *Ancient Perspectives on Egypt* (eds., Matthews, R. and Roemer, C.), London: UCL Press: 21–37.

— (2014) "Reflections on the context of a late Dynasty 0 Egyptian colony in the Southern Levant: interpreting some evidence of Nilotic material culture at select sites in the Southern Levant (ca. 3150 BCE – ca. 2950 BCE)," in *The Nile Delta as a Centre of Cultural Interactions between Upper Egypt and the Southern Levant in the 4th Millennium B.C.* (ed., Mączyńska, A.), Poznań: Poznań Archaeological Museum: 37–55.

Braun, E. and E. C. M. van den Brink (1998) "Some comments on the late EB I sequence of Canaan and the relative dating of tomb Uj at Umm el Ga'ab and Graves 313 and 787 from Minshat Abu Omar with imported ware: Views from Egypt and Canaan," *ÄL* 7: 71–94.

Braunstein, S. L. (1998) "The dynamics of power in an age of transition. An analysis of the mortuary remains of Tell el-Far'ah (South) in the Late Bronze and Early Iron Ages," Dissertation, Columbia University.

Bresciani, E. (1997) "Foreigners," in *The Egyptians* (ed., Donadoni, S.), Chicago, IL: University of Chicago Press: 221–53.

Breasted, J. H. (1906a) *Ancient Records of Egypt. Vol I: The First to the Seventeenth Dynasties*, Chicago, IL: The University of Chicago Press.

— (1906b) *Ancient Records of Egypt. Vol II: The Eighteenth Dynasty*, Chicago, IL: The University of Chicago Press.

— (1906c) *Ancient Records of Egypt. Vol IV: The Twentieth through the Twenty-sixth Dynasties*, Chicago, IL: The University of Chicago Press.

— (1948) "Bronze base of a statue of Ramesses VI discovered at Megiddo," in *Megiddo II: Seasons of 1935–1939, Text* (ed., Loud, G.), Chicago, IL: University of Chicago Press: 135–8.

Brown, W. (2010) *Walled States, Waning Sovereignty*, Cambridge, MA: MIT Press.

Brumfiel, E. M. (2001) "Aztec hearts and minds: Religion and the state in the Aztec empire," in *Empires: Perspectives from Archaeology and History* (eds., Alcock, S. E., D'Altroy, T. N., Morrison, K. D., and Sinopoli, C. M.), Cambridge: Cambridge University Press: 283–310.

Brunton, G. (1937) *British Museum Expedition to Middle Egypt. First and Second Years, 128, 129. Mostagedda and the Tasian Culture*, London: B. Quaritch Ltd.

Bryan, B. M. (2006) "Administration in the reign of Thutmose III," in *Thutmose III: A New Biography* (eds., Cline, E. H. and O'Connor, D.), Ann Arbor, MI: University of Michigan Press: 69–122.

Budka, J. (2014) "The New Kingdom in Nubia: New results from current excavations on Sai Island," *EVO* 37: 55–87, 190.

— (2017) "Crossing borders: Settlement archaeology in Egypt and Sudan," *Near Eastern Archaeology* 80 (1): 14–21.

Budka, J. and F. Doyen (2012–2013) "Life in New Kingdom towns in Upper Nubia —new evidence from recent excavations on Sai Island," *ÄL* 22–3: 167–208.

Burke, A. A. and K. V. Lords (2010) "Egyptians in Jaffa: A portrait of Egyptian presence in Jaffa during the Late Bronze Age," *Near Eastern Archaeology* 73 (1): 2–30.

Burke, A. A., M. Pielstöcker, A. Karoll et al. (2017) "Excavation of the New Kingdom fortress in Jaffa, 2011–2014: Traces of resistance to Egyptian rule in Canaan," *AJA* 121 (1): 85–133.

Caminos, R. A. (1954) *Late Egyptian Miscellanies*, London: Oxford University Press.

— (1977) *A Tale of Woe from a Hieratic Papyrus in the A. S. Pushkin Museum of Fine Arts in Moscow*, Oxford: Griffith Institute.

Campbell, E. F. (1964) *The Chronology of the Amarna Letters With Special Reference to the Hypothetical Coregency of Amenophis III and Akhenaten*, Baltimore, MD: The Johns Hopkins Press.

Carneiro, R. L. (1970) "A theory of the origin of the state," *Science, New Series* 169, No. 3947: 733–38.

Chaix, L. (2004) "Bucrania," in *Sudan: Ancient Treasures: An Exhibition of Recent Discoveries from the Sudan National Museum* (eds., Welsby, D. A. and Anderson, J. R.), London: British Museum Press: 89.

Cifola, B. (1988) "Ramses III and the Sea Peoples: A structural analysis of the Medinet Habu inscriptions," *Orientalia, Nova Series* 57 (3): 275–306.

Clayton, J., A. de Trafford, and M. Borda (2008) "A hieroglyphic inscription found at Jebel Uweinat mentioning Yam and Tekhebet," *Sahara* 19: 129–34.

Cline, E. H. (2014) *1177 B.C.: The Year Civilization Collapsed*, Princeton, NJ: Princeton University Press.

Cooper, J. (2012) "Reconsidering the location of Yam," *JARCE* 48: 1–21.

Cooper, J. and H. Barnard (2017) "New insights on the inscription of a painted Pan-Grave bucranium, Grave 3252 at Cemetery 3100/3200, Mostagedda (Middle Egypt)," *African Archaeological Review*. Published first online: DOI 10.1007/s10437–017–9261–3.

Cromer, E. B. (1910) *Ancient and Modern Imperialism*, New York: Longmans.

Crouch, D. P. (1991) "Roman models for Spanish colonization," in *The Spanish Borderlands in Pan-American Perspectives* (ed., Thomas, D. H.), Washington, DC: Smithsonian Institution: 21–35.

Crouch, D. P., D. J. Garr, and A. I. Mundigo (1982) *Spanish City Planning in North America*, Cambridge, MA: MIT Press.

Cumming, B. (1982) *Egyptian Historical Records of the Later Eighteenth Dynasty. Fascicle I*, Warminster: Aris & Phillips Ltd.

Dakhleh Oasis Project (n.d.) "Report presented to the Supreme Council of Antiquities, Egypt, on the 2000 season of the Dakhleh Oasis Project," unpublished report, http://artsonline.monash.edu.au/ancient-cultures/files/2013/04/dakhleh-report-2000.pdf, accessed August 7, 2016.

D'Altroy, T. (2003) *The Incas*, Malden, MA: Blackwell Publishing.

D'Altroy, T. and T. K. Earle (1985) "Staple finance, wealth finance, and storage in the Inka political economy [and comments and reply]," *Current Anthropology* 26 (2): 187–206.

Darnell, J. and Manassa, C. (2007) *Tutankhamun's Armies: Battle and Conquest During Ancient Egypt's Late Eighteenth Dynasty*, Hoboken, NJ: Wiley.

David, A. (2009) "Egyptian 20th Dynasty wall paintings," in *Excavations at Tel Beth-Shean 1989–1996. Volume III: The 13th–11th Century BCE Strata in Areas N and S* (eds., Panitz-Cohen, N. and Mazar, A.), Jerusalem: Israel Exploration Society: 706–13.

Davies, B. G. (1992) *Egyptian Historical Records of the Later Eighteenth Dynasty. Fascicle IV*, Warminster: Aris & Phillips Ltd.

— (1994) *Egyptian Historical Records of the Later Eighteenth Dynasty. Fascicle V*, Warminster: Aris & Phillips Ltd.

Davies, N. de G. (1905) *The Rock Tombs of El Amarna II: The Tombs of Panehesy and Meryra II*, London: Egypt Exploration Fund.

— (2002) *The Tomb of Rekh-mi-re at Thebes, Vol. I*, reprint, North Stratford, NH: Ayer Company Publishers, Inc.

Davies, W. V. (2003) "Sobeknakht's hidden treasure," *British Museum Magazine* Summer: 18–19.

Davies, W. V. and R. F. Friedman (2002) "The Narmer palette: An overlooked detail," in *Egyptian Museum Collections around the World*. Vol. 1 (eds., Eldamaty, M. and Trad, M.), Cairo: Supreme Council of Antiquities: 243–46.

Deagan, K. (2001) "Dynamics of imperial adjustment in Spanish America: Ideology and social integration," in *Empires: Perspectives from Archaeology and History* (eds., Alcock, S. E., D'Altroy, T. N., Morrison, K. D., and Sinopoli, C. M.), Cambridge: Cambridge University Press: 179–94.

Der Manuelian, P. (1987) *Studies in the Reign of Amenophis II*, Hildesheim: Gerstenberg.

Dever, W. G. (1992) "The Late Bronze—Early Iron I horizon in Syria-Palestine: Egyptians, Canaanites, 'Sea Peoples,' and Proto-Israelites," in *The Crisis Years: The 12th Century B. C.: From Beyond the Danube to the Tigris* (eds., Ward, W. A. and Joukowsky, M. S.), Dubuque, IA: Kendall/Hunt: 99–110.

Diamond, S. (1974) *In Search of the Primitive: A Critique of Civilization*, New Brunswick: Transaction Books.

Dietler, M. (2005) "The archaeology of colonization and the colonization of archaeology: Theoretical challenges from an ancient Mediterranean colonial encounter," in *The Archaeology of Colonial Encounters* (ed., Stein, G.), Santa Fe, NM: SAR Press: 33–68.

Diodorus Siculus (1933) *The Library of History of Diodorus Siculus. Vol. 1*, Books 1–2.34 (trans., Oldfather, C. H.), Cambridge, MA: Harvard University Press.

Dothan, M. (1993) "Mor, Tel," in *New Encyclopedia of Archaeological Explorations in the Holy Land III* (ed., Stern, E.), New York: Simon and Schuster: 1073–4.

Dothan, T. (1982) *The Philistines and their Material Culture*, Jerusalem: Israel Exploration Society.

— (2008) *Deir el-Balah: Uncovering an Egyptian Outpost in Canaan from the time of the Exodus*, Jerusalem: The Israel Museum.

Dothan, T. and B. Brandl (2010) *Deir el-Balah: Excavations in 1977–1982 in the Cemetery and Settlement II: The Finds. Qedem 50*, Jerusalem: Institute of Archaeology, Hebrew University of Jerusalem.

Dothan T. and M. Dothan (1992) *People of the Sea: The Search for the Philistines*, New York: Macmillan.

Doyle, M. W. (1986) *Empires*, Ithaca, NY: Cornell University Press.

Drews, R. (1993) *The End of the Bronze Age: Changes in Warfare and the Catastrophe, ca. 1200 B.C.*, Princeton, NJ: Princeton University Press.

Dreyer, G. (1992) "Recent discoveries at Abydos cemetery U," in *The Nile Delta in Transition: 4th–3rd Millennium B.C.: Proceedings of the Seminar Held in Cairo 21.–24. October 1990, at the Netherlands Institute of Archaeology and Arabic Studies* (ed., van den Brink, E. C. M.), Tel Aviv: E. C. M. van den Brink: 293–9.

— (2008) "Early writing in Ancient Egypt," in *Journey of Writing in Egypt* (eds., Azab, K. and Mansour, A.), Alexandria: Bibliotheca Alexandrina: 14–23.

Dunham, D. (1967) *Second Cataract Forts. Volume II: Uronarti, Shalfak, Mirgissa*, Boston, MA: Museum of Fine Arts.

Edgerton, W. F. (1947) "The Nauri Decree of Seti I: A translation and analysis of the legal portion," *JNES* 6 (4): 219–30.

Edwards, E. N. (2004) *The Nubian Past: An Archaeology of the Sudan*, New York: Routledge.

Elgavish, D. (2008) "Justification for war in the Ancient Near East and in the Bible," *Jewish Law Association Studies* 18: 37–69.

Elton, H. (1996) *Frontiers of the Roman Empire*, Bloomington, IN: Indiana University Press.

Emery, W. B. (1965) *Egypt in Nubia*, London: Hutchinson of London.

Emery, W. B., H. S. Smith, and A. Millard (1979) *The Fortress of Buhen: The Archaeological Report*, London: Egypt Exploration Society.

Epigraphic Survey (1930) *Earlier Historical Records of Ramesses III. Medinet Habu. Volume I*. Chicago, IL: University of Chicago Press.

Evans–Prichard, E. E. (1940) *The Nuer: A Description of the Modes of Livelihood and Political Institutions of a Nilotic People*, Oxford: Clarendon Press.

Fairman, H. W. (1938) "Preliminary report on the excavations at Sesebi (Sudla) and ʿAmārah West, Anglo-Egyptian Sudan, 1937–8," *JEA* 24 (2): 151–6.

— (1939) "Preliminary report on the excavations at ʿAmārah West, Anglo-Egyptian Sudan, 1938–9," *JEA* 25 (2): 139–44.

— (1948) "Preliminary report on the excavations at ʿAmārah West, Anglo-Egyptian Sudan, 1947–8," *JEA* 34: 3–11.

Figueras, P. (2000) *From Gaza to Pelusium: Material for the Historical Geography of North Sinai and Southwestern Palestine (332 BCE–640 CE)*, Beer-sheva: Ben-Gurion University of the Negev Press.

Finkelstein, I. (1988) *The Archaeology of Israelite Settlement*, Jerusalem: Israel Exploration Society.

Finley, M. I. (1976) "Colonies: An attempt at a typology," *Transactions of the Royal Historical Society* 26: 167–88.

Firth, C. M. (1927) *The Archaeological Survey of Nubia, Report for 1910–1911*, Cairo: Government Press.

Flannery, K. V. (1999) "Process and agency in early state formation," *Cambridge Archaeological Journal* 9 (1): 3–21.

Förster, F. (2007) "With donkeys, jars and water bags into the Libyan Desert: The Abu Ballas Trail in the late Old Kingdom/First Intermediate Period," *BMSAES* 7: 1–36.

— (2008) "Preliminary report on the seal impressions found at site Chufu 01/01 in the Dakhla region (2002)," *GM* 217: 17–25.

Frandsen, P. J. (1979) "Egyptian imperialism," in *Power and Propaganda: A Symposium on Ancient Empires* (ed., Larsen, M. T.), Copenhagen: Akademisk Forlag: 167–90.

Fried, M. H. (1967) *An Essay in Political Anthropology*, New York: Random House.

Friedman, R. (2003) "Excavating an elephant," *NN* 15: 9–10.

— (2005) "Finding lost souls," *NN* 17: 11–12.

— (2009) "Hierakonpolis Locality HK29A: The Predynastic ceremonial center revisited," *JARCE* 45: 79–103.

Foucher de Chartres (1969) *A History of the Expedition to Jerusalem, 1095–1127* (trans., Ryan, F. R.), Knoxville, TN: University of Tennessee Press.

Fullerton, W. M. (1913) *Problems of Power: A Study of International Politics from Sadowa to Kirk–Kilissé*, London: Constable & Company, Ltd.

Gadot, Y. (2010) "The Late Bronze Egyptian estate at Aphek," *TA* 37: 48–66.

Galán, J. M. (1994) "The heritage of Thutmose III's campaigns in the Amarna Age," in *Essays in Honor of Hans Goedicke* (eds., Bryan, B. and Lorton, D.), San Antonio, TX: Van Siclen Books: 91–102.

— (1995) *Victory and Border: Terminology Related to Egyptian Imperialism in the XVIIIth Dynasty*, Hildesheim: Gerstenberg.

— (2002) "Mutilation of pharaoh's enemies," in *Egyptian Museum Collections around the World. Vol. 1* (eds., Eldamaty, M. and Trad, M.), Cairo: Supreme Council of Antiquities: 441–50.

Gardiner, A. H. (1920) "The Ancient military road between Egypt and Palestine," *JEA* 6: 99–116.

Giddy, L. (1987) *Egyptian Oases: Bahariya, Dakhla, Farafra, and Karga during Pharaonic Times*, Warminster: Aris & Philips Ltd.

Gillam, R. (1995) "Priestesses of Hathor: Their function, decline and disappearance," *JARCE* 32: 211–37.

Given, M. (2004) *The Archaeology of the Colonized*, New York: Routledge.

Goetze, A. (trans.) (1969) "From the Instructions for the Commander of the Border Guards," in *Ancient Near Eastern Texts Relating to the Old Testament*. Third edition (ed., Pritchard, J. B.), Princeton, NJ: Princeton University Press: 210–11.

— (1980) "The struggle for the domination of Syria (1400–1300 B.C.)," in *The Cambridge Ancient History*, Vol. II, Part 2A, Third edition (eds., Edwards, I. E. S., Gadd, C. J., Hammond, N. G. L., and Sollberger, E.), Cambridge: Cambridge University Press: 1–20.

Goldwasser, O. (1984) "Hieratic inscriptions from Tel Sera' in Southern Canaan," *TA* 11: 77–93.

Gonen, R. (1984) "Urban Canaan in the Late Bronze Age," *BASOR* 253: 61–73.

— (1992a) "The Late Bronze Age," in *The Archaeology of Ancient Israel* (ed., Ben-Tor, A.), New Haven, CT: Yale University Press: 211–57.

— (1992b) *Burial Patterns and Cultural Diversity in Late Bronze Age Canaan*, Winona Lake, IN: Eisenbrauns.

Gophna, R. (1987) "Egyptian trading posts in Southern Canaan at the dawn of the Archaic Period," in *Egypt, Israel, Sinai. Archaeological and Historical Relationships in the Biblical Period* (ed., Rainey, A. F.), Tel Aviv: Tel Aviv University: 13–21.

Gordon, A. H. (1983) "The context and meaning of the ancient Egyptian word inw from the proto-dynastic period to the end of the New Kingdom," Dissertation, University of California, Berkeley.

Gosden, C. (2004) *Archaeology and Colonialism: Cultural Contact from 5000 BC to the Present*, Cambridge: Cambridge University Press.

Grayson, A. K. (1991) *Assyrian Rulers of the Early First Millennium BC. Vol I (1114–859 BC)*, Toronto: University of Toronto Press.

— (1995) "Assyrian rule of conquered territory in ancient Western Asia," in *CANE II* (ed., Sasson, J. et al.), New York: Charles Scribner's Sons: 959–68.

Green, J. D. M. (2006) "Ritual and social structure in the Late Bronze and Early Iron Age Southern Levant: The cemetery at Tell es-Sa'idiyeh, Jordan, Volume 1: Text," Dissertation, University College London.

— (2013) "Social identity in the Jordan Valley during the Late Bronze and Early Iron Ages: Evidence from Tall as-Sa'īdiyyah cemetery," *Studies in the History and Archaeology of Jordan* 11: 419–29.

Greenberg, M. (1955) *The Hab/piru*, American Oriental Series 39, New Haven, CT: American Oriental Society.

Grzymski, K. (1997) "The Debba Bend in the New Kingdom," in *Essays in Honour of Prof. Dr. Jadwiga Lipińska* (ed., Aksamit, J. et al.), Warsaw: National Museum in Warsaw: 93–100.

Gurney, O. (1990) *The Hittites*. Second edition, New York: Penguin Books.

Gwin, P. (2011) "Former Qaddafi mercenaries describe fighting in Libyan War," *The Atlantic*, August 31, http://www.theatlantic.com/international/archive/2011/08/former-qaddafi-mercenaries-describe-fighting-in-libyan-war/244356/, accessed August 23, 2016.

Habachi, L. (1969) *Features of the Deification of Ramesses II*, Glückstadt: J. J. Augustin.

— (1980) "The military posts of Ramesses II on the coastal road and the western part of the Delta," *BIFAO* 80: 13–30.

Hafsaas, H. (2006) *Cattle Pastoralists in a Multicultural Setting: The C-Group People in Lower Nubia 2500–1500 BCE*, Ramallah: Birzeit University.

Hansen, M. H. (2006) *Polis: An Introduction to the Ancient Greek City-State*, Oxford: Oxford University Press.

Haring, B. J. J. (1997) *Divine Households. Administrative and Economic Aspects of the New Kingdom Royal Memorial Temples in Western Thebes*, Leiden: Nederlands Instituut voor het NabiJe Oosten.

Harrell, J. A. and R. E. Mittelstaedt (2015) "Newly discovered Middle Kingdom forts in Lower Nubia," *SN* 19: 30–9.

Harrison, T. P. (1993) "Economics with an entrepreneurial spirit: Early Bronze trade with late Predynastic Egypt," *The Biblical Archaeologist* 54 (2): 81–93.

Hartung, U. (2002) "Imported jars from Cemetery U at Abydos and the relations between Egypt and Canaan in Predynastic times," in *Egypt and the Levant. Interrelations from the 4th through the Early 3rd Millennium B.C.E.* (eds., van den Brink, E. C. M. and Levy, T. E.), London: Leicester University Press: 437–49.

Hasel, M. G. (1998) *Domination and Resistance: Egyptian Military Activity in the Southern Levant ca. 1300–1185 B.C.*, Leiden: Brill.

Hassan, F. (2007) "Droughts, famine and the collapse of the Old Kingdom: Re-reading Ipuwer," in *The Archaeology and Art of Ancient Egypt: Essays in honor of David B. O'Connor*. Vol I (eds., Hawass, Z. and Richards, J.), Cairo: Supreme Council of Antiquities: 357–77.

Hassan, F. et al. (2006) "Modelling environmental and settlement change in the Fayum," *Egyptian Archaeology* 29: 37–40.

Haverfield, F. et al. (1910) "Ancient imperialism," *The Classical Review* 24 (4): 105–116.

Hayes, W. C. (1953) *The Scepter of Egypt: A Background for the Study of the Egyptian Antiquities in the Metropolitan Museum of Art. Vol 1: From the Earliest Times to the End of the Middle Kingdom*, New York: Metropolitan Museum of Art.

— (1960) "A selection of Thutmoside ostraca from Dēr El–Baḥri," *JEA* 46: 29–52.

— (1973) "Egypt: Internal affairs from Thutmosis I to the death of Amenophis III," in *The Cambridge Ancient History, Vol. II, Part 1: The Middle East and the Aegean Region, c. 1800–1380*. Third edition (eds., Edwards, I. E. S., Gadd, C. J., Hammond, N. G. L., and Sollberger, E.), Cambridge: Cambridge University Press: 313–416.

Hein, I. (1991) *Die ramessidische Bautätigkeit in Nubien*, Wiesbaden: Otto Harrassowitz.

Hendrickx, S. and L. Bavay (2002) "The relative chronological position of Egyptian Predynastic and Early Dynastic tombs with objects imported from the Near East and the nature of interregional contacts," in *Egypt and the Levant. Interrelations from the 4th through the Early 3rd Millennium B.C.E.* (eds., van den Brink, E. C. M. and Levy, T. E.), London: Leicester University Press: 58–80.

Hendrickx, S., J. C. Darnell, and M. C. Gatto (2012) "The earliest representations of royal power in Egypt: The rock drawings of Nag el-Hamdulab (Aswan)," *Antiquity* 86: 1068–83.

Herodotus (2007) *The Landmark Herodotus: The Histories* (ed., Strassler, R. B.; trans., Purvis, A. L.), New York: Anchor Books.

Heuser, B. (2010) *The Evolution of Strategy: Thinking War from Antiquity to the Present*, Cambridge: Cambridge University Press.

Hierakonpolis Expedition (n.d.) "HK6: The elite Predynastic and Early Dynastic cemetery," http://www.hierakonpolis-online.org/index.php/explore-the-predynastic-cemeteries/hk6-elite-cemetery, accessed July 30, 2016.

Higginbotham, C. (2000) *Egyptianization and Elite Emulation in Ramesside Palestine: Governance and Accommodation on the Imperial Periphery*, Leiden: Brill.

Hobsbawm, E. J. (2000) *Bandits*, New York: The New Press.

Hoffmeier, J. K. (1999) *Israel in Egypt: The Evidence for the Authenticity of the Exodus Tradition*, Oxford: Oxford University Press.

— (2004) "Tell el-Borg on Egypt's eastern frontier: A preliminary report on the 2002 and 2004 seasons," *JARCE* 41: 85–111.

— (forthcoming in 2018) "A possible location for the sea and land battles of the Sea Peoples with Ramesses III in North Sinai," *BASOR* 380.

Höflmayer, F. (2015) "Exchange, extraction, and the politics of ideological money laundering in Egypt's New Kingdom Empire," in *Policies of Exchange: Political Systems and Modes of Interaction in the Aegean and the Near East in the 2nd Millennium B.C.E.*, *Proceedings of the International Symposium at the University of Freiburg Institute for Archaeological Studies, 30th May–2nd June 2012* (eds., Eder, B. and Pruzsinszky, R.), Vienna: Austrian Academy of Sciences Press: 135–48.

Hölbl, G. (2001) *A History of the Ptolemaic Empire* (trans., Saavedra, T.), New York: Routledge.

Hope, C. (2007) "Egypt and 'Libya' to the end of the Old Kingdom: a view from Dakhleh Oasis," in *The Archaeology and Art of Ancient Egypt: Essays in honor of David B. O'Connor*. Vol I (eds., Hawass, Z. and Richards, J.), Cairo: Supreme Council of Antiquities Press: 349–415.

Hope, C. and A. Pettman (2012) "Egyptian connections with Dakhleh Oasis in the Early Dynastic period to Dynasty IV: New data from Mut al-Kharab," in *The Oasis Papers 6: Proceedings of the Sixth International Conference of the Dakhleh Oasis Project* (eds., Bagnall, R. S., Davoli, P., and Hope, C. A.), Oxford: Oxbow: 147–65.

Horowitz, W. (1996) "An inscribed clay cylinder from Amarna Age Beth Shean," *IEJ* 46 (3/4): 208–18.

Horvath, R. J. (1972) "A definition of colonialism," *Current Anthropology* 13 (1): 45–57.

Howe, S. (2002) *Empire. A Very Short Introduction*, New York: Oxford University Press.

Hubschmann, C. (2010) "Igai: A little-known deity of Dakhleh Oasis," *Rosetta* 8: 42–61.

Hyslop, J. (1990) *Inka Settlement Planning*, Austin, TX: University of Texas Press.

James, F. W. (1966) *The Iron Age at Beth Shan: A Study of Levels VI–IV*, Philadelphia, PA: University Museum.

Jaritz, H. (1993) "The investigation of the ancient wall extending from Aswan to Philae. Second preliminary report," *MDAIK* 49: 107–19.

Jeuthe, C. (2012) *Balat X. Ein werkstattkomplex im Palast der 1. Zwischenzeit in Ayn Asil*, Le Caire: IFAO.

Jeuthe, C., G. Le Provost, and G. Soukiassian (2013) "Ayn Asil, palais des gouverneurs du règne de Pépy II. État des recherches sur la partie sud," *BIFAO* 113: 203–38.

Jeuthe, C. (2014) "Initial results: The Sheikh Muftah occupation at Balat North / 1 (Dakhla Oasis)," *Archéo-Nil* 24: 103–14.

Johnson, C. (2004) *The Sorrows of Empire: Militarism, Secrecy, and the End of the Republic*, New York: Metropolitan Books.

Johnson, D. H. (ed.) (1993) *Governing the Nuer: Documents in Nuer History and Ethnography, 1922–1931 by Percy Coriat*, Oxford: Journal of the Anthropological Society of Oxford.

Junker, H. (1925) *Ermenne: Bericht über die Grabungen der Akademie der Wissenschaften in Wien auf den Friedhöfen von Ermenne (Nubien) im Winter 1911/12*, Vienna: Hölder-Pichler-Tempsky.

Kadry, A. (1982) *Officers and Officials in the New Kingdom*, Budapest: Université Loránd Eötvös.

Kahn, D. and O. Tammuz (2008) "Egypt is difficult to enter: Invading Egypt—a game plan (seventh–fourth centuries BCE)," *JSSEA* 35: 37–66.

Kaper, O. E. and H. Willems (2002) "Policing the desert: Old Kingdom activity around the Dakhleh Oasis," in *Egypt and Nubia: Gifts of the Desert* (ed., Friedman, R.), London: British Museum Press: 79–94.

Kaplan, P. (2003) "Cross-cultural contacts among mercenary communities in Saite and Persian Egypt," *Mediterranean Historical Review* 18 (1): 1–31.

Karmon, Y. (1956) "Geographical aspects in the history of the coastal plain of Israel," *IEJ* 6 (1): 33–50.

Kemp, B. J. (1972) "Fortified towns in Nubia," in *Man, Settlement, and Urbanism* (eds., Ucko, P. J., Tringham, R., and Dimbleby, G. W.), London: Duckworth: 651–6.

— (1978) "Imperialism and empire in New Kingdom Egypt (c. 1575–1087 B. C.)," in *Imperialism in the Ancient World* (eds., Garnsey, P. D. A. and Whittaker, C. R.), Cambridge: Cambridge University Press: 7–57.

— (1989) *Ancient Egypt: Anatomy of a Civilization*, New York: Routledge.

— (1997) "Why empires rise," *Cambridge Archaeological Journal* 7 (1): 125–31.

Kendall, T. (1997) *Kerma and the Kingdom of Kush, 2500–1500 B.C.: The Archaeological Discovery of an Ancient Nubian Empire*, Washington DC: National Museum of African Art, Smithsonian Institution.

Kessel, J. L. (1997) "Restoring seventeenth-century New Mexico, then and now," *Historical Archaeology* 31 (1): 46–54.

Killebrew, A. E. (2004) "New Kingdom Egyptian-style and Egyptian pottery in Canaan: Implications for Egyptian rule in Canaan during the 19th and early 20th Dynasties," in *Egypt, Israel, and the Ancient Mediterranean World: Studies in Honor of Donald B. Redford* (eds., Knoppers, G. N. and Hirsch, A.), Leiden: Brill: 309–43.

— (2005) *Biblical Peoples and Ethnicity. An Archaeological Study of Egyptians, Canaanites, Philistines and Early Israel, 1300–1100 B.C.E.*, Atlanta, GA: Society of Biblical Literature.

Killebrew, A. E., P. Goldberg, and A. M. Rosen (2006) "Deir el-Balah: A geological, archaeological, and historical reassessment of an Egyptianizing 13th and 12th century B.C.E. center," *BASOR* 343: 97–119.

Kislev, M. E., O. Simchoni, Y. Melamed, and L. Maroz (2009) "Botanical remains," in *Excavations at Tel Beth-Shean 1989–1996. Volume III: The 13th–11th Century BCE Strata in Areas N and S* (eds., Panitz–Cohen, N. and Mazar, A.), Jerusalem: Israel Exploration Society: 764–71.

Kitchen, K. A. (1993) *Ramesside Inscriptions Translated and Annotated, Vol I: Ramesses I, Sethos I and Contemporaries*, Cambridge, MA: Blackwell Publishers.

— (1996) *Ramesside Inscriptions Translated and Annotated, Vol II: Ramesses II, Royal Inscriptions*, Cambridge, MA: Blackwell Publishers.

— (1998) "Amenhotep III and Mesopotamia," in *Amenhotep III: Perspectives on His Reign* (eds., O'Connor, D. and Cline, E. H.), Ann Arbor, MI: University of Michigan Press: 250–61.

— (2000) *Ramesside Inscriptions Translated and Annotated, Vol III: Ramesses II, his contemporaries*, Cambridge, MA: Blackwell Publishers.

— (2003) *Ramesside Inscriptions Translated and Annotated, Vol IV: Merneptah and the Late Nineteenth Dynasty*, Cambridge, MA: Blackwell Publishers.

— (2008) *Ramesside Inscriptions Translated and Annotated, Vol V: Setnakht, Ramesses III, and Contemporaries*, Cambridge, MA: Blackwell Publishers.

Koch, I. (2014) "Goose keeping, elite emulation and Egyptianized feasting at Late Bronze Lachish," *TA* 41: 161–79.

Kochavi, M. (1990) *Aphek in Canaan. The Egyptian Governor's Residence and Its Finds*, Jerusalem: The Israel Museum.

Köhler, E. C. (2004) "On the origins of Memphis—the new excavations in the Early Dynastic necropolis at Helwan," in *Egypt at its Origins: Studies in Memory of Barbara Adams* (eds., Hendrickx, S. et al.), Dudley, MA: Peeters: 395–415.

Knoblauch, C. (2017) "The burial customs of Middle Kingdom colonial communities in Nubia: Possibilities and problems," in *Nubia in the New Kingdom: Lived Experience, Pharaonic Control and Indigenous Traditions* (eds., Spencer, D., Stevens, A., and Binder, M.), Leuven: Peeters: 575–90.

Knoblauch, C. and L. Bestock (2013) "The Uronarti Regonal Archaeological Project: Final Report of the 2012 Survey," *MDAIK* 69: 103–42.

Knoblauch, C. and L. Bestock (2017) "Evolving communities: The Egyptian fortress on Uronarti in the Late Middle Kingdom," *SN* 21: 50–8.

Kraemer, B. and K. Liszka (2016) "Evidence for administration of the Nubian fortresses in the late Middle Kingdom: The Semna Dispatches," *Journal of Egyptian History* 9: 1–65.

Kuhlmann, K. P. (2002) "The 'Oasis Bypath' or the issue of desert trade in pharaonic times," in *Tides of the Desert—Gezeiten der Wüste. Contribution to the Archaeology and Environmental History of Africa in Honor of Rudolph Kuper* (ed., "Jennerstrasse 8"), Köln: Heinrich-Barth-Institut: 125–70.

— (2005) "Der 'Wasserberg des Djedefre' (Chufu 01/01). Ein Lagerplatz mit Expeditionsinschriften der 4. Dynastie im Raum der Oase Dachla," *MDAIK* 61: 243–89.

Kuhrt, A. (1995) *The Ancient Near East c. 3000–330 BC*. Volume Two, New York: Routledge.

Laisney, D. (2010) *Cartographie de Balat. Balat IX*, Cairo: IFAO.

Lamb, D. (1988) *The Arabs: Journeys Beyond the Mirage*, New York: Random House.

Langgut, D., I. Finkelstein, and T. Litt (2013) "Climate and the Late Bronze collapse: New evidence from the Southern Levant," *TA* 40: 149–75.

Lattimore, O. (1962) *Studies in Frontier History: Collected Papers 1928–1958*, New York: Oxford University Press.

— (1979) "Geography and the ancient empires," in *Power and Propaganda: A Symposium on Ancient Empires* (ed., Larsen, M. T.), Copenhagen: Akademisk Forlag: 35–40.

Lehmann, G., S. A. Rosen, A. Berlejung, B.-A. Neumeier, and H. M. Niemann (2010) "Excavations at Qubur al-Walaydah, 2007–2009," *Die Welt des Orients* 40: 137–59.

Lernau, O. and D. Golani (2004) "The osteological remains (Aquatic)," in *The Renewed Archaeological Excavations at Lachish (1973–1994)* (ed., Ussishkin, D.), Tel Aviv: Emery and Claire Yass Publications in Archaeology: 2456–89.

Levy, E. (2016) "The Mekal stela," in *Pharaoh in Canaan: The Untold Story* (ed., Ben–Tor, D.), Jerusalem: The Israel Museum: 110–11.

Levy, T. E. et al. (1997) "Egyptian-Canaanite interaction at Nahal Tillah, Israel (ca. 4500–3000 B. C. E.): An interim report on the 1994–1995 excavations," *BASOR* 307: 1–51.

Lichtheim, M. (1975) *Ancient Egyptian Literature. Vol I: The Old and Middle Kingdoms*, Berkeley, CA: University of California Press.

— (1976) *Ancient Egyptian Literature. Vol II: The New Kingdom*, Berkeley, CA: University of California Press.

— (1988) *Ancient Egyptian Autobiographies Chiefly of the Middle Kingdom: A Study and an Anthology*, Freiburg: Universitatsverlag Freiburg Schweiz.

284 | *References*

Lightfoot, K. G. and A. Martinez (1995) "Frontiers and boundaries in archaeological perspective," *Annual Review of Anthropology* 24: 471–92.

Lilyquist, C. (2003) *The Tomb of Three Foreign Wives of Thutmose III*, New York: Metropolitan Museum of Art.

Linseele, V. and W. Van Neer (2003) "Gourmets or priests? Fauna from the Predynastic Temple," *NN* 15: 6–7.

Lipton, G. (2010) "The excavation of the cemetery," in *Deir el-Balah: Excavations in 1977–1982 in the Cemetery and Settlement. Volume I: Stratigraphy and Architecture* (eds., Dothan, T. and Brandl, B.), Jerusalem: Institute of Archaeology, Hebrew University of Jerusalem: 3–46.

Liszka, K. (2012) "'We have come to serve pharaoh': a study of the Medjay and Pangrave as an ethnic group and as mercenaries from c. 2300 BCE until c. 1050 BCE," Dissertation, University of Pennsylvania.

— (2017) "Egyptian or Nubian? Dry-Stone architecture at Wadi el-Hudi, Wadi es-Sebua, and the Eastern Desert." *JEA*: https://doi.org/10.1177/0307513317714407

Liverani, I. (2004) "Hillat el-Arab," in *Sudan: Ancient Treasures: An Exhibition of Recent Discoveries from the Sudan National Museum* (eds., Welsby, D. A. and Anderson, J. R.), London: British Museum Press: 138–47.

Lorton, D. (1974) *The Juridical Terminology of International Relations in Egyptian Texts through Dyn. XVIII*, Baltimore, MD: Johns Hopkins University Press.

Luttwak, E. N. (1979) *The Grand Strategy of the Roman Empire from the First Century A.D. to the Third*, Baltimore, MD: Johns Hopkins University Press.

Luvaas, J. (ed. and trans.) (1999) *Fredrick the Great on The Art of War*, Boston, MA: Da Capo Press.

Machiavelli, N. (1998) *The Prince*. Second edition (trans., Mansfield, H. C.), Chicago, IL: University of Chicago Press.

Mączyńska, A. (2014) "Some remarks on the visitors in the Nile Delta in the 4th millennium BC," in *The Nile Delta as a Centre of Cultural Interactions between Upper Egypt and the Southern Levant in the 4th Millennium B.C.* (ed., Mączyńska, A.), Poznań: Poznań Archaeological Museum: 181–216.

Maigret (1747) *Treatise on the Safety and Maintenance of States by the Means of Fortresses* (trans., anonymous), London: L. J. Davis and B. Stichall.

Martin, G. T. (1991) *The Hidden Tombs of Memphis. New Discoveries from the Time of Tutankhamun and Ramesses the Great*, London: Thames & Hudson Ltd.

Martin, M. A. S. (2004) "Egyptian and Egyptianized pottery in Late Bronze Age Canaan: Typology, chronology, ware fabrics, and manufacture techniques. Pots and people?," *ÄL* 14: 265–84.

— (2011) *Egyptian-Type Pottery in the Late Bronze Age Southern Levant*, Wien: Österreichischen Akadamie der Wissenschaften.

Mattingly, D. J. (2011) *Imperialism, Power, and Identity: Experiencing the Roman Empire*, Princeton, NJ: Princeton University Press.

Maxfield, V. A. (2003) "Ostraca and the Roman Army in the Eastern Desert," *Bulletin of the Institute of Classical Studies. Supplement* 81: 153–73.

Mazar, A. (1997) "Four thousand years of history at Tel Beth-Shean: An account of the renewed excavations," *The Biblical Archaeologist* 60, no. 2: 62–76.

— (2009) "Introduction and overview," in *Excavations at Tel Beth-Shean 1989–1996. Volume III: The 13th–11th Century BCE Strata in Areas N and S* (eds., Panitz–Cohen, N. and Mazar, A.), Jerusalem: Israel Exploration Society: 1–32.

McDonald, M. M. A. (1996) "Relations between Dakhleh Oasis and the Nile Valley in the mid-Holocene: A discussion," in *Interregional Contacts in the Later Prehistory of Northeastern Africa* (eds., Krzyzaniak, L, Kroeper, K., and Kobusiewicz, M.), Poznań: Poznań Archaeological Museum: 93–9.

— (2001) "The mid-Holocene Sheikh Muftah cultural unit of Dakhleh Oasis, South Central Egypt: A preliminary report on recent fieldwork," *Nyame Akuma* 56: 4–10.

— (2002) "Dakhleh Oasis in Predynastic and Early Dynastic times: Bashendi B and the Sheikh Muftah cultural sites," *Archéo-Nil* 12: 109–20.

McFate, S. (2015) "Reining in soldiers of fortune," *The New York Times*, April 17, http://www.nytimes.com/2015/04/18/opinion/reining-in-soldiers-of-fortune.html, accessed August 22, 2016.

McGuire, R. H. (1989) "The greater Southwest as a periphery of Mesoamerica," in *Centre and Periphery. Comparative Studies in Archaeology* (ed., Champion, T. C.), London: Routledge: 39–64.

Mill, J. S. (1910) *Utilitarianism, Liberty, and Representative Government*, New York: E. P. Dutton & Co.

Millet, N. B. (1990) "The Narmer Macehead and related objects," *JARCE* 27: 53–9.

Mills, A. J. (1999) "Pharaonic Egyptians in the Dakhleh Oasis," in *Reports from the Survey of the Dakhleh Oasis, Western Desert of Egypt: 1977–1987* (eds., Churcher, C. S. and Mills, A. J.), Oxford: Oxbow: 171–8 with appendix, 251–65.

— (2012) "An Old Kingdom trading post at 'Ain el–Gazzareen, Dakhleh Oasis," in *The Oasis Papers 6: Proceedings of the Sixth International Conference of the Dakhleh Oasis Project* (eds., Bagnall, R. S., Davoli, P., and Hope, C. A.), Oxford: Oxbow: 177–80.

Mills, A. J. and O. Kaper (2003) "'Ain el-Gezzareen: Developments in the Old Kingdom settlement," in *The Oasis Papers 3: Proceedings of the Third International Conference of the Dakhleh Oasis Project* (eds., Bowen, G. E. and Hope, C. A.), Oxford: Oxbow, 123–9.

Miroschedji, P. de (2002) "The socio-political dynamics of Egyptian-Canaanite interaction in the Early Bronze Age," in *Egypt and the Levant. Interrelations from the 4th through the Early 3rd Millennium B.C.E.* (eds., van den Brink, E. C. M. and Levy, T. E.), London: Leicester University Press, 39–57.

Moeller, N. (2005) "The First Intermediate Period: A time of famine and climate change?," *ÄL* 15: 153–67.

— (2016) *The Archaeology of Urbanism in Ancient Egypt from the Predynastic Period to the End of the Middle Kingdom*, New York: Cambridge University Press.

Monnier, F. (2010) *Les Forteresses Égyptiennes—du Prédynastique au Nouvel Empire*, Bruxelles: Éditions Safran.

Moran, W. L. (ed. and trans.) (1992) *The Amarna Letters*, Baltimore, MD: Johns Hopkins University Press.

Moreno García, J. C. (1997) *Études sur l'administration, le pouvoir et l'idéologie en Égypte, de l'Ancien au Moyen Empire*, Liège: C.I.P.L.

— (1999) *ḥwt et le milieu rural égyptien du IIIe millénaire: économie, administration et organisation territoriale*, Paris: Champion.

— (2013) "Land donations," *UCLA Encyclopedia of Egyptology* (eds., Frood, E. and Wendrichs, W.), Los Angeles, http://digital2.library.ucla.edu/viewItem. do?ark=21198/zz002hgp07, accessed August 19, 2016.

— (2007) "The state and the organization of the rural landscape in 3rd millennium BC pharaonic Egypt," in *Aridity, Change and Conflict in Africa: Proceedings of an International ACACIA Conference Held at Königswinter, Germany October 1–3, 2003* (eds., Bollig, M. et al.), Köln: Heinrich-Barth-Institut: 313–30.

Morkot, R. G. (1987) "Studies in New Kingdom Nubia 1. Politics, economics and ideology: Egyptian imperialism in Nubia," *Wepwawet* 3: 29–49.

— (1991) "Nubia in the New Kingdom: The limits of Egyptian control," in *Egypt and Africa: Nubia from Prehistory to Islam* (ed., Davies, W. V.), London: British Museum Press: 294–301.

— (1995) "The foundations of the Kushite state: A response paper of László Török," *CRIPEL* 17 (1): 229–42.

— (2001) "Egypt and Nubia," in *Empires: Perspectives from Archaeology and History* (eds., Alcock, S. E., D'Altroy, T. N., Morrison, K. D., and Sinopoli, C. M.), Cambridge: Cambridge University Press: 227–51.

— (2012) "Sesebi," in *Ancient Nubia: African Kingdoms on the Nile* (eds., Fisher, M., Lacovara, P., D'Auria, S. et al.), Cairo: American University in Cairo Press: 315–19.

— (2013) "From conquered to conqueror: The organization of Nubia in the New Kingdom and the Kushite administration of Egypt," in *Ancient Egyptian Administration* (ed., Moreno García, J. C.), Leiden: Brill: 911–63.

Morris, E. F. (2005) *The Architecture of Imperialism: Military Bases and the Evolution of Foreign Policy in Egypt's New Kingdom*, Leiden: Brill.

— (2006a) "'Lo, nobles lament, the poor rejoice: State formation in the wake of social flux," in *After Collapse: The Regeneration of Complex Societies* (eds., Schwartz, G. M. and Nichols, J. J.), Tucson, AZ: University of Arizona Press: 58–71.

— (2006b) "Bowing and scraping in the Ancient Near East: An investigation into obsequiousness in the Amarna Letters," *JNES* 65: 179–95.

— (2010a) "Insularity and island identity in the oases bordering Egypt's Great Sand Sea," in *Thebes and Beyond: Studies in Honour of Kent R. Weeks* (eds., Hawass, Z. and Ikram, S.), Cairo: Supreme Council of Antiquities: 129–44.

— (2010b) "Opportunism in contested lands B.C. and A. D. Or how Abdi-Ashirta, Aziru, and Padsha Khan Zadran got away with murder," in *Millions of Jubilees: Studies in Honor of David Silverman*. Volume 1 (eds., Hawass, Z. and Wegner, J. H.), Cairo: Supreme Council of Antiquities: 413–38.

— (2013) "Propaganda and performance at the dawn of the state," in *Experiencing Power, Generating Authority: Cosmos, Politics and the Ideology of Kingship in Ancient Egypt and Mesopotamia* (eds., Hill, J., Jones, P., and Morales, A. J.), Philadelphia, PA: University of Pennsylvania Museum of Archaeology and Anthropology: 33–64.

— (2014) "Mitanni enslaved: Prisoners of war, pride, and productivity in a new imperial regime," in *Creativity and Innovation in the Reign of Hatshepsut* (eds., Galán, J. M., Bryan, B. M., and Dorman, P. F.), Chicago, IL: University of Chicago Press: 361–79.

— (2015a) "Exchange, extraction, and the politics of ideological money laundering in Egypt's New Kingdom Empire," in *Policies of Exchange: Political Systems and Modes of Interaction in the Aegean and the Near East in the 2nd Millennium B.C.E., Proceedings of the International Symposium at the University of Freiburg Institute for Archaeological Studies, 30th May–2nd June 2012* (eds., Eder, B. and Pruzsinszky, R.), Vienna: Austrian Academy of Sciences Press: 167–90.

— (2015b) "Egypt, Ugarit, the god Ba'al, and the puzzle of a royal rebuff," in *There and Back Again—the Crossroads: Proceedings of an International Conference Held in Prague, September 15–18, 2014* (eds., Mynářová, J., Onderka, P., and Pavúk, P.), Prague: Charles University in Prague, Faculty of Arts: 315–51.

— (2017) "Prevention through deterrence along Egypt's Northeastern Border. Or the politics of a weaponized desert," *JEMAHS* 5 (2): 133–47.

— (forthcoming) "Théorie insulaire et affordances des oasis du désert égyptien," (trans., Garond, L.) in *Mer et désert de l'Antiquité à nos jours: visions croisées* (eds., Tallet, G. and Sauzeau, T.), Rennes: Presses Universitaires de Rennes.

Muhs, B. (2016) *The Ancient Egyptian Economy 3000–30 BCE*, Cambridge: Cambridge University Press.

Murnane, W. J. (1990) *The Road to Kadesh: A Historical Interpretation of the Battle Reliefs of King Seti I at Karnak*. Second edition revised, Chicago, IL: Oriental Institute of the University of Chicago.

— (1995) *Texts from the Amarna Period in Egypt*, Kolkata: Scholar's Press.

Na'aman, N. (1981) "Economic aspects of the Egyptian occupation of Canaan," *IEJ* 31 (3/4): 172–85.

— (1988) "Pharaonic lands in the Jezreel Valley in the Late Bronze Age," in *Society and Economy in the Eastern Mediterranean (c. 1500–1000 B.C.). Proceedings of the International Symposium held at the University of Haifa from the 28th of April to the 2nd of May 1985* (eds., Heltzer, M. and Lipinski, E.), Leuven: Peeters: 177–85.

— (1994) "The Hurrians and the end of the Middle Bronze Age in Palestine," *Levant* 26: 175–87.

O'Connor, D. (1974) "Political systems and archaeological data in Egypt: 2600–1780 B.C.," *World Archaeology* 6 (1): 15–38.

— (1983) "New Kingdom and Third Intermediate Period, 1552–664 BC," in *Ancient Egypt: A Social History* (eds., Trigger, B., Kemp, B., O'Connor, D., and Lloyd, A.), Cambridge: Cambridge University Press: 183–278.

— (1993) *Ancient Nubia: Egypt's Rival in Africa*, Philadelphia, PA: University Museum of Archaeology and Anthropology, University of Pennsylvania.

— (1998) "Amenhotep III and Nubia," in *Amenhotep III: Perspectives on His Reign* (eds., O'Connor, D. and Cline, E. H.), Ann Arbor, MI: University of Michigan Press: 261–70.

Oded, B. (1979) *Mass Deportations and Deportees in the Neo-Assyrian Empire*, Wiesbaden: Dr. Ludwig Reichert Verlag.

— (1992) *War, Peace, and Empire: Justifications for War in Assyrian Royal Inscriptions*, Wiesbaden: Dr. Ludwig Reichert Verlag.

Oren, E. D. (1973) *The Northern Cemetery of Beth Shan*, Leiden: Brill.

— (1984) "'Governor's residencies' in Canaan under the New Kingdom: A case study of Egyptian administration," *JSSEA* 14: 37–56.

— (1987) "The 'Ways of Horus' in Northern Sinai," in *Egypt, Israel, Sinai. Archaeological and Historical Relationships in the Biblical Period* (ed., Rainey, A. F.), Tel Aviv: Tel Aviv University: 69–119.

— (1989) "Early Bronze Age settlement in Northern Sinai: A model for Egypto-Canaanite interconnections," in *L'urbanisation de la Palestine à l'âge du Bronze ancien: Bilan et perspectives des recherches actuelles. Actes du Colloque d'Emmaüs (20 – 24 Octobre 1986)* (ed., Miroschedji, P. de), Oxford: British Archaeological Reports: 389–405.

— (1993) "Northern Sinai," in *The New Encyclopedia of Archaeological Excavations in the Holy Land, Vol. 4* (ed., Stern, E.), New York: Simon & Schuster: 1386–96.

Oren, E. D. and Y. Yekutieli (1992) "Taur Ikhbeineh—earliest evidence for Egyptian interconnections," in *The Nile Delta in Transition: 4th–3rd Millennium B.C.: Proceedings of the Seminar Held in Cairo 21.–24. October 1990, at the Netherlands Institute of Archaeology and Arabic Studies* (ed., van den Brink, E. C. M.), Tel Aviv: E. C. M. van den Brink: 361–84.

Pantalacci, L. (2013) "Balat, a frontier town and its archive," in *Ancient Egyptian Administration* (ed., Moreno García, J. C.), Leiden: Brill: 197–214.

Patterson, T. C. (1991) *The Inca Empire: The Formation and Disintegration of a Pre-Capitalist State*, New York: Berg.

Peden, A. J. (1994) *Egyptian Historical Inscriptions of the Twentieth Dynasty*, Jonsered: Paul Åstroms.

Pettman, A. J. (2012) "The date of the occupation of 'Ain el-Gazzareen based on ceramic evidence," in *The Oasis Papers 6: Proceedings of the Sixth International*

Conference of the Dakhleh Oasis Project (eds., Bagnall, R. S., Davoli, P., and Hope, C. A.), Oxford: Oxbow: 181–208.

Pierce, K. V. L. (2013) "Living and dying abroad. Aspects of Egyptian cultural identity in Late Bronze Age and Early Iron Age Canaan," Dissertation, UCLA.

Pieri, A. (2011) "A special person in a special place: The dwarf of HK6," *NN* 23: 7–8.

Plutarch (1960) "Pericles," in *The Rise and Fall of Athens: Nine Greek Lives* (trans., Scott-Kilvert, I.), Harmondsworth: Penguin: 165–206.

Porat, N. (1992) "An Egyptian colony in Southern Palestine during the Late Predynastic–Early Dynastic Period," in *The Nile Delta in Transition: 4th–3rd Millennium B.C.: Proceedings of the Seminar Held in Cairo 21.–24. October 1990, at the Netherlands Institute of Archaeology and Arabic Studies* (ed., van den Brink, E. C. M.), Tel Aviv: E. C. M. van den Brink: 433–40.

Posener-Kriéger, P. (2004) *I papyri di Gebelein—Scavi G. Farina 1935*. Turin: Soprintendenza al Museo delle Antichità Egizie.

Prichard, J. B. (ed.) (1969) *Ancient Near Eastern Texts Relating to the Old Testament*. Third edition, Princeton, NJ: Princeton University Press.

Procopius (1914) *History of the Wars, Vol. 1: Books 1–2* (trans., Dewing, H. B.), Cambridge, MA: Harvard University Press.

Quibell, J. E. (1898) "Slate palette from Hieraconpolis," *ZÄS* 36, 1: 81–4, pl. 12, 13.

— (1905) *Archaic Objects, Vol. 1*, Cairo: Imprimerie de l'Institut Français d'Archéologie Orientale.

Redford, D. B. (1959) "Some observations on Amarna chronology," *JEA* 45: 34–7.

— (1979) "A gate inscription from Karnak and Egyptian involvement in Western Asia during the early Eighteenth Dynasty," *JAOS* 99 (2): 270–87.

— (1990) *Egypt and Canaan in the New Kingdom*. Beer-sheva: Ben-Gurion University of the Negev Press.

— (1992) *Egypt, Canaan, and Israel in Ancient Times*, Princeton, NJ: Princeton University Press.

— (2003) *The Wars in Syria and Palestine of Thutmose III*, Boston, MA: Brill.

Reisner, G. A. (1910) *The Archaeological Survey of Nubia. Report for 1907–1908. Vol. I*, Cairo: National Printing Department.

Renfrew, C. and Cherry, J. F. (eds.) (1986) *Peer Polity Interaction and Socio-political Change*, Cambridge: Cambridge University Press.

Riemer, H. (2004) "News about the Clayton rings: Long distance desert travellers during Egypt's Predynastic," in *Egypt at its Origins: Studies in Memory of Barbara Adams* (eds., Hendrickx, S. et al.), Dudley, MA: Peeters: 971–89.

Rothenberg, B. (1988) *The Egyptian Mining Temple at Timna*, London: Institute for Archaeo-Metallurgical Studies [and] Institute of Archaeology, University College, London.

Routledge, B. (2015) "A fishy business: The inland trade in Nile perch (Lates niloticus) in the Early Iron Age Levant," in *Walls of the Prince: Egyptian Interactions with Southwest Asia in Antiquity: Essays in Honour of John S.*

Holladay, Jr. (eds., Harrison, T. P., Banning, E. B., and Klassen, S.), Leiden: Brill: 212–33.

Rowe, A. (1940) *The Four Canaanite Temples of Beth-shan. Part 1: The Temples and Cult Objects*, Philadelphia, PA: University of Pennsylvania Press.

Rose, P. (2017) "Sesebi: Ceramics, chronology and society," in *Nubia in the New Kingdom: Lived Experience, Pharaonic Control and Indigenous Traditions* (eds., Spencer, D., Stevens, A., and Binder, M.), Leuven: Peeters: 465–73.

Roy, J. (2014) *The Politics of Trade: Egypt and Lower Nubia in the Fourth Millennium BC*, Leiden: Brill.

Saggs, H. W. F. (1984) *The Might that Was Assyria*, London: Sidgwick and Jackson.

Sahlins, M. (1972) *Stone Age Economics*, Chicago, IL: Aldine Atherton, Inc.

Said, E. (1993) *Culture and Imperialism*, New York: Vintage Books.

Sancisi-Weerdenburg, H. (1995) "Darius I and the Persian Empire," in *CANE II* (ed., Sasson, J.), New York: Charles Scribner's Sons: 1035–50.

Sandars, N. K. (1985) *Sea Peoples: Warriors of the Ancient Mediterranean 1250–1150 BC*, London: Thames & Hudson.

Santora, M. (2009) "Big U.S. bases are part of Iraq, but a world apart," *The New York Times*, September 8, http://www.nytimes.com/2009/09/09/world/middleeast/09bases.html, accessed August 22, 2016.

Savage, S. H. (1997) "Descent group competition and economic strategies in Predynastic Egypt," *Journal of Anthropological Archaeology* 16: 226–68.

Säve-Söderbergh, T. (1941) *Ägypten und Nubien: Ein Beitrag zur Geschichte altägyptischer Aussenpolitik*, Lund: Håkan Ohlssons Boktryckeri.

— (1949) "A Buhen stela from the Second Intermediate Period (Khartūm No. 18)," *JEA* 35: 50–58.

— (1960) "The Paintings in the Tomb of Djehuty-hetep at Debeira," *Kush* 8: 25–44.

— (1962) "Preliminary report of the Scandanavian Joint Expedition. Archaeological survey between Faras and Gamai, January–March 1961," *Kush* 10: 76–105.

— (1963) "Preliminary report of the Scandinavian Joint Expedition. Archaeological survey between Faras and Gamai, November 1961–March 1962," *Kush* 11: 47–69.

— (1967–8) "Preliminary report of the Scandinavian Joint Expedition. Archaeological Investigations between Faras and Gemai, November 1963–March 1964," *Kush* 15: 211–50.

— (1989) *Middle Nubian Sites. The Scandinavian Joint Expedition to Sudanese Nubia, Vol. 4: 1*, Uddevalla: Bohusläningens Boktryckeri AB.

— (1991a) "Historical and cultural background," in *New Kingdom Pharaonic Sites: The Finds and the Sites. SJE Volume 5: 2* (eds., Säve-Söderbergh, T. and Troy, L.), Uppsala: Scandanavian Joint Expedition to Sudanese Nubia: 1–13.

— (1991b) "The tomb of Amenemhet and the prince of The-khet," in *New Kingdom Pharaonic Sites: The Finds and the Sites. SJE Volume 5: 2* (eds., Säve-Söderbergh, T. and Troy, L.), Uppsala: Scandanavian Joint Expedition to Sudanese Nubia: 182–211.

— (1992–1993) "A case study of pharaonic imperialism. The Egyptian domination of the Debeira district in Lower Nubia during the 18th Dynasty," *Orientalia Suecana* 41–42: 254–72.

Schulman, A. R. (1988) "Hittites, helmets, and Amarna: Akhenaten's first Hittite war," in *Akhenaten Temple Project II: Rwd-Mnw, Foreigners and Inscriptions* (ed., Redford, D. B.), Toronto: Toronto University Press: 53–79.

— (1992) "Still more Egyptian seal impressions from 'En Besor," in *The Nile Delta in Transition: 4th–3rd Millennium B.C.: Proceedings of the Seminar Held in Cairo 21.–24. October 1990, at the Netherlands Institute of Archaeology and Arabic Studies* (ed., van den Brink, E. C. M.), Tel Aviv: E. C. M. van den Brink: 395–417.

Schumpeter, J. (1966) *Imperialism and Social Classes. Two Essays by Joseph Schumpeter*, New York: Meridian Books.

Scott, J. C. (1998) *Seeing Like a State: How Certain Schemes to Improve the Human Condition Have Failed*, New Haven, CT: Yale University Press.

— (2009) *The Art of Not Being Governed: An Anarchist History of Upland Southeast Asia*, New Haven, CT: Yale University Press.

— (2017) *Against the Grain: A Deep History of the Earliest States*, New Haven, CT: Yale University Press.

Seidlmayer, S. (2003) "The First Intermediate Period (c. 2160–2055)," in *The Oxford History of Ancient Egypt* (ed., Shaw, I.), New York: Oxford University Press: 108–36.

Seierstad, Å. (2004) *The Bookseller of Kabul* (trans., Christophersen, I.), London: Virago.

Several, M. W. (1972) "Reconsidering the Egyptian Empire in Palestine during the Amarna Period," *Palestine Exploration Quarterly* 104: 123–33.

Shaw, I. (ed.) (2003) *The Oxford History of Ancient Egypt*, New York: Oxford University Press.

Shaw, I. and R. Jameson (1993) "Amethyst mining in the Eastern Desert: A preliminary survey at Wadi el-Hudi," *JEA* 79: 81–97.

Shinnie, P. L. (1951) "Preliminary report on the excavations at 'Amārah West, 1948–49 and 1949–50," *JEA* 37: 5–11.

Silverman, D. P., J. W. Wegner, and J. H. Wegner (2006) *Akhenaten and Tutankhamun. Revolution and Restoration*, Philadelphia, PA: University of Pennsylvania Museum of Archaeology and Anthropology.

Simpson, W. K. (1963) *Heka-Nefer and the Dynastic Material from Toshka and Arminna*. New Haven, CT and Philadelphia, PA: The Peabody Museum of Natural History of Yale University and the University Museum of the University of Pennsylvania.

Simpson, W. K. (ed.) (2003) *The Literature of Ancient Egypt: An Anthology of Stories, Instructions, Stelae, Autobiographies, and Poetry*. Third edition, New Haven, CT: Yale University Press.

Singer, I. (1988a) "Merneptah's campaign to Canaan and the Egyptian occupation of the southern coastal plain of Palestine in the Ramesside Period," *BASOR* 269: 1–10.

— (1988b) "The political status of Megiddo VIIA," *TA* 15 (1): 101–12.

Sinopoli, C. (1994) "The archaeology of empires," *Annual Review of Anthropology* 23: 159–80.

— (2001) "Imperial integration and imperial subjects," in *Empires: Perspectives from Archaeology and History* (eds., Alcock, S. E., D'Altroy, T. N., Morrison, K. D., and Sinopoli, C. M.), Cambridge: Cambridge University Press: 195–200.

Skalník, P. (1989) "Outwitting the state: An introduction," in *Outwitting the State* (ed., Skalník, P.), New Brunswick: Transaction Publishers: 1–21.

Sloane, W. M. (1894) *Life of Napoleon Bonaparte, Volume 1*, New York: The Century Company.

Smekalova, T. N. and S. Smekalov (n.d.) "Dakhleh Oasis Project Columbia University Excavations at Amheida 2005 Magnetic survey," unpublished report, http://www.amheida.org/inc/pdf/Geophysical_survey_2005.pdf, accessed August 6, 2016.

Smith, H. S. (1972) "The rock inscriptions of Buhen," *JEA* 58: 43–82.

— (1976) *The Fortress of Buhen. The Inscriptions*, London: Egypt Exploration Society.

Smith, S. T. (1990) "Administration at the Egyptian Middle Kingdom frontier: Sealings from Uronarti and Askut," in *Aegean Seals, Sealings, and Administration* (ed., Palaima, T. G.), Liège: Universite de Liège: 197–216.

— (1991) "A model for Egyptian imperialism in Nubia," *GM* 122: 77–102.

— (1995) *Askut in Nubia: The Economics and Ideology of Egyptian Imperialism in the Second Millennium BC*, London: Kegan Paul.

— (1997) "State and empire in the Middle and New Kingdoms," in *Anthropology and Egyptology: A developing dialogue* (ed., Lustig, J.), Sheffield: Sheffield Academic Press: 66–89.

— (2003) *Wretched Kush: Ethnic Identities and Boundaries in Egypt's Nubian Empire*, New York: Routledge.

— (2013) "Revenge of the Kushites. Assimilation and resistance in Egypt's New Kingdom Empire and Nubian ascendancy over Egypt," in *Empires and Diversity: On the Crossroads of Archaeology, Anthropology, and History* (ed., Areshian, G. E.), Los Angeles: Cotsen Institute of Archaeology at UCLA: 84–107.

— (2015) "Hekanefer and the Lower Nubian princes. Entanglement, double identity or topos and mimesis?" in *Fuzzy Boundaries. Festschrift für Antonio Loprieno, Volume 2* (eds., Amstutz, H., Dorn, A., Müler, M. et al.), Hamburg: Widmaier Verlag: 767–79.

— (2017) "The fortified settlement at Tombos and Egyptian colonial strategy in New Kingdom Nubia," Abstract book for "From Microcosm to Macrocosm: Individual Households and Cities in Ancient Egypt and Nubia," 1–3 September 2017, Munich, Germany, http://acrossborders.oeaw.ac.at/conference-2017.

Smith, S. T. and M. Buzon (2014) "Colonial entanglements: 'Egyptianization' in Egypt's Nubian empire and the Nubian Dynasty," in *The Fourth Cataract and Beyond: Proceedings of the 12th International Conference for Nubian Studies* (eds., Welsby, D. and Anderson, J. R.), Leuven: Peeters: 431–42.

— (2017) "Colonial encounters at New Kingdom Tombos: Cultural entanglements and hybrid identity," in *Nubia in the New Kingdom: Lived Experience, Pharaonic Control and Indigenous Traditions* (eds., Spencer, D., Stevens, A., and Binder, M.), Leuven: Peeters: 615–30.

Smither, P. C. (1945) "The Semnah Despatches," *JEA* 31: 3–10.

Snape, S. (2004) "The excavations of the Liverpool University Mission to Zawiyet Umm el-Rakham 1994–2001," *ASAE* 78: 149–60.

— (2011) *Ancient Egyptian Tombs: The Culture of Life and Death*, Malden, MA: Wiley-Blackwell.

Soukiassian, G. (1997) "A governors' palace at 'Ayn Asil, Dakhla Oasis," *Egyptian Archaeology* 11: 15–17.

Soukiassian, G., M. Wuttmann, and L. Pantalacci (2002) *Le palais des gouverneurs de l'époque de Pépy II: les sanctuaires de ka et leurs dépendances*, Le Caire: Institut français d'archéologie orientale.

Sowell, T. (1998) *Conquests and Cultures: An International History*, New York: Basic Books.

Spalding, K. (1984) *Huarochirí: An Andean Society under Inca and Spanish Rule*, Stanford, CA: Stanford University Press.

Spence, K. et al. (2011) "Sesebi 2011," *SN* 15: 34–8.

— (2017) "Sesebi before Akhenaten," in *Nubia in the New Kingdom: Lived Experience, Pharaonic Control and Indigenous Traditions* (eds., Spencer, D., Stevens, A., and Binder, M.), Leuven: Peeters, 449–63.

Spence, K. and P. Rose (2009) "New fieldwork at Sesebi," *Egyptian Archaeology* 35, 21–4.

Spencer N. (2009) "Cemeteries and a late Ramesside suburb at Amara West," *SN* 13: 47–61.

— (2010) "Nubian architecture in an Egyptian town? Building E12.11 at Amara West," *SN* 14: 15–24.

— (2017) "Building on new ground: The foundation of a colonial town at Amara West," in *Nubia in the New Kingdom: Lived Experience, Pharaonic Control and Indigenous Traditions* (eds., Spencer, D., Stevens, A., and Binder, M.), Leuven: Peeters, 323–55.

Spencer, N., A. Stevens, and M. Binder (n.d.) "Amara West: Living in Egyptian Nubia," guide published online under the auspices of the British Museum, http://www.britishmuseum.org/pdf/Amara_West_Living_in_Egyptian_Nubia. pdf, accessed August 19, 2016.

— (2017) "Introduction: History and historiography of a colonial entanglement, and the shaping of new archaeologies for Nubia in the New Kingdom," in *Nubia in the New Kingdom: Lived Experience, Pharaonic Control and Indigenous Traditions* (eds., Spencer, D., Stevens, A., and Binder, M.), Leuven: Peeters, 1–61.

Starkey, J. L. and L. Harding (1932) *Beth-pelet II*, London: British School of Archaeology in Egypt.

Stein, G. J. (1999) *Rethinking World-Systems: Diasporas, Colonies, and Interaction in Uruk Mesopotamia*, Tucson, AZ: The University of Arizona Press.

— (2002) "Colonies without colonialism: A trade diaspora model of fourth millennium B.C. Mesopotamian enclaves in Anatolia," in *The Archaeology of Colonialism* (eds., Lyons, C. L. and Papadopoulos, J. K.), Los Angeles, CA: Getty Research Institute Publications: 27–64.

— (2005a) "The archaeology of colonial encounters," in *The Archaeology of Colonial Encounters: Comparative Perspectives* (ed., Stein, G. J.), Santa Fe, NM: SAR Press: 3–31.

— (2005b) "The political economy of Mesopotamian colonial encounters," in *The Archaeology of Colonial Encounters: Comparative Perspectives* (ed., Stein, G. J.), Santa Fe, NM: SAR Press: 143–71.

Stevens, A. (2017) "Female figurines and folk culture at Amara West," in *Nubia in the New Kingdom: Lived Experience, Pharaonic Control and Indigenous Traditions* (eds., Spencer, D., Stevens, A., and Binder, M.), Leuven: Peeters, 407–27.

Stevenson, A. (2013) "Egypt and Mesopotamia," in *The Sumerian World* (ed., Crawford, H.), New York: Routledge: 620–36.

— (2016) "The Egyptian Predynastic and State Formation," *Journal of Archaeological Research* 24, no 4: 421–68.

Strudwick, N. C. (trans.) (2005) *Texts from the Pyramid Age*, Atlanta, GA: Society of Biblical Literature.

Subrahmanyam, S. (2001) "Written on water: Designs and dynamics in the Portugese *Estado da Índia*," in *Empires: Perspectives from Archaeology and History* (eds., Alcock, S. E., D'Altroy, T. N., Morrison, K. D., and Sinopoli, C. M.), Cambridge: Cambridge University Press: 42–69.

Suetonius (2007) "Divus Augustus," in *The Twelve Caesars*, revised edition (trans., Graves, R.), New York: Penguin Books: 43–103.

Sun Tzu (2014) *The Art of War* (trans., Giles, L.), Enhanced Ebooks. Reprint of 1910 ed.

Tacitus, C. (1970) *The Agricola and the Germania* (trans., Mattingly, H.), New York: Penguin Books.

Thompson, J. L. (2002), "Neolithic burials at Sheikh Muftah: A preliminary report," in *Dakhleh Oasis Project: Preliminary Reports on the 1994–1995 to 1998–1999*

Field Seasons (eds., Hope, C. A. and Bowen, G. E.), Oxford: Oxbow Books: 43–5.

Thurston, H. (2004) *Secrets of the Sands: The Revelations of Egypt's Everlasting Oasis*, New York: Arcade Publishing.

Török, L. (2009) *Between Two Worlds: The Frontier Region between Ancient Nubia and Egypt 3700 BC – AD 500*, Leiden: Brill.

Trigger, B. G. (1976) *Nubia Under the Pharaohs*, London: Thames & Hudson.

— (1993) *Early Civilizations: Ancient Egypt in Context*, Cairo: American University in Cairo Press.

— (2003) *Understanding Early Civilizations: A Comparative Study*, Cambridge: Cambridge University Press.

Troy, L. (1991) "The cemetery at Fadrus (No 185)," in *New Kingdom Pharaonic Sites: The Finds and the Sites. SJE Volume 5: 2* (eds., Säve–Söderbergh, T. and Troy, L.), Uppsala: Scandanavian Joint Expedition to Sudanese Nubia: 212–93.

—(2003) "Resource management and ideological manifestation. The towns and cities of ancient Egypt," written for The Development of Urbanism from a Global Perspective ("Urban Origins in Eastern Africa" final conference in Mombasa, 1993, English version 2003: 1–58, http://www.ibg.uu.se/digitalAssets/9/9590_TroyAll.pdf, accessed August 3, 2016.

Tubb, J. N. (1990) "Preliminary report on the fourth season of excavations at Tell es-Sa'idiyeh in the Jordan Valley," *Levant* 22: 21–42.

Ussishkin, D. (2004) "A synopsis of the stratigraphical, chronological and historical issues," in *The Renewed Archaeological Excavations at Lachish (1973–1994)* (ed., Ussishkin, D.), Tel Aviv: Emery and Claire Yass Publications in Archaeology: 50–122.

Valbelle, D. (2002) "Pharaonic regality: The nature of power," in *The Pharaohs* (eds., Ziegler, C. and Tiradritti, F.), London: Thames & Hudson: 95–111.

Valloggia, M. (1999) "Dakhla Oasis, Balat," in *Encyclopedia of the Archaeology of Ancient Egypt* (ed., Bard, K.), New York: Routledge: 254–8.

Van Neer, W., M. Udrescu, V. Linseele et al. (2015) "Traumatism in the wild animals kept and offered at Predynastic Hierakonpolis, Upper Egypt," *International Journal of Osteoarchaeology*, published online in Wiley Online Library (wileyonlinelibrary.com), DOI: 10.1002/oa.2440.

van Pelt, W. P. (2013) "Revising Egypto-Nubian relations in New Kingdom Lower Nubia: From Egyptianization to cultural entanglement," *Cambridge Archaeological Journal* 23 (3): 523–50.

Vercoutter, J. (1957) "Upper Egyptian settlers in Middle Kingdom Nubia," *Kush* 5: 61–9.

— (1958) "Excavations at Sai 1955–7: A preliminary report," *Kush* 6: 144–69.

— (1959) "The gold of Kush," *Kush* 7: 120–53.

Vita, J.-P. (1999) "The society of Ugarit," in *Handbook of Ugaritic Studies* (eds., Watson, W. G. E. and Wyatt, N.), Leiden: Brill: 455–98.

Vogel, C. (2003) "Fallen heroes? Winlock's 'slain soldiers' reconsidered," *JEA* 89: 239–45.

— (2004) *Ägyptische Festungen und Garnisonen bis zum Ende des Mittleren Reiches*, Hildesheim: Gerstenberg.

von der Way, T. (1992) "Excavation at Tell el-Fara'in/Buto in 1987–1989," in *The Nile Delta in Transition: 4th–3rd Millennium B.C.: Proceedings of the Seminar Held in Cairo 21.–24. October 1990, at the Netherlands Institute of Archaeology and Arabic Studies* (ed., van den Brink, E. C. M.), Tel Aviv: E. C. M. van den Brink: 1–10.

von Zielbauer, P. (2007) "In Iraq, American military finds it has an alcohol problem," *The New York Times*, March 12, http://www.nytimes.com/2007/03/12/world/americas/12iht-alcohol.4885466.html?pagewanted=all&_r=1, accessed August 22, 2016.

Wainwright, G. A. (1923) "The Red Crown in early prehistoric times," *JEA* 9: 26–33.

Warburton, D. (2001) *Egypt and the Near East: Politics in the Bronze Age*, Paris: Recherches et Publications.

Ward, W. A. and M. S. Joukowsky (eds.) (1992) *The Crisis Years: The 12th Century B.C.: From Beyond the Danube to the Tigris*, Dubuque, IA: Kendall/Hunt.

Ward, W. (1966) "The Egyptian inscriptions of Level VI," in *The Iron Age at Beth Shan: A Study of Levels VI–IV* (ed., James, F. W.), Philadelphia, PA: University Museum: 161–79.

Warfe, A. R. (2003) "Cultural origins of the Egyptian Neolithic and Predynastic: An evaluation of the evidence from the Dakhleh Oasis (South Central Egypt)," *The African Archaeological Review* 20 (4): 175–202.

Weber, D. J. (1992) *The Spanish Frontier in North America*, New Haven, CT: Yale University Press.

Webster, J. (2001) "Creolizing the Roman provinces," *AJA* 105 (2): 209–25.

Weglarz, L. R. (2017) "Continuity and change: A reevaluation of cultural identity and 'Egyptianization' in Lower Nubia during the New Kingdom," Dissertation, University of Chicago.

Wegner, J. (1995) "Regional control in Middle Kingdom Lower Nubia: The function and history of the site of Areika," *JARCE* 32: 127–60.

— (forthcoming) "The stela of Idudju-iker: Foremost—one of the Chiefs of Wawat. New evidence on the conquest of Thinis under Wahankh Antef II," *RdÉ* 68.

Weinstein, J. M. (1981) "The Egyptian empire in Palestine: A reassessment," *BASOR* 241: 1–28.

— (1991) "Egypt and the Middle Bronze IIC/Late Bronze IA transition in Palestine," *Levant* 23: 105–15.

— (1992) "The collapse of the Egyptian empire in the Southern Levant," in *The Crisis Years: The 12th Century B.C.: From Beyond the Danube to the Tigris* (eds., Ward, W. A. and Joukowsky, M. S.), Dubuque, IA: Kendall/Hunt: 142–50.

— (1998) "Egypt and the Levant in the reign of Amenhotep III," in *Amenhotep III. Perspectives on His Reign* (eds., O'Connor, D. and Cline, E. H.), Ann Arbor, MI: The University of Michigan Press: 223–36.

Wells, P. S. (1999) *The Barbarians Speak: How the Conquered Peoples Shaped Roman Europe*, Princeton, NJ: Princeton University Press.

Welsby, D. (n.d.) "Kawa: The Pharaonic and Kushite town of Gematon. History and archaeology of the site," site guide published online under the auspices of the Nubian Archaeological Development Organization and the British Museum, http://www.sudarchrs.org.uk/wp-content/uploads/2014/06/Kawa_QSAP_English_booklet.pdf, accessed August 19, 2016.

Welsby, D. A. and I. Welsby Sjöström (2006–2007) "The Dongola Reach and the Fourth Cataract: Continuity and change during the 2nd and 1st millennia BC," *CRIPEL* 26: 379–98.

Wengrow, D. (2006) *The Archaeology of Early Egypt: Social Transformation in North-East Africa, 10,000 to 2650 BC*, New York: Cambridge University Press.

Wente, E. F. (1990) *Letters from Ancient Egypt*, Atlanta, GA: Scholars Press.

Wiesehöfer, J. (2001) *Ancient Persia from 550 BC to 650 AD* (trans., Azodi, A.), New York: I. B. Tauris Publishers.

Wildung, D. (1977) *Egyptian Saints: Deification in Pharaonic Egypt*, New York: New York University Press.

Wilkinson, T. A. H. (1996) *State Formation in Egypt. Chronology and Society*, Oxford: British Archaeological Reports.

— (1999) *Early Dynastic Egypt*, New York: Routledge.

Williams, B. B. (1986) *The A-Group Royal Cemetery at Qustul: Cemetery L. The University of Chicago Oriental Institute Nubian Expedition. Vol. III*, Chicago, IL: Oriental Institute of the University of Chicago.

— (1988) "Narmer and the Coptos colossi," *JARCE* 1988: 35–59.

— (1992) *New Kingdom Remains from Cemeteries R, V, S, and W at Qustul and Cemetery K at Adindan*, Chicago, IL: Oriental Institute of the University of Chicago.

— (1999) "Serra East and the mission of the Middle Kingdom fortresses in Nubia," in *Gold of Praise: Studies on Ancient Egypt in Honor of Edward F. Wente* (eds., Teeter, E. and Larson, J. A.), Chicago, IL: Oriental Institute of the University of Chicago: 435–53.

— (2006) "The Cave Shrine and the Gebel," in *Timelines: Studies in Honour of Manfred Bietak* (ed., Czerny, E.), Dudley, MA: Peeters: 149–57.

— (2012) "Second Cataract forts," in *Ancient Nubia: African Kingdoms on the Nile* (eds., Fisher, M., Lacovara, P., D'Auria, S. et al.), Cairo: American University in Cairo Press: 340–7.

Wimmer, S. J. and G. Lehmann (2014) "Two hieratic inscriptions from Qubur el-Walaydah," *ÄL* 24: 343–8.

Woodward, J., M. Macklin, N. Spencer, M. Binder, M. Dalton, S. Hay, and A. Hardy (2017) "Living with a changing river and desert landscape at Amara

West," in *Nubia in the New Kingdom: Lived Experience, Pharaonic Control and Indigenous Traditions* (eds., Spencer, D., Stevens, A., and Binder, M.), Leuven: Peeters: 227–57.

Yahalom-Mack, N. and N. Panitz-Cohen (2009) "Groundstone implements," in *Excavations at Tel Beth-Shean 1989–1996. Volume III: The 13th–11th Century BCE Strata in Areas N and S* (eds., Panitz–Cohen, N. and Mazar, A.), Jerusalem: Israel Exploration Society: 719–36.

Yasur-Landau, A. (2010) *The Philistines and Aegean Migration at the End of the Late Bronze Age*, New York: Cambridge University Press.

Yekutieli, Y. (2002) "Settlement and subsistence patterns in North Sinai during the Fifth to Third Millennia BCE," in *Egypt and the Levant. Interrelations from the 4th through the Early 3rd Millennium B.C.E.* (eds., van den Brink, E. C. M. and Levy, T. E.), London: Leicester University Press: 422–33.

Žaba, Z. (1974) *The Rock Inscriptions of Lower Nubia (Czechoslovak Concession)*, Prague: Charles University of Prague.

Zeedani, S. (2007) "A Palestinian perspective on checkpoints," *Palestine-Israel Journal of Politics, Economics and Culture* 13 (4): 89–95, http://www.pij.org/details.php?id=980, accessed August 22, 2016.

Abbreviations

AJA = *American Journal of Archaeology*
ÄL = *Ägypten und Levante*
ASAE = *Annales du Service des antiquités de l'Egypte*
BASOR = *Bulletin of the American Schools of Oriental Research*
BES = *Bulletin of the Egyptological Seminar*
BIFAO = *Bulletin de l'Institut Français d'Archéologie Orientale*
BMSAES = *British Museum Studies in Ancient Egypt and Sudan*
CANE = *Civilizations of the Ancient Near East*
CRIPEL = *Cahiers de Recherches de l'Institut de Papyrologie et d' Égyptologie de Lille*
EA = El Amarna (refers to the numbering of letters)
EVO = *Egitto e Vicino Oriente*
GM = *Göttinger Miszellen*
IEJ = *Israel Exploration Journal*
IFAO = *Fouilles de l'Institut français d'archéologie orientale du Caire*
JAEI – *Journal of Ancient Egyptian Interconnections*
JARCE = *Journal of the American Research Center in Egypt*
JAOS = *Journal of the American Oriental Society*
JEA = *Journal of Egyptian Archaeology*
JEMAHS = *Journal of Eastern Mediterranean Archaeology and Heritage Studies*

JNES = *Journal of Near Eastern Studies*
JSSEA = *Journal of the Society for the Study of Egyptian Antiquities*
MDAIK = *Mitteilungen des Deutschen Archäologischen Instituts, Abteilung Kairo*
NN = *Nekhen News*
RdÉ = *Revue d'Égyptologie*
SN = *Sudan and Nubia*
TA = *Tel Aviv*
UF = *Ugarit–Forschungen*
ZÄS = *Zeitschrift für Ägyptische Sprache und Altertumskunde*

Index

Page references to Figures are followed by the letter 'f' in italics. References to Notes contain the letter 'n', followed by the number of the note.